REVOLUTION GOES EAST

Studies of the Weatherhead East Asian Institute, Columbia University

The Studies of the Weatherhead East Asian Institute of Columbia University were inaugurated in 1962 to bring to a wider public the results of significant new research on modern and contemporary East Asia.

REVOLUTION GOES EAST

Imperial Japan and Soviet Communism

Tatiana Linkhoeva

CORNELL UNIVERSITY PRESS ITHACA AND LONDON

First published 2020 by Cornell University Press

Library of Congress Cataloging-in-Publication Data

Names: Linkhoeva, Tatiana, 1979– author.
Title: Revolution goes east : imperial Japan and Soviet communism / Tatiana Linkhoeva.
Description: Ithaca [New York] : Cornell University Press, 2020. | Series: Studies of the Weatherhead East Asian Institute, Columbia University | Includes bibliographical references and index.
Identifiers: LCCN 2019020874 (print) | LCCN 2019980700 (ebook) | ISBN 9781501748080 (pbk) | ISBN 9781501748097 (epub) | ISBN 9781501748103 (pdf)
Subjects: LCSH: Communism—Japan—History—20th century. | Japan—Politics and government—1912–1945. | Soviet Union—History—Revolution, 1917–1921—Influence. | Soviet Union—Foreign relations—Japan. | Japan—Foreign relations—Soviet Union.
Classification: LCC HX413 .L44 2020 (print) | LCC HX413 (ebook) | DDC 320.53/22095209041—dc23
LC record available at https://lccn.loc.gov/2019020874
LC ebook record available at https://lccn.loc.gov/2019980700

For my late mother, Svetlana Linkhoeva,
and for my father, Leonid Linkhoev

Contents

Acknowledgments

Many people and institutions assisted in writing this book. I had two intellectual godfathers at the University of California, Berkeley: Andrew Barshay, who inspired me to study the Japanese Left, and Yuri Slezkine, who made Russia and Russian history exciting again for me. My two intellectual godmothers were Mary Elizabeth Berry and Victoria Frede-Montemayor, who helped me find my own voice in writing history and are simply everything that I aspire to be. My special thanks go first and foremost to them. John Connelly, Alan Tansman, and Wen-hsin Yeh in Berkeley encouraged this project from its inception. At Ludwig Maximillian University in Munich, Germany, Andreas Renner provided invaluable support to complete the book manuscript. My colleagues at New York University deserve my special gratitude for welcoming and supporting me: Ayse Baltaciuglu-Brammer, Zvi Ben-dor Benite, Jane Burbank, Frederick Cooper, Stephen Gross, Irvin Ibarguen, Rebecca Karl, Monica Kim, Yanni Kotsonis, David Ludden, Andrew Needham, Anne O'Donnell, and Susanah Romney. Conversations and friendship with colleagues at other universities stimulated my thinking: Anna Belogurova, Sheldon Garon, Carol Gluck, Yumi Kim, Mary Knighton, Paul Kreitman, Yukiko Koshiro, George Lazopoulos, Janis Mimura, Jason Morton, Mariko Naito, Saito Shohei, Seiji Shirane, Sören Urbansky, Miriam Voerkelius, Louise Young, and Max Ward. I am fortunate to have Brandon Schechter as my dear friend and colleague. In Japan, I have benefited from the counsel of Arima Manabu, Ishikawa Yoshihiro, Nakami Tatsuo, Tomita Takeshi, Umemori Naoyuki, and David Wolff.

I presented individual chapters at various meetings at UC Berkeley, Columbia, LMU in Munich, the University of Köln and Heidelberg, the University of Kyushu, and Waseda University. I am grateful for the opportunities to present my ideas and for the helpful questions I received. Two anonymous readers from Cornell University Press offered incisive comments for the improvement of the manuscript. I also wish to thank Kenneth Ross Yelsey from the Weatherhead East Asian Institute and Roger Haydon at Cornell University Press for their assistance in publishing this book.

Over the course of research and writing, I have received support from UC Berkeley, LMU in Munich, and NYU. A one-year research fellowship from the Japan Foundation gave me the chance to undertake my research in Japan. I want to thank the Tokyo University of Foreign Studies for the offer of a visiting researcher position. A postdoctoral fellowship from the German Excellence

Initiative at LMU provided two wonderful and productive years in Munich. I also express appreciation to the Schoff Fund at The University Seminars at Columbia University, and the Center for the Humanities at NYU for their help in the publication of this book. Material in this work was presented at the History of Modern Japan seminar at Columbia University.

I am indebted to my partner, Alvaro Bonfiglio, for his immense patience and kindness, and to my two children, Gabriel and Mika Francesca, who were born during my doctoral years. The book is dedicated to my late mother, Svetlana, and my father, Leonid, in my native Buriatia—without their unconditional love none of this would be possible.

Note on Transliteration

Japanese names follow the customary Japanese order, surname first, unless the person uses Western name order in Western-language publications.

REVOLUTION GOES EAST

INTRODUCTION
Two Russias

Proletarians and oppressed people of the world, unite!

—First Congress of the Peoples of the East, Baku, September 1920

The Russian Revolution of 1917 raised a profound question: was socialism a means to promote national unity and wealth, or was its goal to achieve global human liberation from both capitalism and imperialism? In imperial Japan, as elsewhere in the non-Western world, the answer was neither obvious nor uniform. This question, however, was even more complicated in Japan because the Russian Revolution happened at a time when Japan approached the fiftieth anniversary of its own great revolution, the Meiji Revolution of 1868, and when the Japanese public began to contemplate the historical foundations and future of their own modernized imperial state. As such, the Russian Revolution provoked fierce debates among supporters and opponents alike about the relationships among the state, society, individuals, and the national community; and finally, the objectives of the Japanese imperial project. This book explores Japan's disparate responses to the Russian Revolution during the 1920s and demonstrates how the debate about Soviet Russia and its communist ideology became a debate over what constituted modern Japan.

After their successful takeover of power in October 1917, Russian Bolsheviks declared a war not only on capitalism, but no less significantly a war on imperialism.[1] Russian Bolsheviks, however, envisioned their revolution as the first in a series of world proletarian revolutions. The Bolshevik leader Vladimir Lenin specifically insisted that without the success of proletarian revolutions in Europe, the Russian Revolution and the Bolshevik regime would not be able to survive. However, by 1920, as communist revolutions failed to materialize in Europe, and as the Red Army was gaining control over Eastern Siberia and the Russian Far East, the center of gravity of the Russian Revolution shifted to East Asia. It was in East Asia, as well as in the Middle East, where the Russian Revolution merged with and acquired the character of an anti-imperialist struggle. And it was the anti-imperialist message that Russian Bolsheviks skillfully employed in East Asia to win over Japanese, Korean, Chinese, and Mongol national liberation movements.[2] Consequently, the anti-imperialist struggle became the cornerstone of the Japanese, Korean, Chinese, and Mongol communist parties, established between 1921 and 1922 with the help of Russian Bolsheviks.[3]

In 1917, imperial Japan was the only Asian empire, having already formally incorporated Taiwan and Korea and enforced aggressive policies in northeastern China and the Russian East. After the collapse of tsarist Russia, Japan took advantage of the power vacuum in East Asia. Between 1918 and 1925, as part of the Allied intervention to contain the Bolshevik Revolution, Japan deployed considerable armed forces to the Russian Far East, Eastern Siberia, and northern Manchuria. Unlike other foreign interventionist forces, however, Japan actively interfered in the Russian Civil War, which prompted Russian Bolsheviks to declare imperial Japan to be a major threat to the survival of the Soviet state and the world proletarian revolution. "Japanese imperialism," Lenin declared in 1918, was distinguished by an "unheard of bestiality combining the most modern technical implements with downright Asiatic torture."[4] Thus, Japan's actions in Russia contributed in a way to the shape that the Soviet regime eventually took, characterized by a civil-military ruling model and permanent fear of "capitalist encirclement." Soviet leaders, however, quickly realized that imperial Japan was Russia's most formidable neighbor of any in the east or west, and if the Soviet regime wanted to survive, cooperation rather than confrontation must become the guiding principle of Soviet-Japanese relations.

Simultaneously, the Russian Bolsheviks hoped that Japan, as the only industrially advanced country in Asia, and its working class would become the vanguard for a communist and anti-imperialist revolution in the region. Their hopes were supported by the significant political crisis that Japan was going through as the revolution was unfolding in Russia. After the Great War, growing dissent and discontent in the Japanese metropole were aided by wartime inflation and a postwar depression that created what Marxists of the time called a "revolutionary situation." Peasant unrest surged during the Rice Riots of 1918, which involved over one million people and were directly caused by the deployment of Japanese troops to the Russian East. Workers were organizing and staging an increasing number of strikes and walkouts. Students from middle- and upper-class families and elite universities were radicalizing, and shortly afterward they became the main pool for the Japanese communist movement. Incited by the revolution, in

1918 one of the most famous radical student organizations, the Shinjinkai (New People Society), proclaimed the arrival of a new era in which a just society, a society for the people, was to be built in Japan.

From 1919 forward, antigovernment democratic movements were rapidly turning "red," including the Shinjinkai, which renamed its journal *Democracy* to the Russian word for "the people," *Narod*. Discrete movements dedicated to universal suffrage, socialism, labor, students, and women; the liberation of outcasts (Burakumin) and tenant farmers, each advanced demands for more political, social, and economic justice and equality. Nongovernmental grassroots organizations such as the liberal Reimeikai (1918), the pan-Asianist Yūzonsha (1919), the Japanese Socialist League (1920), the National Socialist group (1919), the Japanese Communist Party (JCP, 1921–22), and many other smaller organizations, sprang up around the country, from Hokkaido to Kyushu, to challenge the existing political and economic order. By the mid-1920s, the wide usage of words like *capitalism*, *proletariat* and *bourgeoisie*, *class* and *class struggle*, *revolution*, and *political violence* showed how deeply and quickly a Western and specifically Marxist vocabulary and vision of social and historical development had penetrated the public consciousness. Within the first few years, one of the main effects of the Russian Revolution in Japanese society was to promote a new understanding of the social structure, in which society was divided not simply between the poor and the rich but between fundamentally antagonistic social classes. Under the revolution's impact, socialism began to be seriously considered in Japan as a solution to economic and political problems and an alternative to capitalism.

The novelty of the 1920s was that plans for domestic reforms began to be tightly linked to Japan's foreign policy. In terms of international affairs, many in Japan perceived that Japan's bureaucratic diplomacy failed to secure the country's well-deserved rights on the Asian continent and in the Pacific; first at the Paris Peace Conference in 1919 and then at the Washington Naval Conference of 1921–22. The Anti-Immigration Act of 1924 in the United States further fueled growing anti-Western sentiments among the public and decision makers. More and more public commentators and policy makers called for a new foreign policy, independent from the Anglo-American powers—which, they argued, would solve growing domestic problems as well. Japan's foreign policy was perceived as an extension of its domestic policy—one could not exist without the other. In this context, the new Soviet state, with its radical anticapitalist and anti-imperialist ideology, came to be seen by many in a new—and positive—light, as an alternative to the Western hegemonic order.[5]

The chief claim of this book is that in Japan's responses to the Russian Revolution, both geopolitical and ideological factors played equally important roles. Previous scholarship has tended to look at these factors separately, which resulted in a rather simple and even static picture: on one hand, there was a story of conflict between two ideological rivals, communist Russia and anticommunist Japan, and on the other hand, an uncomplicated story of the quick emergence of the uniformly communist Japanese Left. To complement the existing scholarship, this book brings together Japan's interwar foreign policy and domestic political and ideological changes, and it highlights their entanglement in Japan's responses to the Russian Revolution. Another intervention this book stages is to draw attention to the crucial importance of Korean and Chinese factors in Japan's reaction to communism. I argue that both Japanese political and military policy makers, as well as the Japanese Left and Right, responded not simply to the events in Russia but to the revolutionary ferment they caused in colonial Korea and China. In this sense, it was not only revolutionary Russia but revolutionary Korea and China that conditioned Japan's reactions to the Russian Revolution. Ultimately, diverse interpretations and responses to the revolution, in which both geopolitical and ideological factors played a role, reveal a riven Japan in which disparate visions of its future competed intensely with each other.

The book is thus divided into two parts. Part I concerns the diverse responses of Japanese foreign and domestic policy makers to the revolutionary process in Russia during the 1920s. Japan's official relations with Soviet Russia were formulated by different interest groups—from liberals to conservatives, officials of the Foreign Ministry and army and naval offices, party politicians—and, finally, various pressure groups. It often has been assumed as a given in Western scholarship that the interwar Japanese political and military elite were *naturally* anticommunist. By examining proposed policies of these various groups vis-à-vis communist Russia, it becomes clear that their attitudes were much more nuanced, not as self-evident as has been presumed, and even counterintuitive.

Part II, in contrast, deals with Japanese leftists' debates over the meaning of the Russian Revolution and the merits of socialism and communism. Despite its characteristic inward orientation and preoccupation with domestic politics, I argue that Japanese leftist debates were greatly influenced by international politics of the day. The Soviet advance in East Asia and mass communist conversion in Korea and China had an enormous impact on Japanese leftist discourse. The Russian Revolution had the effect of an ideological earthquake in Japan, and in East Asia in general, after which the landscape looked very different: some moved to the Far Left, and many gravitated to the Far Right. However, this process took some time to settle down because the Russian Revolution itself was ongoing throughout the 1920s, sending mixed messages to leftists around the world, including Japan.

Japan's engagement with international communism, both abroad and at home, had an enormous impact, leaving permanent imprints on its political, intellectual, social, and cultural landscape. Together, Parts I and II tell the story of entanglement, showing how the communist revolution, its containment, and issues of the national community, nation, empire, and imperialism became integrally connected in interwar Japan.

The nature of communist Russia presented a real conundrum for all figures active in Japanese politics, but the question of its geopolitical aspirations was particularly pressing to those engaged in policy making, discussed in Part I of this book. The question was greatly complicated by the fact that from the start, the new Bolshevik leadership exercised a double diplomacy. Leon Trotsky, as people's commissar for foreign affairs, declared in November 1917: "I will issue a few revolutionary proclamations to the peoples of the world and then shut up shop."[6] To bring about a world revolution, the Soviet government created the Third Communist International (the Comintern) in March 1919. The Comintern quickly developed into a global organization, the first of its kind—with ideologically devoted members, seemingly bottomless funds (as well as arms), and military instructors experienced in the Russian Civil War, which allowed the organization to mount impressive operations. But as proletarian revolutions did not materialize in Europe, the Bolshevik leaders' objective became to remain in power, even if it meant unleashing terror against their own people, including their own comrades. Preoccupied with the survival of the new regime, Soviet diplomacy strove for full acceptance internationally as a state equal to the world's great powers. Consequently, it had to compromise its revolutionary message and dissociate the Soviet state from the radical Comintern. Nevertheless, even as the Soviet government conducted conventional diplomacy and signed treaties with capitalist countries, the Comintern continued to toil to destabilize those same countries until it was finally dissolved by Stalin in 1943.

The Bolsheviks' new form of international diplomacy derived from its two chief goals: survival of the Soviet regime, and facilitation of the world proletarian revolution. They appealed to governments for establishment of normal diplomatic relations while trying to incite their citizens to initiate socialist revolutions at home. This dual foreign policy was soon expressed in the creation of mutually exclusive organizations: the People's Commissariat for Foreign Affairs (later Ministry of Foreign Affairs) and the Comintern. The former took steps to secure formal relations with foreign powers, trying to convince them that the Soviet Union was a normal diplomatic power—pragmatic, cynical, and not at all revolutionary—to secure Russia's national interests. Meanwhile, in an effort to spread the worldwide revolution, the Comintern engaged in aggressive foreign propaganda and conducted an activist policy, most importantly in China, to create an impressive radical anti-imperialist and anti-Japanese network in East Asia ready to take power as opportunity might present. As such, during the 1920s, the

Comintern presented the Ministry of Foreign Affairs with a host of problems, not least as a result of the presence of uncontrollable Comintern agents within foreign missions and the negative impact on diplomacy of Soviet foreign propaganda. In East Asia, the Soviet government had to balance an impossible act: to intervene in China to advance a socialist revolution and yet to attempt a policy of rapprochement with the Japanese Empire to secure Russia's borders and its interests on the Chinese Eastern Railway (CER). Few were fooled by the Soviet leaders' insistence that the Comintern acted on its own and was an independent foreign organization. Japanese political and military leaders were often driven mad by the apparent contradiction between the conciliatory statements of Soviet diplomatic officials and the Comintern's subversive actions in Japan, Korea, and China, monitored closely by Japanese intelligence. But it is important to realize that the distinction was there and used by both friends and foes of the Soviet state. Much of the Japanese attitude toward revolutionary Russia was determined by the way in which the relationship between the Soviet state and the Comintern was understood.

In assessing the "true" intentions of the new Bolshevik leadership in East Asia, there emerged essentially two approaches among key contributors to the debate over Japanese foreign policy and the need to contain Soviet encroachment. Importantly, these two approaches essentially mirrored the Soviet dual diplomacy.

The first view considered communist Russia as another state, perhaps less normal but nevertheless a state in its traditional meaning, whose foreign and domestic politics were determined by its unique geopolitical condition. Japanese policy makers argued that as a Eurasian superstate, the Soviet Union, like its predecessor imperial Russia, prioritized the security and integrity of its territories and inherited spheres of influence. While not downplaying the radicalism and danger of the communist ideology, the proponents of this view—such as Gotō Shinpei, Shidehara Kijūrō and even General Tanaka Gi'ichi—argued that the Soviet state's objectives differed from the objectives of the Comintern. Throughout the 1920s, some party politicians, business leaders, and nongovernmental groups began to advocate rapprochement with the communist state, based on the convenient separation of the Soviet national state and the Comintern as an international revolutionary organization. These Japanese imperial policy makers were, in a way, cynical realists who regarded the Soviet state's interests as selfish and imperialist, in the same way that imperial Russia's had been. Consequently, the basic understanding behind the recognition of the USSR in 1925 was similar to that behind the Russo-Japanese rapprochement between 1907 and 1917, and the Soviet-Japanese Neutrality Pact of 1941—that is, a deal could be made with the Russian communists for coexistence on the Asian continent, based on the division of spheres of influence.

The second approach held that the Soviet state was truly radical, and the sole purpose of its existence was to make the world "red." Taking Trotsky's declarations seriously, the proponents of this view—mainly officials of the Foreign Ministry (Motono Ichirō), conservative bureaucrats from the Home and Justice Ministries, liberal commentators (Yoshino Sakuzō and Fukuda Tokuzō), the army (Araki Sadao), and national socialists (Takabatake Motoyuki)—did not differentiate between the Soviet state and the Comintern. They considered the Comintern and communism to be the main ideological threat to Japan's national polity. Concern over the effect of communist ideology on domestic society united such disparate groups as liberals and the conservative bureaucracy, the army, and rightist groups. They understood communism as fundamentally a foreign, alien "disease" against which the national community must be protected. Anxiety over the red menace led to heightened concern about the boundaries and foundations of the national community and the domestic suppression of any leftist (and later rightist) opposition, as well as the emergence of various political anticommunist imaginaries, from traditional monarchist to fascist. As this book argues, the emergence of the police state in Japan in the 1930s was not simply a consequence of the conservative push against new liberal and leftist programs, but the result of concerted efforts by liberals and conservatives alike, national socialists, and rightist groups to defend the nation from international communism by launching its own ideological revolution at home; and for some, by imperial expansion abroad.

The army's attitude toward communist Russia combined these two approaches. Before and after the Russian Revolution of 1917, the army was consistent in regarding imperial Russia, and later the Soviet Union, as an existential threat to the security of the Japanese nation and its economic interests in China and Korea. For military leaders like Yamagata Aritomo and Araki Sadao, the very geopolitical situation of the Russian state—be it imperial or communist—its vital interests and dependence on the Asian continent, determined the Japanese army's antagonistic attitude. The army's anti-Russian sentiments became truly anticommunist and anti-Soviet once the revolution, with its anti-imperialist and anti-Japanese message, recruited to its cause Korean and Chinese national liberation and leftist fighters. The frontier Kwantung Army's actions in Manchuria were justified by the defense of not only Japan but the whole of Asia and even the world (the first Soviet satellite state was, after all, the Mongolian People's Republic) against Russian communist imperialism. The navy, however, did not share the army's preoccupation with Soviet Russia, and at times even openly promoted pro-Soviet policies, to the army's great agitation. The army's anticommunism thus overlaid and combined with its old anxieties about the northern neighbor, dating back to the late nineteenth century, while exposing the disunity within the military in regard to the objectives of national defense policies.

These two approaches to understanding the Soviet state informed both developments: the domestic ideological changes, and Japan's international political strategies. But I conclude that more often than not, domestic anticommunist policies had few repercussions for Japan's foreign policy, which followed its own objectives. Even the army, the strongest anticommunist force in interwar Japan, was eventually forced to accept the geopolitical framework worked out between imperial Japan and imperial Russia *before* 1917, based on the division of spheres of influence in East Asia. This was maintained until 1945, with some modifications.

This book therefore complicates the commonly held assumption about anticommunism in imperial Japan. It often has been assumed that military and civilian policy makers alike were ideological anticommunists, and that their anticommunist convictions shaped Japan's foreign policy during the interwar period. More often than not, Western historians have considered anticommunism in imperial Japan as a given, without questioning its internal and external origins, its evolution as Soviet state building progressed, and nuances in interpretation of the Russian Revolution and Soviet communism within Japanese political, military, and intellectual elites. This oversight, I believe, is partly due to the way in which Soviet-Japanese relations have been approached. Taking the ideological differences between communist Russia and imperial Japan as an established fact, scholars have paid much attention to the history of Soviet-Japanese military conflicts, and their diplomatic and ideological confrontation and rivalry, rather than to their cooperation and mutual interests in the region.[7]

Ultimately, Japan's responses to the Russian Revolution were determined by geography and geopolitics, in which regional and global factors, as well as matters of national interest and security, determined Japanese policy makers' relations with the Soviet state and communist ideology. In dealing with Russian communists, Japanese decision makers took into consideration multiple factors, in which the advantages of cooperation with the Soviet Union in order to ensure gains for their empire often outweighed any possible ideological loathing on their part. Confrontation could easily be changed to cooperation, and today's foes could become tomorrow's friends—especially if big money (fishery and oil) became involved, a common neighbor (China) suddenly ran amok, or a third power (the United States) claimed political and moral authority over the world order.

"The Russian Revolution was the biggest and most dramatic event in my life. Before, we often talked about a revolution, but we had no idea how to do it, how it would look, where it would happen. It was an imaginary thing, a fantasy. . . . At a labor union study meeting I even could not speak about the Revolution as tears overwhelmed me," wrote Yamakawa Hitoshi, one of the main leaders of the Japanese communist movement, in his postwar memoir.[8] Modern Japan had a significant and long-standing current of oppositional thinking and action well before the Russian Revolution. Notably, the People's Rights Movement of the 1870s and 1880s, which protested the cliquism of the Meiji government and demanded political enfranchisement, was foundational to the emergence of socialist discourse in Japan. Since then, concerned with worsening social and economic problems, Japanese political activists had been seized by a passion for participating in national politics. The socialist movement, however, suffered a major blow when a group of anarchists-socialists was convicted of plotting to assassinate the Meiji emperor and executed in 1911, in what is known as the High Treason Incident. Only in 1917, with the Russian Revolution, did the Japanese opposition revive, and the revolution became a catalyst—moving it to another, more radical, level. Under its impact, socialism began to be seriously considered in Japan as a solution to economic problems and an alternative to capitalism. The revolution's significance, however, also lay elsewhere. The Bolsheviks' success provided a model for organization and tactics to achieve what Japanese non-government groups and activists had always sought: participation in national politics in order to improve social and economic conditions.

In Japan, there exists an enormous scholarship on the Japanese Left which, however, has tended to limit the story of Japanese radicalism to national history, rarely studying it until recently in the context of the empire and international politics, let alone in conjunction with the ideological and military penetration by Russian Bolsheviks into the region.[9] In English-speaking scholarship, communism is still treated as marginal in comparison to the great significance attributed to the liberal-democratic and nationalist/fascist movements of the interwar period.[10] To underscore the Bolsheviks' massive impact on Japanese politics and society, the second part of this book focuses on early leftist discussions of the Russian Revolution taking place in the 1920s.[11] I examine three main interpretations of the Russian Revolution offered by anarchists (Ōsugi Sakae and Takao Heibē), national socialists (Takabatake Motoyuki), and communists of the early JCP variety (Yamakawa Hitoshi). By bringing to light fierce debates among these three interpretations over the meanings and merits of the Russian Revolution—and socialism in general—in resolving economic, political, and social problems, I demonstrate how the interwar Left in Japan developed, broadened its horizons, and finally contributed to the shape that interwar society eventually took. My intention is to offer further nuance to the existing consensus that the failure of the Japanese Left to mount any meaningful resistance to the increasingly oppressive and militarized state was due to the power of the imperial state and the effectiveness of its police apparatus. While acknowledging the validity of this argument, my chief claim is that the battle, in fact, was lost first within the Left.

To underscore my claim, I shift attention from the relationship between the state—either Japanese or Soviet—and leftist movements to the early leftist *internal* intellectual debates vis-à-vis Soviet Russia. By examining early leftist discourses on the Russian Revolution, I demonstrate that despite leftists' enthusiasm for the Russian Revolution and its supranational and anticapitalist vision, these discourses contained and were stymied by a simultaneous commitment to the nation and the national community. This conflation of Marxism and nationalism was, of course, a global post–World War I phenomenon, especially in those countries where socialism amalgamated with the goals of national independence and rapid modernization. By contrast, in interwar Japan, the main agenda of leftist groups and activists was the claim to political and social leadership in an imperial society. They sought to inaugurate a new politics to bring about social and moral regeneration, as well as economic and political justice. For these activists, the Russian Revolution was the inspiration and model for the organization of mass national politics, which was a new post–World War I phenomenon. They placed the utmost priority on politics—that is, on trying to bring the people (the masses) into politics and letting politics penetrate deep into social and cultural life. They considered themselves representatives of the will of the masses, whether workers or the Japanese people as a whole. Within the leftist debates over the supposedly internationalist Russian Revolution, therefore, the nation and national politics were a given premise and their main objective.

Finally, the Russian Revolution's supranational vision became the crucible of Japanese socialism and forced Japanese radicals to confront and reformulate the relationships between internationalism, nation, and empire. Ultimately, in leftist discourse, supranational concerns often became dependent on and subordinate to national and imperial ones. I argue, however, that their initial doubts about the universalism of the Russian Revolution and the authority of Russian communists formed the main reason for Japanese socialists' eventual rejection of communist internationalism. Their doubts, in turn, were based on the deeply rooted conviction of cultural, national, racial, and civilizational differences between Japan and Russia, and between Japan and the rest of Asia. One of the main claims of this book is that resistance to Soviet Russia and Soviet communism became such a dominant trope among leftist political intellectuals and activists that it overshadowed the awareness and urgency of challenging Japan's own imperial project and growing nationalism. In the end, concern over Soviet communism and the Soviet state's growing influence in East Asia led the majority of radicals to prioritize the nation and its interests above the immediate concerns of the international proletariat.

The question of when the Russian Revolution ended is important in understanding the revolution's impact in Asia. Sheila Fitzpatrick, an authoritative historian of the Russian Revolution, argued that it ended in 1937–38 with the Great Stalinist Purges, while all its twists and turns—including the New Economic Policy in 1921, Lenin's death and Stalin's rise, the First Five-Year Plan and the "Cultural Revolution" in the late 1920s—were merely stages of a twenty-year process of revolution.[12] In Part II, however, I argue that for Japan and its leftists, the Russian Revolution ended in 1928–29, because by that time, as revolutionary fervor was waning inside Russia as well, a consensus was reached about the meanings and merits of the Russian Revolution for modern Japan. The consensus was abrupt and forced, mainly because of Japan's renewal of belligerence in China beginning in 1927. The subsequent leftist debates were less concerned with the Russian Revolution per se than with Japanese imperialism abroad and its repercussions within Japanese society.

I believe, however, that the way in which Japanese leftists approached their subsequent dilemmas—including the relationship with Stalinism and Chinese communism, the outbreak of war in China, and the rise of the military-bureaucratic regime at home (to name a few)—was determined by their initial reaction to the Russian Revolution. Ultimately, intense debates and disagreements vis-à-vis the Russian Revolution and Soviet communism about what type of revolution Japan needed, and how Japan was different from Russia and the rest of Asia, essentially prevented Japanese radicals from confronting critically their own assumptions and prejudices. In the 1930s, against the backdrop of economic depression, the escalating siege mentality, and the emergence of the military-bureaucratic regime, the anti-Bolshevik national Left was badly equipped to mount any meaningful opposition to the Japanese government and its military commitment to the imperial offensive on the Asian continent.

The amalgam of reactions to the Russian Revolution described in this book reveals Japan at a crossroads. There was no agreement, either among factions of the government, bureaucracy, and the military, or among members of socialist and rightist movements, about what to make of communism and Soviet Russia. Their discordance ultimately reflects the ideological and geopolitical uncertainties in which Japan found itself in the 1920s, lacking both a core programmatic vision for its society and national state, and a single, coherent policy of regional integration. The Russian Revolution thus heralded the emergence of alternative visions of what modern Japan ought to be.

Part I

"OUR NORTHERN NEIGHBOR"

BEFORE 1917

Umi no hi kogoru   hokkoku mo
Harukaze ima zo   fuki wataru
Sanbyaku-nenrai   bakko seshi
Roshia wo utan   toki wa kinu
Over the north country
whose seas are frozen
Spring wind blows
It is time to beat Russia
Rampant for three hundred years.

—Mori Ōgai, "Regiment Song of the Second Army," 1904

It struck me, too, that Dostoevsky's youth is no stranger, this youth whose mind is in turmoil because of Western ideas and who, in the midst of this intellectual agitation, has utterly lost his home. How very closely he resembles us. Indeed, I repeatedly ran into scenes that made me feel that the author was describing me, that he had me firmly in his grasp.

—Kobayashi Hideo, *Literature of the Lost Home*, 1933

In 1771, a Polish adventurer born in Hungary, Maurice Benyovsky, escaped his prison in Siberia, where he was sent for taking part in a Polish rebellion against tsarist Russia, and shortly afterward arrived in Japan with some bad news for the Japanese. The Russians, warned Benyovsky, were planning to attack the Japanese from the north and subjugate the Japanese nation in the very near future. Even though the country had enjoyed a period of relative security in its external borders due to its policy of seclusion since 1635, Benyovsky's claims struck a nerve in Japan. Thus began the Japanese history of the "northern problem" (*hoppō no kyōi*, or the "threat from the North"), an awareness that due to Russia's possession of territories on the Asian continent and its geographical proximity to Japan, Russo-Japanese relations must follow their own logic, distinct from those Japan would have with European powers and later the United States. The crucial part of that awareness was the early realization that Russia was a Eurasian empire in possession of vast Asian populations and territories, and that it had a long, tightly connected history of relations with the Mongol and Chinese Empires. Russia's perplexing cultural and geographical position split Japanese attitudes toward it from then on essentially into two opposing camps: those who conceived of the Russian state and society as aggressive and expansionist and therefore a direct threat to the Japanese nation, and those who considered cooperation with Russia to be vital for the stability and prosperity of Japan and East Asia in general. As the next two chapters demonstrate, the Russian Revolution of 1917 and the arrival of international communism in Asia did not significantly alter this basic framework, which defined Japan's attitudes toward Russia as much during the imperial period of Russian history as it did during the Soviet period.

The Japanese discovered that they had neighbors to the north in the early eighteenth century.[1] Russian explorers reached the Pacific Ocean in 1638, penetrating the Far East in their search for a passage to the American continent. Between 1711 and 1768, the Russians occupied a group of islands northeast of the island of Ezo, now Hokkaido, which they named Kurily, or Smokies. Benyovsky's arrival in Japan on his way to Europe, coupled with a Russian request for trade in 1778 and Russian landings in Sakhalin five years later, prompted the military rulers of Japan to explore their northern possessions and defenses. Several Japanese expeditions to survey the islands of Ezo and Sakhalin followed in the late eighteenth century, producing the first Japanese accounts about the geography, climate, and population of Ezo, Sakhalin, and the Kurile Islands.[2] Knowledge about Russia, however, was acquired mainly from Dutch and Chinese books.

One of the earliest firsthand Japanese accounts of Russia was recorded by an educated merchant, Daikokuya Kōdayū, whose boat crashed near Kamchatka in 1783. After spending several years in Siberia, he traveled to Saint Petersburg, where he was granted an audience with Catherine the Great. Upon his return home in 1792, based on the information Kōdayū provided to Tokugawa official scholars, a detailed report on Russia (totaling eleven volumes) was produced strictly for government use.[3] Kōdayū's celebrated return to Japan spurred public interest in the northern neighbor, resulting in the publication of many books on Russia, which were heavily focused on geography, history, and the military; in comparison, earlier Dutch-Western studies focused largely on science.[4] It is important to note, however, that Japanese officials' worries about Russia were less focused on the possibility of a military threat to Japan and more concerned with the expansion of Russian influence to the east, which the Japanese feared might lead to the loss of Japanese influence over Ainu lands (the northern parts of today's Hokkaido and some of the Kurile Islands). The Tokugawa government was afraid that the Ainu people, whose position within the Tokugawa administrative system was not settled, would want to come under the control of what was perceived by the Tokugawa officials as the more civilized Russian Empire.[5] To counteract this, Japanese Tokugawa officials argued that the Ainu people had been traditionally under the patronage of Matsumae, a Tokugawa domain on the southern tip of Ezo Island, and therefore the Ainu land was Japanese territory.[6]

Since the 1850s, Japan had to contend with Russia's growing imperial ambitions in Asia. With the 1689 Treaty of Nerchinsk, Russia settled its borders with Qing China, dividing the Mongols and their territories. Taking advantage of China's defeats in the Opium Wars (1839–42, 1856–60) and its paralysis during the Taiping Rebellion (1851–64), Russia signed the Beijing Convention of 1860 and acquired the Trans-Amur and Trans-Ussuri regions, establishing at its eastern edge a city port named Vladivostok (literally, "ruler of the East"). In 1853, Russian Vice Admiral Evfimii Putyatin and his mission arrived at Nagasaki, only one and a half months later than Commodore Matthew Perry from the United States, to start negotiations that resulted in the Treaty of Shimoda of 1855. The treaty settled the Russian and Japanese national boundary in the Kurile Islands, opened three Japanese ports for Russia, and established extraterritoriality rights for both Japanese and Russians. As the result of the negotiations between the Russian government and the Tokugawa officials, the Kurile archipelago was divided between Russia and Japan, while Sakhalin was left under the joint sovereignty of both nations. Thus, Japan's entrance into international politics coincided with Russia's push to China, Korea, and Japan; from that point on, Japan's view of international relations in East Asia had to revolve around Russia's thrust into the region.[7]

The Meiji Restoration (Meiji ishin) of 1868 became one of those great historical events, the impact of which extended far beyond the Japanese islands and far beyond the date of its accomplishment. In 1867, a military uprising by a group of samurai opponents put an end to the long-lived Tokugawa shogunate. As a way to unite the country in the face of the Western advance into Japan and the East Asian region, the new leadership declared the restoration of imperial rule. The new Meiji imperial government, established in 1868, declared the political, economic, social, and military modernization of the country as its chief aims, exemplified in the slogan "rich country, strong army" (fukoku kyōhei). What started as a local power struggle and a local modernizing program transformed Japan into a powerful modern imperial nation-state, whose example many in the non-Western world soon aspired to emulate.

Japanese Meiji leadership, however, never felt secure about Japan's standing. Witnessing the "scramble for China," the new modernizing political and intellectual elite saw Western powers, including Russia, as predators ready to take advantage of weakened Japan. Fear of colonization, formal or informal, became a sort of paranoia, permeating the general public, the political elite, and the military. To widen its defense perimeter, Japan embarked on imperial expansion, first in Hokkaido in 1869 and then in the Ryūkyū Islands in 1879. Japan's colonization of Hokkaido led to new border negotiations with Russia: in 1875 the Russian

Empire obtained undisputed sovereignty over Sakhalin Island, which gave it an exit to the Pacific Ocean, while Japan retained the Kurile Islands. Unhappy with the outcome, the Japanese would remember this treaty as treacherous because Russia, they claimed, had used the weakness of Japan for its own gain.[8] Hasegawa Tatsunosuke, better known under his pen name Futabatei Shimei, the "father of modern Japanese literature," was motivated to enter the Foreign Languages School (Gaigo Gakkō) after the 1875 treaty and devote himself to the study of the Russian language out of a deep-seated "feeling of suspicion and animosity" toward the Russian imperial state.[9] (Despite this antipathy, Futabatei become the chief cause of Japan's infatuation with Russian literature, translating more than thirty major Russian literary works into Japanese.)

As Korea began to loom large in Japan's foreign policy, so too worries increased regarding Russia's plans for the Korean Peninsula. Various missions dispatched by the Foreign Ministry to Russia and Korea since 1870 had discovered that Russia and Korea shared a border, and that there was growing Korean immigration to the Russian Far East. The Foreign Ministry and the newly established army (1871) became alarmed by the possibility of Russia using Korean immigration to encroach on Korean territory, which would have been perceived as a direct threat to Japan's security.[10] One of the consequences of the discovery of the shared Russo-Korean border was the emergence of the "Korean Question" among the political and military elite. Outlining the basic principles of the Japanese modern military in 1871, Yamagata Aritomo (1838–1922)—then chief of the General Staff, twice prime minister, and one of the most powerful men in Meiji Japan—stated that Japan needed to expand its military capability in order to protect its territory from foreign aggression, specifically from Russia's southward advance.[11] The 1876 Treaty of Kanghwa between Japan and Korea, which gave Japan special privileges in Korea and was a classic "unequal treaty," was also in part an outcome of Japan's Russian policy.

More information on Russia and its people became available to the Japanese public as economic and cultural relations expanded in the second half of the nineteenth century. While visiting Russia, Japanese officials, journalists, businessmen, and travelers noted the peculiarity of the Russian state and its society, its difference from West European countries, as well as its poverty and the extreme mismanagement of its imperial territories. Many Japanese traveled through Russia by way of Siberia and were appalled by the poverty of Russian peasants, the corruption of the authorities, and the vast differences between "Asiatic" and European Russia. In the famous classification of nations published in the government organ *Meiji gekkan* (Monthly magazine of Meiji, 1868), Russia was ranked in the second category (*kaika no kuni*) along with Italy, Spain, Portugal, and the countries of Latin America.[12] One of the most important and influential intellectuals of the nineteenth century, Fukuzawa Yukichi (1834–1901), who visited Russia as part of the Takenouchi mission (1860–61) dispatched by the Tokugawa government, popularized in his bestselling books the notion of an autocratic and barbaric Russia. Fukuzawa foresaw that poverty in Russia might become a major cause for antigovernment rebellions that would turn the autocratic state to even more repressive measures against its own people.[13]

However, the most detailed descriptions of Russia and its activities in China, Korea, and Central Asia were provided not by civilians but by military sojourners.[14] One of the first accounts of Russia was written by Vice Admiral Enomoto Takeaki, the Japanese plenipotentiary in the 1875 Treaty, who stayed in Russia for three years and on his journey back in 1878 wrote *Siberian Diaries* (Shiberia nikki). He documented different aspects of Russian life, including information about the Russian army, possibilities of trade with Russia, and the economy and ethnic population of Siberia. Because of their intelligence value, the diaries were restricted for army intelligence use and only appeared in 1935 as an army publication.[15] In 1892–93, Major Fukushima Yasumasa made a trip on horseback from Berlin to Vladivostok to gather military intelligence on the building of the Trans-Siberian Railway. His journey made him a national hero and he was documented daily by leading newspapers, which took this opportunity to inform their readers about conditions in Russia.[16] One of the important consequences of these direct observations and writings was that framing Russia as backward vis-à-vis not only the West but also Japan became a common trope among the ruling elite as well as the general public. Repeated observations about Russian backwardness caused many travelers and readers to admire Russia less, appreciate Meiji Japan more, and feel pride in Japan's achievements in modernization. The Japanese were fond of pointing out that Japan became a constitutional monarchy in 1889, seventeen years earlier than Russia, which established its first constitution only in 1905 and as a direct result (the contemporary Japanese also liked to stress) of the Russo-Japanese War of 1904–5. This general preconception about the backwardness of Russia and its peculiar historical and geographical conditions played a crucial role in the reception of the Russian Revolution not only among the political establishment and the general public but also the Japanese Left.

The general preconception of a backward Russia was in stark contrast to the business opportunities many Japanese saw in the Russian Far East. The Japanese community in the Far East, especially in Vladivostok, steadily grew, along with the Chinese and Korean communities. Japanese industrial trusts such as Mitsubishi and Mitsui, eagerly interested in the exploitation of timber and oil on Sakhalin, were also forerunners of Japan's economic expansion in the region.[17] Among the Japanese retailers who settled in the Russian Far East were traders, tourist organizers, joiners, smiths, tailors, and owners of laundries, and collectively they owned one-fifth of all enterprises in the Maritime Province. But the most numerous and prosperous group that had vital interests in establishing relations with Russia were fishermen and the fishing business communities. In the decade before the Russian Revolution, every year up to fifteen thousand Japanese fishermen worked in fisheries leased by Japanese companies in Russia.[18] And it was big business circles, especially the powerful fishery business, that later would become the most forceful and successful advocate for rapprochement with communist Russia.

After a short period of amicable relations, the construction of the Trans-Siberian Railway (1891–1902) set off a fierce rivalry between Russia and Japan over the control of Korea and Manchuria. The point of contention was that a part of the Trans-Siberian Railway went through China's territory, which became the Chinese Eastern Railway (CER), acquired through a Russian concession ("the alienation zone"). As the famous journalist Kuga Katsunan noted in retrospect, "the 24th year of Meiji [1891] was, in fact, the year when the Eastern Question was born."[19] By constructing the railway, Russia planned to curb England's growing dominance in the Chinese market, maintain a permanent fleet in Vladivostok, and prevent foreign control of the Far East—a region vulnerable because of population sparseness and weak lines of communication. The Trans-Siberian Railway enabled Russia to reinforce its eastern borders without reliance on a maritime route, which was constrained by the British navy. Now Russia was in a position to greatly increase its political and military influence in the East Asian region. The construction of the railway sparked concerns among the Japanese public and government. As the Japanese understood it, the new railway would not simply connect Vladivostok with Moscow and Europe; it would make possible the transfer of weapons and troops from the western part of Russia to Asia. As Kuga wrote, it was the news of the railway that "made the Japanese nation become aware of foreign affairs," giving birth to further fears that Japan was under direct military threat from Russia. As a matter of fact, the Russians had indeed moved to the Far East in order to use the area as a base for Russian expansion into Manchuria. Foreseeing Russian intentions, General Yamagata Aritomo warned Emperor Meiji in 1892 that in a decade, the completion of the railway would enable Russia to penetrate Manchuria, Mongolia, and China proper.[20] The Russian advance in Manchuria was considered by the Japanese as the first step in the colonization of Korea, itself only over 120 miles away from the Japanese island of Kyushu. Their fears climaxed with the Ōtsu Incident in 1891, when the future Nicholas II traveled to Japan to celebrate the opening of the Trans-Siberian Railway. He was attacked and injured by one of his Japanese guards, who thought his visit was intended to plan a possible invasion of Japan. The Russian government was satisfied by the measures taken, which included the resignations of the home minister and foreign minister, and the suicide of a Japanese woman who begged the Russians for forgiveness on behalf of the whole nation.[21]

The Sino-Japanese War of 1894–95, and more so the Triple Intervention that followed, brought to the surface the basic conflict between Japan's and Russia's objectives for the Asian continent. Japan's stunning victory in the war against Qing China, the spectacle of Japanese military power, and the extent of Japanese demands and ambitions induced a turnabout in Russian policy. As a result of its victory, Japan received huge indemnities from China and acquired its first colony, Taiwan, and the Liaodong Peninsula, including Port Arthur. Russia decided to intervene, and the Russian-German-French Triple Intervention (initiated by Russia) forced Japan to return the Liaodong Peninsula. Shortly after the Triple Intervention, in 1898, Russia leased the peninsula and obtained the right to build a branch of the Chinese Eastern Railway, which extended southward from the newly founded city of Harbin (aptly called the Manchurian Petersburg for the great Russian presence in it) to Port Arthur. Although the CER was a private company and the land legally belonged to the Chinese state, it secured not only the Russian officials' control of the state of affairs on the railway zone but also Russian domination of Manchuria in general. Moreover, because the Trans-Siberian Railway ended in Vladivostok, the Russian imperial state managed to increase its influence in the Pacific as well. The situation began to look even more dire to the Japanese leadership as Russian economic and military activities in Korea intensified: Russian army officers were sent to reorganize the Korean army in 1896, the Russian-Korean border was militarized, and concessions to exploit timber, mineral resources, and lumber were granted to Russian companies.

Russia was the biggest imperialist offender, in Japan's view, along with Britain, but the attitude toward Russia was rather complex and went through major swings from positive to negative, and back to positive—not least because both, as emerging major powers, had to settle territorial claims in the East Asian region. The Triple Intervention thus saw the emergence of an anti-Russian faction among Japanese policy makers, as well as an influential pro-Russian faction. The pro-Russian faction included Prime Minister Itō Hirobumi, the elder statesman Inoue Kaoru, who had extensive connections to the business world, and Yamagata Aritomo. This faction was soon reinforced by Gotō Shinpei (1857–1929), Itō Hirobumi's protégé, whose interest in Russia arose while he served as the first president of the South Manchurian Railway (1906–8). Itō, Yamagata, Inoue, and later Gotō opposed confrontation with Russia and instead sought peaceful cooperation in Korea and Manchuria. In 1896, Yamagata attended the coronation of Nicholas II, where the Yamagata-Lobanov agreement was signed, later succeeded by the Nishi-Rosen agreement of 1898. Both agreements provided a basic framework for a divided sphere of influence in the region, which would recognize Russia's special interests in Manchuria and Japan's in Korea. These efforts, however, were thwarted by the unfolding events in China: the Boxer Rebellion of 1900, which prompted Japan's and Russia's military intervention into Chinese affairs along with that of other Western powers.

After the suppression of the antiforeign movement in China, the Russian troops remained stationed in Manchuria, which exacerbated Japanese public concern for the fate of China, and by extension Korea. Distressed by the Boxer Rebellion, the socialist Kōtoku Shūsui penned the instantly famous book *Imperialism: Monster of the Twentieth Century* (Nijū seiki no kaibutsu tekokushugi, 1901), in which he argued that Japan's mission was to be a model and guide for China, preserve its territorial integrity, and act as a mediator between China and Western powers.[22] The seeming reluctance of the Russians to evacuate (the evacuation also was forestalled by logistical difficulties in the mismanaged Russian Empire) convinced many in the Japanese army and the government, including Yamagata Aritomo, that Russia was entertaining predatory plans for Korea by establishing control over Manchuria. The voices for adoption of a strong foreign policy toward Russia gained momentum. Konoe Atsumaro, president of the House of Peers, and his followers assembled in 1903 a group of seven university professors, six of whom were from Tokyo Imperial University's prestigious faculty of law, and made them call on government leaders individually to lobby for war. The professors made their program public, which made an impact because at that time it was highly unusual for civilian outsiders to express openly their opinion on foreign policy.[23]

The most formidable pressure on the government came, however, from within the army. The most consequential outcome of the army's agitation was its new fixation not simply on Korea but now on Manchuria, both as a defense perimeter for Korea and as a valuable goal in itself. In 1903, high-ranked army and navy officers with responsibility for war planning and some middle-ranked members of the foreign ministry formed a secret society, the Kogetsukai.[24] Tanaka Gi'ichi, future prime minister, minister of war, and foreign affairs minister, was instrumental in its activities. A protégé of Yamagata Aritomo, Tanaka had intimate knowledge of Russia and its military capabilities. He was sent to Russia as an observer from the Second Section (intelligence) of the Army General Staff, and served in the Russian army, in the Novocherkassky Infantry Regiment, for five years between 1897 and 1902. Upon returning home in 1902, Tanaka, who by then was fluent in Russian, became head of the Russian Section of the Army General Staff, and his views were very influential in the development of Japan's plans for waging war with Russia. Tanaka argued that a successful war with Russia would secure the territorial integrity of Korea and establish Japan's position in northeast Asia—that is, in the whole of Manchuria. This was a consistent objective of

Tanaka's, which became evident in his later push for the Siberian Intervention in 1918. Kogetsukai members lobbied for their cause behind the scenes, approaching statesmen and finding support from Foreign Minister Komura Jutarō, War Minister Terauchi Masatake, and future Home Minister General Kodama Gentarō, chief of staff of Japan's Manchurian army. The strong anti-Russian views of middle-grade officers had thus been incorporated into the official position taken by military leaders, which in turn put considerable pressure and influence on government policy.[25]

Grassroots nationalist organizations that sprang up in the same decade also constituted a formidable lobby and exerted continuing pressure on the government. The most notorious of these was the Kokuryūkai (Black Dragon Society, also known as the Amur River Society, 1901), whose intention was to drive the Russians to the Amur River, then the frontier between Manchuria and Siberia. Other notable nationalist organizations included the Rōninkai (Society of Masterless Samurai, 1908), and the pro-government Tairo Dōshikai (Society of Comrades against Russia, originally called the People's League, 1900), which was also created with the assistance of Konoe Atsumaro. The unifying philosophy of Japanese nationalists was that Japan must contain Russia, expel it from the East, and "lay the foundation for a grand continental enterprise taking Manchuria, Mongolia, and Siberia as one region."[26] Part of their influence was based on continuous support from army headquarters, the Ministry of War, and the Foreign Ministry. In exchange for information and public agitation, the Ministry of War often secretly subsidized these organizations. Politicians also used nationalist organization for their own aims. Konoe, for example, was a close friend of the "father" of Japanese radical nationalism, Tōyama Mitsuru, leader of the Gen'yōsha. Konoe rallied Tōyama's support for his aggressive line, so that Tōyama visited Itō Hirobumi and threatened him for his alleged sympathy with Russia. Following rumors of assassination plots, Itō received police protection.[27]

Agitation in Japan for war with Russia, as well as Russia's inflexible diplomatic position, made war seem unavoidable.[28] War fever encompassed both countries. Spoiled by Japan's gains after its victory in the Sino-Japanese War, many in Japan agitated for a declaration of war. Moreover, for educated elites, the existing image of backward and despotic Russia made it easy to argue that the Russian people were in need of liberation and help from the Japanese army. The poet Ishikawa Takuboku and the liberal professor Yoshino Sakuzō believed that the imminent war with Russia was "for justice, for civilization, for equality, for the ultimate ideal." Later, Yoshino even characterized the 1905 Russian Revolution as the consequence of Japanese liberation efforts.[29] Tokutomi Roka, in his letter to his literary idol Leo Tolstoy in 1906, wrote: "I firmly believed we ought to defeat Russia. I loved the Russian people introduced by you and by other great writers of your country, but I enthusiastically insisted that we should never tolerate the tyranny of the Russian government. I was therefore satisfied with Japan's so-called victory and regretted during the peace negotiations that Russia did not bow low enough."[30] Many thus shared a conviction that Japan represented the civilized world and needed to take on its historical mission to fight backward—but at the same time imperialist—Russia in the name of progress, and peace in Asia. The war fever also revealed changing Japanese attitudes toward their empire: not only was territorial expansion welcomed, but warfare as the means to accomplish that became acceptable.

The Russian public was also guilty of agitation for war. There were those among the educated public who believed that Russians were liberators to Asians oppressed by the Chinese yoke, and that Russia's mission was to defend Europe against "the sea of the yellow race," which at that time designated imperial Japan. Japan stood for the generalized Asiatic hordes and came to be viewed as modern, cunning, intelligent, and therefore a more dangerous threat to Western Christian civilization. It was in Russia during the years leading to the Russo-Japanese War that the idea of Japan as a country of "Yellow Peril" took off and became a common phrase among the intelligentsia, members of high culture, and high-ranking bureaucrats.[31]

The impact of the Russo-Japanese War of 1904–5 on both countries cannot be overemphasized. Russia's loss in the war shook the empire to its very foundations, precipitating the Russian Revolution of 1905, the granting of the first constitution, the fracturing of Russian society and the Russian Empire, and ultimately, the overthrow of the Romanov dynasty in 1917. Russia's defeat exposed its weakness to the whole world. Once in awe of the Russian tsars—Peter the Great, for example, was a very popular figure in early Meiji Japan as a great modernizer—the Japanese soon abandoned sentiment for further ridicule of Russia's feudal and reactionary ways. Japan's victory had a particularly strong impact in the non-Western world—setting an example of what was perceived as a successful struggle by an Asian country against the "white man's domination," against Western predatory imperialism. Many in Japan agreed with this interpretation, but importantly, this sentiment was coupled with the feeling of national pride in Japan's final elevation to the status of a Great (by definition imperialist) Power. Heightened popular nationalist sentiments expressed themselves in public outrage over the provisions of the Treaty of Portsmouth, according to which Japan did not receive indemnities from Russia. However, in the protests that followed (one of the most famous being the Hibiya Riot of September 1905), one thing became clear: popular anger during the riots was directed at the government and the police but not at the emperor. Governments could be changed and blamed for troubles and failures, but for the public, the emperor endured beyond governments, politics, and class distinctions. The emperor was thus singled out by the ordinary people in their quest for justice and protection. If prior to the Russo-Japanese War the emperor was the symbol of national unity, after it he came to be regarded as the ruler of a great imperial power, on a par with or superior to other world empires.[32]

The Russo-Japanese War marked a shift in Japan's foreign policy toward establishing a strong foothold in Manchuria. According to the Treaty of Portsmouth, Japan acquired recognition of its paramount interest in Korea and possession of the southern half of Sakhalin. But the most momentous change was Japan's acquisition of the Russian rights to and concessions in southern Manchuria, leasehold of the Kwantung Territory (comprising 3,400 square kilometers of the Liaotung Peninsula, including the city of Dalniy, renamed Dairen by the Japanese), and a narrow railway zone from Port Arthur to Changchun, about 150 miles south of Harbin. Although the Portsmouth peace treaty was negotiated without official participation by the Chinese government, the Qing government later agreed to the terms of the treaty, additionally giving Japan the right to build a railway from Antung, near the Korean border, to Mukden; opening various timber preserves; and secretly agreeing it would not build lines parallel to the South Manchurian Railway (SMR). The Kwantung Territory governor-generalship, under the leadership of a general or lieutenant-general, administered the new acquisitions and commanded the army stationed in the areas between 1906 and 1919. In 1919, the Office of the Kwantung Governor-General became a civilian administration, while the Kwantung Army went under the jurisdiction of the newly established Kwantung Army Command, which became responsible for the protection of the Kwantung Leased Territory and the railway zone. As a result, the Kwantung Army Command began to consider, as its self-appointed task, that the economic development of Manchuria depended on it. Moreover, senior staff officers of the Kwantung Army held a strong conviction that Russia would attempt to regain control over southern Manchuria and took as its main task to prepare for such a "revenge war." With this aim in mind, the Kwantung headquarters demanded expansive military and administrative rights in Manchuria, much wider than railway zones would normally have.[33]

Responsibility for economic development in the Kwantung Leased Territory and railway zone was entrusted to a semigovernmental organization called the South Manchuria Railway Company (SMRC, in Japanese Mantetsu). Gotō Shinpei was appointed as its president, but he also was the army's pick. The army's chief of staff, Kodama Gentarō, who was also the chairman of the committee to establish the SMRC, pushed Gotō's candidacy. Kodama instructed Gotō that the tasks of the SMRC—the management of the railway, opening up of mines, improvement of agriculture, encouragement of Japanese settler migration to southern Manchuria—all these were means toward achieving the ultimate goal, which was to ward off Russia's southern advance.[34] Gotō, however, went beyond the call of duty, and as president of the SMRC formulated a policy of rapprochement with Russia. As the first step under Gotō's presidency, the SMRC's research department was established in 1906, becoming the most powerful center in Russian (and Chinese) studies, and providing crucial data and analysis for governmental and military foreign policies. Simultaneously, the Japan-Russia Association (Nichiro kyōkai) was established in Tokyo in 1906, with the direct support of the government, the military, and the imperial court.[35]

Gotō's undertakings in establishing more amicable relations with Russia symbolized, in fact, the start of a new phase in Russo-Japanese relations.[36] Itō Hirobumi and Gotō Shinpei succeeded in concluding the first Russo-Japanese agreement of 1907, which stipulated mutual recognition of each other's spheres of interest in Manchuria, Russian recognition of Japan's control over Korea, and Japanese recognition of Russia's special status in Outer Mongolia. Even the army conceded that working relations should be established with Russia. In 1907, the Army General Staff worked out a basic plan for Japan's national defense, authored by Tanaka Gi'ichi and redrafted by Yamagata. The "Imperial National Defense Plan" of 1907 stipulated that while Russia was still the main target of Japanese military preparedness, measures must be taken to settle the old feud and reach an understanding.[37] Not only did Japan's victory change the structure of power politics in East Asia, satisfying for a while Japan's ambitions on the continent, but the amicable phase was mainly due to the arrival of a third power in the region, the United States. The second Russo-Japanese agreement was signed in July 1910. The Foreign Ministry, previously skeptical about rapprochement with Russia, this time pushed for the entente, motivated to jointly protect Russian and Japanese interests in East Asia from the United States. In 1910, U.S. Secretary of State Philander C. Knox proposed to "neutralize" the SMR and CER, now controlled by Japan and Russia respectively, by creating an international syndicate to loan China the funds to purchase the SMR and CER. Until the loan was repaid, the railways would be controlled by an international body dominated by foreigners. Greatly alarmed by the United States' aggressive proposition, Japan and Russia strongly rejected the proposal, which prompted Britain and France to withdraw their initial support. The US proposal eventually died, but this incident demonstrated how developing Russo-Japanese cooperation, and their united opposition to any external pressure, became the foundation of a new order in East Asia. As a result, both countries were willing to overlook quite serious actions by the other side. In 1909, when Itō Hirobumi was assassinated by a Korean nationalist from Vladivostok at a train station in the Russian-Chinese city of Harbin during his meeting with Russian Minister of Finance V. N. Kokovtsov, the Japanese government took no diplomatic actions against Russia. When Japan annexed Korea in August 1910, Russia did not express any objections.[38]

The momentous event in China in 1911—the fall of the Qing dynasty and the establishment of a republican government—in effect destroyed China's political unity for the next two decades, the consequences of which both imperial Russia and imperial Japan had to grapple with instantly. During this period, China was run by various rival regimes, while its northern territories were controlled by competing warlords, whose chances for survival and dominance greatly depended on their cooperation with either Russia or Japan. The Japanese army jumped at this opportunity with proposals to establish pro-Japanese puppet-states in Manchuria and now-independent Mongolia but was checked by the Foreign Ministry and the government, who did not want troubles with Russia, Britain, and the United States, and preferred to secure economic rights by political means. Outer Mongolia's declaration of independence from China in 1911 prompted Japan's Foreign Ministry to sign the third agreement with Russia in 1912, which sought to separate Japanese and Russian interests in Inner and Outer Mongolia.[39]

The outbreak of World War I was another "golden" opportunity for Japan to solidify its political and economic power in East Asia. Japan declared war on Germany in August 1914, as did Russia, and moved rapidly into Shandong Province in China, acting on behalf of the Allies. While European powers were fighting the war in Europe, Japan consolidated its power in China. Partially satisfying its notorious "Twenty-One Demands" from January 1915, Japan signed the Sino-Japanese Treaty of 1915, which granted it special rights in southern Manchuria and Shandong Province, prolonging the term of exploitation of the SMR and the right of Japanese citizens to mine, live on, and rent land in the railway zone. Highly dependent on Japan's military aid, especially munitions, and looking for guarantees to help protect its eastern border and preserve a status quo relationship with Japan, Russia issued a statement in regard to the demands: "The Russian government considered the Demands as appropriate to be claimed to the Chinese government."[40]

Besides China, there was another issue (albeit less prominent and visible) that the Russian and Japanese governments had to deal with.[41] Although after Japan's victory in the Russo-Japanese War, and especially after the annexation of Korea in 1910, Russia relinquished its intention to meddle in Korean affairs, the Korean question remained on the table, simply because colonial Korea had shared borders with Russia. Russo-Japanese relations were marred mainly by the issue of Korean immigration.[42] Since the 1860s, Russia had offered incentives to attract Korean and Chinese immigrants to make up for the lack of cheap labor in the sparsely populated region. Korean immigrants settled in the Russian Maritime

Province as early as the 1860s, but the big influx of population happened after Japan's victory in the Russo-Japanese War, especially in 1908–9, when large numbers of regular Japanese troops forced Korean guerrillas out of their homeland and into China and Russia. In 1902, there were 32,410 Koreans residing in Russia; in 1910, this number grew to 80,000; by 1923, there were some 107,000 Koreans in Russia (17 percent of the total population); and by 1926, that number had risen to 168,000.[43] Vladivostok became the center of congregation for Korean political refugees and participants in the struggle against the Japanese regime, including top opposition leaders. Beginning in 1908, regular skirmishes took place between Korean guerillas operating from Russian territory and Japanese troops stationed on the Korean side. Attacks on the Japanese significantly intensified after Japan annexed Korea in 1910.[44] The Japanese government not only pressured the Russian government to police Korean insurgents, but also acted on its own. Japanese troops often shelled Korean villages on the Russian side of the border from Korean territory. The Japanese consul-general in Vladivostok and the Japanese Vladivostok Resident Association made attempts to establish control over Koreans in the Maritime Province and to prevent the growth of an anti-Japanese movement among Korean immigrants. Assaults on and murders of Japanese residents in the Maritime Province by Koreans were also steadily increasing.[45] After Itō's assassination by a Korean nationalist, the authorities of the Maritime Province, anxious to preserve good relations with Japan, worked on curbing Korean insurgent activities. In 1911, Russia and Japan signed the Treaty of Extradition, allowing the extradition of political criminals who aimed to suppress the activities of Russian socialists in Japan, as well as rebellious Koreans in Russia.[46] However, the Russian government did not agree to extradite guerrillas to the Japanese administration in Korea. In 1914, the Japanese embassy in Petrograd requested the extradition of twenty-one leaders of the anti-Japanese movement. Russian authorities arrested a number of the leaders and deported some of them to Manchuria, but no one was extradited to the Japanese authorities in Korea.[47] Russia found itself in the middle of a struggle between Japan and Korea and, despite the rapprochement, did not openly take Japan's side in the conflict. Korea and Korean insurgents were the Japanese Empire's weakest issue in 1917, and it was there that the Russian Bolsheviks struck first.

Diplomatic, economic, and military cooperation between Russia and Japan reached its acme in 1916 with the conclusion of the Russo-Japanese Alliance, which specified measures to be taken in case a third power, namely the United States, tried to establish its influence, whether political or economic, over China. The mastermind of the alliance was none other than Yamagata Aritomo. In February 1915, Yamagata submitted to the Cabinet a memorandum in which he proposed to form an alliance with Russia that would obligate the two nations to lend military support to protect the territorial integrity of China. To break the resistance of the reluctant Foreign Ministry, which was mindful of the existing Anglo-Japanese Alliance, Yamagata arranged the visit of Grand Duke George Mikhailovich, a member of the Russian imperial house, in January 1916. The royal "charm offensive" was aided by Japanese popular media and agitation by financial circles for an alliance with Russia. Not only were Japan and Russia formally allies in the war against Germany, but it was also widely realized that such an alliance would bring great economic benefits, specifically through the conclusion of new, important fishery agreements and the promotion of extensive trade in arms and food.[48]

Japanese attitudes toward Russia therefore were conditioned by multiple factors, not least geographical. Mutual economic and political interests determined by their geographical proximity and shared ambitions in the region, mainly in Korea and China, were responsible for wide swings in the attitude toward Russia on the part of Japanese policy makers, from antagonistic to friendly and back. The most important factor in Russo-Japanese relations was what lay between them: China, the "sick man of Asia." Yamagata's warming up to Russia in 1915 was part of the government's new tactic to strengthen Japan's position on the continent through the newly defined policy of coexistence and co-prosperity (kyōzon kyōei), in which Japan would act as a benevolent partner to republican China. Gotō, as home minister in Terauchi Masatake's Cabinet, formulated the idea of an "east Asian economic alliance," and in October 1916 he began working on establishing a Sino-Japanese investment bank.[49] Coexistence and co-prosperity in East Asia obviously could not be done without the inclusion and/or understanding of Russia.

In sum, the Japanese political, military, diplomatic, and business establishment had divergent motives and interests regarding Russia.[50] The army was consistent in its agitation for war and in considering Russia, whether imperial or Soviet, as an existential threat to the security of the Japanese nation and its economic interests in China and Korea. As we shall see, the navy disagreed with this view and regarded cooperation with Russia as essential to an anticipated war with the United States. The Foreign Ministry supported the army's anti-Russian position, but largely because it gave priority to cooperation with the Anglo-American powers, Britain and the United States. As the Foreign Ministry had great influence over the SMRC and the Kwantung Army, and since it was committed to Sino-Japanese cooperation as the only key to Japan's stability, the ministry was able to restrain the Kwantung Army's agitation against Chinese Manchurian warlords and imperial Russia for a while. However, it is important to note that anti-Russian policies among the decision makers were not based on any higher principle but were largely used as leverage in Japan's negotiations with

Russia and Western powers to secure Japan's interests on the Asian continent. The balance of power in East Asia between Russia and Japan was based on the division of "spheres of influence" and the shared desire to stop a third party advance in China, which remained in place until October 1917.[51] As Siberia and the Russian Far East were plunged into political chaos afterward, Japan was prompted to reconfigure its sphere of influence in northeast Asia once again.

Parallel to the official Russia policy, which veered between negative and positive attitudes based on the geopolitical considerations of the day, there existed another trend that regarded Russia in a more positive light. Historians and literary scholars have noted the rich cultural relations that developed between Russia and Japan from 1868 onward. Sho Konishi, for example, has compared the influence of Russian culture on Japan between the mid-nineteenth and early twentieth centuries to the impact of China on the intellectual life of Tokugawa Japan prior to 1860 and to the American cultural presence after the Asia-Pacific War.[52] Although his scholarly focus is on revolutionary anarchist encounters, Konishi demonstrates that a vital point of convergence between Russia and Japan was the fact that intellectuals and social critics in both countries worked out alternative progressive visions to Western modernity. One should add that many educated Japanese people were powerfully attracted to the critique of the West developed in Russia and sought to find connections between this critique and Russia's revolutionary energies, which the Japanese found useful in their own critique of Japan's modernized state and Western imperialist powers. Members of the Japanese intelligentsia, students, feminists, antiestablishment activists, government bureaucrats, colonial administrators, Pan-Asianist agitators, and even occasionally army officers developed a strong and lasting interest in Russian intellectual, cultural, literary, and social revolutionary movements, especially those informed by anti-Western sentiments. They astutely recognized that Russian anti-Westernism derived from the empire's peculiar cultural, historical, and geopolitical position, which for many Japanese resembled their own country's peculiar position vis-à-vis the West and the rest of Asia. While the popular fascination with Russian culture and revolutionary thought had a limited impact on Japanese foreign policy, I argue that the long-standing Japanese interest in Russia's cultural and intellectual production nevertheless paved the way for the favorable reception of ideas and ideologies, including socialism and communism, originating in Russia.

Russian literature became the main conduit for Japan's burgeoning interest in Russia, revealing to Japanese readers similarities in cultural circumstances between the two countries. From the 1880s onward, translations of Russian writers became extremely popular, selling out almost immediately after publication. Every educated person in Japan knew the names of Leo Tolstoy, Nikolai

Turgenev, Nikolai Gogol, Anton Chekhov, and Fyodor Dostoevsky. Between 1868 and 1950, almost three hundred Russian writers were translated into Japanese.[53] As some historians have suggested, although "Russia lost the war in 1905, it soon conquered Japan through its literature."[54] Tolstoy was by far the most translated foreign writer in the entire history of modern Japanese translation practice, and the enormous impact his writing and religious thought had in Japan has been discussed thoroughly by Sho Konishi.[55] Japanese editions of Dostoevsky were one of his first foreign translations; prior to World War II, the number of copies sold of Dostoevsky's works in Japan was the highest in the world.[56] Dostoevsky's popularity peaked in Japan in the 1930s, in part due to the translations of the works of Leon Shestov, the existentialist philosopher and commentator on Dostoevsky and Friedrich Nietzsche. The philosopher Miki Kiyoshi noted that Dostoevsky and Shestov, and their engagement with European modernity, aptly captured the anxieties and contradictions of the 1930s in Japan and dubbed this period the era of "Shestovian Angst."[57] Famous Japanese literary figures such as Uchida Roan, Tokutomi Roka, Mori Ōgai, Shimazaki Tōson, and Arishima Takeo acknowledged the profound influence Russian literature had on their own literary engagement with Western modernity. As the literary scholar Paul Anderer writes, "late-nineteenth-century Russian life, like that of Japan since the Restoration, seemed up in the air, removed from concrete experience, and Dostoevsky was widely regarded as the great chronicler of this cultural homelessness. His characters were abstracted from life by reason of imported dreams of progress and civilization; his city seemed inhabited not by the living but by the possessed."[58]

The popularity of Russian literature in Japan also had a lot to do with the investment of many Russian writers in exploring the suffering of the common people and exposing the ethical and social contradictions of a society in transition. By offering complex social critiques, such writings contributed to the birth of social science in Japan. Largely responsible for introducing Japanese readers to the Russian literature of the "insulted and humiliated" was Futabatei Shimei (1864–1909), a prolific translator and teacher of the Russian language. Futabatei has been called the first modern Japanese writer, and his novel *The Drifting Cloud* (Ukigumo, 1887) is said to be partially based on Ivan Goncharov's 1859 novel *Oblomov*. One of Futabatei's students was Yokoyama Gennosuke (1871–1915), one of the founders of social research in Japan, whose highly influential and still valuable *The Lower Strata of Japanese Society* (Nihon no kasō shakai, 1898), exposed poverty and poor working conditions around the country. The famous poet Ishikawa Takuboku, who before his death in 1912 claimed to have become a socialist, wrote that it was Russian writers who opened his eyes to social problems in Japan. Russian literature—its penetrating depiction of cultural homelessness and the suffering of commoners in the modern age—resonated with many people in Japan and contributed to the favorable reception of Russian revolutionary ideas among the Japanese reading public.

Russian populism (*narodnichestvo*) played an enormously important role in the Japanese political imagination of the late nineteenth century. Russian populism developed as a critical engagement with and active resistance to capitalist development in Russia and Western Europe and was one of the first attempts in Russia to put into practice radical alternatives to Western capitalist modernity. In Japan, Russian populist ideas became known in 1878, when the first very sympathetic reports of the Russian nihilist movement (*Rokoku kyomutō*) reached Japan. Russian populist ideas were disseminated by a growing number of translations. Between 1881 and 1883 alone, sixty-five books on Russian populism were published in Japan. After the Sino-Japanese War in 1896, Tokutomi Roka published Sergei Stepnyak-Kravchinsky's novel *The Career of a Nihilist* in the influential newspaper *Kokumin shinbun*, run by his more famous brother Tokutomi Sohō. Translations of the populist Pyotr Lavrov's writings, Stepnyak's *Underground Russia*, and *La Russie politique et sociale*, by the member of the terrorist organization People's Will Lev Tikhomirov, followed. In 1902, Kemuyama Sentarō published the first academic study of populists and anarchism in *Early Modern Anarchism* (Kinsei museifushugi). Taking Russian populism as a model, Japan's own genre of the political novel also began to emerge.

Russian populist ideas found a warm reception in the Freedom and People's Rights Movement (Jiyū minken undō, 1874–84), which, although inspired by the French and American revolutions, found the current Russian populist movement more relevant to its cause. Japanese political activists felt an affinity with the Russian populists because both were from the newly formed class of intelligentsia and had a self-appointed task to fight for the good of the common people. Russian populists' quick slide into terrorism, most notoriously exemplified by the assassination of Alexander II in 1881, made an enormous impact on Japanese political activists and the general public, as well as state officials.[59] Proponents of the People's Rights Movement immediately pointed out that the Japanese government's continuous refusal to grant political rights to a broader population might result in the same terrorist outcomes as they witnessed in Russia. Covering the trial of Vera Zasulich, who shot the governor of Saint Petersburg in 1878 in protest against the maltreatment of a political prisoner, one Japanese newspaper asked: "Is not it just by chance that this heroic woman was born in Russia?"[60] Who knows, the Japanese democratic agitators continued, where such actions could be replicated next?

Their warnings were justified because there were people in Japan who sympathized with the Russian populists' terrorist actions. Not only did they approve of political violence in Russia, but they also endorsed political violence per se. In

1882, for example—in imitation of the People's Will, the terrorist group behind the assassination of Alexander II—the Nihilist Party of the Far East was formed in Nagasaki.[61] The extent of the Russian populist terrorist influence on Japanese radical imagination became evident during the so-called High Treason Incident of 1910 (discussed later), when a group of Japanese radicals were accused of plans to assassinate Emperor Meiji with a bomb. During the notorious trial, the only woman executed for the conspiracy, Kanno Suga, acknowledged that her role models were Vera Zasulich and Sofia Perovskaya, who was also executed in 1881 for her role in the assassination of Alexander II.[62]

Even Meiji nationalist groups took notice of Russian populism. Uchida Ryōhei, cofounder of the notorious nationalist Kokuryūkai in his book On Russia (Roshia ron, 1901), based on his travels from Vladivostok to Saint Petersburg, expressed admiration for Russia's political aggression—even its potential for violence. "An extremist nation demands an extremist revolution," he wrote of Russia. "Their revolution will spill incomparably more blood than the French revolution."[63] Uchida also praised the radical student movement in Russia and lamented the faint-hearted Japanese students who, he believed, were obedient servants of a bureaucracy and lacked courage and independence of spirit. In addition to predicting a revolution and the collapse of tsarist Russia, Uchida suggested that Japan should assist in these developments, acting as a paternalistic benefactor to an immature and disorderly state. "In accomplishing the aim of liberating and guiding Russia," he wrote, "we should not refrain from war if it should seem a timely means."[64]

Prior to 1917, Japan's political and cultural engagement with Russian revolutionary thought and movements peaked around the time of the Russo-Japanese War. The war became especially transformative for Japan's own socialist movement, radicalizing it and bringing it into the fold of the international socialist movement.

Socialist ideas were first introduced in Japan in the 1880s and 1890s, but in the context of the larger democratic People's Rights Movement, which strove for the people's right to participate in the political and economic life of the country. Western socialism was understood, first and foremost, as an explanation of the cause of social problems (shakai mondai) and as a means and a program of social and moral regeneration.[65] Troubled by the corruption and cliquism of contemporary politics and the growing impoverishment of the people, the early socialists believed that a social revolution (kakumei), which would overthrow corrupt politicians and inject fresh blood into the government, was a necessary step in returning to the principles of the Meiji Revolution. Their aspirations, they believed, did not contradict the kokutai—the official ideology centered on the imperial family and the body politic. In fact, they regarded themselves to be in a

struggle against the exploitative structure of the capitalist economy, which threatened the economic and moral health of the *kokutai*. They envisioned socialism
as paving a path to national economic prosperity without posing a threat to the
Meiji constitutional monarchy.[66]

The beginning of the Japanese socialist movement is considered to be the
establishment of the Society for the Study of Socialism (Shakaishugi kenkyūkai)
in 1898, which was organized to "study the principles of socialism and whether or
not they may be applied to Japan."[67] In 1900, the society was renamed the Socialist Association (Shakaishugi kyōkai), and took a more active stance in disseminating knowledge about Western socialism. In the spring of 1901, the members
of the association—among them the future JCP representative to the Comintern Presidium Katayama Sen, Kōtoku Shūsui, and Abe Isoo—established the
Shakai minshutō (Social Democratic Party), whose platform was modeled after
the Erfurt declaration of the German Social Democratic Worker's Party (later
renamed the Social Democratic Party, or SPD). Employing the Public Order
and Police Law of 1900, which curtailed radical social movements for the next
two decades, the Japanese government banned the country's first socialist party
within hours of its establishment. The Meiji government was deeply concerned
by the party's quite radical demands, which included the abolition of the House
of Peers, the adoption of universal suffrage, and a reduction in the number of
armed service personnel. The government, however, was greatly alarmed because
it feared that the party might come under the direct influence of the SPD of Germany, which by 1900 was the biggest party in the world. In 1906, the socialists
made another attempt to create a legal party, the Nihon Shakaitō (Japan Socialist
Party), but it was banned within a year.

The Russo-Japanese War transformed Japanese socialists into true radicals.
In the wake of the government's suppression of their activities, they abandoned the idea of moral reformation of the government within the imperial
institution and instead began to agitate against the economic (capitalist) and
political (imperial) system of Meiji Japan. As the cost of the war mounted
and disappointment grew on both sides, pioneering feminists and socialists
in Japan and Russia began to voice more forcefully their skepticism not only
of the war but also of the imperial governments behind it. Kōtoku Shūsui,
Sakai Toshihiko, and a few others organized Japan's first antiwar movement,
founding the antiwar newspaper *Heimin shinbun* (1903–5) and the Heiminsha
(The Commoner's Association), the publishing company behind the newspaper.[68] The Heiminsha came to national attention when it translated and published in its entirety Leo Tolstoy's famous antiwar pamphlet "Bethink Yourself!"
(June 1904). Tolstoy's declaration that the "war was [being fought] for an alien
land over which Russians have no right" was an attack on Russian colonialism,

and it powerfully stirred Japanese antiwar and anti-imperialist sentiments. Tolstoy's essay inspired the most famous Japanese antiwar proclamation, the feminist writer Yosano Akiko's 1904 antiwar poem "Never Let Them Kill You, Brother!" (Kimi shinitamō koto nakare). The poem radically suggested that the interests of the individual must not be subordinated to the interests of the state. Other famous pacifists, including the Christian Uchimura Kanzō and Christian socialist Kinoshita Naoe, whose novel *Pillar of Fire* (Hi no Hashira, 1904) was an open attack on the Japanese government, worked in close collaboration with the Heiminsha.[69] Besides Tolstoy, the Heiminsha produced editions of Russian revolutionary and antiwar literature, introducing to Japanese audiences the writings of Vladimir Lenin, Alexander Herzen, Mikhail Bakunin, Georgy Plekhanov, and others. The Heiminsha's translation and publication of *The Communist Manifesto* in 1905 was the final straw for the police. The editors were fined and jailed, and the newspaper was disbanded. But the cat was out of the bag at this point, so to speak. Numerous socialist circles, Marxist reading groups, and similar organizations began to develop from Hokkaido to Kyushu, as did a number of successor publications, such as *Chokugen*, the Marxist *Shakaishugi kenkyū*, and the Christian socialist *Shin kigen*.

The Russo-Japanese War also brought the Japanese socialist pacifist movement into a close relationship with the international socialist movement, including Russian, Asian, and American radicals. Russian revolutionary thought had a great impact among early Japanese socialists, who in their struggle against the imperial government found many affinities with Russian radicals' fight with the tsarist government. On March 13, 1904, the Japanese socialists issued a proclamation of solidarity with the oppressed Russian people:

> Yes! We are comrades. Brothers. Sisters. Never have we reason to fight each other. The demon that is our common enemy now pours forth his evil flames . . . reaches out his poisonous hands, and outrages the living millions. Now is the time for us, and socialists the world over, to band together in strength. Marx's words, "workers of the world, unite," shall now, indeed, be realized.[70]

The text was reprinted in an American socialist paper, and a welcoming response from the Russian Social Democrats was printed in their publication *Iskra*, which was translated into Japanese and published in July 1904 in *Heimin shinbun*. *Iskra*, the first all-Russian illegal Marxist newspaper, was founded in Geneva by the young Russian Social Democratic Party, established in 1898. It had a board of six editors, among whom were the more famous and moderate Georgy Plekhanov, Vera Zasulich, and the still-unknown junior editor, Vladimir Ulyanov, who wrote under the penname of Vladimir Lenin. *Iskra*'s response stated in part:

Hearing their voices [the letter from the Heiminsha] among the cries of war in both Japan and Russia, we truly feel as if [we are] touching upon the exquisite music of a messenger from the world of goodness and beauty. And that world of goodness and beauty will inevitably be realized tomorrow, although it exists as present only in the class-conscious minds of the submerged masses. Even though we do not know when this tomorrow may come, our social democratic parties all over the world are endeavoring to bring it forth as soon as possible. We are digging the grave for . . . the present social organizations, and are organizing the power which ultimately will bury them.[71]

This exchange resulted in the invitation of the Japanese delegation to the Sixth Congress of the Second International in Amsterdam in August 1904. Katayama Sen was nominated the first vice-president of the congress, and his public embrace of the famous Russian Marxist Georgy Plekhanov, who acted as the second vice-president, was an apt demonstration to those attending of the success of socialist internationalism.[72] The dawn of the much-awaited "tomorrow" finally came (or appeared to have arrived) with the Russian Revolution of 1905, which had a tremendous impact on Japanese and other non-European socialists. Kōtoku saw the Russian Revolution of 1905 as the forerunner of all the coming social revolutions in the world, including the one in imperial Japan. "The Russian Revolution will not be confined to Russia, and the flames of the proletarian revolution will escalate all over the world," he wrote in *Hikari* in January 1906.[73] The Russian Revolution of 1905 was hardly noticed in Europe; while in contrast, in Japan, China, India, Persia, and Turkey it was regarded as the first successful part of a worldwide struggle against political despotism.

The Russo-Japanese War and the Russian Revolution of 1905 became occasions for Japanese, Russian, and Asian socialists to meet and band together. The Russian populist revolutionary Nikolai Sudzilovsky-Russel (1850–1930) came to Japan from the United States in 1905 to conduct revolutionary propaganda among Russian prisoners of war (POWs). His Nagasaki publication *Volya* closely cooperated with the socialist *Hikari*, as well as with *Kakumei Hyōron* and the Chinese revolutionary newspaper *Minbao*. In response to a personal request from Lenin, Kōtoku had *Heimin shinbun* publish hundreds of documents that Russian revolutionary émigré groups had distributed among Russian POWs.[74] Propaganda literature intended for Russian POWs was smuggled from Siberia to Hokkaido, then delivered to the Russian camp in Nagasaki on the southern island of Kyushu.[75] Japanese socialists often acted as intermediaries between Chinese, Russian, and other European revolutionary exiles. Grigory Gershuni (1870–1908), a member of the Russian Socialist Revolutionary Party, met Sun

Yat-sen (1866–1925) in Japan in 1906. Song Jiaoren (1881–1913), the future Guomindang leader, met in 1906 through his Japanese friend Miyazaki Tamizō (1865–1928) the Polish revolutionary Bronislaw Pilsudski (1866–1918).[76] Kōtoku's group delivered lectures to Chinese students in Tokyo as part of the Socialist Lecture Series (Shakaishugi Kōshūkai), as well as to the Chinese Society for the Study of Socialism, established in 1907 in Tokyo. In 1906, the anarchist Ōsugi Sakae opened the first school of Esperanto in Japan, which attracted many Japanese and Chinese students with its vision of a supranational society. Japanese socialists were among the founding members of the Asiatic Humanitarian Brotherhood (Ashū Washinkai), organized in Tokyo in 1907 by Chinese, Japanese, Vietnamese, Philippine, and Indian anticolonial activists. As Rebecca Karl remarks, the Asiatic Brotherhood was an unprecedented attempt to forge a vision of an anti-imperialist Asia that would consciously avoid "replicat[ing] would-be hegemonic Japanese state Asianisms of the time, which were often defined against China and intended to distance Japan theoretically and historically from its neighbors in order to tie it more firmly to Europe and capitalist/imperialist expansion."[77] Undoubtedly, these early (1905–10) attempts at regional cooperation planted the seeds for later socialist anti-imperialist movements.

By 1917, Japan had considerable knowledge and experience with socialism as a theory and a revolutionary program, including the versions that originated in tsarist Russia. Japanese socialists also identified themselves as such, producing several works on the history of their own movement by the early 1900s. They also considered the Japanese socialist movement as an important member of the international socialist movement, actively participating in the workings of the Second International. Japanese socialists looked up to Russian populists and to the makers of the Russian Revolution of 1905. The main draw for Japanese socialists and the emerging intelligentsia was the Russian radical critique of both political despotism and Western capitalism. It struck a great chord with many in Japan, who grappled with similar issues of worsening "social problems," a sense of cultural homelessness, and relentless pressure from the modernizing state to comply with its goals. At the same time, as we will see in the following chapters, Japan's immersion in European socialist discourse, according to which Russia's political and economic backwardness disqualified it from being a frontrunner in a future proletarian revolution, caused confusion among Japanese socialists when in October 1917 Lenin announced that the first socialist revolution in history had been accomplished in Russia.

In this chapter I have identified two most important perceptions of Russia, which, I believe, help us make sense of Japan's complex attitudes toward Russian communism. First, Japanese policy makers were always conscious of the geopolitical "destiny" of the imperial and Soviet Russian state. No matter what regime was in power in Russia, the Japanese contended, as a Eurasian state it would always act to preserve and safeguard its geopolitical interests. Viewed from this perspective, there was a remarkable continuity in Japan's approaches to imperial and Soviet Russia. This leads us to the second prevalent assumption among Japanese decision makers and the general public—that Russia was neither West nor East—which determined its peculiar cultural anxieties. Like Japan, Russia was a latecomer not only to the process of industrialization but also to political and social modernization, producing penetrating analyses and critiques of modern predicaments that resonated deeply with the sentiments of the Japanese across different social classes. As we see in the next chapter, Japan's initial response to the revolutionary events in Russia in 1917 was determined by the framework established in the previous decades.

REVOLUTION AND INTERVENTION

Workers, prepare for the last assault!
Slaves, unbend your knees and spines!
Proletarian army, rise in force!
Long live the revolution
with speedy victory,
The greatest and most just of all the wars
Ever fought in history!

—Vladimir Mayakovsky, *Vladimir Ilich Lenin*, 1924

On March 18, 1917, the leader of the majority Seiyūkai party and future prime minister Hara Takashi (1856–1921) wrote in his diary, "a revolution has erupted in Russia, and the tsar has abdicated. The situation in Russia is strange. Just as [we saw] in the aftermath of the Russo-Japanese War, a revolution has once again come and constitutional politics are taking hold in Russia. This time, the abdication of the tsar is truly a great political change. There are complicated reasons for this change, but it seems to emanate from the rise of the pro-German [antiwar, pacifist] group."[1] Little did Hara know that the February Revolution anticipated events that would drastically reshape the history of the world, including Japan, in the twentieth century. Hara Takashi's remark reveals that the Japanese political elite saw similarities between the February uprising and the Russian Revolution of 1905, which forced the tsarist autocracy to pull out of the Russo-Japanese War, issue Russia's first written constitution, and establish a parliament. While welcoming the prospect of Russia's political modernization, Japan was concerned about whether Russia could continue to contribute to the ongoing Great War despite its escalating domestic chaos. At the same time, Japan came to be interested in exploring opportunities for expansion in northeast Asia as Russia's power waned in that region. Between 1917 and 1922, the army and the Foreign Ministry formulated a plan for engaging with the Russian Revolution, which included the following objectives: eliminating Russian influence in East Asia, extending Japan's own economic interests in China and the Russian eastern territories, and forestalling the spread of Bolshevism in colonial Korea and China.

On March 8 (February 23 according to the Julian calendar in force at the time), what came to be called the February Revolution broke out in the Russian capital of Petrograd.[2] The insurrection was simultaneously a workers' strike and a soldiers' mutiny. The incompetent reaction of the authorities revealed the imperial state's structural decay as well as the elite's lack of commitment to the tsarist regime. World War I, in which the Russian army had already lost more than two million troops by 1917, had a direct and decisive impact on the Russian revolutionary events of that year and on the subsequent Civil War, which lasted from 1918 to 1922. During the Great War, workers' strikes grew in frequency and militancy, while the influence of the radical revolutionary parties increased among workers and soldiers. During the February uprising, amid lawlessness and chaos, two centers of power emerged: the Petrograd Soviet of Workers' and Soldiers' Deputies, and the Provisional Government. The radicalized majority of the Provisional Government was in favor of destroying the monarchical system and founding a republic in Russia. Deserted by his supporters, the last tsar of Russia, Nicholas II, abdicated on March 15. As there was no longer a unified tsarist authority to hold the empire and its people together, state power disintegrated. The February Revolution thus marked both the end of the old regime and the beginning of a new revolutionary process.[3]

In early 1917, Japan had looked anxiously at the events in Russia, contemplating the future of the war, the prospects of the Russian imperial state, and what Japan should make of the unfolding situation. Numerous reports, telegrams, and letters were exchanged between Japanese diplomatic and military officials in Russia and Japan. However, because the February Revolution occurred in the midst of the most destructive war in history, its foreign contemporaries, including the Japanese, perceived it as an episode in that war rather than an event in its own right. Initially, Japanese journalists, diplomats, and military staff reported from Russia that the February uprising was being carried out by patriotic masses who believed that only a total reorganization of the government would bring victory over Germany.[4] The Allies and the Central Powers alike welcomed the February Revolution. The former (Japan, Britain, France, Italy, and the United States) hoped that the removal of an unpopular tsar would make it possible to reinvigorate Russia's war effort; the latter (Germany, Austria-Hungary, the Ottoman Empire, and Bulgaria) hoped it would take Russia out of the war altogether. The Japanese government, together with other West European governments, quickly acknowledged the Provisional Government because it promised to "sacredly observe the alliances that bind us to other powers."[5] The diplomatic archives reveal that the Japanese government had high hopes for the revolution, anticipating that it would encourage Russia to modernize and consequently make it better able to continue the war.[6] Thus, both the political elite and the general public welcomed the February uprising and the end of imperial authority as a sign of Russia's belated entry into the modern age, rather than the beginning of the end of the established international and domestic order.

Remarkably, in the midsummer of 1917, Japan's political and military establishment expected that the Provisional Government would not hold on to power for long and that most probably the Bolshevik group would attempt a coup. The pro-German pacifist group Hara mentions in his March 1917 diary entry was none other than the Bolsheviks led by Vladimir Lenin, and thus the Bolshevik coup did not come as a total surprise to the Japanese establishment. The Japanese government and the army were well informed about the situation in Russia from the reports sent by Uchida Kōsai (1865–1936), the Japanese ambassador to Russia between December 1916 and February 1918, the consulates in Vladivostok and Harbin, and numerous intelligence officers operating inside Russia. Uchida Kōsai witnessed firsthand the revolutionary upheaval and supported the people's cause against the corrupted tsarist government. In his reports to Foreign Minister Motono Ichirō (1862–1918), Uchida also expressed doubt about the authority of the Provisional Government and concern over the growing strength of the pacifist Soviet Council. Japanese military officers, although supportive of the February Revolution as an act of the "people" against the corrupt tsarist government, regarded militant pacifist workers as ideologically aligned with Germany. Ishizaka Zenjirō, army major general and military attaché at the Japanese embassy in Petrograd, expressed his enmity toward Lenin and the Bolshevik group for their alleged collaboration with Germany. Generally, diplomatic officials and the military were most concerned with the situation in the Russian army and were horrified at the demoralization suffered by Russian troops as a result of prolonged war and lack of patriotism. They were also concerned that arms might become widely available to the civilian population. And since the Russian people had a "very low level of literacy and were ignorant and volatile," the only possible outcome, they warned, would be widespread violence.[7]

Concerned about the CER and the Trans-Siberian Railway, Foreign Minister Motono sent the president of the SMRC, Kawakami Toshitsune (1861–1935), to Russia, where he remained between June and October 1917. Kawakami delivered his report to the Ministry of Foreign Affairs on November 15, 1917, eight days after the start of the October Revolution, but it was based on his observations in the preceding few months. In many ways, his report was an informative and accurate depiction of the social and political situation in Russia. Besides commending the February uprising as a democratic revolution against tsarist despotism, Kawakami informed the Japanese government of the wide spread of socialist ideas among the working class and the army. Kawakami pointed out that the army and railway workers were thoroughly radicalized and had been sabotaging the war effort. Reporting after the November 6 storming of the Winter Palace in Saint Petersburg, Kawakami predicted that the militant Bolshevik party would most likely stay in power and conclude a separate peace with Germany. In Kawakami's account, and in what became the general understanding of the 1917 events among the Japanese ruling elite, the popularity of socialist ideas in Russia was due to the Bolsheviks' promise of peace with Germany, which exposed the "unpatriotism" and dangerous internationalism of socialist theory in general.[8]

What the Japanese army and Foreign Ministry were really interested in, however, was how to make best use of the opportunities that had opened up in northern Manchuria and the Russian Far East, as the Russian central authority in those places, remote from the capital, was rapidly disintegrating. As early as March 1917, Ishizaka advised the Tokyo government to seriously consider exploring new opportunities in Siberia and Harbin because the Russian influence was bound to wane there.[9] However, throughout 1917 both Uchida and Ishizaka strongly advised against armed intervention, hoping to avoid a full-scale war.[10] Kawakami, in contrast, recommended that the Japanese army enter the Russian Far East if and when Russia concluded a separate peace with Germany. Concerning Russian public opinion, he predicted that anti-German "patriotic" Russians would welcome the Japanese forces. As Russia was disintegrating, there was no state authority to prevent the country from plunging into the kind of chaos and disorder that could affect neighboring countries. Therefore, Kawakami insisted, in order to maintain peace in the region, Japan had every right to colonize the Russian Far East, Siberia, and northern Manchuria, or at least to acquire special rights in those territories.[11] Kawakami's ideas were echoed in the press. The newspaper *Osaka Asahi shinbun* speculated as early as the summer of 1917 that the Bolsheviks' rise to power would lead to Russia becoming a sort of German colony, which would endanger Japan and its colonies and therefore justify the deployment of troops to the Russian Far East.[12] It was not Uchida's recommendations but Kawakami's observations, derived from the vital interests of the SMR in northern Manchuria and the Russian Far East, that shaped subsequent attitudes and policies of the Foreign Ministry toward revolutionary Russia. Kawakami's report, and the position of the Foreign Ministry in general, reveals that Japanese decision makers viewed Eastern Siberia and northern Manchuria as one territory, and that control over the railroads was a major factor in Japan's foreign policy. Chinese claims to Manchuria were ignored, and it was assumed that territories formerly under Russian influence would and should be brought under Japanese influence.

Domestically, news of the February Revolution caused quite a stir, and the event was quickly linked by the Japanese liberal press to the country's ongoing domestic problems. The February Revolution—an uprising of the people against a corrupt feudal government and its bureaucracy—coincided with the rise of agitation in Japan for the Taishō Revolution, the aim of which was to empower the people through universal suffrage. In 1917, Japan was in the middle of a general election campaign. The Kokumintō (National Party), organized by Inukai Tsuyoshi and Ozaki Yukio as an oppositional party to the landlord-backed Seiyūkai, advocated British-style parliamentary politics and attracted a variety of business owners and liberal supporters in big cities. However, in April 1917, Prime Minister Terauchi Masatake, former governor-general of Korea (1910–16) and a leading member of the Yamagata Aritomo clique, extended his support to the Seiyūkai, making it the majority party in the Diet. The general public was greatly dissatisfied with the election and questioned the entire Japanese constitutional order, in which the victory of the ruling party was predetermined. In the summer of 1917, students of the prestigious Waseda University occupied the campus to foment a "Waseda Revolution." The strike committee compared the aging prime minister Terauchi to Alexander Kerensky, leader of the Provisional Government, and cried out for a Japanese Kerensky.[13] For the *Osaka Asahi* and *Tōyō Keizai Shinpō* newspapers, the Terauchi government was an embodiment of all that was currently wrong in Japan. The liberal journalist Ishibashi Tanzan (1884–1973) wrote:

> Count Terauchi, his cabinet, and their bureaucrats have violated the people's right to be loyal to their sovereign and love their country [*chūkun aikoku*] by arbitrarily designating whatever does not suit them as lèse majesté and a crime. . . . They have perpetrated despotic oppression no better than that of the Russian bureaucracy. I speak freely from deep concern for the security of the throne and hope that the bureaucrats, especially Prince Yamagata and Count Terauchi, will reflect on this situation.[14]

The newspapers, however, did not extend their critique of the political system to the emperor or the institution of the monarchy. Instead, bureaucracy and oligarchy were blamed for usurping and abusing power. The liberal Yoshino Sakuzō, for example, argued that Japanese and British constitutional monarchies were modern, democratic, and progressive, whereas the Romanov and the Habsburg monarchies were feudal and backward and therefore destined to disappear. Even Ishibashi supported the Japanese monarchy as the country's unifying principle because it proved to be very useful and effective during the Meiji Restoration. When a Russian in Saint Petersburg asked the journalist Ōgimachi Suetada if the Japanese also wanted to abolish their monarchy, Ōgimachi answered that the Romanov tsar and the Japanese emperor were completely different and no comparison between them was even possible.[15] It is striking that no one in Japan, not even Japanese socialists, thought about comparing the ruling dynasties in Russia and Japan, let alone following the Russian example in overthrowing the monarchy. In this context, the February Revolution was often compared with the Meiji Restoration of 1868, which represented, in its official interpretation, the defeat of a feudal military samurai regime and the victory of modernizing revolutionaries under the leadership of the emperor. Hence, in the popular view the equivalent of the Russian autocracy was the feudal Tokugawa government, not the Japanese emperor. The Japanese media repeatedly pointed out that Russia lagged some half a century behind Japan in terms of civilizational development. The perceived backwardness of the obsolete Romanov monarchy explains why the Japanese and the rest of the world reacted with relative indifference to the execution of Nicholas II and his family in the summer of 1918. The Japanese government and media dismissed the murders as simply another consequence of the ongoing violent revolution.

Japanese commentators did not fail to remark, however, on the importance and value of socialist ideas and organizations. In an interview with *Jiji Shinpō*, the Waseda professor Nagase Hōsuke (a former editor for the General Staff attached to the Balkans and a historian of France) compared the February Revolution with the French Revolution, in which people demanded not simply bread but freedom.[16] The journalist Ishibashi also pointed out that the driving force of the democratic February Revolution was a "socialist party" and that the soviets were the main authority—which would be successful, he predicted, in pushing for a separate peace between Germany and Russia. In mid-1917, Nobori Shomu, a professor of Russian language at the prestigious military academy, published a book under the title *The Russian Revolution and Social Movement* (Rokoku kakumei to shakai undō), in which he examined the history of the Russian revolutionary movement and the Russian Social Democratic Labor Party and insisted that the revolutionary changes in Russia would not stop there. For the next few years, the book was widely read not only by the increasing number of radical students and intellectuals but also by members of the Japanese Cabinet, the Home Ministry, and War Ministry, where Nobori started serving as a consultant in 1919.[17] The most penetrating analysis came, unsurprisingly, from the Japanese socialist circle. The socialist Takabatake Motoyuki (discussed in chapter 7) emphasized the central role of the workers' and soldiers' soviets and, starting in the summer of 1917, focused his attention on the new political group, the Bolsheviks. Takabatake pointed out that the Bolshevik leader Vladimir Lenin's antiwar position meant not only withdrawal from the imperialist war but also recognition that such a withdrawal "is impossible . . . without the overthrow of capital." As such, Takabatake predicted, the February Revolution was not the end of revolutionary upheaval in Russia, but just the beginning.[18]

On the night of November 6–7, 1917, the Bolsheviks seized power through a military insurrection. They occupied key governmental institutions without much resistance, taking over telegraph offices and railroad stations and surrounding the Winter Palace, where the Provisional Government was in session. The all-Bolshevik Council of People's Commissars assumed the central governmental functions, with Vladimir Lenin as its chairman and Leon Trotsky as the people's commissar (minister) of foreign affairs. Lenin immediately proposed a declaration of peace with Germany and signed a decree nationalizing all agricultural land. The Bolsheviks, however, organized the uprising through the Military-Revolutionary Committee of the Petrograd Soviet, and news went out that it was in fact the soviets, not the Bolsheviks, that had taken power. Indeed, the soviets immediately took power in the provinces, and local soviets were not always dominated by Bolsheviks.[19] Socialists from a wide range of leftist factions supported a government consisting of all socialist parties and resisted the Bolsheviks' claim to dominance. In January 1918, the Bolsheviks dispersed by military force the elected Constituent Assembly and established a single-party Bolshevik regime, declaring war on everyone who was unwilling to accept their rule. Following Marxist doctrine, Lenin expected that the international proletarian revolution would soon break out and come to the aid of Russia, which was economically and socially backward and unable to build socialism on its own. Until the international revolution happened, the Bolsheviks' task was to hold on to power by establishing a dictatorship of the proletariat.[20]

In their declared war against capitalist imperialist countries, starting in late November 1917 the Bolshevik government began disclosing secret treaties concluded between tsarist Russia and foreign powers, including the Russo-Japanese secret treaty of 1916. Exposing these secret treaties, the Bolsheviks rightly thought, would reveal the predatory capitalist and imperialist nature of the great powers to the international public. At the same time, despite internal opposition, Lenin went through with his promises to end the war with Germany. The armistice from December 15, 1917, and the Treaty of Brest-Litovsk signed on March 3, 1918, brought the long-awaited peace to Russia, but it also gave great advantages to Germany. According to the treaty, Russia ceded to the Central Powers Finland, the Baltic states, Russian Poland, the Ukraine, much of Belorussia, as well as territory in the Caucasus; which together accounted for one-third of Russia's cultivated land, half of its industry, and 80 percent of its coal production. Concerned with the rogue start of Bolshevik foreign diplomacy and panicked at the prospects of Germany's ascendance, Britain and France began to agitate in December 1917 for military intervention against Russia.

The October Revolution became an international problem not only with Russia's withdrawal from the war, but also when Bolshevized railway guards in Harbin and the soldiers' and workers' soviets attempted unsuccessfully to seize power over the administration of the CER in November 1917 and oust its leader, General Dmitry Horvath. The British, French, and American consuls in Harbin feared that Bolshevik control of the CER would prevent future delivery of essential war matériel stockpiled at Vladivostok and Harbin, and that the Japanese would immediately seize the opportunity to gain control of the CER and expand its influence in East Asia. The Allies thus encouraged Chinese troops in the region to fight the Bolsheviks off, occupy the area, and assert Chinese authority in place of the previous Russian control, which they did in January 1918. A year later, in the spirit of the new Bolshevik doctrine based on open diplomacy, nonannexation of territories, and the self-determination of peoples, the Soviet government renounced Russia's right to the CER without compensation and relinquished all previous Russian concessions in China (the infamous Karakhan Manifesto of July 1919).[21] This created a sensation in China and greatly alarmed the Japanese government. Although the Soviet government almost immediately (in March 1920) denied that such a generous offer was ever issued, the Japanese government feared that the soviets' meddling in China's affairs would come at the expense of Japan's interest in the region and encourage the Beijing government to reclaim concessions given to Japan. As these events demonstrated, since late 1917 the CER and northern Manchuria were becoming the main focus of the renewed rivalry between Japan, Soviet Russia, and China and thus one of the most crucial factors in determining Japanese attitudes toward Soviet Russia.

Outside the two capitals, Petrograd and Moscow, the new Bolshevik government was weak. By the end of 1918, the Russian Socialist Federal Soviet Republic (RSFSR) was the same size as medieval Muscovy, and few people believed that the regime could survive. News of the October coup did not reach remote areas of Siberia and the Russian Far East for weeks, and people in the north of Siberia remained in ignorance of it for months. In November and December 1917, the minor but very militant Bolshevik groups tried to take power in several Siberian and Far Eastern cities with mixed success, finally resorting to a fragile coalition with non-Bolshevik socialist groups.[22] The first counterattacks against the Bolsheviks and the socialist coalitions came in early 1918 from Cossacks and tsarist army officers in Transbaikalia and the Russian Far East. This separate offensive coincided with the birth of several White Armies in European Russia. In Siberia, the son of a Transbaikal Russian Cossack and a Buryat-Mongol mother, Grigory Semenov, a Cossack captain himself and a military commissar of the Provisional Government in Transbaikalia, emerged as the leader of the anti-Bolshevik forces. In Western Siberia in the city of Omsk, in September 1918 a provisional all-Russian government was established, which came under the leadership of Admiral Alexander Kolchak in November 1918.[23] Lacking coordination and plagued by internal rivalries, especially between Kolchak and Semenov, the anti-Bolshevik forces had little chance of success without major support from abroad. Although hoping initially for British and American support, in the end it was Japan that proved to be their most willing partner.

There was confusion and uncertainty among Japanese decision makers about what to make of the new Bolshevik regime. What do the Bolsheviks want? What do they intend to do? Can they be trusted? Following the example of its Western Allies, Japan refused to formally recognize the new government, and official diplomatic relations consequently lapsed. However, the attitude of the political and military establishment was not univocal, and by early December 1917 opinion on the matter split. The army and Foreign Ministry insisted on taking advantage of the power vacuum in East Asia to expand Japan's colonial control, both formal and informal, into Siberia and the Russian Far East. The civil government opposed this move, reluctant to meddle in Russian internal affairs and risk jeopardizing relations with the United States and Britain.

As I demonstrate in this chapter, there was little awareness on the Japanese side that the Bolshevik takeover was the harbinger of a radically new ideology, and in fact, little interest in learning about it. The Japanese government considered the October events a reaction to the Great War, and like its European allies was deeply suspicious of the Bolshevik regime. The suspicion was based, however, not on hostility to their radical ideology but rather on the perception that the Bolshevik upstarts seemed to be extremely pro-German, and perhaps even acting on German orders.

The reality was that Japan's eventual intervention in the Russian Revolution in the summer of 1918, its deep involvement in the Russian Civil War, its military brutality and the subsequent memory of it in Russia, and the overextended stay of the Japanese army on Russian territory (the last Japanese troops left Russia in 1925) were one of major factors in transforming the initial Bolshevik rule into a militarized bureaucratic regime, ready to resort to coercion, even terror, to remain in power, as well as in winning popular support. The Civil War was fought on many geographical fronts, among which the Siberian and Far Eastern were one of the bloodiest and most prolonged. The success of the revolution and the survival of the Soviet regime would thus be secured not in the west but in the east, by the ousting of the Japanese army.

Few among Japanese decision makers foresaw in early 1918 that the ill-planned invasion of Russian territory for the purpose of immediate territorial gain would unite Russian, Korean, and Chinese pro-independence and nationalist activists, validating and strengthening Soviet communist appeal in East Asia. It is within this context—as the revolution was starting to pivot toward a struggle against Japanese imperialism, drawing into its orbit Asian national independence movements—that the attitude of Japanese establishments toward Soviet communism took form. In the end, Japan's response to the Russian Revolution contributed to what this revolution eventually became.

Because of the disruption of telegraph lines in the first two weeks of the revolution, news of the ongoing events in Moscow and Petrograd reached Japan with delay. The government had its first contact with Uchida Kōsai only on November 23, when the telegraph line with Petrograd was restored. The Japanese consul in Moscow managed, however, to telegraph on November 9: "I received news from the Russian capital that on November 7 the Social Party's [*shakaitō*] radical group [*kagekiha*] occupied imperial banks, post offices, telegraph and telephone offices, train stations, released prisoners, arrested the prime minister from the Kadet [Constitutional Democratic] Party. Petrograd's soviets are restless too and considering preventive measures."[24]

Japanese officials and the general public learned about the revolution largely from Japanese newspapers, which in turn obtained information from their partners in London, Harbin, and Shanghai. On November 11, *Tokyo Asahi shinbun* finally identified Lenin and Trotsky as leaders of the Bolshevik Party and informed its readers that the main demands of the Bolsheviks were an immediate truce with Germany and distribution of all land to the propertyless. Confusion and false rumors continued to circulate in Japanese media through November; reports of Lenin's overthrow, his exile to Finland, and arrest in Germany occasionally made the headlines.[25] Drawing from British sensationalist reports, Japanese newspapers detailed rumored atrocities committed by the Bolsheviks, their new policy of "nationalization" of women, and pogroms—as well as rumors of an international Jewish conspiracy, in which Lenin, Trotsky, and Grigory Zinoviev acted on behalf of Jewish world bankers. The most persistent stories were that Lenin and the Bolsheviks were, in fact, German agents. Lenin's actions, in particular, promulgated this rumor; it was a known fact that Germany, interested in supporting factions opposing the war, let Lenin and other members of the radical émigré community cross Germany from Switzerland by train in April 1917.[26] Newspaper reports described the October Revolution as a bloodless coup that happened without mass participation and was therefore illegitimate, in stark contrast with the February uprising. The Bolsheviks were seen to be lacking a mass political base: a power-hungry, militant group doomed to collapse soon. Their success was deemed largely accidental and in no way was the coup considered an epoch-changing event.[27] Not unlike their Western counterparts, Japanese media condemned Lenin and the Bolsheviks for their egoism, the selfishness of their anti-Allied actions, and their lack of patriotism, while hysterically predicting the imminent arrival of German troops at Japan's door via its new Russian colony.[28]

The government chose the tactic of waiting to see what the reaction of other countries would be. On November 13, the Advisory Council on Foreign Relations (Rinji Gaikō chōsa iinkai), composed of the highest-ranking politicians and responsible for Japan's foreign policy, held its regular meeting, during which the Russian Revolution was not even mentioned. What was discussed, however, was the conclusion of the purchase of the rail line between Harbin and Changchun—presumably from the old tsarist government. Even after Trotsky announced the start of armistice negotiations with the Central Powers on November 21 and the immediate urgent meeting of the Allied Powers, where France pressed for a joint intervention, Japanese policy makers remained undecided about what to do. Foreign Minister Motono instructed the Japanese ambassador in France on November 29 not to criticize Lenin and the new Soviet regime publicly and not to call Lenin a usurper. That same day, Motono authorized Uchida in Petrograd to make contact with the new regime—without, however, publicly recognizing this act. When during the Allies' meeting on December 3, France further pressed Japan to agree on a joint occupation of the Trans-Siberian Railway, the Japanese ambassador declined, arguing that the occupation would mean an open war with Russia, which Japan wanted to avoid.[29]

Motono's position, however, began to alter as it became more evident that the Bolsheviks were going to stay in power. On December 9, Trotsky announced that the new government was canceling all obligations and debts of the tsarist and provisional governments, including vast sums owed to Japan from the arms trade. The Bolshevik cancellation of foreign obligations and debts damaged major Japanese enterprises such as Mitsui and Mitsubishi, whose property was subsequently confiscated. Moreover, the Soviets published secret tsarist diplomatic archives, including a secret Russo-Japanese anti-American agreement from 1916, which unnerved many in the Foreign Ministry. In the meetings of the Advisory Council on December 17 and 27, Motono raised for the first time the question of intervention in Russian territory, arguing that Lenin's peace and violation of international responsibilities were serious grounds for an intervention. To support his argument, Motono appealed to Kawakami's report written during his tour in Russia. Besides, Motono argued, Japan must intervene to stop German military advance into the East and protect the huge stockpile of war matériel in Vladivostok's port.[30] The latter concern was genuine, but the government, and especially the military, were more concerned about the matériel falling into the hands of increasingly restless Korean independence groups than with the Germans.

Leader of the majority Seiyūkai party Hara Takashi, Prime Minister Terauchi Masatake, and Yamagata Aritomo rejected Motono's arguments, stating that the intervention would worsen relations with the United States, already suspicious of Japan's Asian policy after the Twenty-One Demands to China. They added, however, "If the Bolshevik wave reaches the Russian Far East and northern Manchuria, our empire cannot remain tranquil in the face of German penetration of our side," thus indicating that the government was ready to resort to military action if the empire's interests were challenged by other powers.[31] The Advisory Council authorized the drawing up of plans for potential objectives in Siberia and the Far East, which included the acquisition of Sakhalin, attachment of the CER and the rail line south of Harbin to the SMR (if the Allies objected to Japan's control of the CER, joint control by a British-French-American consortium would be considered), and the army's sole control of the Trans-Siberian line in Eastern Siberia. The Cabinet and the council, however, still hesitated and in March 1918 once again rejected Motono's persistent push to intervene, arguing that currently there was no threat from either Germany or Soviet Russia to Japan's national security, and that it would be foolish to invade another country without clear reason and jeopardize peace in the region.[32] Defeated, Motono resigned in April and died four months later from cancer.

What was behind Motono's push for the intervention? He did not leave behind any diaries or personal records, but we can make reasonable speculations about his motivation. Motono was the longest-serving Japanese ambassador to Russia (1906–16). Except for Tanaka Gi'ichi, Motono knew Russia better than any other Japanese government official. He was personally responsible for the Russo-Japanese treaties of 1907, 1910, and 1916. In his ten years in Saint Petersburg, Motono learned to speak fluent French and acquired many friends in Russian high aristocratic society. He did not speak Russian well and was not interested in Russia outside of the imperial court—he had no knowledge of Russian writers, nor he was interested in the liberal or radical intelligentsia. According to the memoirs of Satō Naotake (1882–1971), titled *Two Russias* (Futatsu no Roshia, 1948), Motono was deeply shaken by the collapse of the Russian Empire and was driven by his desire to save aristocratic Russia and by his hatred of the new regime.[33]

Or so wrote Satō. Documents in the archives of the Foreign Ministry, however, make it clear that it was actually Satō Naotake himself, then consul-general in

Harbin, who had pushed Motono to advocate for the intervention in his reports and telegrams.[34] In Satō's memorandum from April 1918 to the Advisory Council, he claimed that further inaction would mean the de facto recognition of the Bolshevik regime, which in turn, due to Siberia's geographical proximity to Japan, would pose a grave threat to Japan's social independence (*shakai dokuritsu*). Satō reminded the government of the High Treason Incident of 1910, when a group of anarchist-socialists plotted to assassinate the emperor, and warned of the destruction that socialist thought could wreak on domestic society. He stressed that Bolshevik authority and the military were weak, and therefore the time was opportune to strike.[35] Besides Satō, the head of the Japanese trade mission in Vladivostok, Shimada Gentarō, had been pleading for an urgent intervention since December 1917, claiming that the Russian population in the Far East was open to the idea of secession from Russia and the establishment of a separate state.[36] The sense of urgency in Motono's outlook created by the reports from Harbin and Vladivostok was exacerbated when he learned about British plans to intervene in southern Russia and support the White general Alexei Kaledin to crush Bolshevism and keep Russia in the war.

Better understanding of the Foreign Ministry's position vis-à-vis Russia can be gained by examining the views of Motono's successor, Gotō Shinpei. Known for his pro-Russian position and his opposition to the intervention as home minister (1916–18), Gotō began to advocate for the intervention on assuming the foreign affairs portfolio. This sudden change of position may be explained by Gotō's decision to put his individual opinions aside and represent the Foreign Ministry's outlook. In his first meeting with the press, Gotō announced:

> The penetration of Eastern Siberia by a country hostile to Japan constitutes an imminent danger to Japan, China, and the Allies, and that is why at this point we cannot ignore it. There are no changes in our and the Allies' understanding that Russia is a great country, and we are committed to helping Russia reform and restore its state institutions. I believe it is Japan's duty and responsibility to offer help to Russia's reconstruction.[37]

Gotō's pronouncements, however, repeated almost word for word Motono's arguments. This was hardly a coincidence because both Motono's and Gotō's memorandums to the Advisory Council and the Cabinet, as well as their speeches at press conferences, were prepared by the same middle-rank Foreign Ministry officials: Kimura Eiichi (1879–1947), an Asian specialist in the Foreign Ministry who became the director of the South Manchurian Railway in 1930; and Matsuoka Yōsuke (1886–1946), then secretary to the foreign minister. The latter, of course, was the infamous Matsuoka Yōsuke, the future wartime foreign minister, who pulled Japan out of the League of Nations in 1933 and concluded an alliance with Nazi Germany in 1940 and the Neutrality Pact with the Soviet Union in 1941. Importantly, Matsuoka and Kimura advocated intervention not for any ideological reason but rather out of concern over the possible economic penetration of Siberia by the United States. They were sure that the United States would eventually send troops to Siberia, which, coupled with the dispatch of US railway technicians (who were, in fact, invited by the Russian Provisional Government just before its collapse), would enhance its position in the region and prevent the expansion of Japanese influence on the continent.[38] Echoing these concerns, Gotō urged the Advisory Council to adopt an independent foreign policy without being bound by considerations regarding the relationship with the United States and Britain. He also emphasized that the intervention was not aimed against the Russian people or the new Soviet regime but was rather meant to ensure Siberia's independence by providing economic and military relief.[39]

Regarding Bolshevik ideology, Gotō did not consider it to be a threat to Japan, or even China, and thus he never regarded the Russian Revolution as an epochal event. He thought the whole communist idea of abolition of private property was against human social nature, and that therefore the regime would not last long. He, like many others, believed that the Bolshevik regime was politically and militarily weak and lacking mass support, and that anti-Bolshevik forces were more numerous, stronger, and enjoyed wider approval.[40] Crucial for our understanding, however, is Gotō's remark that Siberia must be kept independent—not so much from Germany's military advance as from "dangerous" German ideas. The Japanese army's task in Siberia would be to prevent German radical socialist ideas and their promoters from entering the Asian continent. With this aim, Gotō proposed to tighten the Japanese border, prevent any contact between German/Russian radicals and Japanese socialists, and establish stricter censorship of the Japanese press.[41] In fact, since January 1918, as the Korean independence movement was gaining momentum both in the Korean diaspora in the Russian Far East and in colonial Korea, the Japanese military and some members of the government suggested that the pro-independence movement was the work of German radical agents, not Russians. Therefore, in the first few months after the revolution, both the October coup and the Korean independence movement were considered likely to be the workings of the German socialist party rather than the Russian Bolshevik Party.

Although strongly opposed to Motono's and then Gotō's plan for intervention, Japanese Ambassador Uchida Kōsai also believed that Germany and German socialist ideas were behind the October Revolution. After witnessing firsthand the two revolutions in Petrograd during his stay there between February 1917 and February 1918, Uchida returned to Japan via the Trans-Siberian Railway.

On arriving in Harbin, he gave a series of candid interviews that generated great interest in Japan and abroad.[42] Regarding communist ideology, Uchida stated that Bolshevism's main tenet was the abolition of private property, and that the origins of this idea lay in the German radical tradition. This German intellectual invention was able to "contaminate" Russia because Russia had found itself in a grave situation: the inept autocratic government, the toll of the Great War, and the lack of political will among statesmen and the military meant that there was no resistance to the spread of German socialist ideas in Russia. He further pointed out that traditionally Russian thought and literature had been concerned with social problems, which made it susceptible in the current historical context to the German socialist solution. Curiously, he blamed German prisoners of war for disseminating communist propaganda, which, Uchida claimed, he witnessed with his own eyes during his trip back home on the Trans-Siberian Railway.

However, Uchida also said that the German threat to Japan, which the newspapers had covered with much sensationalism, was insubstantial; and that despite the Treaty of Brest-Litovsk, Germany would not dominate Russian territory or politics. Uchida was in a better position to judge than the government at home: after leaving Petrograd, he stopped in the town of Vologda for a week to observe the Russo-German negotiation of armistice. The Bolshevik regime, Uchida continued (again contradicting media reports), had mass support because it promised peace, not because the Russian people supported socialist ideas, and was likely to be the only centralized authority that would remain after the dust had settled. He largely blamed the Bolshevik takeover on the incompetence of the imperial and provisional governments but had no doubt that Soviet Russia would emerge again as a major power in world politics. Uchida also criticized the Western media and politicians for spreading false rumors about Japan's ill intentions toward Russia, causing anti-Japanese feelings among the Russian people and leadership. Uchida also declared that the recognition of Soviet Russia by world powers was only a matter of time and that the Japanese government must stay on friendly terms with the Soviet government. However, although opposed to intervention, Uchida did not call for the immediate recognition of Bolshevik Russia but advised waiting for revolutionary fervor to subside and for the revolutionary government to stabilize.[43]

The Foreign Ministry's position, as expressed by Motono, Gotō, and Uchida, was largely unconcerned with communist ideology per se. Communism was regarded not as the consequence of internal economic and social tensions or a reaction to capitalist industrialization but largely as the result of foreign—specifically German—socialist propaganda. Since communism was brought in from outside, the Bolshevik regime was considered to be either temporary or ideologically superficial. The Japanese leadership, therefore, was careful to distinguish between the Bolshevik ideological elite and the Russian people, declining to recognize the former for the time being, but making sure to express their encouragement and support to the latter.

Besides the Foreign Ministry, the main progenitor of the intervention was the Japanese Army General Staff (Sanbō Honbu) under the leadership of Field Marshal Uehara Yūsaku and his deputy, General Tanaka Gi'ichi. As Uehara revealed in his memoirs, the General Staff's plan to dispatch forces to Siberia was intended to "rebuild stability in Siberia, and enhance Japan's pre-eminent position on the continent."[44] The General Staff proposed the creation of an independent, communist-free Siberian state to the east of Lake Baikal, which would flourish economically through an alliance with Japan. The idea that the Bolsheviks were, in fact, German agents and carriers of German radical social ideas permeated military circles as well. In the spring of 1918, in a position paper probably written for presentation to the army minister, Tanaka advocated a policy of support for Asiatic Russians willing to "defend their fatherland against the eastward advance of German-Austrian influence," by which he meant Bolshevism. Tanaka asked that all continental diplomatic and military representatives be instructed to make this policy clear to the Russian people and to work toward securing their cooperation.[45] A Siberian buffer state would thus come into existence, protecting China and Korea from German/Bolshevik ideological and military expansion. Moreover, the establishment of a Siberian republic, the General Staff reasoned, would increase pressure on China to accept Japanese economic and strategic influence in Manchuria and Inner Mongolia. Considering that Finland, Poland, and the Baltic states gained independence after the Russian Revolution, such plans seemed not unrealistic to the Japanese military.

As the government was reluctant to intervene and concerned with the United States' reaction, the army took matters into its own hands. In mid-November 1917, the General Staff developed a plan to intervene under the pretext of protecting Japanese residents in the Far Eastern territory. The plan was to send troops to Vladivostok and Khabarovsk in Russia, and to Harbin and Chichihar in northern Manchuria, and take control of local railway and telegraph lines.[46] In early December 1917, Tanaka gave orders to send secret agents (*tokumu kikan*) to all major stations along the Trans-Siberian Railway between Irkutsk and Vladivostok. Major-General Nakajima Masatake, reassigned from his post in Petrograd, became the operational chief in Vladivostok. Nakajima's task was to establish contact with anti-Bolshevik forces and, if necessary, provide arms, cash, and technical advice. In February 1918, Nakajima made a wager on Ataman Semenov, who with Japanese backing emerged as the major anti-Bolshevik force in Siberia.

Meanwhile, the army's plans for Russia were tightly entangled with its objectives in northern Manchuria. In December 1917, Tanaka urged the cabinet that

Japan "must take over" the CER after the Russian withdrawal. Disintegration of Russian power in the East, he argued, offered an excellent opportunity to gain a foothold in Harbin and over the CER for any future expansion in northeastern China and Asiatic Russia.[47] With this aim in mind, the General Staff began to work on winning over the White forces on the CER. In March 1918, Nakajima and Kawakami Toshitsune, still the president of the SMR, met with General Horvath in Harbin and pledged their support in return for major concessions to Japan on the CER. The future war minister Araki Sadao, then a lieutenant colonel fresh from his assignment in Russia, became the Japanese army's representative in Harbin attached to Horvath.[48] Araki's stint in Russia and later in Harbin during the first years of the revolution were formative in his later rabid anticommunist and anti-Soviet position. The Japanese government eventually gained what they wanted, albeit not for long. Although the CER had been under Chinese control since January 1918, the Japanese army was successful in compelling the Chinese government to sign the Sino-Japanese Joint Defense Agreement in May 1918, which allowed Japan to gain better control over the CER and establish a strong foothold in northern Manchuria.[49]

The Bolshevik advance into the Russian Far East prompted the Japanese government to react swiftly. After the establishment of Soviet rule in Vladivostok in January 1918, the Japanese government authorized the dispatch of two battleships to the port of Vladivostok to protect Japanese residents and businesses. The navy, however, was prohibited from engaging in any further actions. After the murder of some Japanese residents by a Russian mob, in April the marines landed in Vladivostok and occupied the city. The General Staff pressed for further intervention, but both the Ministries of the Army and the Navy and the Cabinet rejected the proposal, giving stern instructions to the consulate in Vladivostok not to interfere in Russian domestic affairs.[50] The landing, however, made a huge impact on the Russian population, spurring nationalist feelings and strong anti-Japanese sentiments. In turn, the Bolsheviks used this opportunity given them by the Japanese military, skillfully manipulating the public's fear of Japanese invasion. Consequently, the Bolsheviks eliminated competition from other leftist factions and by the summer of 1918 established an exclusive Bolshevik authority in the Far East, albeit temporarily before the renewal of the Japanese offensive.

In the first half of 1918, the General Staff's efforts to push for a full-scale intervention were futile because the majority of the government and the council—among whom the leader of the Seiyūkai party, Hara Takashi, and the elder statesman Yamagata Aritomo were the most vocal—strongly opposed the intervention. They warned that it would cause financial disaster and jeopardize relations with the United States, and that Japan was not equipped to conduct a large-scale war without economic aid from the United States and Britain. The consensus was that Japan would not intervene unless the Unites States accepted its share of responsibility for the decision. For a while, the government managed to keep control of the General Staff, which steered clear of implementing its plans in Siberia. With the appointment of Tanaka as army minister in the Hara Cabinet in September 1918, the government brought the General Staff under its control. For the most part, the General Staff and the Army Ministry followed government orders but were irked by the requirement that the United States give its approval to their actions in East Asia.

By June 1918, it seemed that the intervention would not happen—the retreating German troops did not represent a threat anymore, nor did the struggling Bolshevik regime seem to be a source of any real danger. The 1918 summer events in Siberia, however, fundamentally changed the situation. In May 1918, some thirty thousand to fifty thousand former Austro-Hungarian prisoners of war, known as the Czecho-Slovak Legion, clashed with the Bolsheviks in Western Siberia and, with Allied encouragement, sealed off the whole of Siberia along the Trans-Siberian Railway from Soviet power. The rescue of the legion became a convenient rallying point for the governments of Britain, France, Japan, and the United States to officially join the intervention. Woodrow Wilson was hostile to the Bolshevik leadership, especially after the peace treaty the Bolshevik regime concluded with Germany, but did not want to get involved in the Russian Civil War and resisted British-French pressure for a Japanese-American expedition to the Russian Far East. However, the evacuation of the Austro-Hungarian prisoners of war and, more importantly, the need to restrain and keep an eye on Japanese activities in the Russian Far East and northern Manchuria convinced the US leaders to send troops. On July 8, 1918, the US government invited Japan to undertake a joint armed intervention.[51]

Wilson's decision enabled the General Staff, the army, and the Foreign Ministry to proceed with their own agenda. Their opponents in the Japanese government could not object to the US invitation and could not let the United States conduct the operation without Japanese participation. And so, between 1918 and 1922, approximately 125,000 soldiers, belonging to the armies of ten countries, were deployed to Siberia and the Russian Far East as part of the Allied intervention in the Russian Civil War.[52] Despite the agreement among the Allied intervention forces that the number of troops be limited to seven thousand, and despite the opposition from the Cabinet and the Privy Council, the Army General Staff, asserting the "right of supreme command" (tōsuiken), launched a full-scale assault deploying more than seventy-two thousand troops (one-third of all of Japan's active service troops) to Vladivostok and the Transbaikal region. By the end of October 1918, the Japanese army had occupied the region between Irkutsk and Vladivostok along the Trans-Siberian Railway and the city of Nikolaevsk at the mouth of the Amur River (some 1,600 kilometers to the north of Vladivostok), as well as the Chinese Eastern Railway line in northern Manchuria, including the city of Harbin. The US decision to intervene finally granted the Japanese army a new opportunity to realize its long-cherished plans for assuming control over the whole of Manchuria, while control over the Russian Far East was an unexpected bonus, which the army was not going to let slip by.

The Japanese government officially announced its decision to intervene in Russia on August 2, 1918. The draft of the announcement was reworked several times, but with results that were satisfactory to few. The main reason for the intervention was ostensibly the rescue of the Austro-Hungarian prisoners of war. In addition, Japanese troops were to provide assistance to the Russian people, "tired" of revolutionary events. Notably, Bolshevism and the threat it presented were not mentioned—the Japanese government was very careful not to include any confrontational statements against the Soviet government. Any mention of northern Manchuria, which seemed to be included in the erased drafts, was also suppressed. Gotō clarified that the Siberian Intervention was a foreign war with a just cause, while the interventionist force was a "new Salvation Army," "in accordance with the new principle of people of the world being all brothers," and that their goals were thus completely different from that of a punitive expedition and invasion.[53] It was presumed that the Japanese troops were in Russia to "save" it, yet no one in the government or the Diet publicly identified from whom or from what Russia must be saved. The declaration promised withdrawal once order was restored and renounced any desire to infringe on Russian territorial sovereignty and Russian internal affairs. There was cheerful confidence among many in Tokyo that the Bolshevik regime was not to survive the intervention, and that Japanese plans for the region certainly would be realized.

The Japanese "offensive" was both economic and military. To obtain local Siberian support for Japan and to counteract US relief efforts, an economic mission was organized to provide relief to the local people and spur economic activity in the region. A Special Commission for Siberian Economic Aid (Rinji Shiberia Keizai Enjō Iinkai), largely run by Matsuoka Yōsuke and Kimura Eiichi, worked closely with the Japanese army on the ground.[54] The commission was "to establish a basis for Japanese economic activities in opposition to the acquisition of concessions by the United States and other countries." The commission's agenda thus reveals Matsuoka's fears (not entirely unjustified) of US penetration in the region, in terms of finance and trade. In December 1918, the commission set up the Russo-Japanese Trading Company; in 1919, the Far East Business Development Corporation and the Russo-Japanese Bank were organized for the purpose of entering the mining, oil production, forestry, fisheries, and related transport industries. All major players of the day—including the business conglomerates Mitsui, Mitsubishi, Sumitomo, Kuhara, and Furukawa—were involved in the activities of the commission, injecting a large amount of money into Siberia and fully cooperating with the army.[55] It must be added that the Foreign Ministry had ultimate control over the commission, and Minister Uchida and Deputy Minister Shidehara Kijūrō would often check its overly aggressive economic plans for Russia.[56] It was during this period, while working together on Siberian affairs, when the moderate Shidehara (whose conciliatory style of diplomacy would later be dubbed "Shidehara diplomacy") and the more aggressive Matsuoka developed fundamental disagreements about Japan's foreign policy that would later play out in a more visible and dramatic way.

In pursuit of its agenda, Japan became the only country that actively intervened in the Russian Civil War. In August–September 1918, a Japanese-Cossack offensive swept away Soviet rule in the Far East and Transbaikalia. In one infamous incident, the Japanese burned alive a local Bolshevik commander, Sergei Lazo, in the firebox of a locomotive. This incident became a cornerstone of Soviet revolutionary mythology and forever imprinted the negative image of the Japanese in Russian public memory. The Advisory Council and the Cabinet tried to curb the General Staff's support of the White Cossacks—specifically, Grigory Semenov, Ivan Kalmykov, Ivan Gamov, and Roman Ungern-Sternberg, whose names became synonymous with the worst atrocities of the Civil War—but the command in Siberia and especially the secret intelligence officers not only ignored the order but continued to offer financial and military assistance to these leaders. Atamans, who controlled parts of the CER and played havoc with the communication and supply line between the Allied forces and the White Army in Western Siberia, were also a useful way for the Japanese to put pressure on the Allies and the White administration of Harbin to gain more control of the CER.[57] The General Staff also tried to cultivate the national aspirations of the indigenous peoples, but they had little idea how to win them over. Despite the pan-Asianist rhetoric, they regarded Siberian indigenous people as simple "tribes" of "wild" peoples. Japanese soldiers and officers felt a cultural superiority in reference to them, and there were numerous cases of plunder by Japanese soldiers.[58]

The actions of the Japanese military in Siberia, however, backfired greatly. Japanese support for the atamans, as well as abuses by the Japanese army, drove the local population into the arms of the Bolsheviks. Japan's ultimate failure to achieve its military and economic aims was the result of its inability to develop an effective political strategy in the region. The country's economic efforts seemed insignificant or insincere against the backdrop of the Japanese army's everyday brutality. The most significant economic gain was the establishment of Japan's total monopoly over the Russian fishery industry, but this looked more like a plundering of resources than an effort to rebuild the Russian economy. All in all, Japanese efforts in Russia relied principally on military force and short-term alliances with local anti-Bolshevik forces, which did not lead anywhere due to persistent mutual suspicions.

In the summer of 1918, as the government was dispatching troops to Russia, the unprecedented scale of the Rice Riots, caused by the inflation of rice prices, seemed to some contemporaries to signal the coming of a leftist revolution to Japan. The biggest popular riot in modern Japanese history, the Rice Riots involved over one million people from Hokkaido to Kyushu, prompting the government to dispatch more than 100,000 men to 170 places in 23 prefectures to suppress the uprising.[59] At the end of the day, thirty civilians were killed and five thousand rioters were tried. The protesters were far from trying to implement a leftist revolution and were not prompted to act by an emergent "class consciousness," but some contemporary observers were unnerved by the timing—too close to the Russian Revolution—and by the possibility of connections to socialism. Although socialist leaders were not engaged in the riots, the police arrested or administratively detained several of them, including Ōsugi Sakae, Arahata Kanson, and Yamakawa Hitoshi.

After the riots brought down the unpopular Terauchi government, a new Cabinet came to power, with Hara Takashi as prime minister, Uchida Kōsai as foreign minister, and Tanaka Gi'ichi as army minister. Despite his earlier opposition to the intervention, Hara carried on with plans to create a buffer state between East Asia and Soviet Russia to deter the advance of communism—the influence of which, it was suspected, was present in the Rice Riots. Uchida, who had resigned from his ambassadorship in protest against the intervention, now too as the new foreign minister proceeded with implementing the government's policy of aggression in Russia. For the Paris Peace Conference in January 1919, Uchida wrote a memorandum arguing that a Siberian republic, which Japanese military forces were assisting in creating, would serve as a bulwark against the communist revolution and expansion of Soviet power in Siberia and Outer Mongolia. In the new republic, the Japanese delegation assured Western powers in Paris that equality of opportunities for *all* foreigners would be ensured—the right to live freely, trade, and conduct business.[60]

With the aim of establishing a pro-Japanese buffer state, in mid-1919 the Hara Cabinet began its support of the Omsk government and its leader Admiral Kolchak. The main influence in Hara's decision to support Kolchak and pursue the idea of a buffer state was none other than Satō Naotake, who had so much influence over

Motono. Now an ex-consul-general in Harbin, Satō moved to Omsk to lend support to Kolchak and act as his adviser. As he had previously argued to Motono, Satō insisted that the Bolsheviks were *kaji dorobō*, thieves who take advantage of a conflagration. Satō pinned his hopes on Kolchak as the only force capable of uniting Russia and establishing order. Importantly, Kolchak promised to uphold all imperial obligations and repay all outstanding state debts, in addition to giving substantial concessions to the fish and oil industries, and offered assurances that Japan would retain control over the eastern part of the Trans-Siberian Railway and the CER.[61]

In addition, Hara disapproved of the General Staff's support of the volatile Cossacks, especially after news of their atrocities with the help of the Japanese forces began to circulate in Europe and the United States. The political friction at home between the government (Hara and Uchida) and the army (Tanaka, Araki Sadao in Harbin, and the General Staff) had its counterpart in Siberia: Kolchak was supported by the former, and his rival Ataman Semenov by the latter. Nevertheless, both Japanese parties showed hesitation and lack of conviction that their actions were right. Kolchak's regime proved to be short-lived, as it failed to mobilize grassroots support during its one-year existence, and by the end of 1919 his forces were defeated; he was executed in Irkutsk in January 1920. Semenov's hold on Transbaikalia lasted as long as the Japanese forces were present in the region. As soon as they withdrew, Semenov's luck ran out later in 1920. He followed the Japanese army to Vladivostok, Harbin, and later to Tokyo.[62]

The fall of Kolchak heralded a new phase of the Civil War and foreign intervention. The Red Army steadily advanced from the Urals to Eastern Siberia, and finally the Pacific. In contrast, the White armies and the interventionist forces were plagued by internal divisions and rivalries, confused and inconsistent policies, and domestic pressure in the Allies' home countries to end the intervention, particularly after the signing of the Armistice in Europe in November 1918. In January 1920, the United States resolved to evacuate its forces from Siberia, and in April all Allied troops, except the Japanese, were withdrawn.

The Soviets were not ready to face the Japanese army because they were preoccupied with the raging Polish-Soviet war (1919–21). To avoid a full-scale confrontation with Japan, the Soviet leadership decided to create a temporary buffer state in the territory east of Lake Baikal. On April 6, 1920, the Congress of Toilers of the Baikal Region proclaimed the Far Eastern Democratic Republic (FER). In the wake of the approaching Washington Conference and mounting international and domestic criticism of the intervention, the Japanese government recognized the FER and in July 1920 started negotiations with its leaders.[63] The Japanese army agreed to withdraw from Transbaikalia on the condition that the FER would remain democratic and free of communism. Limited now to the

Russian Far East (where the army installed a pro-Japanese rightist government in 1921) and northern Manchuria, the Japanese army and government were determined to hold on to these territories.

The so-called Nikolaevsk Incident in the spring of 1920 provided an opportunity to prolong the Japanese intervention. Japanese forces had occupied Nikolaevsk in the summer of 1918, largely to protect the considerable Japanese fishery business in the region, until the town was attacked by guerrillas under Yakov Triapitsyn. In what is known as the Nikolaevsk massacre, more than seven hundred Japanese officers and town residents were killed, in addition to several hundred Russian inhabitants. The Japanese army seized this opportunity to start a propaganda offensive back home. Newspapers ceaselessly reported gruesome stories about the murdered five thousand Japanese citizens (rather than the actual seven hundred), including women and children. The number of murdered Russian people was omitted. Press conferences of war journalists attracted considerable crowds. Around the country, memorial services were held with members of the imperial family in attendance. The murdered military were enshrined in the Yasukuni shrine, where the spirits of executed war criminals would be enshrined in the postwar period.[64]

In 1920, self-defense became the new rationale for the Japanese military to remain in the Russian Far East. The military announced to the Japanese public that "Now we establish the region from the Russian maritime area to Vladivostok as our self-defense territory. This is separate from the expedition's previous objective. It has been developed from the desire to clearly establish the region of Japanese self-defense."[65] Under this pretext, the Japanese army occupied and held the northern part of Sakhalin until 1925. South Sakhalin had been under Japanese control since 1905. Under the auspices of the navy, the extraction of natural resources (i.e., oil) in Sakhalin and colonization by Japanese settlers intensified.[66] On one hand, the Nikolaevsk Incident bolstered the argument for Japanese annexation of a portion of the Russian Far East to shield the Japanese inhabitants of Manchuria and Korea from similar destruction at the hands of the Bolshevik Russians, Koreans, and Chinese. Soviet writers even expressed the opinion that the Japanese deliberately provoked the Nikolaevsk conflict to justify further occupation of Russian territory.[67]

On the other hand, the "self-defense" rhetoric had some grounds behind it. By 1920, the Japanese government seemed to have become genuinely concerned that the revolution was spilling beyond Russian borders into China and Korea, thus directly jeopardizing the security of the Japanese Empire.[68] The Bolsheviks were active among Russian and Chinese railway workers at the CER. The railway's communist party branch was responsible for numerous strikes and propaganda handbills and appeals, which were directed against the White tsarist management of the CER and Japan's imperialist designs with respect to China. The communist branch also called for active support of the proletarian revolution in Russia.[69] Reports of Korean anti-Japanese activities began to be dispatched to Japan in early 1918. Several thousand radicalized Koreans and Chinese in the Russian Far East joined some two hundred Bolshevik-led partisan groups numbering about fifty thousand people. Recent Korean immigrants with knowledge of the Japanese language served as translators, agents, and informants, providing invaluable help to the Bolsheviks.[70] The FER's national-revolutionary army had a Korean-Chinese regiment (later the International Regiment of the Fifth Red Banner Army), which was composed of 65 percent Chinese and 30 percent Koreans and had its own military academy in Irkutsk that by the end of the 1920s had trained 163 Chinese and Korean officers.[71] A few hundred Koreans organized their own partisan groups, some of their members returning to colonial Korea to participate in the national liberation movement. Often they would conduct anti-Japanese guerrilla activities on Korean territory, then quickly retreat to Chinese or Russian territories.

Cities on the Manchurian frontier and in the Russian Far East also offered refuge to Korean independence groups committed to militant resistance. In 1922, the so-called First Chinese Revolutionary Division of Kirin Province was formed in the Russian Far East. Initially composed of around three thousand fighters, once they moved to northern China, according to Soviet reports, their numbers increased to twenty-one thousand (twelve thousand foot soldiers and nine thousand mounted fighters).[72] As a German journalist informed the Japanese in September 1922, the Soviets established many propaganda schools in Moscow, Tomsk, Omsk, Irkutsk, and Tashkent with the aim "to stir up Korea against the Japanese rule."[73] Colonized Koreans hardly needed propaganda to spur their anti-Japanese sentiments; according to Soviet sources, the number of Korean volunteers was so high that the majority of them had to be placed on reserve. Historians have largely attributed the rise of Korean and Chinese pro-independence movements—the Korean independence demonstrations on March 1, 1919; the May Fourth Movement in China; and the proclamation of an independent Korean government in Khabarovsk in 1920—to the Wilsonian moment of 1919. However, it is obvious that Japanese contemporaries perceived those events quite differently—namely as the direct consequence of the Russian Revolution and the Bolsheviks' plan to implement a world proletarian revolution. For the Japanese leaders, the colonized Koreans were the perfect "dagger" in the hands of the Russian communists pointed at the heart of the Japanese Empire.[74]

Foreign Minister Uchida Kōsai "ordered the consuls in Manchuria and Vladivostok to do everything possible to crush rebellious Korean organizations within their jurisdiction."[75] In 1919–20, the police force of the Korea Govern-ment-General repeatedly crossed the border and conducted raids on suspected radical camps in Manchuria. Japanese officials knew that many Koreans were enlisted in the Red Army and that "certain Koreans who were in collusion with the Bolsheviks had actually attempted an armed invasion of the Korean bor-der and burned a Japanese consulate."[76] The Seoul Press reported on Octo-ber 2, 1920, that three hundred to four hundred Koreans allegedly under the leadership of some Russians attacked and burnt the Japanese embassy in the town of Hunchun in the Jiandao region. In a matter of days, Chinese sol-diers joined the rioters and again attacked Japanese troops and the Japanese embassy. Japanese officials insisted that the rioters were Korean Bolshevik partisans and included fifty Russians. A wave of protests spread around the whole of northern Manchuria, involving around forty thousand people. In response, the Japanese army in Korea crossed the border and joined Jiandao region consular police forces in what came to be called the Jiandao Expedition (*Kantō shuppei*). After a brutal and murderous large-scale military operation, the Japanese army retreated to Korea in the spring of 1921.[77] After the events in Jiandao, Hara was so concerned with the susceptibility of the Koreans in Manchuria to Bolshevism that he entertained the idea of trying to annex the Jiandao area to Korea by lease or purchase.[78] As another example of Japanese preoccupation with radicals on the borders, a Sino-Korean-Japanese security organization, the Manshū hominkai (Manchuria People's Protection Society), was established to safeguard the borders against the guerilla Bolshevik Kore-ans. The Protection Society was basically a death squad; all apprehended were shot.[79] On top of that, the success of the Korean communist organization in Shanghai, established in 1921 with the aid of the Comintern, as well as their position as a conduit between Japanese leftists and the Soviet Union (discussed in chapter 4), was considered by the Japanese Foreign Ministry and police to be a direct threat to the stability of metropolitan society itself.[80]

The greatest consequence of the Japanese government's engagement with the radicals on the borders was, however, its decision to support the Manchurian warlord Chang Tso-lin, hoping with his help to protect Manchuria and Korea against Bolshevik subversion.[81] Little did the Japanese foreign policy makers sus-pect that, eight years later in 1928, their own army officers would assassinate the "treacherous" Chang Tso-lin, which paved the way to Japan's aggression in China in the 1930s.

For the common people in Japan, the objectives of the intervention were always unclear, and dubious at best. The Austro-Hungarian prisoners of war safely left Russia in 1919, the Great War was over in November 1918, Soviet

Russia and communism were never identified as enemies, and the army's aspirations for domination in northern Manchuria were never made public. The pacification of the imperial borders and suppression of Korean and Chinese anti-Japanese activities were not convincing arguments for the deployment of such huge numbers of armed forces and material resources. At home, the educated public was quite rightly concerned that the intervention would threaten peace in East Asia and incite hatred of the Japanese among Russian and Chinese people, thereby destroying the good relations rebuilt after the Russo-Japanese War.

In the general mood of antimilitarism and the growing demand for reducing the military budget, the intervention became hugely unpopular among members of the Diet and the public, concerned with the immense waste of money in a time of postwar economic recession. To the people, both the army and the navy looked like *zeikin dorobō* (tax robbers), and there was widespread criticism of them in Japanese society. The image of the imperial army was damaged so much that officers were often reluctant to wear uniforms in the streets. The Siberian Intervention (*Shiberia shuppei*) was often called *Shiberia shippai* (Siberian failure).[82] By 1921, all three political parties—Kokumintō, Kenseikai, and Seiyūkai—joined in their call to limit the military budget. Even the prime minister, Admiral Katō Tomosaburō, joined the chorus in July 1922, blaming the army for conducting its own "double diplomacy" (*nijū gaikō*) and constantly interfering in diplomatic relations with China. Moreover, in the navy's view, not only had the Siberian adventure wasted a great part of the state military budget that could have been allocated to naval expenditures, but it jeopardized the relationship with the United States, with whom the navy pursued a policy of détente.

The growing suspicion and antagonism in Europe and the United States about Japan's continued occupation of Siberia finally led to increasing pressure on Japan to withdraw. Already during the Paris Peace Conference, the Hara Cabinet conceded and reduced troop strength in Siberia by one half. In addition, in March 1919, Japan relinquished its exclusive military control over the Trans-Siberian Railway and the CER and agreed to the establishment of the Interallied Railway Committee to control the CER. During the Washington Naval Arms Limitation Conference in 1921–22, under strong pressure from the former Allies, Japan promised to withdraw from Russian territory and trim naval expenditures. Finally, Chief of Staff Marshal Uehara accepted the military budget reduction and ended his opposition to the withdrawal from Siberia. On June 24, 1922, the Japanese government proclaimed the withdrawal of all Japanese troops from the Maritime Province of Siberia and from northern Manchuria. In November 1922, the Japanese evacuation was completed, except from Sakhalin Island where extraction of oil by Japanese companies continued. In December 1922, the FER joined the USSR, and communist rule was established in all of Russia's territory. A year later, in 1924, control over the CER—so coveted by Japan—went from the Interallied Railway Committee to the USSR and China, after they signed the Sino-Soviet Agreement (discussed in the next chapter). The Japanese army's Siberian adventure ended in a fiasco, taking the lives of more than two thousand of its own soldiers and many more Russians, Siberian indigenous people, Koreans, and Chinese.

The Siberian Intervention was a strange war: no clear enemy was identified, Bolshevism and communism were never mentioned, and no greater cause was declared. Although it was an obvious war against Russia and its people, as the violence became indiscriminate, the Japanese government tirelessly and cynically pronounced its friendship with the Russian people and insisted it was acting in their interest. Any mention of the Soviet state, either positive or negative, was carefully omitted in official documents, which presumed for the Japanese government the continuous existence of imperial Russia. After all, the imperial Russian embassy in Tokyo lasted the longest among all Russian embassies, closing its doors only in 1925.[83] But at the same time, and more importantly, the Japanese government never publicly stated its opposition to or fundamental disagreement with the ideological principles of the new Soviet state.

By 1922, it was obvious to everyone (except perhaps the army) that Japan had lost its undeclared war on Soviet Russia. Lacking a clear and consistent approach to the Soviet Union and Soviet communism, the Japanese decision makers did not possess the inner conviction that their actions in Siberia were correct and quickly lost control over the escalating violence. As the Bolshevik regime gained political and military momentum in Siberia and the Russian Far East, not least because of the brutal and short-sighted actions of the Japanese interventionist army, the Japanese government had to accept the fact that the Bolshevik government would probably stay in power for the foreseeable future.

The initial military reaction to the Russian Revolution was undertaken by the army and the Foreign Ministry. Their motives, however, had less to do with a fear of the communist threat to the Japanese islands and more with the spread of communism and Soviet influence in Korea and China, where communism overlapped with national liberation movements and stimulated the fight against Japanese rule. Initial ambition for an informal empire in Siberia was consequently replaced by the urgency to keep the militant anti-imperialist/anti-Japanese ideology away from Korea and China. However, Japan's initial strong response failed, and the alternative pro-Soviet approach began to be worked out among some influential Japanese political groups, signifying major dissolution of the consensus about expansion on the continent. The new approach required, however, a certain understanding and interpretation of Soviet and international communism, to which we now turn.

3

THE ANTI-WESTERN REVOLUTION

An alliance of the Japanese people with the peoples of the Soviet
Union would be a decisive step on the way to the liberation of the
East. Such an alliance would mean the beginning of the end for
world capitalism. This alliance would be invincible.

—Stalin's interview to *Tokyo nichi nichi* newspaper, July 1925

Sometime in the spring of 1922, three men—two Japanese and one Russian—
met in a boardroom in central Tokyo to discuss how to advance stalled negotiations between Japan and Soviet Russia. The two Japanese men were a member of
the House of Representatives, the national populist Nakano Seigō (1886–1943)
and a pan-Asianist journalist, Mitsukawa Kametarō (1888–1936). The Russian man was the communist Vasily Antonov, who officially arrived in Tokyo in
March 1922 to establish a branch of the telegraphic agency of the Far Eastern
Republic (DALTA), but who unofficially acted as a representative of the Soviet
government. At the meeting, Mitsukawa asked Antonov whether Soviet Russia
intended to pursue the world socialist revolution. Antonov replied that the Soviet
government, as a matter of fact, did not plan to instigate world proletarian revolutions but would morally support national revolutions in Asia. Greatly satisfied
with the answer, Mitsukawa informed the readers of the prestigious magazine
Tōhō jiron about the Soviets' benevolent intentions in Asia. In the same issue,
at Mitsukawa's recommendation, Antonov's article "The Nature of the Russian Revolution" (Rokoku kakumei no seishitsu) was published, which largely
emphasized Soviet support of the liberation of colonial peoples.[1]

Mitsukawa, Nakano, and Antonov talked a great deal more about the Russian
Revolution and the intentions of the Soviet government during the course of
Antonov's one-year stay in Tokyo. The content of these conversations was surely
identical to what Mitsukawa reported in his article, as Antonov's mission in Tokyo
was to convince Japanese decision makers to reconsider their view of the Soviet
government. In June 1922, Antonov met with Matsudaira Tsuneo, the director of

the Anglo-American Department in the Ministry of Foreign Affairs, and passed on to him Moscow's wishes to resume the halted negotiations. As a result, Japanese and Soviet delegations met in September in Vladivostok to set up a further conference. At the same time, Gotō Shinpei, then mayor of Tokyo, reached out to the Soviet government to arrange an unofficial visit to Japan of its representative, Adolf Ioffe. With Ioffe's arrival in Japan in February 1923, Antonov's mission was over, and he bid farewell to his acquaintances Mitsukawa and Nakano. Gotō's work, however, had just started. Gotō, Mitsukawa and other pro-Soviet politicians and public commentators now had a task: to accomplish rapprochement with Russia in a way that would convince the public, the Foreign Ministry, the army, and other doubters, including in China and the United States, at a time when the last Japanese soldiers were still evacuating from mainland Russia.

The Soviet dual and contradictory diplomacy, conducted by both the Soviet Ministry of Foreign Affairs and the Comintern, muddled Japan's response to the Russian Revolution. As we have seen, the first state response to the Bolshevik takeover was formulated by the military and the Foreign Ministry and resulted in the failed Siberian Intervention. But as the Bolshevik regime showed no sign of collapse, and quite to the contrary engaged in feverish activities in China, many in Japan campaigned for a qualitatively new relationship with Soviet Russia. This campaign was deeply entangled with the unfolding issues of domestic economic policies, as well as Japan's foreign policies vis-à-vis the Asian continent and the United States. To convince the doubters, especially liberals and conservatives from the Home and Justice ministries (discussed in chapter 4), the Japanese proponents of the rapprochement with Russia, inside and outside the government, preferred to focus on the USSR as a state—whose leadership, they argued, had abandoned its revolutionary zeal and slogans in order to survive in the hostile international environment. Pan-Asianists, who are discussed in the first half of this chapter, considered the Russian Revolution as an anti-Western revolt that, they argued, made Soviet Russia an obvious ally of Japan. Regarding Western imperialist powers as Japan's biggest enemies, pan-Asianists agitated for Soviet-Japanese cooperation, and even for the creation of a Eurasian bloc, in order to resist the Anglo-American world order that was undermining Japan's (and, by extension, Asia's) safety and well-being. This was a powerful argument, and it gained strong, influential supporters in government and business circles during the interwar and wartime periods. The second part of this chapter deals with Gotō Shinpei, and the subsequent efforts of the government to find grounds for peaceful coexistence with Soviet Russia in East Asia. Pan-Asianists' and pro-Soviet politicians' coordinated efforts thus demonstrate not only the fact that Soviet Russia loomed large in Japan's overall foreign policy, but also that foreign affairs began to be viewed as the key and only solution to Japan's domestic issues.

The Russian Revolution, with its vision of international solidarity and an alternative social order, coincided with the rise of another movement in Japan—pan-Asianism. Pan-Asianist ideas in Japan date back to the end of the nineteenth century, when terms such as "pan-Asianism" (*Han-Ajiashugi*, or *Zen-Ajiashugi*), "Asian solidarity" (*Ajia rentai*), and "Raising Asia" (*kō-A*) were coined and employed by various political organizations and individuals concerned with Japan's foreign policy vis-à-vis Western powers and Japan's Asian neighbors.[2] There were two fundamental concepts underlying most strands of Japanese pan-Asianism. First, as Mitsukawa explained, pan-Asianism was based on the belief that "Asia constitutes culturally, politically, economically, geographically and racially a single community that shares the same fate."[3] Second was the conviction that Western imperialism threatened Asia, and that the only defense against Western encroachment was the unity of Asian peoples. As a political vision of a united front of Asian nations against Western imperialism, pan-Asianism had strong links with Asian anticolonial nationalism. In most Japanese versions of pan-Asianism, however, Japan was imagined as the leader of an Asian alliance, but the form of the union and the nature of Japan's leadership varied.[4]

Pan-Asianism became a viable and eventually mainstream approach to foreign politics in the post–World War I period, which seemingly exposed the decline of the Western liberal-capitalist and imperial global order and presented the chance for alternative programs to be realized. The Russian Revolution made an especially strong impact on pan-Asianists because it presented itself as a radical break from and challenge to Western capitalism and imperialism. This chapter explores the Soviet moment in Japanese pan-Asianist circles during the 1920s, centered on the writings of Mitsukawa Kametarō, who extensively addressed the issue of the relationship between the Japanese Empire and Soviet Russia on the Asian continent. Mitsukawa was a well-known journalist, the founder of a number of important right-wing societies, and an educator with extensive connections—from liberal university professors to senior military officers, and from Chinese and Indian revolutionaries in exile in Japan to the *tairiku rōnin*, Japanese pro-expansionist adventurers in China.[5] As a member of an Indian liberation fighters' support group, in 1916, Mitsukawa met Tōyama Mitsuru (1855–1944), leader of the nationalist Gen'yōsha (Dark Ocean Society); Uchida Ryōhei (1879–1937), founder of the nationalist Kokuryūkai (Black Dragon Society); nationalist politician Nakano Seigō; Home Minister Gotō Shinpei; and the infamous Ōkawa Shūmei (1886–1957). Moreover, as a journalist for the naval publication *Kaikoku shinpō*, Mitsukawa grew close to the highest echelons of the navy, among whom were Admiral Saitō Makoto, later the president of the Russo-Japanese Society after the death of Gotō Shinpei, and Admirals Nakazato Shigeji and Sakonji Seizō, who became presidents of the North Sakhalin Oil Enterprise.[6] These influential groups—Gotō Shinpei, the navy, the Meiji nationalist organizations, fishery business, and pan-Asianist circles—finally formed a pro-Russian lobby, pushing successfully for the normalization of Soviet-Japanese relations in 1925.

The pan-Asianism of Mitsukawa, Ōkawa, and other members of their circle initially grew out of their encounter with the plight of Indian anticolonial exiles, which fed their already brooding anti-British and in general anti-Western attitudes.[7] Mitsukawa and Ōkawa founded a number of important rightist organizations, such as the Rōsōkai (Old and Young Association, established in 1918) and the Yūzonsha (Society of Those Who Yet Remain, established in 1919), with the infamous radical nationalist Kita Ikki (1883–1937), among others. More consequential, however, was the fact that both Mitsukawa and Ōkawa worked at Takushoku University (Colonial Development University since 1919, formerly known as Oriental Society Technical School), where Gotō served as president. Takushoku University was tasked with educating administrators for Japan's colonial empire and, in fact, Professor Ōkawa was later promoted to researcher, and then director, of the SMR Research Institute, which Gotō founded in 1906.[8] Mitsukawa also had a very close relationship with Gotō. What makes Mitsukawa an especially significant figure is that he became the author of the memorandums on Soviet-Japanese relations that Gotō used in his arguments with the Cabinet and the Foreign Ministry, while pushing for stronger cooperation with Soviet Russia. Mitsukawa also worked closely with Gotō when he was preparing for his trip to Russia at the end of 1927 to meet Joseph Stalin and People's Commissar for Foreign Affairs Georgy Chicherin. What then were Mitsukawa's ideas about Soviet-Japanese cooperation on the Asian continent that would inform his work with Gotō?

In 1918, having for some time questioned the justness of the Eurocentric international order, Mitsukawa, Ōkawa, and other like-minded anti-imperialist pan-Asianists enthusiastically supported the Russian Revolution as a major assault on Western imperialism, appropriating along the way the categories of the Marxist-Leninist critique of imperialism. Mitsukawa expressed genuine admiration for Lenin and the Bolsheviks, lauding them as true patriots who saved Russia from total disintegration and destruction.[9] Ōkawa also admired how the Bolsheviks won despite foreign intervention, the counterrevolution, and conquered hunger and devastation by conviction and bravery alone, "teaching us that with this degree of faith and bravery the impossible can become possible."[10] In this regard, Mitsukawa, as well as Ōkawa and Kita Ikki, saw parallels between the Russian and Meiji revolutions: both were simultaneously modernizing and national revolutions; the former was accomplished by a group of Bolsheviks under the leadership of Lenin, while the latter was a coup d'état of lower samurai and a dedicated civilian elite. Kita Ikki, for example, wrote: "Those who jump to the conclusion that a coup d'état is an abuse of power on behalf of conservative despotism ignore history.... We see in the present Russian Revolution the example of Lenin using machine guns to dissolve a parliament filled with obstructionist forces."[11]

Mitsukawa's support of the Russian Revolution found its way into a political pamphlet he published in May 1919. Titled *Why Do We Make Bolsheviks Our Enemy?* (Naze ni Borushevizumu wo teki to nasu ka), the pamphlet argued for Japan's cooperation with Soviet Russia and the immediate withdrawal of Japanese troops from Russian territory.[12] Mitsukawa asserted that Bolshevism was not a threat to the Japanese Empire and nation: "Against those who argue that Bolsheviks are like pests and that, if you touch them, the empire's *kokutai* would be in danger, I say that making the Bolsheviks an enemy exposes the empire to even graver danger."[13] Alienating the Bolsheviks could potentially be a grave mistake with serious repercussions for domestic life and foreign affairs. Mitsukawa also suspected that the foreign intervention in Russia was designed by the Anglo-American powers to constrict the Japanese presence in Asia.

A positive outlook on the Bolshevik takeover was shared by most nationalist-minded commentators. The first ever publication of Trotsky's writings in Japanese was his article "Bolsheviks and World Peace," translated by Endō Kichisaburō, a radical nationalist and renowned oceanologist from Hokkaido University, published in December 1917 in the rightist magazine *Dai Nippon*, where Mitsukawa worked. Arguing that the Bolsheviks' goal was to pull Russia out of the war and restore its national strength, Endō berated the hysteria in the Japanese media about the Bolsheviks being pawns of Germany.[14] But despite considering the Meiji and October revolutions as similar in causes and objectives, for Mitsukawa, Kita, Endō, and other nationalists, the key to the success of the Meiji Revolution was the powerful unifying force of the Japanese imperial institution. Unlike Western or Russian monarchies, Mitsukawa wrote, the Japanese monarchy had the innate character of goodwill toward its people, and only it was able to mobilize the whole nation and restore its unity. In this regard, pan-Asianists upheld a commonly shared view that the Romanov dynasty was more equivalent to the feudal Tokugawa rule rather than the Meiji monarchy.[15]

In the first postrevolutionary years, the Yūzonsha group, formed by Mitsukawa, Ōkawa, and Kita Ikki in 1919, also embraced revolutionary fervor. Mitsukawa saw that Japan was in danger of adopting of a Western, capitalist way of life: the chase after profit and the pursuit of selfish individualism, which in foreign policy manifested in politicians, oligarchs, and big business bowing before the Great Powers and abandoning Japan's national interests. Mitsukawa's 1918 article on this subject, "The Coming of the Age of Revolution" (Kakumei jidai no tōrai), begins by characterizing the late 1910s as an era in which the old Meiji revolutionary

spirit and order were finally exhausted: people's thoughts and actions were morally depraved and money-driven, politicians were corrupt, and the emperor
had fallen out of touch with the Japanese people due to the usurpation of state
power by wealthy oligarchs. Postwar economic depression, the resentment felt by
impoverished peasants and workers toward the new rich (*narikin*), the Rice Riots,
and people's discontent with the Siberian Intervention, Mitsukawa and Ōkawa
claimed, would together serve as the impetus for a social revolution.[16]

Ideas espoused by Mitsukawa and other members of the Yūzonsha were part
of what the historian Itō Takashi called the emerging "national renovationist"
(*kokka kaizō*) movement.[17] As Ōkawa himself explained, fervor for national renovation was embraced by different political groups united by concern over Japan's
domestic policies and international standing.

> During World War I, following the rapid development of Japanese capi-
> talism, social problems and social movements were on the rise. Second,
> under the impact of World War I, the Russian communist revolution, the
> collapse of Austria-Hungary, the Spanish revolution, and the Italian fas-
> cist dictatorship altered social structures all around the world. Because
> of these developments, various reconstruction organizations sprang up
> in Japan. This reconstruction movement can be divided roughly into
> the following segments. First was anarchism, whose leader was the now
> deceased Ōsugi Sakae. Second was the communist party, and third
> were social-democratic organizations that later developed into various
> proletarian parties. Fourth was national socialism [*kokka shakaishugi*],
> centered around Takabatake Motoyuki. Fifth was the Yūzonsha group,
> whose political program echoed that of national socialism. Despite this
> resemblance, the spiritual foundations of the Yūzonsha were different,
> as it was based on Japanese tradition.[18]

Here Ōkawa explained that by the end of World War I, pan-Asianists, nationalists, communists, and national socialists had shared the call for a radical revolution to end the rule of the "corrupt privileged strata" (bureaucratic, financial,
and political party cliques) that enslaved the people. The goals of a reformed
state were a reduced bureaucracy, state regulation of big business, elimination
of party politics, and rule by a dedicated group of politicians in the name of the
emperor. The revolution's purpose thus was to "purify" the corrupted body politic, "cleanse" and revitalize the state, and return society to its original premises.

Mitsukawa offered an even cruder distinction between postwar political
groups in pointing out that contemporary opinion about the management of
society split into two approaches: *kokkashugi* (statism), which included socialists
and pan-Asianists, and *minshushugi* (democracy), espoused by proponents of

Western-type liberal democracy.[19] Pan-Asianists' main objection to the "democracy" movement was not that it was a political theory of an essentially foreign intellectual and political tradition. To the contrary, pan-Asianists and nationalists actively supported the universal suffrage movement. Their main fear was that Japan's liberal-democratic movement and its leaders could be used by Western imperialist powers to gain influence over the hearts and minds of the people of Japan and other Asian nations. Instead of a liberal-democratic program, the "renovationists" offered a better solution, what Mitsukawa called totalitarian politics (*dokusai seiji*).[20] In envisioning a centralized state beyond party politics, based on a planned economy and military-industrial base, it is no wonder that "renovationists" expressed greater sympathy with Soviet state-building.[21]

The impact of the Russian Revolution can be detected in the new vocabulary that pan-Asianists began to employ in the early 1920s. Although they often publicly dismissed communist ideas, especially those pertaining to class warfare and the abolition of monarchy, in many instances they appropriated the Leninist framework of world revolutionary struggle. Pan-Asianists perceived the West and the East to be engaged in different historical tasks: Europe was undergoing social revolutions, while Asia was undergoing national liberation revolutions. Both depended on each other, and together they amounted to a world revolution.[22] Their argument very much resembled Lenin's claim that revolutions in the West would result in the immediate establishment of a socialist or communist order; in the East, in colonial and semicolonial countries, the bourgeois-democratic movements would play the leading role in national liberation.[23] There are also striking similarities between Lenin's and the pan-Asianists' classification of nations. At the start of World War I, Lenin argued that the world is divided not only into different social classes but into different nations as well: the *entirely exploiter* bourgeois nations and the *entirely exploited* proletarian nations. Pan-Asianist thinkers seized on Lenin's distinction and identified Japan as a "proletarian" state, oppressed by Western capitalist imperialism, sharing this status with the likes of China, India, Egypt, and Soviet Russia. Hence, for pan-Asianists the idea of Asia was not just based on a shared language, culture, or religion—"Asia" was composed of every region that suffered at the hands of Western imperialism. In relation to Russia, Mitsukawa argued that the Russian Revolution transformed Russia from a Western imperialist power into a proletarian, oppressed, and therefore—by definition—*Asian* nation.[24]

Moreover, the idea that Russia was geographically and culturally part of Asia was not, of course, novel and was in fact developed by Russian philosophers and literati in the late nineteenth century as part of their critique of Western modernity. Mitsukawa and other pan-Asianists were aware of Russia's Eurasianism—that Russia was not of Europe nor of Asia but constituted a separate geographical and civilizational entity, Eurasia—according to another member of the Yūzonsha, Shimano Saburō (1893–1982), one of the pioneers of Russian studies in Japan. As a student of Russian language and literature, Shimano spent the years between 1911 and 1918 in Vladivostok, Moscow, and Saint Petersburg, at one point on a scholarship from the SMRC, whose president, Kawakami Toshitsune (another supporter of rapprochement with Russia), Shimano personally knew. He was a student of the Russian philosopher Semyon Frank and the famous Buddhologist Fyodor Shcherbatsky, and he was acquainted with the religious philosophers Nikolai Berdyaev and Sergei Bulgakov, whose critique of the Russian Revolution, combined with the assertion of the uniqueness of the Russian civilization, made a big impact on Shimano's political outlook. After witnessing the February and October revolutions, Shimano relocated to Siberia in 1919, now as an SMR employee in the role of Japanese army translator and messenger attached to Ataman Semenov's army in Transbaikalia. After witnessing the dark side of the Bolshevik Revolution in the capital, and the atrocities committed by both the Red and the White armies in Siberia, Shimano was intensely averse to revolution as a political method but never identified himself as an anticommunist. After his return to Tokyo, he continued to work for the SMR, but his career largely revolved around translation of Russian Eurasianist émigré literature, most notably Nikolai Trubetskoy's *Europe and Mankind* (1920), a devastating critique of Eurocentrism. Shimano's reports on Eurasianism and his translations appeared mainly in the journals of the SMR, but many were reprinted later by pan-Asianist publishers.[25] However, we can only speculate to what extent his views influenced Japanese pan-Asianist thought on Russia. But what is undeniable is that Japanese pan-Asianists were aware that a similar tradition of viewing world history as a confrontation between the East and the West existed in Russia as well.

The Russian Revolution's uniqueness lay in the fact that it was, for pan-Asianists, not a class war against capitalism but the first successful anti-Western, anti-imperialist revolt. In *Stolen Asia* (Ubawaretaru Asia, 1921), Mitsukawa declared that globally the post–World War I years were a time of liberation of societies from the oppression of wealth and liberation of nations (*minzoku kaihō*) from the oppression of foreign powers. It so happened that Russia became the leader of these two movements because of the success and strength of the Russian Revolution. Mitsukawa wrote in 1921:

> What is the world revolution? It is the destruction of the egoistic and selfish desires in the whole world, and the creation of ideal states on earth where justice and peaceful coexistence would be fulfilled. It is the elimination of racist discrimination, resolution of uneven development,

and realization of fairness of existence of the humankind. This world revolutionary spirit was affected by the Great War, brooded by it, nurtured, and then erupted as an independent movement. The old powers must be replaced by the new. The forerunner of this movement was without doubt Russia, where the global revolutionary spirit broke out in March 1917. The first page of the history of the world revolution begins in Nordic snowy Russia.[26]

In other words, the Russian Revolution was the first in a series of upcoming global revolutions that together would alter the course of world history by superseding the Western hegemonic order.[27] The Bolsheviks' support of anti-colonial movements in Turkey, Persia, and Afghanistan in 1921 seemed to support the pan-Asianists' conviction that the Russian Revolution was part of the emerging Asian awakening.[28] By emphasizing the anti-imperialist and therefore pro-Asian impulse of the Russian Revolution, Mitsukawa and Ōkawa intended to defuse its perceived threat and even express affinity with its objectives. Their attitude reveals the great confidence that the pan-Asianists had in the stability of Japanese society and polity—a confidence that the national socialists, for example, lacked, likely because they were more acutely aware of the country's social contradictions. Mitsukawa's pro-Soviet position, his claim that Soviet Russia did not pose a threat to Japan's monarchical body politic (*kokutai*)—or, for that matter, to any statist principles because it was itself built on them—as well as his personal friendship with many renowned socialists, led some to even label him a communist.[29]

Pan-Asianist commentators somewhat qualified their view once the Soviets successfully established their first two satellite states—the Tuvan People's Republic (est. in 1921, joined the USSR in 1944) and the Mongolian People's Republic (est. in 1924)—and gained control over Central Asia in the years between 1919 and 1925. If before the pan-Asianists had stressed the anti-imperialist impulse of the Russian Revolution, from the mid-1920s on they argued that the abolition of capitalism within Russia did not mean that Russia had abandoned its imperialist pursuits and interests abroad. In his reappraisal of the Soviet regime, Mitsukawa reproached: "Moscow people do not want to be called imperialists, but as long as they control the vast territory of Siberia and Mongolia, they cannot deny they are being imperialist."[30] In fact,

> There is no difference between imperialism and socialism. The opposite of imperialism is the small country principle; the opposite of socialism is capitalism. Russia and the U.S. are both big countries and big powers and, as such, both practice imperialism. We wrongly used to think that capitalism alone requires imperialist tactics to increase

its economic power and that, on this basis, it is the enemy of socialism. [We also used to think that] imperialism was equated with monarchy. Postrevolutionary Russia does not replace tsarist Russia and is as imperialist.[31]

However, for pan-Asianists, there was still a qualitative difference between Soviet and Western varieties of imperialism. The former was dictated by its geographical circumstances, largely originated in resistance to the latter, and therefore was moral and justified. Western imperialism, in contrast, was predatory. Having vindicated the USSR's foreign policy, Mitsukawa insisted that the Soviet advance in Asia was reminiscent, and in fact a continuation, of tsarist foreign policies, which were not incompatible with Japan's benevolent imperial designs for the same region.

Supporters of Asian regionalism began actively to work and lobby for Japan's rapprochement with Russia. Another vocal supporter of the Bolsheviks, Nakano Seigō had, since his election to the Diet in 1920, been advocating for replacing the Japanese-British alliance, which would expire in 1922, with a Japanese-Russian alliance. In 1922, he and Ogata Taketora, another influential journalist and later right-wing politician, created the organization Yūshinsha (New Society), whose purposes were to advance the withdrawal of Japanese troops from Siberia, recognize the USSR, cancel all Russian debts, and promote cooperation between Russia, China, and Japan. Nakano and Mitsukawa, also a member of the Yūshinsha, became deeply involved in the Russo-Japanese negotiations, regularly meeting with Soviet representative Antonov during his stay in Tokyo in 1922–23, and acting as intermediaries between the Japanese government and Soviet state representatives.[32]

One episode in particular reveals the Yūshinsha's role as an important intermediary. The anarchist Takao Heibē, during his trip to Russia in the winter of 1922, met Lenin himself and (possibly at Lenin's request) made contact with his old acquaintance, none other than Nakano Seigō, in order to reach influential politicians through him. Nakano and Takao met at a Rōsōkai group, established by Mitsukawa and Ōkawa in October 1918, and kept in contact based on their shared support of the Bolshevik regime and opposition to the Siberian Intervention. Nakano, in turn, contacted Gotō Shinpei. Although Gotō had received information about the situation in Russia from the SMR research institute, he was unaware of the full intentions of the Soviet leaders. According to Takao's communication, Lenin and other Bolshevik leaders wanted to assure the Japanese government that they had no plans to incite a revolution or support a military takeover in Japan. Instead, the Soviet government was interested in the normalization of diplomatic relations in order to focus on rebuilding the country, which had been devastated by the revolution and previous wars. The historian Matsuo Takayoshi speculates that this information convinced Gotō and other influential politicians to move toward recognizing the USSR.[33]

What is remarkable about this episode is not only the ease with which an anarchist vagabond (Takao) could communicate with a nationalist Diet member (Nakano) and one of the most prominent politicians of the time (Gotō), but also the friendly relations and mutual accord that existed between people from presumably opposite ideological positions. How unconcerned Gotō was about mingling with leftist circles, and how normal this was at the time, can be gleaned from the fact that when Soviet Foreign Deputy Adolf Ioffe arrived in Japan in February 1923, Gotō used the anarchists Takao and Taguchi Unzō (the Japanese representative to the Third Comintern Congress) as his go-betweens with Ioffe.[34] Gotō, in fact, knew the leftist circles very well. His adopted daughter was married to the eldest brother of a top communist leader, Sano Manabu, named Hyōta, and it was known that Gotō personally funded the most famous Taishō anarchist, Ōsugi Sakae.[35] Very suggestive is the fact that as Gotō, in his capacity as foreign minister, was authorizing the dispatch of troops to Siberia, he was making contact with the very influential liberal politician Ōzaki Yukio in 1919 to create a workers' party—which, they agreed, would become part of a new government orientation toward implementing a policy of state socialism. Their plan and negotiations were known to the public, which indicates that at that time the inclusion of socialist ideas in a political program was rather an acceptable norm.[36]

Mitsukawa's support of the recognition, however, split the Yūzonsha. When Ioffe arrived in Japan to discuss the terms of Japan's recognition of the USSR, disagreements erupted between Ōkawa and Mitsukawa on one side, and Kita Ikki on the other.[37] Kita used Ioffe's visit as an opportunity to vent his long-held antipathy toward Russia, largely because he followed with alarm the growing Soviet influence in Chinese politics. Kita's view of Russia was further influenced by the way the Russians had treated his close friend and disciple (*deshi*) Iwata Fumio. On Kita's suggestion, Iwata traveled twice to Siberia (in July 1921 and September 1922) for intelligence gathering for the Japanese army; on his second trip, he was captured and imprisoned in the Siberian town of Chita for six months. Kita attended a celebration after Iwata's return from Chita in January 1923, just a week or so before Ioffe's visit to Japan. Importantly, however, it was Gotō who pleaded with Ioffe to release Iwata. Ioffe, in turn, requested from Moscow the release of Iwata in order to facilitate the recognition negotiations.[38] Whether Kita was aware of Gotō's role in the release of his friend is unknown.

Nevertheless, in his "Open Letter of Warning to Ioffe," thirty thousand copies of which were distributed across Japan, Kita compared Ioffe to a cat and likened

Gotō and other Japanese politicians who had invited him to Japan to rats. Kita urged Ioffe to go home while he still had his life and stated that his main concern was Russia's aggressive advance in China. For Kita, Russia was an enemy to China, and thus an enemy to Japan. Any cooperation or alliance between Russia and Japan was impossible. To his mind, postrevolutionary Russia was the heir to tsarist Russia, as the Bolsheviks claimed all former Romanov-controlled territory as their own while refusing to take responsibility for Russia's former international obligations. To stop Soviet Russia, which he regarded as essentially imperialist, Kita even proposed an economic alliance with the United States as a prerequisite to a possible war with either Britain or Russia. In contrast, Ōkawa and Mitsukawa seemed more concerned about the United States, because they believed that Japan had more fundamental disagreements with the American liberal-capitalist order and therefore faced an imminent war with it.[39]

Kita Ikki had a very negative view of the Russian Revolution and the popularity of socialist ideas in Japan from the beginning. Divergent assessments of the revolution and Soviet Russia contributed, among other factors, to a split within the pan-Asianist movement in 1923. In a letter from February 1920, addressed to his closest friend, who had been arrested for anarchist propaganda, Kita regretted that the brightest young people in Japan were captivated by the Russian Revolution, socialism, and anarchism—all of which, he insisted, were foreign intellectual products and thus inapplicable to Japanese reality. Karl Marx and Pyotr Kropotkin were utopian and old-fashioned, Kita thought, and implementing their ideas of class struggle, internationalist proletarian brotherhood, and destruction of centralized institutions could bring only harm to a nation.[40] Moreover, he recalled that Kropotkin had supported the Russian war effort in World War I and had therefore abandoned proletarian internationalism. Kita then proceeded to discredit the world significance of the Russian Revolution. He did not understand, he wrote, why "people admire an inferior revolution of an inferior people." Russia was a barbaric country, he argued, with 80 percent of its people illiterate, cruelly treated by their own government, like animals. Lacking the capacity to govern themselves, they were dependent on the Germans to manage them. "These are different things—the battle of gods and the battle of people in hell," he wrote. Before admiring the revolution, he advised his friend that one first needed to study Russia and its history. The revolution was an internal political reorganization that brought an outsider group to power; but in terms of foreign affairs, Kita predicted, Russia would maintain its expansionist and imperialist drive.[41]

Kita's view, however, was in the minority, while the pro-Russian, pan-Asianist trend gained ascendancy. Kita has received more attention in English scholarship than Mitsukawa and Ōkawa, as one of the "founders of Japanese fascism," and for his alleged influence on various terrorist right-wing groups, such as the

Ketsumeidan (Blood Brothers Band) and the Sakurakai (Cherry Blossom Society), both composed of young army officers who, in the 1930s, sought to bring terror to Japan's high politics and big business. Regarded as the inspirational mastermind behind the failed coup of February 26, 1936, Kita Ikki was executed in August 1937. Historians, however, have raised doubts about the degree of his involvement in and influence on the terrorist acts of the 1930s.[42] After the collapse of the Yūzonsha in 1923, Kita Ikki lived in reclusive isolation and devoted himself to the practice of apocalyptic Nichiren Buddhism. In contrast, Mitsukawa and Ōkawa remained at the center of political life in the capital. Ōkawa continued to enjoy respect and influence among intellectuals, politicians, the military, and various Asian exiles. Besides lecturing to future colonial administrators at the Takushoku University and acting as the director of the highly influential research institute of the SMR, he taught at a small private academy on the grounds of the imperial palace. Among his students were army officers such as Araki Sadao, Hata Sanetsugu, and Watanabe Jōtarō—all of whom later attained the rank of general and had a great influence on Japan's foreign and domestic policy in the 1930s.[43] Mitsukawa also remained politically active, expanding his network to high military and political echelons. The acme of his political career was his membership in the famous Dai Ajia Kyōkai (The Greater Asian Association), which included Prime Minister Prince Konoe Fumimaro and General Matsui Iwane, and acted as a "brain trust" for the cabinet, similar to the better-known Showa Kenkyūkai. Thus, within the pan-Asianist group the faction that advocated for Soviet-Japanese rapprochement and a regional Asian bloc became the most active and politically influential throughout the interwar period. Pan-Asianist discussions became closely entangled in Soviet-Japanese negotiations, initially promoted by Gotō Shinpei.

In December 1917, the new Soviet government had already approached Japan's ambassador to Russia, Uchida Kōsai, regarding recognition and new trade treaties. Despite the tense situation in Siberia, in June 1918 and again in February 1920 the Bolsheviks offered Japan concessions in Siberia and the Far East, including in the fishery and oil industries. On February 24, 1920, People's Commissar for Foreign Affairs Chicherin published an open letter to the Japanese foreign minister, "Soviet Peace Offer to Japan," which stated: "The peoples of Russia cherish no aggressive designs against Japan. The Soviet government has no intention of interfering in the internal affairs of the Japanese people. It fully recognizes the special economic and commercial interests of Japan in the Far East, interests surpassing in several respects those of other countries."[44] For the time being, the Japanese government left the Soviet note unanswered.

But as the other powers were beginning to negotiate with Soviet Russia, Tokyo realized that to continue to ignore Soviet proposals for negotiations would leave

Japan at a disadvantage. Concerned with securing its interests in the Russian Far East, northern Manchuria, and Inner Mongolia, in 1921 the Japanese government entered talks with the Bolshevik government via the Far Eastern Republic about the withdrawal of its troops, economic concessions, and recognition of the Soviet government. As one historian succinctly put it, "while the commanders of the Japanese forces were burning Bolsheviks alive, Tokyo diplomats were systematically trying to find out whether the comrades of these victims of Japanese brutality might not come back to the political path of Nicholas II's alliance with Japan."[45] This new, reversed diplomatic approach was based, however, on a certain understanding of what communism was and would do, and what Soviet leaders were and would do.

Here I argue that throughout the 1920s, a faction of politicians, business leaders, and nongovernmental groups began to advocate rapprochement with the communist state based on the convenient separation in the official rhetoric of, on one hand, communism as an international ideology, with its organ the Comintern as an international revolutionary organization and, on the other hand, the Soviet Union as a national state. Soviet officials also did their utmost to distance themselves from the Comintern, which, they claimed, was an international organization that had nothing to do with the USSR. This basic separation was also instrumental in the 1930s—when Japan claimed that the Anti-Comintern Pact of 1936 was directed against the international organization of the Comintern, not the USSR—and later, when in pursuit of a nonaggression pact (finally settling on a neutrality pact) with the Soviet Union, Japanese officials claimed that the Neutrality Pact of 1940 was signed with the USSR as another "normal" state, not with a rascal revolutionary outsider. Certainly, this understanding was not universal. As will be discussed in the following chapters, the military and national socialists did not distinguish between the Soviet state and communist ideology. But even then, it was hard to tell where the military's hostility toward communism ended and where its traditional agitation against "the neighbor from the North" started.

Government policies relating to Russia were not limited to Soviet-Japanese relations but were placed in the larger context of Japan's policy vis-à-vis China, Britain, and the United States. For Gotō Shinpei, the rapprochement with Soviet Russia was important most of all to secure Japanese interests in Asia.[46] In his memorandum to the Cabinet from March 1923, Gotō identified Japan's foreign policy tasks as follows: "1) to solidify the foundations for undertaking economic development in Asiatic Russia; 2) to eliminate the source of future troubles by forestalling possible American moves toward Russia; and 3) to prevent any machinations on the part of the Chinese before they can achieve a rapprochement with Russia."[47] There was a growing concern about the United States' intentions in Manchuria and the Russian Far East, especially after its acquisition of concessions in Sakhalin.[48] But most of all, Gotō feared that a Sino-Soviet rapprochement would result in Japan's isolation in East Asia. He blamed the Foreign Ministry for relying on cooperation with Britain and the United States at the expense of Japan's interests on the continent. In truth, Gotō argued, only a collaboration between Soviet Russia and Japan would be able to bring some order to the chaos that was Chinese politics, an effect of which was to allow an opening to the United States to penetrate Chinese market.[49]

> If a Japanese-Soviet rapprochement can be realized, it will be instrumental in the first place, in forestalling the plot the Chinese are now engineering and, second, in bringing about a favorable situation for us for getting easy access to economic concessions. To advance national interests, Japan took steps to establish friendship with Russia in the days of tsarist Russia without questioning its aggressive policy.[50]

The Balkanization of China, as Gotō remarked, threatened Japan's economic position, and to prevent such disintegration, cooperation with Russia (be it imperial or Soviet) was an absolute prerequisite.

Considering Japan's vital interests on the continent, Gotō appealed to geography. No one canceled the fact that part of Soviet Russia's territory was in Asia, and that it had extensive borders with China, Korea, and Japan, wrote Gotō. As such, the Bolshevik regime inherited from the tsarist government the same sets of concerns and objectives. One has only to remember how the Soviet government denied the Karakhan statement from 1919 about giving up the CER and began to assert its legal heritage of the tsarist concessions in China's territory. Therefore, Gotō continued, it was more natural for Japan to ally with Soviet Russia and pursue a common China policy and shared interests on the Asian continent, rather than to align with geographically distant Anglo-American powers.[51]

For Gotō and other pro-Russian influential groups, potential economic and political gains overshadowed concerns about communist subversion. Marxist doctrine and the political character of the Bolshevik regime were not considered insurmountable obstacles for a mutually beneficial economic and political partnership. This view reached its ascendancy when Gotō served as home minister in the cabinet of Yamamoto Gonnohyōe (in office September 1923–January 1924). But even before that, since 1922 Gotō's position had been backed by Prime Minister Takahashi Korekiyo (November 1921–June 1922), who resolved on the "peaceful development of the continent" under the "tōa keizai ryoku" (Asian economic cooperation) policy, which required cooperation with the Soviet Union. The next prime minister, Admiral Katō Tomosaburō (in office June 1922–August 1923), was also Gotō's supporter, himself driven by the navy's desire for concessions over Sakhalin's oil resources, on which it was coming increasingly to depend.[52] Incidentally, the North Sakhalin Oil Company presidency was occupied by people from the navy, who were eager to maintain nonconfrontational relations with the new Soviet government.[53] Not coincidentally, it was the navy's initiative to have the Imperial Defense Policy revised in 1923, identifying the United States as Japan's chief "hypothetical" enemy, and thereby initiating a reassessment of relations with the Soviet Union. The army resisted these changes and insisted that the wording be modified to include the possibility of war against two or even three enemies at once, which meant keeping the Soviet Union on the list of hypothetical enemies (albeit not as the chief one), along with the United States and China.[54]

In addition, behind Gotō stood the formidable support of the business community, especially the fishery business, which was the least preoccupied with communist ideology. In fact, it was the same business circles that pushed the Japanese government to establish diplomatic relations with the Soviet Union after 1945. Representatives of the Far East Business Development Corporation (established in 1919 to explore business opportunities in Russia during the Siberian Intervention), and which included all major business companies of the day—Mitsui, Mitsubishi, Furukawa, Kuhara, Sumitomo, the SMR, Yokohama Bank, Bank of Colonial Korea, and many others—visited Ioffe during his stay in Japan and expressed interest in metallurgy, forestry, railroads, and especially in establishing a Soviet-Japanese shipbuilding company.[55] The Soviet government welcomed these prospects eagerly, and the subsequent development of the Russian Far East was to a great extent funded by Japanese money.

Related to this was the support Gotō received from the old Meiji nationalist groups. On one hand, the Gen'yōsha and Kokuryūkai had always regarded the Siberian Intervention as harmful to Japan's interests and openly supported the recognition of the USSR. Although expressing some concern over communist propaganda, these groups were deeply involved in the fishery business and had a keen interest in oil concessions in Sakhalin. High-ranking members of the Gen'yōsha and Kokuryūkai were employed in different fishery companies or had large investments tied to the fishery industry. According to Ioffe's reports, in November 1922 in Beijing he met with a member of the Kokuryūkai who proposed to buy Sakhalin Island, which Ioffe refused to discuss. Nevertheless, the Meiji nationalist groups acted as intermediaries and were inconspicuously involved in inviting Ioffe to Japan.[56]

On the other hand, Gotō's pro-Russian activities drew criticism from newly established nationalist groups that had proliferated since 1919. Most vocal among the critics was Kita Ikki, discussed above. Unlike the old Meiji nationalist groups, the Taishō nationalist groups were often organized around anticommunist ideas and were backed by the Home Ministry and/or on the payroll of the police, who were growing anxious about the domestic communist movement. One of the nationalist groups, the Sekka Bōshidan, in February 1923 twice attacked Gotō's house, smashing furniture and doors and injuring Gotō's eldest son, who met them in place of his father.[57] As a friend of Gotō's, the military officer Satō Yasuburo warned Gotō that the new radical right was manipulated by his political enemies. Satō called the agitating nationalist groups crazy and deranged and advised Gotō to be very careful. He also recommended starting a counterpropaganda attack that would emphasize the advantages of the alliance with Soviet Russia and Gotō's explanation of communism.[58] Spurred by the reluctance of the Foreign Ministry to go ahead with the recognition, as well as by indirect attacks from the Home Ministry, Gotō resolved to address the issue of communism publicly.

The opportunity for a counterattack came immediately. Gotō made public his views on communism in the introduction he wrote to the Japanese edition of a work by a prominent American historian, Charles A. Beard, titled *Cross Currents in Europe Today*, published in Boston in 1922. The Japanese edition, titled *The Political Situation in Proletarian Russia after the War*, was published by numerous newspapers on February 7, 1923, and quickly became in Japan the most authoritative interpretation of the Bolshevik regime. Ioffe gave Lenin a copy of the English edition of Beard's work after Ioffe's return from Japan. Ioffe mentioned with annoyance in his reports that Gotō gave public speeches and interviews about the Soviet Union, using Beard's "ridiculous misconceptions" about Soviet communism—adding that he, Ioffe, had to repudiate them in his own interviews.[59]

What mostly annoyed Ioffe was Gotō's denial of the uniqueness of the Russian Revolution. Instead, Gotō saw the Russian Revolution as modernizing and nationalist in the manner of the Meiji Revolution. Gotō argued that if one looked at the first years of the Bolshevik regime, one could not help but see similarities between the October Revolution and the Meiji Revolution. Both, Gotō judged, had the same objective: to "expel barbarians" (foreigners) and restore the country by promoting "loyalism" to the state and its leaders.[60] In 1927, Gotō likened Trotsky, ousted by Stalin, to the hero of the Meiji Revolution, Saigō Takamori, who in opposition to the Meiji government went into exile and died during the Satsuma Rebellion in 1877.[61] Gotō wisely refrained from looking for analogies to Lenin and Stalin in recent Japanese history.

In terms of communist ideology, using Beard's writings Gotō argued that international communism was not sustainable, was illusory at best, and would not be able to eventuate in a state form. Socialists had already failed when the majority of them supported the Great War in 1914, and communists had failed in bringing about a world proletarian revolution. The Japanese leadership carefully followed the internal struggles of the Russian Communist Party but took them as signs of the party's decline and degeneration. For example, in 1926 Gotō cheerfully reported that Grigory Zinoviev, who served as the first head of the Comintern, had just been released from his duties. Gotō argued that Zinoviev's loss of power signified the decline in importance of the revolutionary Comintern.[62] During his trip to Russia in the winter of 1927–28, Goto confirmed in his reports long-circulated rumors of the struggle between Trotsky and Stalin.[63] Gotō, in fact, arrived just a few days after the infamous Fifteenth Party Congress (December 2–19), which expelled supporters of the Left Opposition to Stalin, led by Trotsky and Zinoviev. As Gotō was taking the Trans-Siberian Railway back to Japan in January 1928, Trotsky and his family were taking the same railroad to his exile in Kazakhstan.

Trotsky was no less well known in Japan than Lenin; the two were frequently mentioned together as the makers of the Bolshevik Revolution. In fact, in November 1923, War Minister Tanaka Gi'ichi himself, in an interview that he gave in fluent Russian to a Russian representative of the Russian Telegraph Agency (ROSTA), professed his great admiration for the organizational skills of his colleague in Russia, Leon Trotsky. Tanaka finished the interview, which was published in the hugely popular newspaper *Tokyo nichi nichi* in commemoration of the sixth anniversary of the Russian Revolution, with the words: "Please tell your people, I am a friend of Russia."[64] Nevertheless, Trotsky was associated with the old revolutionary guard and the idea of a permanent world revolution, while Stalin emerged by 1927 as the more conciliatory figure, a more proper partner for Japan in its ambitions in Asia. The downfall of Trotsky was greeted therefore by many in Japan as another sign of normalization of Soviet Russia.

In his communications with the Cabinet and his public addresses, Gotō repeatedly noted that things said and promised during a revolution are rarely realized, and that this was true for Russia, which by now had lost its original hostility to capitalism and, in fact, was implementing economic reforms that were not too far from state capitalism. The economic reforms that Gotō and many others in the government viewed positively were specifically centered around the New Economic Policy (NEP), which allowed "capitalist relations" in Russia.[65] Gotō made sure to stress in his public speeches and interviews that because of NEP, Soviet Russia had not a communist but a state capitalist system. Charles Beard went even further and claimed that under NEP Russia was transforming into a state capitalist country, where petty industries would flourish under private initiatives, and large industries, railways, and natural resources would be exploited by foreign concessionaires under state supervision.[66]

As the declaration of world revolution was a thing of the past, Japan had no cause for concern, Gotō reassured his audience. He criticized his own country's narrow-minded, anticommunist so-called patriots, asserting that they lacked confidence in their history and tradition.[67] "If we need to be concerned over the spread of communism, it means we have weakness inside our own country to be taken care of."[68] He continued elsewhere: "It is ridiculous to think that our country can become red because of the establishment of relations with Russia. It is obvious that, just as we did not become a republic because of the relationship with the United States, we will not become communist because of relations with Russia."[69] Gotō was not alone in his critical commentaries. Mochizuki Koraō, a member of the Diet, wrote in the magazine *Taiyō* in April 1923:

> The national character of Japan and the traits of her people, which are unchanged since the foundation of the country, may be likened to the color of the sun that absorbs all colors, red or white, and in the veins of the 65,000,000 nationals there is not a drop of blood that forgets the nation, for the souls of the Imperial ancestors repose in them ... If the rulers of the country ... see to it that the living conditions of the people are stabilized, then a thousand Ioffes are not to be feared.[70]

Gotō further pointed out that in many West European countries communist parties exist and act within the law, which has the power to limit their activities should they become a threat to national security.

Echoing pan-Asianist arguments, Gotō underscored the benevolent objectives of the Russian Revolution. "Since communist Russia has stood for the cause of opposition to aggression and of coexistence and co-prosperity with other nations, there is no reason to fear bad effects from a rapprochement and to hesitate to open trade with the Soviets."[71] Gotō's supporter, the politician Mochizuki Koraō, was even more unequivocal: "Many of the world powers, while chanting paeans to justice and humanity, do not really give equal treatment to different races, but Russia has no racial prejudice, and since the establishment of the Moscow dynasty 300 years ago equal rights have been extended to all races as an expression of the traditional spirit of the Russian people."[72] Communist Russia was one of the mistreated nations of the non-Western world and as such a natural ally for Japan. Gotō pointed out that fears of communist subversion were based on scant knowledge of Russia and argued that Japan ought to develop academic studies of Russia. In fact, Gotō lamented, to date there had not been a sober and extensive analysis and public discussion of the Russian Revolution in Japan, which made it difficult to dispel popular misconceptions about Soviet good intentions.

Meanwhile, in 1924, Gotō's earlier warnings about the possibility of Sino-Soviet rapprochement and subsequent isolation of Japan were coming true. The Soviets scored two important diplomatic victories in China in 1924, which added a sense of urgency to Japan's recognition of the Soviet Union, even from the previously reluctant Foreign Ministry and the military, especially Tanaka Gi'ichi. The first Guomindang Congress of January 1924 formally launched the Comintern-designed alliance between the Guomindang and the Chinese communists, propelling Russian and Chinese communists to greater importance within the Guomindang Party. Meanwhile, in May 1924, the Beijing government recognized the USSR and decided that although the CER should be redeemed by China, its future would "be determined by the Republic of China and the USSR to the exclusion of any third party or parties." The Beijing government and Soviet Russia agreed to joint management of the CER under a Russian manager and five Chinese and five Russian directors.[73] The Japanese government realized that in this situation—active Soviet policy in China and China's positive response to it—a new diplomacy was in order, actively involving communist Russia.

Although the Taishō period is considered to be the era of party politics, much of the foreign policy course depended on personalities. The Foreign Ministry's reluctance to recognize the USSR was largely due to its minister, Uchida Kōsai (in office September 1918–September 1923). He and Matsudaira Tsuneo, director of the Anglo-American department, resisted Gotō's efforts. Although realizing that recognition of the USSR became inevitable once Britain established trade relations with Soviet Russia in 1922, Uchida preferred not to rush for rapprochement and the signing of a treaty. Some historians have attributed this to the Foreign Ministry's preference for cooperative diplomacy with Western powers at the expense of Russo-Japanese relations. Another reason, however, was Uchida's concern over communist ideology. Uchida, and especially his assistant Matsuoka Yōsuke, criticized Gotō and the successive prime ministers for overlooking the seriousness of communist ideology in their preparations for recognition.[74] Tōgō Shigenori, then the chief of a section under Matsudaira and a future foreign minister, explained the basis for divergent opinions among the decision makers: "While Prime Minister Katō Tomosaburō and Mr. Gotō did not seriously concern themselves with communist activities, preferring to consider policy toward the Soviet Union in terms of accommodating conflicting interests in the Far East, the foreign ministry approached the Russian question more broadly, insisting that ideological issues also be taken into account."[75]

Besides Uchida's personal experience in Russia, another possible reason for delaying rapprochement was the Foreign Ministry's greater knowledge of the developments in Asia. The Foreign Ministry's concern with international communism was fed by continuous reports from its consulates in Korea and China and by its extensive intelligence network. As Eric Esslestrom explains, since 1919 the main task of the Japanese consular police in China and Korea had become the suppression of growing Korean and Chinese nationalist and communist movements and prevention of their interaction with Japanese communists.

Foreign Ministry archives reveal that its staff members were aware that as early as May 1920 a meeting had taken place in Shanghai between a Japanese socialist, Korean revolutionaries, and anti-Japanese Chinese. In 1921, reports presented evidence that Korean communists in Shanghai had conspired with Japanese communists to obtain financial support, that some Japanese communists resided in Shanghai, and that certain Koreans had traveled to Tokyo to establish contacts with the nascent Japanese Communist Party (JCP). Between the late spring of 1920 and the summer of 1921, several meetings between Japanese anarchists and communists and Korean Comintern envoys took place in Tokyo and Shanghai, of which the Foreign and Home ministries were aware. Intimate knowledge of subversive activities of colonial and Japanese subjects at home, and in Korea and China, informed Uchida's view that international communism—which brought together Russian, Korean, Chinese, Mongolian, and Japanese leftist radicals—posed a direct threat to the stability of metropolitan society itself.

During Uchida's term, the Foreign Ministry began to cooperate closely with the Home Ministry and the police, who were preoccupied with the domestic communist movement. To bolster domestic security forces and combat widespread escalation of Comintern activities, which found fertile ground in Shanghai, the Home Ministry requested in April 1921 the joint appointment of a Home Ministry police superintendent as a consular police superintendent in Shanghai. In effect, the consular police in China and Korea came to serve as the local branch office of homeland state authority. After the JCP was established in the summer of 1922 as a Comintern branch and a communist network linked Vladivostok, Shanghai, and Tokyo, the Foreign Ministry cooperated to ensure that Japanese police power was unhindered outside national boundaries, as it was within them.[76]

But once Uchida resigned in September 1923 and the new foreign minister, Shidehara Kijūrō (in office June 1924–April 1927 and July 1929–December 1931), came into office, the Foreign Ministry's outlook changed dramatically. Shidehara's first term coincided with the recognition of the USSR by Britain, Italy, Austria, and other countries, and Japan thus felt more confident about following their lead. But Shidehara's personal view on communism should be taken into consideration as well. Shidehara was neither an anticommunist nor a sympathizer; rather, he was concerned about whether communist ideology and its Russian agents could penetrate China. The new leadership in the Foreign Ministry also noted that the growing anti-imperialist agitation was not specifically directed against Japan. Shidehara concluded that fears of the "Bolshevization" of China were greatly exaggerated. First, relying on intelligence reports from China, Shidehara pointed out that the Comintern's agents—especially its main envoy, Mikhail Borodin—did not have much influence and authority within Chinese nationalist circles. Shidehara believed that there was more division than unity within the Guomindang Party, as well as between the Guomindang and the Chinese Communist Party (established in the summer of 1921), and that their alliance was rather a tactical maneuver by the Guomindang nationalist leaders. As the consul general at Canton reported, anti-imperialist agitation was undertaken by the Guomindang mainly to increase its influence and support, rather than to enunciate serious anti-Japanese policies.[77]

Shidehara and Gotō shared the belief that China, in fact, could never become a communist country. In 1924, Shidehara told the US ambassador, Edgar A. Bancroft, that "he did not think Sovietism would take any hold on the Chinese: the Chinaman loves money and has his little property and is the greatest individualist and it is wholly unlikely that he would accept communism; while Dr. Sun [Yat-sen] was a radical idealist and for this reason his political career had been a failure, he did not think Sun was favorable to communism."[78] In April 1927, in conversation with the British ambassador John Tilley, Shidehara repeated that he absolutely did not believe China could ever become communist. And even if a communist government were installed in China, private property and international trade would still be likely to exist there, as the Soviet example (i.e., the ongoing NEP) had shown.[79]

Gotō shared the same view, which he openly professed to the Soviet leadership during his visit to the USSR in December 1927–January 1928. In his meeting with Stalin in January 1928, Gotō had a revealing conversation about China. Stalin asked why Japan had so far resisted Russia's cooperation in establishing order in northern China. Gotō replied that there were still influential groups in the government that favored cooperative diplomacy with the United States and Britain, rather than with Russia. These groups also believed that chaos (*randō*) in China came from the communist movement (*sekka undō*), directed by the Soviet Union. Gotō quickly added that he did not think the Soviet Union was involved in Chinese affairs. However, he indirectly warned Stalin that communism would never take root in China because, he argued, the four-thousand-year-old Chinese civilization was incompatible with the principles of communism. Stalin replied that the Japanese leadership had still not understood the true nature of Chinese nationalism—namely, that it was a reaction to Western and Japanese imperialism, similar to the Japanese nationalist movement during the late Tokugawa upheavals. According to Stalin, revolutionary changes in China, whether nationalist or communist, were rooted in current problems China faced, which had nothing to do with its ancient civilization.[80]

As the above conversation suggests, even though Shidehara and Gotō downplayed the strength and influence of Soviet communism in China and Japan, they could not ignore the issue of communist propaganda. The spread of communist propaganda in Japan, Korea, and China was perhaps the most pressing concern of Soviet-Japanese relations, and opponents of the rapprochement regularly used this issue to their advantage. In his communication with Russian colleagues, Gotō tirelessly insisted on the futility of their efforts to convert China and Japan to communist principles. As he tried to convince Stalin in 1928 to give up the "Bolshevization" of China, so he tried to do in 1923 in regard to Japan, in the wake of Japan's recognition of the USSR. In his letter to Chicherin from August 10, 1923, Gotō wrote that it was unfortunate that Soviet Russia initially took a hostile position and threatened to spread the communist revolution across the globe. He continued to explain in his letter to Ioffe on the same date (August 10, 1923) that Japan had a peculiar social system: "From ancient times, Japan was one big family, the emperor was the father of the family, all land belonged to the state, and private property was forbidden."[81] Even during the feudal period, private property had never been recognized. After the Meiji Restoration, Gotō continued, patriarchy (*kachōshugi*) was promoted by the government and permeated all social classes. Though ancient Japan had a social system reminiscent of the communist organization of society, in the Meiji period Japan had been transformed into a modern state by the deliberate adoption of the European private property system. Gotō implied, therefore, that the government-promoted patriarchy (or family-state system) and the system of private property (capitalism) were the twin foundations of Japan's remarkable modernization. Therefore, Russian communist propaganda (*kyōsanshugi*) in Japan was useless and indeed harmful.[82] In his answer, Chicherin foreshadowed Stalin's reply in 1928, pointing out that communist ideas naturally arise where there is discontent with social injustices and where the national movement is taking root—similar to what Japan had experienced in the early Meiji period. However, in addressing the issue of Comintern propaganda, Chicherin, and later Stalin, insisted that the Soviet government was neutral and did not have any relations with Comintern activities. They reminded the Japanese leaders that the Comintern was an international organization that included communist parties from around the world, while the Soviet government concerned itself with matters of national Soviet interest.[83] To this, Gotō's reply to Stalin in 1928 was "I choose to believe your [Stalin's] words."[84]

Choosing to believe that the Soviet Union was a normal state adhering to norms of international diplomacy, the Japanese government recognized the USSR, and on January 20, 1925, concluded the Soviet-Japanese Basic Convention. The terms of the convention remained largely in force through 1945. Significantly, Japanese and Soviet negotiators formally recognized all former treaties concluded between Japan and tsarist Russia. To quell anxieties over communist propaganda, most notably within the Home and Justice ministries, in article 5 of the convention the Soviet Union pledged to forbid subversive activities in

Japanese territory in return for Japan's promise not to recognize anti-Bolshevik organizations in Japan.

> The High Contacting Parties solemnly affirm their desire and intention to live in peace and amity with each other, scrupulously to respect the undoubted right of a State to order its own life within its own jurisdiction in its own way, to refrain and restrain all persons in any governmental service for them, and all organizations in receipt of any financial assistance from them, from any act overt or covert liable in any way whatever to endanger the order and security in any part of the territories of Japan or the Union of Soviet Socialist Republics.[85]

There were warning signs, however, that things would not go as smoothly as the Japanese had hoped. For example, Lev Karakhan, author of the controversial Karakhan Manifesto and the Soviet ambassador to China in 1925, told Japan's ambassador to China, Yoshizawa Kenkichi, that since the Comintern and the Soviet state were legally different entities, article 5 did not have an effect on the activities of the Comintern. The Japanese government, however, ignored Yoshizawa's report, and took it for granted that article 5 was binding for both the USSR and the Comintern. More embarrassing was an "unconfirmed report" to the Foreign Ministry that the first Soviet ambassador to Japan, Viktor Kopp, en route to Tokyo announced to the Provincial Committee of the Communist Party at Harbin that the Soviet-Japanese Convention, "as [an alliance] with a country with an imperialist system, it is not particularly solid; it will be a mythical treaty . . . merely giving us the possibility for the legal existence in the territory of Japan of the leading organ of the vanguard of the revolution." Kopp continued, "I leave the conduct of the political work in Japan entirely in the hands of the Japanese socialists, giving them only moral support in getting rid of defects, permitted by Japanese workers in party building, again I repeat, making use of Japan as a threat to America in the far East."[86] The Japanese government preferred to ignore this report as well. Despite these warning signs, the Japanese government resolved to establish diplomatic relations with the Soviet Union—while swiftly passing in the Diet the anticommunist Peace Preservation Law only a month later, in February 1925.[87] But even then, despite having proof of Comintern activities in Japan, the Japanese government never resorted to breaking diplomatic relations with Soviet Russia—unlike Britain, which severed relations in 1927 after Comintern propaganda activities were exposed.

From the other side, Russia's objective was to be at peace with Japan as much and for as long as possible. Assuring the Japanese government of communist noninterference in Japan's domestic affairs, Foreign Minister Chicherin announced in the main Soviet newspaper *Pravda*: "There exist deeply rooted differences in form between our political regime and Japan's, and consequently the policies of the two states are based on different principles. We are confident, however, that the Japanese government will loyally adhere to the treaty that has been signed.... We are also confident that each contracting party will strictly follow the rule of noninterference in the internal affairs of the other."[88] In fact, in 1924–28, the Comintern scaled down communist propaganda in Japan, as well as in Manchuria and Korea.[89] As discussed in later chapters, the early JCP collapsed in 1923, although not at the Comintern's initiative. Revived in 1926, the JCP strove for nonmilitant, legal working relationships with proletarian parties. It adopted a more confrontational approach, including the abolition of the monarchy clause, only after the 1932 Comintern Theses on Japan, which were, in turn, issued in the wake of the Manchurian Incident. Meanwhile, in 1926 Chicherin issued instructions to Soviet cultural institutions to circulate positive views on Japan, publish popular and academic books on Japan and its history, increase cultural and scientific ties, and greenlight finalizing agreements on timber, oil, coal, and fishery concessions.[90]

But what was most important, and what overshadowed any potential concerns over communist propaganda, was hinted at in article 2, which recognized the Treaty of Portsmouth, signed after the Russo-Japanese War in 1905. This treaty deprived Russia of South Sakhalin and the southern half of its railroad network in Manchuria, but acknowledged Russia's—and subsequently the USSR's—control over the CER. In effect, by this action Moscow and Tokyo formally re-created the Russo-Japanese spheres of influence that now divided East Asia into Soviet and Japanese parts. Japan retained unhampered control over Korea, southern Manchuria, and eastern Inner Mongolia, while the USSR received Japanese assurances that its claims over Outer Mongolia, northern Manchuria, and western Inner Mongolia would not be challenged by Japan. The Basic Convention was therefore less about economic gains, contrary to what most Western scholars have argued, and more about the political settlement of East Asia.[91]

The impact of the renewal of the Russo-Japanese secret treaties in Asia was significant. Japan agreed to withdraw the last of its troops from the northern part of Sakhalin Island in return for important oil concessions, which marked the end of the period of the Foreign Intervention and the Russian Civil War. Despite China's (albeit secret) protests over the clauses of the convention, the Soviet Union's ambassador to China, Lev Karakhan, also secretly recognized the validity of Japan's Twenty-One Demands to China, and moreover demanded that China recognize unequal treaties signed between China and imperial Russia in regard to the CER.[92] In addition, Japan remained neutral during the 1925–26 and 1929 Sino-Soviet conflicts over the CER, and the USSR remained neutral during the Manchurian Incident. As the Soviets acknowledged, "Without the establishment of normal relations with Japan it would have been impossible to hope for a complete restoration of our rights to the Chinese eastern railway."[93] Both the Soviets and the Japanese fully realized the mutual advantages of cooperation.

The Soviets also realized that Japanese decision makers were irritated by the United States' recent policies—American pressure for Japanese withdrawal from the Russian Far East during the Washington Conference, its anti-Japanese immigration policy of 1924, and growing economic and political competition in China.[94] As Karakhan stated, "For Japan this agreement has at present probably a still greater importance than for us. The threat of isolation is removed by the existence of a power on the Asiatic continent friendly to Japan."[95] The Basic Convention guaranteed Russia's neutrality in case of a Japanese conflict with a "third power," and the delivery of oil to the Japanese navy in such an event—a provision that greatly alarmed Britain, the United States, and France.[96] The convention's division of East Asia undermined the Washington Conference's resolution to enforce the open door policy in China. The Japanese leadership sought to exploit this neutrality clause in the Basic Convention once it began preparations for a war with the United States, and the leaders succeeded in signing a neutrality pact with the Soviet Union in April 1941.

So confident were the Japanese leaders in the benign intentions of their new communist friends that between 1924 and 1929 the government seriously considered the possibility of Japanese immigration to the Russian Far East. As Mitsukawa made plain, the root of social problems in Japan was the overpopulation of the islands. He argued that an overpopulated Japan had no choice: it had to either "expand or perish," which is why it "must expand overseas, no matter what."[97] His solution to the problem of overpopulation was the colonization of China. However, because "when we think of China, we think of Russia," Japan had to deal with Russia, too.[98]

In 1924, Gotō hinted to Chicherin that the exploding population on the Japanese islands presented a serious concern. He complained that the United States, the Pacific islands, and Africa were closed to Japanese immigration and called for a Soviet-Japanese agreement to be a model that would also shame the US government's anti-Japanese legislation. As a conciliatory gesture, the Soviet government made a public offer of a land lease in 1925 through its media arm, the newspaper *Pravda*.[99] In June 1925, Gotō proposed to Soviet Ambassador Kopp a detailed plan for the immigration of two million unemployed Japanese to Siberia, in addition to more than two million acres (860,000 hectares) of land leased for seventy-five years. The proposed plan was circulated in Japanese newspapers beginning in early 1926.[100]

Tanaka Gi'ichi continued to press the Soviet government for land concessions during his visit to Moscow in 1926, explaining that Japanese peasants could be relocated to cultivate rice, which Russia needed, and would teach the local Russian and indigenous population how to grow the crop. The Soviet government was tempted, aware that economically the region needed Japanese investments, but hesitated.[101] Chicherin openly explained to Tanaka that in the Far East, memory of the Japanese intervention was still strong; only four years before, Japanese troops had controlled the region, most of the time by brute force. The Soviet authority there was still shaky (which was true), and it could not guarantee the safety of Japanese peasants. Instead, Chicherin offered territories on the northern bank of the Amur River for the immigration of 325,000 Japanese men and women. After some consultation, Tanaka declined the offer because the proposed territory was too far removed from Japan. After some back-and-forth negotiations, the Soviets withdrew from the arrangement out of fear that the Japanese might overwhelm the sparsely populated area and that the territory would become a channel for penetration into the region by the Kwantung Army, which was stationed relatively nearby.[102] Moscow's decision caused disappointment in Tokyo. The area on the Amur River was finally offered to socialist Zionists, and in 1928, on territory that could have been populated by Japanese immigrants, the Jewish Autonomous Oblast was established.

Since the renewal of official relations between Japan and the Soviet Union, a policy of alliance with inclusion of China began to be entertained in Moscow and Tokyo. In a March 1925 article for *Warekan* titled "The True Significance of the Restoration of Russo-Japanese Relations" (Nichiro shinkō no shinkachi), Nakano Seigō argued that the recognition of the USSR and the implementation of universal suffrage were of equal significance.[103] Both events, he claimed, were victories of public opinion. Moreover, the recognition of the USSR was a turning point in international politics, as it made possible an alliance between Japan, Russia, and China: "The autocracy of the league of imperialist powers has already overwhelmed Japan, Russia, and China, and is forcing them to create a league based on true equality and freedom."[104]

Gotō openly declared in his letter to Chicherin, "that the united power of our two nations might correct mistakes and shortcomings of the Versailles, Washington, and other international conferences." In his letters to Chicherin, Gotō also appealed to the historically special relations between Russia and Japan and to their shared interests:

> The relationship between Japan and Russia is different from relations between Russia and Britain or the United States and other countries. Now not only educated people but the broader masses as well have realized that a good relationship between Japan and Russia serves not only mutual happiness but stabilizes the neighboring country, China, and secures its cultural

existence. The relationship between Japan and Russia serves as the foundation for peace in East Asia, and consequently in the Pacific Ocean.[105]

Gotō asserted that the friendship of the Japanese and Russians signifies the
friendship and reconciliation of Eastern and Western cultures, and therefore
would eliminate mutual misunderstanding and serve as a vehicle for global
peace. He agreed with the critics of Japan's Foreign Ministry who did not believe
that US and Japanese policies in East Asia could be harmonized. Gotō was a
strong advocate of the need to maintain a balance between the "new continent"
represented by the United States and the "old continent" represented by Japan,
Russia, and China.[106]

It is important to underscore that the creation of a Russia-China-Japan bloc
was not a novel idea but rather a revival of Japan's old geopolitical plans for
Eurasia. Already in 1915, Yamagata Aritomo had spelled out the necessity of an
alliance with Russia to secure Japan's interests in Asia. He believed that the future
war would be a race war, between the yellow and the white races, on a much
larger scale than the Great War. Japan needed to secure Chinese cooperation,
but it also needed an alliance with one European power so as to prevent a union
of the white nations in advance of the coming racial conflict. The main result
of Yamagata's thinking and actions, as we discussed above, was a defensive and
offensive alliance with imperial Russia in 1916.[107] In the military, Yamagata's outlook was adopted by Tanaka Gi'ichi. Tanaka has most often been portrayed by
Western historians as a rabid anticommunist, chiefly due to his update to the
Peace Preservation Law in 1928, which stipulated the death penalty for communist activities. The flipside of the coin, however, was that as prime minister
and foreign minister since April 1927, Tanaka actively sought an alliance with
Russia. Prioritizing Japan's economic and political expansion in China, Tanaka
maintained that East Asia's fate was now determined by three countries—Japan,
China, and Russia. "We cannot think of them separately. When we think of Sino-
Japanese relations, we must think of Russia, when we think of Soviet-Japanese
relations, we must think of China."[108]

To advance Soviet-Japanese cooperation, Tanaka sent his two envoys, Kuhara
Fusanosuke and Gotō Shinpei, to Moscow; their tasks included the discussion
of measures against the penetration of American and British capital into Manchuria, trade and fishery agreements, management of the CER, and the new
important issue of a neutrality pact. Tanaka's close friend, Kuhara Fusanosuke,
went first. Kuhara was the founder of Kuhara zaibatsu, one of the largest copper producers in Japan, and because it had a mining business in Siberia, Kuhara
actively supported the Siberian Intervention. In 1927, Kuhara retired and handed
over his mining business to his brother-in-law, Aikawa Yoshisuke, who in 1928

turned their combined business into one of the biggest zaibatsu, Nippon Sangyō, or Nissan (Japan Industries).[109] During his trip to Moscow in the fall of 1927, Kuhara attended the tenth anniversary celebration of the Russian Revolution, together with other invited guests from Japan, mainly people from the spheres of the arts and literature. In private, Kuhara met with Stalin and Anastas Mikoyan, the people's commissar for external and internal trade.[110] Besides negotiating fishery agreements, Kuhara's task was to get Moscow's approval for Japan's plan to exploit the natural resources of Manchuria and Inner Mongolia.[111]Kuhara also ventured to propose to the Soviet leadership Tanaka's project of creating in Manchuria and Eastern Siberia a demilitarized zone.[112] This was a variation on Tanaka's previous idea of a buffer state between Russia and Japan, which he pursued during the Siberian Intervention.

What Tanaka had in mind became clearer as his second envoy, Gotō Shinpei, was preparing for his trip to Russia in 1927. Before going to Russia, Gotō summoned Mitsukawa Kametarō and tasked him with writing a memorandum on the Russo-Japanese partnership in relation to Japan's policy in China.[113] Mitsukawa's memorandum was circulated among influential political and business elites and used by Gotō in his trip to Russia as the basic outline of Japan's propositions.

First, it stated that in 1927 it was safe to say that the world socialist revolution had failed. Mitsukawa pointed to the inconsistencies between the Bolsheviks' internationalist claims and their statist politics and nationalist policies. The Russian Civil War and the prolonged foreign intervention had forced Lenin and the Bolsheviks to turn to statist principles as the only way to survive among hostile capitalist and imperialist countries.[114] Gotō also publicly expressed admiration for the State Planning Committee, or Gosplan, which in 1927 launched the First Five-Year Plan, captivating the interest not only of Japanese reform bureaucrats and the SMR but also the military.[115] Mitsukawa stressed in his memorandum that although Lenin and the Bolsheviks had initially claimed that the ultimate aim of the Russian Revolution was the elimination of the state and its institutions, as well as an uncompromising struggle against nationalism, the Bolshevik government's only choice if it were to strengthen Russia was to adopt statism (*kokkashugi*) and nationalism (*minzokushugi*) as its founding principles.[116] Moreover, Mitsukawa pointed out, the Russian Communist Party had degenerated, and the spirit of the revolution had been exhausted. As evidence of this change, as noted above, Mitsukawa singled out the emerging conflict for power between Stalin and Bukharin, on one hand, and Trotsky and Zinoviev, on the other: the so-called Left Opposition. Therefore, Mitsukawa concluded, Japan's ruling elite and the Japanese people need not worry about the USSR's ambitions for a global communist order. This plan had not been brought to fruition in Russia and would not succeed elsewhere either.[117]

Second, Mitsukawa and Gotō did not fail to mention the high hopes they had for Stalin and for his "scientific" pragmatic approach to foreign policies. In cooperation with the Soviet Union, Mitsukawa and Gotō argued, China could finally be pacified and convinced to accept its neighbors' vital interests in it. The cooperation would also lock out other countries, namely the United States and Britain, as it did in the period between 1905 and 1917. In sum, Gotō and Mitsukawa advocated the creation of a political and economic bloc uniting Soviet Russia, China, and Japan against the world order dominated by the Anglo-American powers. The bloc, it was hoped, would create a sense of community in East Asia by overcoming Asian nationalisms, thus bringing stability to the Japanese Empire.

Moreover, Mitsukawa also spelled out plans widely entertained among policy makers to create a buffer puppet state in Northeast Asia. Mitsukawa specifically saw the puppet state also as a solution to Japan's overpopulation problem. According to his plan, China would give up all of Manchuria and Inner Mongolia to the new state, while Russia would contribute the territory of Eastern Siberia (the territory east of Lake Baikal) and the Russian Far East. This plan was undoubtedly related to Gotō's contemporaneous talks with the Russians about Japanese immigration to the Russian Far East, discussed above. In that vast common space, Mitsukawa proposed, two to three hundred million people—including Japanese, Chinese, Mongolian, Russian, and indigenous peoples—would live together in peace and build a new civilization. Its three pillars would be Russia, China, and Japan—although, Mitsukawa added, because China was weak, administration would in reality be divided between Russia and Japan.[118] Mitsukawa did not see the acquisition of these territories as a result of military conflict but of diplomatic negotiation for mutual benefit. In addition, the claim on those territories was justified by the idea, widely disseminated within Japan, that Eastern Siberia, the Maritime Province, Inner Mongolia, and Manchuria (more accurately, the Three Eastern Provinces) had not historically been integral parts of the Russian and Chinese nations but rather colonies or distinct administrative and ethnic units within the Russian and Chinese Empires. According to this logic, Japan thus simply offered Russia and China an opportunity to co-rule and co-manage those territories more effectively and to the states' mutual advantage.[119] As for those who objected to Japan's colonial policy on moral grounds, Mitsukawa declared that this policy was fundamentally different from the "evil" American and British versions of colonialism. He expressed the heartfelt conviction of many pan-Asianists that Japan was a moral empire (dōtoku teikoku), now teaming up with another "liberator of Asia," the Soviet Union.[120]

By the mid-1920s, the Soviet leaders had greatly moderated their revolutionary rhetoric, thereby helping Japanese pan-Asianists and pro-Russian factions in the government to champion their cause. To a large degree, the change was precipitated by the death of Lenin in January 1924 and Stalin's ascendance to power. In late 1924, Stalin and Bukharin began promoting a new policy of "socialism in one country," distancing themselves from the "militantly internationalist and revolutionary policy that made Soviet socialism dependent on revolution abroad, and aiming toward a more national commitment to build a new socialist society within a single state."[121] In the general exhaustion of the postrevolutionary years, Trotsky's notion of exporting the revolution was losing mass support, while the Soviet leadership under Stalin's guidance worked hard on securing its borders even if it meant concluding treaties with capitalist countries and compromising its revolutionary message. In order to be fully accepted internationally as a state equal to the world's great powers, the Soviet Foreign Ministry did its utmost to disassociate itself and the Soviet state from the Comintern.

In 1918, Lenin expressed the opinion of the majority of the Soviet leadership when he declared imperial Japan, above any other nation, to be the most dangerous threat to the Russian Revolution. "Japanese imperialism," in Lenin's words, was distinguished by an "unheard of bestiality combining the most modern technical implements with downright Asiatic torture."[122] To counter Japan's threat, Lenin even entertained the idea of rapprochement with the United States by offering it the territory of Kamchatka, which would "drive a wedge" between the United States and Japan.[123] Lenin and the Second Comintern Congress also explicitly criticized pan-Asianism and pan-Islamism. The congress defined the pan-Asiatic movement as one trying to combine "the struggle for liberation against European and American imperialism with the strengthening of the power of Japanese imperialism." The Comintern Congress declared that it was the duty of all communists to fight against these movements.[124]

Although Lenin deemed Japan to be one of the worst imperialist powers, Stalin completely reversed Lenin's assessment. Stalin and other Soviet leaders attempted to vindicate Japan's foreign policy, mainly by claiming that it acted not as an independent imperialist force but as an appendage to other, economically more powerful countries. To appease Japan, Stalin even acknowledged that Japanese imperialism, and pan-Asianist ideas of regional integration under Japan's leadership, might become a positive force in the development of revolution in the East, therefore contributing to fomenting a proletarian revolution! At the same time, the United States, which until then had been considered a "neutral" country in terms of the spread of the proletarian revolution in Western Europe, came to be regarded by the Soviet Union as its main political enemy.[125] In July 1925, in an interview with the journalist Katsuji Fuse of *Tokyo nichi nichi*, Stalin (at that time the general secretary of the Communist Party) declared that Japan, by virtue of being an Asian country, was necessarily an oppressed nation, and that this could constitute the basis for an alliance between the two countries. Stalin said that the Japanese were "the most advanced of the peoples of the East" and that they "were interested in the success of movements for the liberation of subjugated peoples . . . An alliance of the Japanese people with the peoples of the Soviet Union would be a decisive step on the way to the liberation of the East. Such an alliance would mean the beginning of the end for world capitalism. This alliance would be invincible."[126] With this aim, beginning in 1925, Soviet representatives approached Japan's Foreign Ministry and the army with a proposition to forge a formal alliance between the USSR, China, and Japan. In Moscow, Foreign Minister Chicherin discussed the issue with Japan's first interim ambassador to Russia, Satō Naotake (the same Satō who while general-consul in Harbin pushed for the intervention in 1918). In Beijing in 1925, Colonel Suzuki Teiichi was approached by a Soviet representative with a plan to form an alliance between the USSR, Japan, and Germany to develop in tandem a revolutionary movement in China. Playing on Japan's anxieties, these proposals necessarily included as their ultimate goal the rooting out of Anglo-Saxon power from the Asian region.[127]

After the Basic Convention of 1925, Stalin thus advanced the possibility of collaboration with imperial Japan based on its embrace of a pan-Asianist, anticolonial position. "Inasmuch as the slogan 'Asia for the Asiatics' means a call to a revolutionary war against imperialism—and to this extent only—there undoubtedly exists a common cause," Stalin explained. Ioffe reiterated this view: "Probably nowhere else in the world does the Soviet Union enjoy the popularity that it enjoys in Japan. Even as the Japanese imperialist state adopts policies to suppress weaker peoples (Korea and China) in the Far East, so long as it comes into conflict with imperialism of still stronger powers it is prepared to turn its face toward the Soviet Union, the only large non-imperialist country in the world."[128] One should not underestimate, however, the sincerity of Stalin's communist beliefs. In the same interview given to the Japanese newspaper, Stalin made a crucial critique of the pan-Asianist program:

> The slogan "Asia for Asians" embraces not only that side. It also contains two additional elements that are absolutely incompatible with the Bolshevik strategy. First, it does not address the issue of Eastern imperialism, as if by considering Eastern imperialism better than Western, it is not necessary to fight against Eastern imperialism. Second, this slogan instills in the workers of Asia a feeling of distrust toward the workers of Europe, alienates the former from the latter, tears apart the international ties between them and thus undermines the very foundations of the liberation movement. The revolutionary tactics of Bolsheviks are aimed not only against Western imperialism, but against imperialism per se, including Eastern. They work not to weaken international ties

between Asian workers and the workers of Europe and America, but to widen and strengthen those ties.[129]

Despite the nationalist bent that Soviet state building took under his guidance, Stalin was, after all, a true believer in communism and emphasized the imperialist nature of the Japanese capitalist state. However, if and when needed, Stalin was ready to collaborate with Japan to some extent.

To achieve both goals—a socialist revolution in China and the defense of Russia's national interests through cooperation with imperial Japan—was hard but, as Soviet-Japanese relations in the 1920s proved, not impossible. The Soviet Union and imperial Japan agreed on a mutual task: to restrain political chaos in China. In 1925, Stalin predicted: "But [Chang Tso-lin] is ruined also because he built his entire policy on quarrels between us [the USSR] and Japan. . . . Only he will keep his position who builds his policy on the improvement of our relations with Japan and on a rapprochement between us and Japan."[130] During the 1920s, many Japanese decision makers could not agree more with Stalin's statement. When the stakes were that high (and they were), communist ideology, I argue, never became a decisive factor in Japan's foreign policy. Japan's pro-Soviet foreign policy diverged, however, from the simultaneous anticommunist domestic crackdown, the theme of the next chapter.

ANTICOMMUNISM WITHIN

The first necessity is developing the new age in consonance with the national character . . . We do not think that something suitable to Russia is valid for China or something fit for Japan is perfectly adaptable to France. On this point we differ from the Marxists. . . . When it comes to ethnic differences derived from history and tradition, we do not think the world is divided only laterally [by class].

—Kiyosawa Kiyoshi, *Why Liberalism?*, 1935

As the government's foreign policy rapidly moved toward reconciliation with the Soviet Union, concern over the effect of communist ideology on domestic society was growing within Japan. This concern over the communist threat in the 1920s united such disparate groups as liberals and the conservative bureaucracy, particularly in the Home and Justice ministries. Liberals pointed to worsening social conditions and ministerial bureaucrats to the degeneration of moral and cultural traditions to explain the appeal of "dangerous thought" to university professors, students, workers, women, outcast groups, and others. Unlike pan-Asianists and politicians concerned with foreign affairs, Japanese liberals and conservatives did not differentiate between the Soviet state and the Comintern, and they considered the Comintern and communism as the main ideological threats to Japan's national polity. The Soviet Union was an embodiment of its ideology, and its foreign policy objectives were to make the world "red." The imperial state, liberals and conservatives urged, must do its utmost to counter this threat.

During the 1920s, communism was perceived as essentially a *foreign* threat to the national community. And it was none other than the leaders of the Taishō liberal-democratic movement, most of whom were university professors and journalists, who first articulated and put forward this idea of communism as an external menace to the national community. However, since 1919, liberals' anticommunist rhetoric had served its own purposes. Waging its own battle for the democratization of Japanese politics, Japanese liberals used the Red Scare to convince the government and the public that only the implementation of universal suffrage would stop the "Bolshevization" of the Japanese nation. The conservative bureaucracy of the Home and Justice ministries, in contrast, became preoccupied with communism around 1922, when the JCP was first established. For the conservatives (although they did not call themselves such), concern over communism overlapped with their general dismay at the dramatically changing post–World War I Japanese society. The conservative bureaucrats' program to combat international communism was an attempt to gain control over an increasingly diverse and diversified society based on reinforcing the unique traditionalist bond between the emperor, the nation, and the land.

The anticommunist trajectory formulated by liberal commentators and conservative bureaucrats culminated in the implementation of the Peace Preservation Law (*Chian ijihō*) of 1925, which suppressed the Japanese leftist movement and criminalized anyone convicted of following Bolshevik ideology. However, even more indicative of domestic anticommunism was the revision of the Peace Preservation Law in 1928. It imposed the death penalty on those who intended to alter the national polity (*kokutai*) but gave only two years' imprisonment to those who wished to alter the capitalist system of private property. Put simply, none of the interwar anticommunists cared about the communists' anticapitalist agenda. What they did care about was the shape of future politics, and who would determine it. Anxiety over international communism exposed for liberals, conservatives, and nationalists alike the unresolved and undefined nature of the Japanese national community and polity in transition. The communist doctrines of class struggle and international brotherhood were particularly worrisome for liberal and conservative commentators, because if not checked, they would further undermine post–World War I Japan's already unstable state and society. The intellectual "panic" brought about by the Russian Revolution led not simply to the domestic suppression of any leftist opposition but, more importantly, to the emergence of various competitive political imaginaries, from national liberal to traditional monarchist to fascist. All of these imaginaries, nevertheless, regarded the state as the rule maker, as the only proper means for social unity, stability, and prosperity.

The Russian Revolution marked a great shift in Japanese interwar liberalism. Since the Taishō political crisis of 1912–13, which inaugurated the beginning of party politics in modern Japan, Japanese liberal commentators—most notably two professors of law at Tokyo Imperial University, Yoshino Sakuzō and Minobe Tatsukichi—centered their efforts on promoting political parties and strengthening the representative government against the old oligarchic, cliquish Meiji politics (*hanbatsu seiji*). In 1918, the first party government was formed under the leadership of Hara Takashi, leader of the majority Seiyūkai Party. However, the great Rice Riots in the summer of 1918, workers' strikes, students' agitation, and the arrival of international communism in Japan exposed the limitations of Japanese liberalism to answer the needs of society at the crossroads. As Marxism and communism began to win over the minds of students, workers, peasants, women, and intellectuals, liberal commentators had to convince these newly emerging social groups that liberal democracy was different from socialist or communist democracies and explain how their definition of a liberal-democratic organization of society was better than a socialist one. As such, the Russian Revolution became the stimulus for the expansion, both political and theoretical, of Japanese interwar liberalism.

Beginning in 1917, Japanese liberals advocated for universal suffrage, a demand to extend democratic rights to as many male subjects of the empire as possible. Liberals were less concerned with social and economic reforms per se, because they believed that the implementation of universal suffrage would have an overall positive effect on social and economic conditions.[1] To succeed with these goals, liberal educators, intellectuals, students, and journalists began to organize various study and meeting groups around the country and to publish in the exploding press media. One of the first and most famous organizations was the Reimeikai (Dawn, founded in December 1918), established by Yoshino and Fukuda Tokuzō. Others included the Kaizō dōmeikai; Warera group (established by Ōyama Ikuo and journalist Hasegawa Nyozekan in 1919); a study group organized around the journal *Shakai mondai kenkyū* and its founder, Professor of Economics Kawakami Hajime at Kyoto Imperial University; and the liberal editorial of the magazine *Tōyō Keizai Shinpō* (the future politician Ishibashi Tanzan was its star journalist). What characterized Taishō liberalism, however, was its commitment to the state, its belief that in Japan it was the responsibility of the imperial state to ensure the well-being of its subjects. Liberals thus promoted representative government under the umbrella of the monarchy, the dominance of mass-based parties, reduced bureaucracy, and a responsible military. The most identifiable component of the definition of interwar liberals was their belief that democratic politics ultimately served the goals of national unity and social harmony.[2]

Taishō liberals' self-identification developed in opposition not to the state but to the socialists. The quarrel between liberals and socialists was never about economics; both, in fact, despised laissez-faire capitalism. Instead, they disagreed about the shape of politics. Japanese-style democracy, liberals anxiously argued, served national interests, while communist democracy professed "empty" and subversive internationalism. Communism in this context became the radical backdrop against which liberal commentators justified and pursued their own demands. The notion of the "red threat" was strategically utilized by liberal commentators: the extended franchise and democratic reforms were the only solution, they argued, that could strengthen and unite the nation against the external destabilizing threat. Taishō liberalism, however, was hardly successful: it failed to win over students, who moved en masse to more appealing left-wing radicalism, and it produced many defectors (for example, Ōyama Ikuo), who became disillusioned not simply with party politics in Japan but with Japanese-style liberalism's theoretical compliance with the increasingly repressive state.

Taishō liberal educators and journalists—Yoshino Sakuzō, Fukuda Tokuzō, Ōyama Ikuo, Kiyosawa Kiyoshi, and others—greeted the February Revolution with great enthusiasm as the "people's revolution" against the corrupt and autocratic tsarist government and bureaucracy. However, after the news of the Bolshevik takeover reached Japan, few of them recognized its revolutionary potential, regarding it instead as part of the ongoing Great War. Like the Japanese government, it took some time for Japanese liberals to accept the new Bolshevik regime as legitimate. Understanding the Great War as a war between the forces of democracy and the forces of autocracy and militarism, Yoshino Sakuzō condemned the October Revolution as an illegitimate coup, an "unpatriotic" action of the Bolshevik militant group. The abolition of the state and its main organs, believed to be at the core of the Leninist program, was a sign of defeatism, he insisted. The Bolshevik Party and its insistence on the dictatorship of the proletariat seemed to many supporters of Western-style parliamentary government to thwart the normal course of democratic and liberal changes in Russian society initiated by the February events.[3]

Once more information on the new Bolshevik state became known in Japan, and as the Bolsheviks solidified their power, Yoshino recognized that Bolshevism was perhaps part of the "trend of the times," part of the evolving international democratic movement, but surely a more extreme version of popular protest. When in a special issue of the magazine *Chūō Kōron* (June 1919), various contributors condemned Bolshevism, likening it to a pestilence, Yoshino disagreed. Addressing the liberal and educated audience of *Chūō Kōron*, Yoshino pointed out that widespread fatigue from the Great War and Lenin's promise to deliver "peace, land, and bread" made understandable the mass support the Bolsheviks enjoyed among the Russian people. In this sense, the October Revolution in Russia was a people's revolution, a lower-class revolt against incompetent authorities, rather than an illegitimate takeover by debased radicals. Japanese liberals recognized that the success of the Bolshevik Revolution originated in Russia's peculiar political and social circumstances. As such, Japanese readers should keep in mind, Yoshino warned, that the Bolshevik Revolution was a social revolution, an ideological solution to the problems of Russian political and social backwardness.

Yoshino pointed out, however, that Bolshevism was different from "orthodox" socialism. Socialism struggled for the same ideals as *minponshugi,* the term that

Yoshino used to describe the type of democracy suited for Japan—democracy in which sovereignty resided not in the people but with the monarchy and imperial government serving the people's welfare. In contrast, the Bolshevist claim of democracy was a sham. Bolshevism as it had been implemented in Soviet Russia was undemocratic because it installed a one-party regime and rejected representative government, claiming that democratic institutions were not in the interests of workers.[4] The prominent liberal journalists Murobuse Kōshin and Ōyama Ikuo initially also attacked Bolshevism as another type of autocracy that rejected the true spirit of democracy. Bolshevist-type socialism resembled Bismarck's policy, Murobuse wrote, and was in reality a form of state capitalism.[5] Ōyama condemned the Russian Revolution as an instance of a "disgraceful baptism of blood." Revolution as a method, he continued, was a "most abhorrent thing," appropriate only for backward and decaying countries like Russia. In Japan, Ōyama continued, it was not necessary to resort to radical measures and dismantle the whole political system, but rather only to remove certain obstacles to the proper functioning of the constitution and democratic politics. In support of liberalism, Ōyama stressed the value of democratization as a barrier to the spread of radical ideas in Japan. If the government did not want to see people turn toward political extremism, warned Ōyama, it must urgently undertake a program of social reform and democratization.[6]

For liberals, class struggle constituted a great threat to the democratic process and the coherence of the national community. For Yoshino and Ōyama, harmony between capital and labor was indeed achievable through democratic mechanisms, whereas the state as a neutral organ served to mediate between conflicting interests. That was contrary to the belief of socialists, who viewed the state always as a tool of a particular class—the bourgeoisie or the workers—and as something that eventually must disappear. Against his socialist and communist competitors, Yoshino advanced a classless political vision:

> The extension of suffrage to the extreme is to destroy class bias. Class interest must be banished from politics. If both capitalists and workers consider only their own class interests, impartial resolution of state affairs becomes impossible. The place to discuss class interest is elsewhere. As a member of this nation, I would like to see the Diet provide impartial and consensual opinion that transcends class bias. . . . In sum, taking into consideration the essential feature of the Diet, its members should not base their thinking on class interests. Even though each member may think of class interests, the Diet as a whole should not wear the color of [a particular] class. In this respect, universal suffrage can be an ideal institution.[7]

Neither the natural rights of every individual nor the expansion of workers' rights was the theoretical basis of universal suffrage. Instead, suffrage should rest on "social cooperation" based on the "organic" relations between individuals and the neutral and therefore benevolent state.

If interwar Japanese liberalism is defined as advocacy for the extension of political rights to the broader male population, then it had its adherents even within the military. Even some army commentators recognized that the army's conservatism did not harmonize with the democratic trends of the time and might undermine its unity and stability. In 1922, retired Lieutenant Colonel Satō Kōjirō wrote *The Military and Social Problems* (Guntai to shakai mondai), one of the army's first responses to social discontent and the new political trends. He lamented the growing division between the army and the people but did not express hostility either to democracy or to socialism. Both ideas, he wrote, in fact existed in Japan from ancient times, and as soon as the people and the army come fully into contact with them, their perceived danger will recede and they will be placed in proper perspective. Satō criticized the army for not allowing a healthy discussion to develop, which would alleviate the feeling of alienation between the military and the people. He reprimanded the army for its cultivated feeling of superiority and exclusivity, its conservatism, and its lack of democratic attitude in dealing with the soldiers and public. As democratic measures, he proposed that officers receive training in social affairs (*shakai kunren*); military youth schools (*yōnen gakkō*), the breeding place of army conservatism, be abolished; and prospective military academy students be selected from regular high school graduates. Satō, however, insisted that future wars would be total wars, and therefore, in order to achieve the total mobilization of Japanese society, giving people a much greater stake in their political society was a necessary requirement. Satō's book caused a sensation in Japan and, in fact, his idea of democratization as a component of mass mobilization found widespread approval in the army, where preoccupation with total mobilization had been growing since World War I.[8]

Satō reacted to developments in the army that originated with the Siberian Intervention. Both the liberal and the nationalist press reported frustration among Japanese troops in Siberia (especially rank-and-file soldiers and junior officers) with their senior officers about the repressive character of the army and the seeming pointlessness of their dispatch to Siberia.[9] Many new conscripts refused to read the oath of loyalty to the army, some mutinied against their superiors, and a few even deserted. There was very low morale in the army: looting the local population and stealing inside the army barracks were common. The army command was aware of the factors that contributed to the internal destabilization of the army. Most of the soldiers came from impoverished peasant families and were influenced by the general mood in favor of "democracy." Some had it even worse: many enlisted soldiers had to pacify the regions participating in the Rice Riots before being sent to Siberia. As Yoshino pointed out, new conscripts, having endured the traumatic experience of suppressing riots by farmers whose plight they understood all too well, adopted a negative view of the army.[10] The army officials branded those who complained as "socialists" or "radicals" and were vigilant about limiting soldiers' contact with the outside world, carefully monitoring soldiers' attitudes and which books and periodicals were sent to them from Japan. The progressive magazines *Kaizō*, *Kaihō*, and *Chūō kōron* were strictly prohibited.[11]

It was true that those in the military had grounds for concern. They knew that the communist Katayama Sen established a small printing workshop in Chita to produce Bolshevik propaganda leaflets, which the Japanese communists tried to smuggle into Japanese garrisons in Siberia and into Japan. However, this propaganda was not effective, because very few leaflets passed the gates of garrisons and reached the soldiers; not a single Japanese officer or enlisted man joined a communist party.[12] To counter the worries of the army command, the Japanese liberal press (including its sympathizers within the army) pointed out that the army's problems in Siberia were a reflection of domestic problems, rather than being related to communism per se. But the liberals also emphasized that communism could become a major problem in the army if political reforms were not extended to those who were enlisted.

One of the first sophisticated analyses of Soviet communism was offered by Fukuda Tokuzō (1874–1930), a professor of economics at Keio University. Fukuda was a very influential public intellectual, an adviser to the government, and the first expert in Marxism, especially its economic thought. Fukuda's articles on the Soviet Union were read by Chief of the General Staff Uehara Yūsaku, among others, and the two had private conversations in 1919.[13] His writings and interpretation of Marxism, along with those of Professor of Economics Kawakami Hajime, also influenced early Chinese and Korean Marxists.[14] Fukuda argued that Russian Bolshevism was an ideology of reaction (*handō shisō*) and could not be understood without knowledge of the Russian national situation and sentiments before and during the Great War. Fukuda rightly pointed out that Russia had been undergoing rapid and uneven industrialization; most of the land and industry still belonged to the big landlords and the aristocracy, which caused great social and political upheavals. "Caught between the capitalist and feudal economic systems, the Russian people's resentment had been growing for a long time. This revolution was triggered by the war and their defeats in it. Thus, the conditions to readily accept the Bolshevik movement were created by Russia's long history."[15] In one of the first Japanese accounts of the Russian Revolution published in Japan, Fukuda explained that the core of communism was the abolition of private property, which was the basis for the total restructuring of society. Communists believed that only with the destruction of private property could human dignity, equality, and freedom be obtained. Russia's peculiar historical and social conditions, Fukuda concluded, made the Bolsheviks' advocacy of class struggle logical and understandable, but only in the Russian context.

Fukuda attributed Japan's failure in Siberia to its misunderstanding of Bolshevism as an ideology and of the Bolsheviks as a political group: the term *kagekiha* (extremists), commonly used in Japan to describe Russian communists, tempted Japanese people to mistake Bolsheviks for libertarian and antistate anarchists and to ignore the fact that the Bolsheviks' main priority was the creation of a proletarian state. Bolshevism, Fukuda wrote, stood for a "Big Principle, for a potent ideology [*shugi*] that had the power to rouse and unite hundreds of thousands of people." The intervention, he maintained, was therefore misguided and pointless; Lenin and Trotsky were not simply upstart outsiders but expressed the hopes and wishes of the Russian people. The tsar was not only a source of evil for the Russian people and the world but also a threat to Japan. Fukuda exhorted the Japanese to be grateful to the Russian communists for eliminating Russian and German despotism and imperialism.[16] Although he was hardly sympathetic to socialism, Fukuda insisted that Japan needed more study of the Soviet Union and its ideology to confront uninformed commentaries, which could be harmful to establishing good relations with the Soviet state.

Nevertheless, since 1919 socialism and its more radical form, communism, had become the most apparent and easily identifiable enemy of the state, and liberal commentators rushed to differentiate themselves from the Left by declaring the sanctity of the constitutional monarchy and the preeminence of the private property system in modern Japan. Like Ōyama above, Fukuda maintained that the antimonarchical doctrine of communism was alien to Japanese society. Fukuda argued that the backbone of Japanese national unity was the monarchical tradition (*kokutai*), which nothing and no one could change. Related to this, Fukuda dismissed the idea that class warfare could develop in Japan: "Japan is a lucky country as it also went through a rapid industrialization, but the clash between the old and the new was not as strong, the progress of the country was steady, and economic life in Japan was healthy. Japanese people's national feelings are completely different and there are no conditions for Bolshevik ideas to thrive in Japan."[17] Class warfare was incompatible with the Japanese way of thinking, and modern Japanese society was healthy enough to avoid such a disastrous development.[18] Moreover, Fukuda asserted that communism would never take root in Japan because the abolition of private property would lead to the collapse of industry, and those accustomed to enjoying the spoils of the capitalist system would never turn against it. Relying on the writings of the Ukrainian Marxist scholar Mikhail Tugan-Baranovsky, Fukuda challenged Marx's theory that capitalism had an internal drive toward self-destruction. Fukuda insisted that capitalism had the potential for transformation and improvement and could develop indefinitely. That last argument embroiled him in what became a famous public debate over Marxist economics with Kawakami Hajime from Kyoto Imperial University (and later many more Marxist economists), which lasted for ten years. To counter Fukuda, Kawakami, who since 1919 had turned from a Christian liberal position to Marxism, employed Rosa Luxemburg's theory of the stagnation and inevitable end of capitalism—which was, in effect, the first introduction of her theory into Japan.[19]

Fukuda thus brushed off the growing popularity of Marxism in Japan. Communist ideas were known in Japan only to a few young, idealistic intellectuals, he wrote in various popular outlets, while the nonorganized workers cared only for immediate economic improvement.[20] Fukuda additionally pointed out that the internationalist claims of Bolshevism were simply false. He insisted that theirs was the age of nation-states, and that individuals always and unavoidably thought in national terms. The communists' aspiration to create a supranational brotherhood was thus unrealistic, and the Bolsheviks' recent nationality policies, their support of nationalist movements abroad, and their overtly nationalist foreign policy directly undermined their internationalist claim.[21] Fukuda thus emerged as one of the main defenders of the capitalist liberal order, which was firmly entrenched in modern Japan, and in his opinion could not be dislodged by communist ideas or movement within Japan.

Fukuda's position was, however, more an instance of wishful thinking than a reflection of the reality of the early 1920s. Students of his own society (Reimeikai) were increasingly abandoning their membership, while discussions at meetings revolved around socialism and communism rather than parliamentary politics. In fact, anxiety among educated elite and public men over socialism's and communism's hold on the Taishō society was steadily growing, and the lack of consensus among them of what to make of that is striking. Take, for example, the public debate that unfolded in the magazine *Roshia hihyō* in July 1919. Several leading journalists, university professors, and army officers were asked to share their thoughts about the possibility of the Bolshevization of Japan. Aoki Seiichi, a member of the powerful Association of Veterans, described how he had gone to Siberia a year earlier and been horrified at the army's demoralization. Japanese soldiers, he asserted, were becoming very susceptible to Bolshevik ideas amid the chaotic environment. Aoki insisted that Bolshevism was a threat to the Japanese Empire because the Siberian Bolsheviks instigated unrest among anti-Japanese Koreans in Siberia and were thus responsible for various Korean uprisings. The rise of the radicalized anti-Japanese movement in China was also the result of the Bolshevization of the East Asian region. Aoki saw a difference between socialism, which dealt with social problems, and Bolshevism, which was socially destructive and antinational. He ended his opinion piece, however, with the insistence that Bolshevism was part of the Jewish conspiracy to overtake the world.[22]

The liberal journalist Murobuse Kōshin doubted the influence of Bolshevism in Japan but, like Aoki, pointed out that the military in Siberia had been strongly drawn to Bolshevism. The success of Bolshevism in Russia, he emphasized, was due to the Bolshevization of Russian soldiers. Bolshevism appealed to Japanese soldiers as well, and thus the common Japanese eventually could be drawn into Bolshevism, too. He also pointed out that, unlike Japanese soldiers, US soldiers in Siberia were not interested in Bolshevism. This difference, he claimed, was due to the relative lack of political freedoms in Japan; the more the Japanese government denied civic freedoms to its people, the greater the possibility of the Bolshevization of young people and workers.[23]

In contrast, the journalist Ōba Kakō argued that Bolshevist ideas were popular in Japan, citing the many popular magazines that dedicated more and more issues to Marxism and the translations of the main Marxist thinkers, which sold out immediately. He also pointed out that the Japanese educated public had cooled toward the liberal democratic movement because they found Bolshevist ideas more relevant. Ōba noted that communist propaganda had nothing to do with this popularity. Compared to Taishō liberalism, Bolshevism seemed truly egalitarian, and thus had more appeal to Japanese soldiers and workers.[24]

Kemuyama Sentarō, a historian of Russian anarchism, expressed his doubts that Bolshevism or socialism were properly understood in Japan, if anyone could talk about their influence at all. Bolshevism, he wrote, was a Russian phenomenon, based on the peculiar history of Russia and the "self-destructive character" of its people. Although there was no doubt that Russian proletarian absolutism shook the "world of capitalists and aristocracy" with its radical ideas and actions, the situation in industrialized and advanced Japan was inopportune for a Bolshevik revolution. However, he warned, as the Japanese were "impressionable people and have a tendency to run from one extreme to another," the government should be watchful.[25] Those few who denied the possibility of the Bolshevization of Japan maintained that there was no organized Japanese working class that could struggle to take political power. The liberal Kayahara Kazan dismissed Japanese workers as timid and ashamed of their status as workers. He also pointed out that socialist and Bolshevik ideas were popular among university professors and students, who were too immature to translate their ideas into an actual political movement. The current "socialist craze" in Japan, Kayahara concluded, would only "confuse already confused minds, make more anxious already anxious people." He called on the government—which, he acknowledged, had been "defining education, morals, and the philosophy of its people"—to step up and create a new ideological framework for the national polity.[26]

These opinion pieces demonstrate how undecided the educated Japanese were about the causes and goals of the Russian Revolution. Understanding the revolutionary upheaval in Russia as the outcome of a particular set of circumstances (uneven industrialization under autocratic rule and the consequences of World War I), Japanese liberal commentators did not fail to emphasize the potential danger communist ideology posed to Japanese society, in which a majority of its people were disenfranchised. In sum, the issue of Bolshevism came hand in hand with the unfolding movement in Japan for wider democratic rights. As Professor Fukuda and retired Lieutenant General Satō had pointed out, most of Japan's population were peasants and workers whose lives and needs could not be ignored any longer by the state and big business; the state did not have any moral right to recruit its young men into the army or demand greater commitment to the needs of the state without providing them with basic political guarantees. The state also must bring big business into implementing labor regulations in accordance with the "trends of the time." A political minority would soon become a political majority, warned Fukuda. The liberals insisted that the Russian Revolution made it all the more clear that the state must initiate new social policies to deal with existing "social problems" and "evil practices" by building a social democratic welfare state, at the core of which was not the protection of private property but rather of human life and human dignity.[27] But as Fukuda, Yoshino and others maintained, imperial democracy (*minponshugi*) and the social welfare state must prioritize the people (*kokumin*) and the state, not the interests of a particular social class. Concerned with the labor problem and, in fact, contributing to the labor legislation that had been worked out in the government, Fukuda warned that the most dangerous outcome of both laissez-faire capitalism and conservatism would be the people's turn to Bolshevism as an attractive alternative or solution.

At the same time, liberals warned the public and government against the danger of Bolshevik internationalism, which Russians would impose by unleashing "world revolution." Even if the Russian Bolsheviks were to succeed in building a proletarian state in Russia, warned Yoshino, the neighboring nonproletarian countries should not be complacent. The Soviet state, operating via its agent, the Comintern, would work on destroying the political and economic regimes hostile to communism. Besides, this would be done by the Comintern agents in order to safeguard the Russian Revolution and provide security for the Soviet state. For their own survival, the Soviet state and the Comintern would never stop their propaganda activities. Yoshino urged the Japanese police to be vigilant about this danger and the Japanese state to take preventive care of its own workers.[28] Fukuda also appealed to the government to carefully monitor home-made socialist "cosmopolitan-unpatriots."[29] All the distinguished participants in the debate at *Roshia hihyō*, although in disagreement as to the degree of influence that Bolshevism exercised in Japan, did agree that the government and the ruling elite should take a more proactive and aggressive anticommunist position.

Liberal commentators were therefore united in pressuring the government to buttress its anticommunist position with a more coherent national ideological framework. The new national ideology should not be based on appeals to patriotism or nostalgia for traditional values but on mobilizing people's commitment to the state and its purpose by extending voting rights. Democratic liberals argued that democratization of the political process would provide a means for the people to identify themselves with the state through participation in national affairs, thus creating national harmony, consensus, and a sense of community. Concerned with strengthening and unifying the nation through active political participation by the empire's subjects, liberals grew anxious at the Bolsheviks' slogans of permanent world revolution. They reckoned that the Russian Revolution, despite its origins in Russia's peculiar historical circumstances, still could become "contagious" as a result of communist Russia's propaganda activities in politically and socially unstable post–World War I Japan. Although expressing confidence in the moral and ideological strength of the Japanese national community, these commentators called for a series of reforms to curb "subversive" thought and actions within Japan. As such, the anticommunist proposals of the leaders of Taishō liberalism agreed with the thinking of the Home and Justice ministries.

In response to the demands of the Taishō democratic liberals, party politicians and conservative intellectuals recognized that democratic changes, part of "the trend of the world," must be included in domestic and foreign policy to counter the rise of domestic labor disputes and international communism.[30] Moreover, the democratization of domestic politics was required to strengthen cooperation with the United States and to improve Japan's international standing. The new Hara Takashi cabinet of September 1918 welcomed the universal suffrage movement, albeit for a short period, while the oppositional parties began to promote liberal labor policy, calling for the legalization of labor unions in an effort to minimize growing social conflict and reduce the appeal of radical thought among workers. The Home Ministry proposed a progressive labor union bill in 1920, which, however, never passed. Nevertheless, the recommendations of liberal commentators on strengthening the national ideological framework aligned with the concerns of the conservative bureaucracy within the government, which soon embarked on its own program to stabilize the increasingly riven society.

Conservative bureaucrats understood communism as a foreign ideology that threatened Japan's cultural traditions and its unique national structure, defined by the timeless ethical bonds between the emperor, the nation, and the land. Preoccupied with what they understood as the degeneration of national morals in the post–World War I period, conservatives warned of communism and the ability of foreign communists to infiltrate Japanese society. To protect, defend, and reinvigorate Japan's unique cultural and political traditions, the conservative bureaucracy embarked on its own response to the Russian Revolution by reinforcing the Meiji family-state orthodoxy.

The preoccupation of the Home Ministry and Justice Ministry with internal order and the domestic labor and socialist movements dates back to 1900, the year in which the Public Order and Police Law declared organization by workers to be a disturbance of public peace and order. The law made unions and strikes illegal and outlawed the circulation of literature agitating for strikes and walkouts, crippling the labor and socialist movements for decades. Under this law, the Social Democratic Party (Shakai Minshutō, established in 1901) was banned within hours. In 1906, the Japan Socialist Party (Nihon Shakaitō) was banned within a year. Socialist newspapers and periodicals were routinely harassed by the police, and their editors fined and put in prison.

In 1910, the Ministry of Justice indicted a group of twenty-four anarchists for having plotted to assassinate the emperor, in what is known as the High Treason Incident (*Taigyaku jiken*). The trial and execution of eleven defenders ended, in effect, the Meiji socialist movement. The purpose of the trial was not so much to punish a conspiracy to kill the Japanese emperor but to crush the nascent Japanese socialist and anarchist movements by eliminating their most important leaders. One of the consequences of the High Treason Incident was the establishment of the first Special Higher Police unit (commonly known as Tokkō) within the Tokyo Metropolitan Police Board (Keishichō) in August 1911. The Tokkō police became responsible for surveilling leftist movements.[31] The public trial in the High Treason Incident became a show trial, warning the public that the state would not tolerate any radical attempts to redefine the national imperial polity. Wary of the ongoing process of the annexation of Korea (1910) and a possible backlash at home and in the colonies, the government resorted to suppression of any dissent to its actions.[32] In the long run, however, the impact of the High Treason Incident had the opposite effect. Because of the publicity it received, interest in socialist ideas and sympathy with the cause of the accused spread well beyond socialist circles, preparing the ground for the approving reception of the Bolshevik Revolution by the increasingly politically active, disenfranchised masses.

After the Russian Revolution of 1917, in the midst of the economic and social crisis and endless political and financial scandals, the Home and Justice ministries became genuinely disturbed by the waves communism had begun making in Japan. As labor and peasant unrest was growing, and homegrown socialists activated and established contacts with Russian and Asian radicals, so the state preoccupation with social movements increased. Several events and developments between 1919 and 1925 converged, producing a general sense of crisis within the state bureaucracy. First, the number and intensity of peasant participants in the Rice Riots greatly impressed the government, so even though domestic socialists had nothing to do with the riots, as a matter of precaution the police arrested many leaders of Japanese socialism in the fall of 1918. But the worst fears of the Home and Justice ministries were realized in May 1921, when police arrested a man named Kondō Eizō in the port of Shimonoseki, because they were suspicious of his excessive spending during a rowdy night of drinking.[33] To their great shock, Kondō turned out to be a communist who had just returned to Japan from Shanghai, where the Russian Comintern agent Grigory Voitinsky had given Kondō the enormous (by contemporary standards) sum of 6,500 yen to organize a communist party in Japan.[34] The conservatives in the government seized the opportunity to draft legislation that would specifically target the new ideological threat.

The state backlash in response to this arrest had important consequences because the bureaucracy now faced the problem of defining not only the foreign ideological threat but also *what* lay behind the threat. In other words, bureaucrats and the police were forced to define both what was communism and what made it different from the more familiar anarchism and socialism, as well as incompatible with the Japanese national community and polity. With this aim, in late 1921 the Justice Ministry in the Hara Cabinet drafted the Bill for the Control of Extreme Social Movements (*Kageki shakai undō torishimarihō*), largely modeled after English laws and legal theories dealing with sedition, which would have punished communist and anarchist propaganda with up to seven years in prison. In February 1922, the next prime minister, Takahashi Korekiyō, sponsored the bill, which passed the House of Peers but at the end was withdrawn by the majority party Seiyūkai leaders for fear that it would fail in the House of Representatives and generate more popular agitation.

Despite their disapproval of communism, liberals joined the nationwide protests against the antisocialist bill. The agitation became a good platform for them to demand that it was time to grant more political rights and freedoms to the people, as the rest of the civilized world had done. The more liberal members of the Diet, together with liberal journalists, argued that rather than mounting a war on new ideas, the government should investigate what lay behind the social protest movement in order to correct unjust economic, social, and political conditions. Not the bill but the extension of suffrage would reverse the tendency toward radicalism, liberals argued. The primary movers of the campaign against the bill were socialists, who also joined the liberal agitation for universal suffrage, albeit not for long. For socialists understood that the labor movement needed to use available parliamentary mechanisms—partly as a platform for rousing the masses, partly as a means of winning short-term reforms. As long as the conservative government resisted democratic reforms, liberals and socialists usually joined forces. The united front of liberals and socialists, however, was short lived: it fell apart once universal suffrage was implemented in 1925, and in some notable cases even before.[35]

The bill faced harsh criticism both inside and outside the Diet for ambiguity in its wording. While drafting the bill, the bureaucrats failed to satisfactorily distinguish between socialism, anarchism, and communism. Neither were they able to define what needed to be defended. The legislators could not clarify or come to a consensus about the "fundamental structure of society" (*shakai no konpon sōshiki*) and the national monarchical polity (*kokutai*), which were presumably under foreign ideological threat. In the end, neither *kokutai* nor *seitai* (form of government)—terms that were to generate considerable debate in 1925—were included in the bill.[36] The proponents of the bill settled on a formulation of the law intended to stem the flow of radical propaganda coming into Japan and prevent the Japanese from working in concert with *foreign* radicals. The law would apply only to those who were in contact with foreign agents, receiving money from outside the country, or importing propaganda materials in order to "subvert the laws of the state" or "alter the fundamental structure of society." In the middle of the growing universal suffrage movement, conservatives made sure to clarify that the bill in no way was to infringe on the freedom of speech and expression of the proletarian masses (*musan kaikyū*).[37]

The main significance of this judicial attempt to pass an antileftist bill was that it clearly identified the binary relationship between "dangerous foreign thought" and domestic objects to be protected, which would form the basis of the later 1925 law.[38] To describe Russian communism, bureaucrats tended often to use the word "plague" (*pesuto*), which in fact captures very well their imagining of communism as an external threat perpetrated by foreign radicals—Russian, Korean, and Chinese—against the Japanese national community. The idea that communism was a foreign disease was already present when in early 1918, then Ambassador to Russia Uchida discussed communism in Russia as essentially German sociopolitical thought brought by Germans, alien to Russian traditional thought. As the bill proposal reveals, in the early 1920s, to prevent Japan from being contaminated by this disease, tightening border controls and establishing surveillance at home and on the Asian continent seemed to the bureaucrats to be sufficient measures.

To counter the increasing tide of opinion favoring reconciliation with communist Russia, the Home Ministry went on the offensive. While the Soviet foreign deputy Ioffe was still in Tokyo, in June 1923 the police carried out mass arrests of leftists, including university professors and prominent public leaders, on the charge of fomenting a communist plot. The arrests took place at the same time as the government announced its decision to go ahead with official negotiations with Ioffe. A reporter from the *Chicago Daily News* captured the "striking paradox" of Japanese policy vis-à-vis communism and the Soviet Union: "while the police authorities connected the alleged plot with agitation for recognition of the USSR, the government by according Ioffe an official status in the negotiations was actually aiding the propagation of 'dangerous thought.'"[39] The arrests were prompted by searching the office of Sano Manabu, a professor at Waseda University and one of the emerging leaders of the Japanese communist movement. Sano was also related to Gotō Shinpei through his older brother. So as Gotō participated in official negotiations with the Soviet leadership, his relative Sano was fleeing from the Japanese police to Shanghai, together with a few other comrades, where they became the target of the Japanese consular police. Although disapproving the actions of the Home Ministry, Gotō did not make any public remarks on this issue. Foreign and domestic policies, while influencing each other, did not interfere in each other's realms.

Even though the state was alarmed at the establishment of the JCP and its contacts with the Comintern, the arrested members of the JCP got off comparatively unharmed. Some cases were dismissed for lack of evidence; of those found guilty, none entered prison until the sentences were confirmed by the high court in April 1926, and even then they did not serve full terms (ranging between eight and ten months), because of a general amnesty granted in honor of the Taishō emperor, who died that year. Most were released on bail and continued to be active in the communist movement.[40] Judging from the lightness of the sentences given in the roundup in the summer of 1923, the concern was not with the domestic radical movement per se but with foreign leftist radicals, who were "trying their best to make our country red."[41] However, a renewed awareness that there was no appropriate law that would be able to specifically deal with the communist movement became part of the backdrop against which the Diet began to debate new anticommunist legislation.

Anxious about the external communist menace, the conservative bureaucracy began rapidly moving to radical rightist politics, resorting to using political violence against its opponents. The Great Kantō earthquake of September 1, 1923, caused extensive damage and confusion and became the backdrop against which the conservative bureaucracy teamed up with the military police and extreme nationalists to choke back the labor and leftist movements. Investigation of the alleged communists arrested in June 1923 was still under way on September 1, when in the aftermath of the earthquake ten union organizers were shot by the police, and the anarchist Ōsugi Sakae, his little nephew, and the feminist anarchist Itō Noe were beaten to death by the military police (the notorious *kenpeitai*). The official investigation ended in shockingly lenient sentences—for the murder of ten labor agitators, the police were ordered simply to issue an apology. The military police officer Amakasu Masahiko, responsible for the death of the anarchists, was released from prison after three years and subsequently occupied high-ranking posts in Manchukuo.

Moreover, it was the minister of justice himself, Hiranuma Kiichirō (1867–1952), who assisted in "restoring public order" by providing funds to rightist organizers of anti-Korean violence (six thousand Koreans were murdered), who staged acts of arson all over Tokyo to add credence to rumors of a Korean uprising. He also protected the military police officers on trial, whose actions brought back, he argued, "a sense of duty and patriotism."[42] In 1926, now head of the Privy Council and the House of Peers, Hiranuma became an adviser to Kenkokukai (National Creation Society), established by the radical right-wing leader Akao Bin, which resorted to numerous acts of violence—including the notorious strike breaking at the Noda Soy Sauce Factory in 1927 and a bungled attempt to set fire to the house of the liberal-turned-socialist Ōyama Ikuo.[43] In another famous example, in 1919 Home Minister Tokonami Takejirō jointly with yakuza bosses founded the Dai Nihon Kokusuikai organization (Greater Japan National Essence Association), which had at its peak approximately two hundred thousand members and primarily acted as a strike breaker and harasser of socialists and labor leaders, as well as outcasts and members of the universal suffrage movement. What is notable is that the conservative bureaucracy used right-wing organizations—the Kokusuikai, Yamato Minrōkai (Yamato National Service Association, 1921), Dai Nihon Seigidan (Greater Japan Justice Group, 1922), and Sekka Bōshidan—rather than the old Meiji-era nationalist organizations, such as the Kokuryūkai or the Gen'yōsha. Because of their stakes in the oil and fishery businesses, the old nationalist groups had generally supported recognition of the USSR, while both the conservative bureaucracy and the new Taishō nationalist groups shared an anticommunist and antisocialist animus and were ready to use violence and terror, primarily against the working class.

However, the murders of the union organizers and anarchists in 1923 had consequences because leftists pushed back, answering violence with violence. To avenge the murders, several of Ōsugi's fellow anarchists organized the Girochinsha (Guillotine Group), which was responsible for attempting to murder Fukuda Masatarō (former martial law commander), blowing up a police station and a prison in Osaka, and setting off a bomb in a Ginza-area train. The whole group (five people in Tokyo, sixteen in Kyoto and Osaka) was captured and tried in 1925, and most of them died in prison.[44] But it was another incident that sent shockwaves through the bureaucracy. Angered by the brutal slaying of the Japanese leftists and Koreans, Nanba Daisuke, a young man whose father was a member of the House of Representatives, attempted in December 1923 to assassinate Crown Prince and Regent Hirohito (future Emperor Shōwa). The failed terrorist act, known as the Toranomon Incident, shook the political elite as an unexpected attack on the state and the monarchy, reminiscent of the High Treason Incident of 1910.[45] Nanba acted alone and was not part of any terrorist ring, but he also confessed that he acted out of his communist conviction, was inspired by Kōtoku Shūsui's alleged attempt on Emperor Meiji in 1910, and wanted to avenge Kōtoku. The direct inspiration came from the socialist Kawakami Hajime's article, "Danpen," published in the April 1921 issue of *Kaizō* magazine, in which Kawakami stressed the role of Russian terrorists in bringing about the Russian Revolution. Nanba Daisuke was promptly executed, and the conservative bureaucracy went to work pushing new anticommunist legislation.

The urgency seemed real, as the Justice Ministry reported that in Japan between 1922 and 1925 there were 291 incidents related to "social thought," which involved the impressive number of 1,815 people. All of these incidents and people, the report stressed, were related to the Comintern and its agent within Japan, the JCP.[46] Foreign Minister Shidehara, while pushing rapprochement with Russia, also agreed that some sort of radical thought-control mechanism should be in place at home.[47] Ambassador to Poland Satō Naotake, who in 1918 as consul general in Harbin had pushed Foreign Minister Motono to start the Siberian Intervention, in 1924 was trying to convince Foreign Minister Shidehara that the Soviet government was simply an alias for the Comintern, intent on aggressive communist propaganda abroad. He advised the implementation of broad measures at home: the revision of school curricula to promote stronger loyalty, patriotism, and nationalism, coupled with aggressive anticommunist propaganda in the press.[48] As the violence was escalating, not least because of direct (by the Comintern) or indirect (through literature) Russian encouragement, the government, it was widely realized, had to set legal boundaries of social and political dissent and reinforce a system of public policing.

In 1924, the Justice and Home ministries started to work on new antileftist legislation that would establish the national imperial polity as requiring protection against communism and criminalize socialist organizing.[49] The Justice and Home ministries jointly introduced a bill to the Diet in February 1925, which was passed in March and enacted in April as the Peace Preservation Law (PPL). The PPL quickly developed into an extensive system of detention, surveillance, and "thought conversion" (*tenkō*) until its repeal in 1945. Article 1 stipulated: "Anyone who has

118

formed a society with the objective of altering the national polity (*kokutai*), or denying the system of private property (*shiyū zaisan*), and anyone who has joined such a society with full knowledge of its object, shall be liable to imprisonment with or without hard labor for a term not exceeding ten years."[50]

What was most significant in the law was that the term *kokutai* was used for the first time as a statutory concept.[51] As Richard Mitchell demonstrates, since the PPL was intended primarily as a strong reaffirmation of the state's basic unity and harmony, not as criminal legislation, "they could not have devised a better term; '*kokutai*' in one word symbolized everything worth protecting." Mitchell continues, "by the inclusion of '*kokutai*' the government was telegraphing to all subjects its intention to preserve the Japanese way of life in the face of rapid change."[52] Legislators, however, had trouble defining *kokutai* because the term referred to both judicial and ethical spheres. On one hand, as in the Meiji Constitution, *kokutai* was defined in judicial terms; on the other hand, it designated something beyond law and history, some "transhistorical and transcendent ethical value that expressed the essential particularity of the Japanese nation."[53] Legislators therefore faced a peculiar conceptual conundrum, which was, in fact, raised by many who opposed the PPL and the general anticommunist and anti-Soviet trend, including Gotō Shinpei. If *kokutai* designates a transcendent ethical value peculiar to the Japanese nation, how is it possible for it to be under threat from communism? No one offered a satisfactory answer because the immediate objective of the authors of the PPL was to "demarcate the boundary between external dangerous thought and something essentially Japanese," whatever the latter meant.[54]

Moreover, as happened during the debates over the Anti-Radical Bill in 1922, the bureaucrats had trouble defining different strands of leftist thought. In the end, the committee had decided not to use the words "anarchism" and "communism" because they had trouble with defining and distinguishing them. Instead, the committee used the phrase "altering the *kokutai*," which had a broader meaning. Justice Minister Ogawa Heikichi cited the case of Nanba, who was at first an anarchist but ended up being a communist. "The communism which we most fear today is that of the so-called Russian Communist Party." This kind of communism, he noted, planned "not just to equally divide property" but also to create a government "with absolute power held by laborers and farmers." Ogawa held that it was a natural development for anarchists to turn to communism, since anarchism was inadequate.[55] In preparing reports on anarchism and socialism, Justice Ministry staff used Marxist writings (both German and Russian) and, ironically, appropriated the socialist critique of anarchism as the correct one.

The passing of the PPL was in line with the traditional suppression of leftist opposition since the Meiji period, but in reality it was grounded in the specific interwar crisis—to which, according to the state bureaucracy, the Russian Revolution greatly contributed. The enactment of the PPL coincided with the passing of a new suffrage law and the renewal of diplomatic relations with Russia. After the recognition of the USSR, it was expected that there would be an increase in the amount of radical thought entering Japan. Meanwhile, universal suffrage ensured that the election would no longer guarantee the victory of the establishment and conservative parties but would give way to oppositional or—even worse—proletarian parties. Therefore, the PPL was concerned with domestic instability, which was, as the conservative bureaucracy contended, a consequence of the infiltration of Russian communist ideas (the same line of thought as in the debates over the 1922 bill), rather than a result of the postwar economic and political crisis.

Despite the tradition of state suppression of the opposition, the road to the enactment of the PPL was not predetermined, and the law did not have universal support. It was enacted in response to intense pressure from the Privy Council and its head, Hiranuma Kiichirō. Hiranuma threatened to veto the universal manhood suffrage act in the Privy Council unless the government enacted the PPL. Hiranuma's and the Justice Ministry's position was supported by some members of the Foreign Ministry (Uchida Kōsai and the consul general in Harbin), some members of the Tokyo Metropolitan Police Office (specifically those who surveilled anarchists), and certain industries.[56] Confronted with Hiranuma's blackmail, the Diet complied in order to push through the universal suffrage bill. When the public learned about the provisions of the proposed PPL, an opposition movement developed among labor groups, scholars, the press, and some members of opposition parties to repeal this "bad law" (akuhō). Notably, among those who publicly opposed the PPL were liberal intellectuals and Diet members, Gotō Shinpei and those who supported rapprochement with Soviet Russia, and members of the police force who surveilled JCP members. The last of these groups maintained that the communist movement inside Japan was insignificant, and the PPL introduced unjustified and exceedingly harsh measures.[57] None of these opponents was persuaded that Japan faced an external ideological threat. What concerned those who opposed the PPL was whether the law was intended as a countermeasure to the enactment of universal suffrage.[58] The public outcry was largely over what effect the bill would have on public speech, academic research, and the reforms that were taking place in electoral policy, particularly in regard to the Universal Manhood Suffrage Act.

The committee responsible for drafting the law gave assurances to the Diet that the PPL was not directed against the expansion of political rights at home but rather targeted external radical threats. The committee specified that the law punished those involved in creating organizations and fomenting agitation.

Scholars and students would still be permitted to perform research and write studies dealing with anarchism, communism, and socialism and would be "free to announce the results of their research." A crime would occur only when someone put subversive ideas into action. "Thus, if you are a scholar researching communism, with no intention of putting such ideas into practice, and then announce the results of your research, there is no connection with this law."[59] In this way, the committee's insistence won support from the liberal opposition. Once the Universal Manhood Suffrage Act was enacted, liberal commentators were fairly quiet about the passage of the PPL. As noted above, they were convinced that the state ought to introduce police measures to end anarchist and communist subversive activities at home, which threatened the national community. Convinced that the state fundamentally served the best interests of the people, liberals could not imagine that the state would use the law as an instrument of violence against its own people.

I would agree with those historians who examine the passage of this far-reaching anticommunist legislation in relation to Japan's foreign policy.[60] The enactment of the PPL was directly related to the recognition of communist Russia in January 1925 and anxiety over the consequences it might bring to Japan. Discussion in the Diet prior to the enactment reveals the connection. When arguing for the passage of the law, Home Minister Wakatsuki Reijirō emphasized the danger posed by the recognition of the USSR, which would increase "opportunities for extremist activists" to enter Japan proper.[61] Justice Minister Ogawa clarified that "in our country there are people gradually appearing who are trying to put anarchism and communism into practice." He then gave an account of the development of the JCP, mentioning specific individuals and their increasing contacts with Soviet Russia. The main line of questioning in the Diet revolved around the law's effectiveness against foreign ideologies, and whether thought was something that could even be regulated; to which Ogawa replied with the same repetitive argument that "These agitators are people greatly to be feared, since we cannot give them the proper punishment for this kind of terrible crime. . . . Under present conditions, there is no law to properly punish this kind of dangerous action."[62] The foreignness of communism was emphasized in the understanding that those Japanese who were implicated in communist activities ceased to be Japanese. For example, a 1930 Tokkō (thought police) manual clarified that "Anyone against our system . . . is not only disloyal, but ceases to be Japanese."[63] When someone pointed out that Japan had assimilated many foreign thoughts, such as Confucianism and Buddhism, the proponents of the PPL in the Diet replied that anarchism and communism "are not things that can be assimilated within Japan's fundamental social structure."[64]

The anxiety over the Soviet Union's interference in Japan's domestic policies had never abated. In February 1928, Japan held its first general election after the enactment of the Universal Manhood Suffrage Act, which raised the number of eligible voters from three million to thirteen million, although women still could not vote. In the general election, half a million votes were cast for the proletarian parties. The proletarian Labor-Farmer Party gained two seats in the Diet. These results caused increased concern in government circles that the revolutionary movement might get out of hand. The real problem was that the Home Ministry suspected that the winning proletarian parties were sponsored by the Comintern. The government mouthpiece *Japan Weekly Chronicle* speculated about the existence of some communist plot to explain such success.[65] As a consequence of anti-Soviet paranoia, on March 15, 1928, the police began a nationwide roundup—1,568 leftists were arrested, and proletarian parties and labor unions were banned.[66] The Ministry of Justice released a statement to clarify the basis of the government repression:

> The Communist Party of Japan, as the Japanese branch of the revolutionary proletarian world party, the Third International, is luring our empire into the whirlpool of world revolution. It strives to change fundamentally the perfect, unblemished character of our nation and to establish a dictatorship of workers and farmers. In line with its basic policy, the Party stands with Soviet Russia and advocates complete independence for the colonies.[67]

Mass arrests of JCP members and socialists continued for another year, and general suppression and harassment was vigorous throughout the wartime period.

Tanaka Gi'ichi, prime minister and foreign minister since April 1927, together with the Home and Justice ministries, devised and introduced into the Diet a revision of the PPL, which would have made attempting to change the *kokutai* a capital offense. The Diet disapproved, but Tanaka gained the cooperation of the Privy Council, and the revised PPL was issued as Emergency Imperial Ordinance No. 129 and temporarily put into effect in June 1928, pending formal approval of the revision by the Diet in January of the following year.[68] Tanaka argued with his opponents in the Diet, citing that the Soviet danger had been confirmed by information emerging from the investigations of those recently apprehended in the 1928 arrests. As Tanaka explained, Soviet representatives were operating inside the country, trying to infiltrate Japan through the Comintern and the JCP.[69] Justice Minister Hara Yoshimichi also insisted that the foreign threat originated in Moscow, then traveled through the Comintern and arrived at its domestic source in the Japanese Communist Party.[70]

But what was most significant in the revised PPL was that crimes against the *kokutai* and "private property system" were separated into their own respective clauses, with the "alteration of the *kokutai*" infringement becoming punishable by death, while an infringement against the private property clause retained its two-year prison sentence. The only time when the "denial of the private property" clause was applied was in December 1925, with the arrests of students from Kyoto Imperial University and Doshisha University who were engaged in political activities within the Student Federation of Social Science (Gakusei shakai-kagaku kenkyūkai, or Gakuren). From that time until its repeal in 1945, almost all of the more than sixty-eight thousand arrests under the PPL were based on the *kokutai* clause.[71] In effect, the 1928 revision signaled that *kokutai* was the central objective of the PPL, demarcating the boundary between dangerous thought and that which needed to be protected. The government, liberals, and nationalists were anxious about the unity and coherence of the national community rather than the defense of the capitalist economic system.

The 1928 revision signaled that the conservative bureaucracy and the military (Tanaka Gi'ichi was, after all, a man of the army) had abandoned the defense of capitalism. Quite to the contrary, by the end of the 1920s, as the Shōwa Financial Crisis of 1927 was unfolding, Japanese leaders scorned laissez-faire economics and urged business to redouble its devotion to the state and community. The business elite found itself rejected by the Left, Radical Right, conservatives, and military. Similar to criticism from the Left, groups on the right criticized business for its preoccupation with profit, but they also pointed to the failure of business to embody the traditional values of selflessness, familism, paternalism, cooperation, and spirituality. Although business traditionally had emphasized its dedication to the common good, on one hand, during the 1920s businessmen found themselves forced to underscore more forcefully their rejection of economic individualism in favor of traditional collectivist values. On the other hand, carefully cultivated images of patriotic dedication enabled big business to blunt the demands of social critics clamoring for labor laws and unions. Welding "distinctively Japanese" norms to employer–employee relations management could stigmatize social legislation inspired by "alien" leftist ideals of workers' rights.[72] That being said, in its campaign against communism the conservative bureaucracy was able to convert big business into its collaborator in the revivification of traditional values.

As a consequence of the 1928 revision of the PPL, the responsibilities of the thought-control police and the military police greatly expanded; agents of the Tokkō police were now in major world cities, such as Beijing, Shanghai, Harbin, Berlin, London, New York, and Chicago. In expanding police activities overseas, the Home and Justice ministries received support from the Foreign Ministry, too. Thought study groups were formed in both the Home and Justice ministries in order to better understand the various genealogies of "dangerous thought"; police agents began to specialize in particular movements and the history and organization of political groups—such as anarchism, socialism, communism, Korean and Taiwanese nationalist movements, rightist movements, and labor unions. Finally, the issue of clarifying the essence of the Japanese state's sovereignty converged in the mid-1930s with the infamous "movement to clarify the *kokutai*" (*kokutai meichō undō*) and the Ministry of Education's publication in 1937 of *Kokutai no Hongi* (The fundamental principles of the kokutai).[73] In the 1930s, the PPL evolved into one of the most important tools of the state to control any dissent—from the Radical Left, liberals, and the Radical Right.

Because Russian communism was considered to be an external foreign threat, it prompted liberals and conservatives alike to reckon with what was under threat, how to define the national community and body politic, and what was the "fundamental structure of our society" that was incompatible with the principles of communism. Faced with these issues, during the 1920s anxiety on the part of the government, conservatives, and liberals shifted from preoccupation with the foreign threat to the realization that modern Japanese society lacked a viable and comprehensive understanding of what *was* the national community, how to define it, and what was required from a national/imperial subject. In the effort to respond to international communism, various programs of liberal paternalism, spiritual mobilization, and cultural regeneration were worked out—ranging from liberal nationalist to conservative to fascist, including the state's own program for reforming those who strayed. The tragedy of interwar liberalism in Japan was that in its keen efforts to distance itself from socialism and communism and in its promotion of a comprehensive national ideological framework, it inadvertently contributed to the emergence of a police state in Japan in the 1930s. Thus, originating in the anxiety over the "communist menace," the PPL policy, with the silent approval of liberal commentators, finally evolved into what is known as the *tenkō*, or "thought conversion" policy, when so-called "thought criminals" were forced to abandon their support of Western leftist and later liberal political thought systems and profess their dedication not simply to the national community but to Japan's imperial expansion and war abroad, understood as indispensable to the survival of that community.[74]

Part II

THE JAPANESE LEFT AND THE RUSSIAN REVOLUTION

ANARCHISM AGAINST BOLSHEVISM

> The sole means is the bomb.
> The means whereby the revolution
> can be funded too is the bomb.
> The means to destroy the bourgeois class
> is the bomb.
>
> —*Revolution* (Kakumei), December 1906

Japanese socialism had a long-standing tradition, harking back to the late 1890s. However, until Lenin's sudden rise to power in 1917, not orthodox Marxism but rather anarchism was considered to be the best solution to capitalism and imperialism.[1] Between 1919 and 1923, anarcho-syndicalism enjoyed great popularity among Japanese workers and students, who were attracted to the anarchist "direct action" (*chokusetsu kōdō*) strategy of industrial organization and strikes, and its rejection of all forms of political activity.[2] The main features of Taishō anarchism were insistence on the primacy of the individual over society; noncentralized, independent labor unions; and the rejection of both Marxist socialism and Russian communism's assumption of a party-based political movement. This chapter demonstrates that post–World War I anarchism (Taishō anarchism), while rooted in the substantial Japanese socialist tradition, was largely developed in conversation with Russian Bolshevism. Ultimately, the anarchists' rejection of the Russian Revolution proved to be their undoing.

Japanese interwar anarchism developed and envisioned itself as a transnational movement. From the early days, following the end of the Russo-Japanese War, Japanese anarchists imagined the struggle against capitalist imperialism in spatial terms, cultivating regional networks across East Asia by forming ties among Russian, Japanese, Korean, and Chinese radicals. This chapter focuses on how Japanese anarchists facilitated the introduction of the Russian Revolution in Japan and argues that for Japanese anarchists Asia-wide resistance to Japanese imperialism was the main appeal of Russian communism. Subsequently, Japanese communism muted this current, because it situated the revolutionary struggle in national historical temporality, thus squarely focusing on domestic issues of capitalist development.

Often missing from the conventional history of Japanese anarchism is its propensity for political violence. Taishō anarchism was born with a bang—that is, the alleged anarchist plot to assassinate Emperor Meiji in 1910, followed by the public trial and execution of twelve radicals. Japanese anarchists were conscious that Japan shared many socioeconomic features and state repression with agrarian and politically backward tsarist Russia, and thus they found inspiration in the terrorist tactics of Russian populists (*narodniki*), the first modern political terrorists in global history. Anarchists also were initially attracted to Bolshevik militant tactics, inherited from the same Russian populists. Hence, considering the strong impulse for anti-imperialist struggle and a bent toward militant tactics, we come to see that Japanese anarchists' attitude toward the Russian Revolution and Soviet Russia was not straightforwardly antagonistic, as historians have generally presumed, but rather more complex and nuanced.

Ōsugi Sakae (1885–1923) and Takao Heibē (1895–1923) were among the first Japanese radicals to go to Shanghai, the Siberian towns of Chita and Irkutsk, and Moscow to make contact with Russian Bolsheviks and Asian radicals and establish regional revolutionary networks. Significantly, it was after these trips that they declared that the end of the Japanese empire could be brought about only by the anticolonial, proletarian struggle of Asian peoples with the help of the Soviet Union. However, due to their disagreements with the JCP and the Russian communists, both men withdrew their support for the Russian and Japanese communist parties just a few years after their historic visits. Takao and Ōsugi were murdered within two months of each other in 1923—by a rightist gang and the military police, respectively. Their funerals turned into mass social gatherings attended by thousands of people who showed up to pay homage to them and express support for their ideas and principles. Their deaths, however, marked the end of the Left's original, noncommunist encounter with the Russian Revolution.

Focusing on the lives and deaths of these two chief representatives of Taishō anarchism, I show how Japanese anarchists rejected Marxism and Russian communism, and how, as a consequence of that rejection, in a matter of a few years their strategy of general strikes (anarcho-syndicalism) changed to individual terrorism, driven by despair. Ultimately, because the remaining anarchists rejected the notion of a vanguard socialist or communist party—or any centralized organization, for that matter—they were not able to unify into a coordinated movement; neither were they successful in the regional anarchist network, itself overrun by communist influence. Anarchists' quarrel with the communists made it easy for the imperial government to suppress its internal enemies and coopt many of its adherents for the sake of the national moral community.

Interest in socialism originated in the 1890s in Japan and was understood as the latest Western thought that aimed at solving social problems (*shakai mondai*) created by the Meiji state's capitalist industrialization. Unlike later leftists, many of the first generation of socialist thinkers were Christians, inspired by Christian humanitarian idealism and seeing in Christ the original communitarian. Socialism therefore was still a vague and heterogeneous concept, denoting a general perception of a collective need to treat justly all members of society and the people's right to participate in the political and economic life of the country. Troubled by the corruption and cliquism of contemporary politics and the growing impoverishment of the people, the early socialists believed that a socialist revolution (*kakumei*) to overthrow corrupt politicians and inject fresh blood into the government would be a necessary step in returning to the democratic principles of the Meiji Revolution. Their aspirations, they believed, did not contradict the *kokutai*, or the official ideology centered on the imperial family and the body politic. In fact, armed with socialist theory, they believed that they struggled against the exploitative and immoral structure of the capitalist economy that threatened the health of the *kokutai* and the national community.[3] Furthermore, because Japanese socialists' introductions to and translations of canonical Marxist and anarchist works were the first to appear in any East Asian language, Japanese socialism strongly influenced Chinese and Korean intellectuals as well. Tokyo became the hub of radical knowledge in East Asia in the first two decades of the twentieth century, drawing in students and radicals from across Asia and introducing the latest anarchist, socialist, and later Marxist theories.[4]

The Russo-Japanese War of 1904–5 led to the radicalization of the Japanese socialist movement. Kōtoku Shūsui, leader of the radical wing, began to advocate new maxims of Japanese socialism: anti-imperialism, antinationalism, antimilitarism, and anticapitalism. Simultaneously, he became attracted to the anarchist creed of Pyotr Kropotkin. However, Kōtoku's turn to anarchism happened in San Francisco, where he stayed in 1905–6 after his escape from police harassment and mingled with immigrant communities of Russian political exiles and Japanese and Chinese workers.[5] The dominant historical narrative maintains that Japanese socialism's conversion to anarchism happened because of Kōtoku's contact in San Francisco with the American organization Industrial Workers of the World. However, Kōtoku gravitated more to Russian political exiles, establishing contact through them with Pyotr Kropotkin himself, who in a 1907 letter asked him to distribute copies of his own journal *Bread and Freedom* among Russian POWs.[6] By the time of his 1904 proclamation of solidarity with the oppressed Russian people, Kōtoku had found more shared circumstances with economically backward Russia and its radicals' fight with the repressive tsarist state, as well as immigrant Asian communities, than with white American laborers. Back in Tokyo, Kōtoku became actively involved in Chinese student leftist activities, simultaneously trying to attract the students to the tenets of anarchism. He would comment that "it is most hopeful that these Chinese are not content with their slogans of People's rights and opposition to the Manchu dynasty and have made a step forward. . . . China is the Russia of the Far East. Japan has become for China what Switzerland was for Russia, namely a training-school of young revolutionaries. . . . I believe, a Nihilist party would shortly make its appearance in China."[7]

In 1906–7, under the impact of the Japanese state's increased suppression and his newly acquired anarchist beliefs, Kōtoku essentially split the Japanese socialist movement into those who followed him in adopting anarcho-syndicalist tactics, and their opponents who insisted on gradualist reform through parliamentary politics. The general features of anarcho-syndicalism were industrial strikes, centrifugal political organization, and rejection of parliamentary politics. It also accepted political violence against opponents. Kōtoku publicized in Japan the resolutions passed at the Amsterdam International Anarchist Congress (August 1907), which approved of general strikes, armed insurrections, and even terrorist actions.[8] Russian terrorist populist groups also legitimized violence in Japanese anarchists' eyes. Prohibited from advocating socialism openly, Kōtoku and other members of the movement came to believe that the only way they could succeed was to take "direct action" in the form of terrorism against the imperial house itself. Japanese anarchists, like their Russian populist counterparts, reached the same conclusion—that their heroic terrorist acts would awaken the people to radical solutions, and the elimination of the imperial system would lead to a thorough and lasting restructuring of the whole imperial society and beyond.[9]

The High Treason Incident of 1910, in which Kōtoku, as the head of a group of twenty-four defendants, was tried for having plotted to assassinate the emperor, ended the early socialist movement but also started Taishō anarchism. Kōtoku's followers—Sakai Toshihiko, Ōsugi Sakai, Takabatake Motoyuki, and Arahata Kanson—had been previously sent to prison after the Red Flag (Akahata) Incident in 1908, which saved them from being incriminated and arrested in the High Treason Incident.[10] Kōtoku's centrality to the plot has been questioned by historians, but it is undeniable that the details of the assassination, including the obtainment of nitroglycerine, were worked out by his friends. For the anarchists and the government, the assassination plan was intrinsically linked to the assassination of one of the most powerful Japanese politicians, Itō Hirobumi, in Harbin in 1909 by a Korean nationalist.[11] The imperial institution and its government found itself under assault from domestic and colonial radicals. After the annexation of Korea in 1910, the assaults by Korean insurgents (who often claimed to be followers of anarchism) intensified. While fighting its new colonial subjects in the steppes of Manchuria and northern Korea, the government at home acted swiftly to suppress domestic anarchist opposition. Branding the defenders as *hikokumin* (nonnationals or traitors), in 1911 the government executed Kōtoku and eleven others, ushering the Japanese socialist movement into its "winter years."

News of Kōtoku's execution and his idea of revolution spread well beyond socialist circles and radicalized many young people. Tokutomi Roka, a renowned novelist, made a famous speech "On Rebellion" (Muhonron) at the elite First Higher School in Tokyo in February 1911, one month after the executions, in which he said: "My friends, Kōtoku and the others have been labeled rebels and executed by the present government. But one should not be afraid of rebellion. . . . To do something new has always been called rebellion. . . . To live is to rebel. Kōtoku and the others died rebelling. They have passed away, but they have also come back to life again. And now their graves are empty."[12]

A number of people turned to anarchism in protest, such as the poet Ishikawa Takuboku (1886–1912), the feminist historian Takamure Itsue (1894–1964), and the champion of minority rights Sumii Sue (1902–1997). Because the trial was so notorious at the time, interest in Kōtoku, socialism, anarchism, and Russian populism sharply increased. In cultural and literary production, anarchist ideas relating to the rejection of hierarchy, authority, status systems, and the state proliferated. Celebrated writers such as Tanizaki Jun'ichirō, Nagai Kafū, Satō Haruo, and Akutagawa Ryūnosuke expressed these tendencies in their literary works and lives. At that time, the pan-Asianist Mitsukawa Kametarō was a journalist for the rightist newspaper *Dai Nihon* and attended all the public sessions of Kōtoku's trial. During the trial, he developed a strong disapproval for the workings of the state bureaucracy and the police and sympathized with Kōtoku's revolutionary ideals. Writing in 1917, Mitsukawa proclaimed that the execution of the socialists in 1911 induced the Japanese people to embrace Kōtoku's version of the violent revolution and consequently to support the Russian Revolution as a reaction to the authoritarian methods of the state.[13]

During the "winter years" of the Japanese socialist movement, which lasted from 1911 to 1919, very little political literature could be published, no political parties or groups could be organized, and defections were numerous. The socialist movement was almost rooted out of existence. Many members of the group were arrested or under constant police surveillance, some recanted (like Nishikawa Kōjirō), some distanced themselves from the movement or disappeared and lost contact with it, and some succumbed to mental illness as a result of government pressure.[14] Young Yamakawa Hitoshi, who would become the main theoretician of the Left after 1917, departed for his home in Okayama after his release from prison and lay low there until he returned to Tokyo in 1916. Although after the death of the Meiji emperor in 1912, many socialists were released from prison and police surveillance ceased, the authorities remained vigilant for any sign of political opposition. It is a well-known story that the very word "society" (*shakai*) was considered subversive because of its association with socialism. A book titled *The Society of Insects* was prohibited simply for having the word in its title.

However, this was also a period when literature and art—which now turned inward to examine individual feelings and anxieties—flourished, exemplified by the emergence of the literary group Shirakaba, I-novels, the Esperanto movement, and diary culture. New philosophical trends that stressed universalism, rationalism, and faith in the primacy of culture were represented by Nishida Kitarō and his school, Taishō vitalism (*Taishō seimeishugi*), educationalism (*kyōyōshugi*), the philosophy of personalism (*jinkakushugi*), and neo-Kantianism. Anarchists also moved into the sphere of thought and culture. Influenced by Nietzsche and Max Stirner, Ōsugi began to preach radical individualism in his influential journal *Kindai shisō* (1912–14), attracting the attention of students, writers, and intellectuals.[15] After the journal's cessation in 1914, Ōsugi started the newspaper *Heimin shinbun* (1914–15) as a continuation of Kōtoku's activities. In 1917, Ōsugi launched a short-lived monthly, *Bunmei hihyō*, and in February 1918 the newspaper *Rōdō shinbun*.

Meanwhile, Sakai Toshihiko organized a small publishing company, Baibunsha, which became the main source of income for many former activists. He also organized regular meetings, attended by some ten socialists, mainly to discuss developments in European socialist movements. In 1914, Sakai began to publish the monthly literary magazine *Hechima no hana*. Renamed *Shinshakai* (New society) a year later and staffed by Sakai, Arahata Kanson, Takabatake Motoyuki, and Yamakawa Hitoshi (since 1916), the magazine published pieces by Katayama Sen, who left Japan in 1914 never to return, and the anarchist Ishikawa Sanshirō, who immigrated to France in 1913. Sakai described his effort in the first issue as "the raising of a small flag on the tip of a worn-out fountain pen," expressing high doubts that any large uprising would result from the activities of his small group. He compared himself and his fellows to a "group of fugitives, loyal to a wretched but ambitious army, who had entrenched themselves in a mountain cave and devised a plan for holding out: 'We have no plans to descend the mountain in the near future to attempt a counterattack on the enemy's front, but in concert with like tribes of fugitives far and near ... we are determined to wait our opportunity patiently.'"[16]

When the February Revolution broke out in Petrograd, Japanese leftists, like the rest of the Japanese public, regarded it as a popular revolt against the corrupt, feudal tsarist government and bureaucracy. The small circle of Japanese socialists that endured the "winter years" of state suppression immersed themselves now in the study of Russian radicalism, being vaguely aware of the differences between numerous factions of the Russian Left.[17] During 1917, their publishing organ *Shinshakai* published numerous articles educating their readers about the worker-oriented Social Democrats and the pro-peasant Socialist Revolutionaries, Lenin's April Theses of 1917, the weak liberal movement in Russia, and the dual government established between workers' soviets and middle-class liberals. Over the course of 1917, Japanese socialists largely focused their attention on Russian Socialist Revolutionaries, whom they considered the heir to the populists and who were very much admired by Japanese radicals.[18] On August 31, 1917, the Bolsheviks had won an absolute majority in the Petrograd and Moscow soviets, calling for "all power to [be held by] the working class, led by its revolutionary party, the Bolshevik-Communists."[19] Only then did Japanese socialists focus on Lenin and the Bolshevik group, although Takabatake wrote as early as August that Lenin was not an anarchist, which was a commonly held view during 1917. Initially, however, the Japanese leftists did not differentiate between Bolsheviks and the soviets. In fact, the soviets, councils of workers and soldiers, attracted great attention from Japanese anarchist socialists. Not the Bolshevik Party but the numerous soviets in the capital and around Russia were considered responsible for the success of the proletarian revolution.

In late April 1917, on their way from the United States back to Russia, Nikolai Bukharin (1888–1938) and Vladimir Volodarsky (1891–1918) visited Japan.[20] Inspired by their encounter with the Russian revolutionaries, Japanese socialists organized a meeting on May 1 in Yokohama to commemorate the February Revolution. The meeting resulted in a resolution from Japanese socialists to Russian workers, written by Yamakawa Hitoshi. Katayama Sen published the resolution in his New York newspaper *Heimin*, and Sebald Rutgers, a Dutch Marxist who stayed for two months in Japan on his way from the United States to Russia in the spring of 1918, read it at the Comintern's First Congress in Moscow in March 1919. The Japanese version was published in *Shinshakai* in December 1917 and signed by "The Committee of the Tokyo Socialists." It read as follows:

> We, Japanese socialists, gathered on May 1 in Tokyo in order to express our deepest sympathy for the Russian Revolution, which we are following with great eagerness. We understand that the Russian Revolution is, on one hand, a political revolution of the bourgeoisie against the medieval autocratic system; but, on the other, it is a proletarian revolution in which workers rose up against the contemporary capitalist system. That the Russian Revolution must become a world revolution concerns not only the Russian socialists but every socialist in the world. The capitalist system is reaching its highest stage of development all around the world,

and we are already living in the age of mature capitalist imperialism. Socialists of the world, if they do not want to become prisoners of imperialist ideas, must take a firm internationalist position. All the power of the international proletariat must stand against international capitalism, our common enemy. When the proletariat starts down this road, it will accomplish its historical mission. Russian socialists have made their utmost effort to end the war. And now they have to convince the proletariat class of the enemy country to do the same, to point its weapons, which brothers in trenches now point at each other, at the ruling class of its own countries. We, socialists all around the world, together with the Russian socialists, trust in the bravery of our comrades.[21]

In addition to the resolution, Japanese socialists also sent a letter through Sebald Rutgers, addressed "To the Russian Comrades." Significantly, the letter, dated July 19, 1918, squarely focused on Japan's imperialist activities and expressed the socialists' regret that they could not stop the Japanese government from sending troops to Siberia, due to the strong suppression of the radical movement in Japan.[22]

The socialists also suddenly found themselves in the public limelight: youth, often from elite circles, grew increasingly interested in their ideas; the police intensified surveillance of their work; and newspapers sought to print articles on socialism and Russian radicalism. The postwar economic depression, the increased number of labor disputes and strikes, and the Rice Riots contributed to a growing preoccupation with politics among the general public, especially students. Inflation and political scandals created a new image of the rich as swindlers, politics as essentially rotten, and the whole system as unfair.[23] In 1919, Yamakawa Hitoshi and Sakai Toshihiko published *Shakaishugi kenkyū*; Hasegawa Nyozekan and Ōyama Ikuo started *Warera*; the Tokyo University-based Shinjinkai initiated their publication *Demokurashī*; Takabatake Motoyuki published *Kokka Shakaishugi*; and Ōsugi Sakae started the newspaper *Rōdō undō*, to name only a few of the most famous leftist publications. Leftist magazines such as *Kaizō* and *Kaihō*, along with the established and widely respected *Taiyō* and *Chūō kōron*, shaped and promoted interest in socialist ideas by publishing articles about social and labor problems and studies of socialism and Marxism. After dedicating a number of its issues to labor disputes from September 1919 onward, the progressive but bankrupt journal *Kaizō* improved its finances and subscription rate immensely.[24] Translations of Marxist classics and studies of Marxism also began to be published on a mass scale.[25] Red Cover Library, a series of books dedicated to socialist thought, was widely popular. So great was the interest in Marxism that in 1920, the Daitōkaku publishing company began to publish the *Collected Works of Marx and Engels*, while Takabatake Motoyuki was commissioned to translate Marx's *Das Kapital* into Japanese.

The labor movement showed a parallel surge in membership and activities. Between July and October 1919 alone, there were over three hundred strikes, more than the total of the preceding several years. In 1919 there were seventy-one labor unions, a huge number in comparison to only five in 1914. The first and largest nationwide labor union, Yūaikai (the Friendly Society), formed in 1912 to reconcile labor and capital, took on an increasingly radical tone as its younger leaders replaced the old moderates.[26] As the number of labor strikes began to grow rapidly in 1919, the workers' impact on politics and society became the center of attention for both the public and the increasingly radicalized students, some of whom even moved into the working-class slums in the Tsukishima area of Tokyo. By and large, questions of social change and social class divisions in Japanese society were brought to the forefront, and growing concern with class relations stimulated interest in socialism as a means of resolving social problems. Specifically, interest in syndicalism surged because it appealed mostly to the growing and volatile urban working class and prescribed immediate plans of action to improve workers' lot.

In 1917, there was worldwide confusion among leftists over the nature of the Russian Revolution. The October Revolution, which was interpreted as the first genuine social revolution in history carried out by workers, appeared to many Japanese socialists as an anarchist revolution. In his articles, Sakai Toshihiko consistently referred to Lenin as an anarchist and pacifist.[27] Moreover, the figureheads of global anarchism—Emma Goldman, Alexander Berkman, and Pyotr Kropotkin—whose writings were widely translated and published in Japan, believed that the revolution had the potential to develop into an anarchist social revolution. One of the most famous Taishō anarchists, Ōsugi Sakae, recollected: "The Russian Revolution was the first socialist revolution that overthrew the capitalist system. Because of this revolution, workers of the world were emboldened and strongly influenced in their thoughts and actions. . . . I myself was one among those who was deeply excited and influenced by the Russian Revolution."[28] Ōsugi mentioned the revolution for the first time in April 1918, at the Meeting to Commemorate the Russian Revolution (Roshia Kakumei Kinenkai), attended by about forty radicals of all persuasions. He praised the revolution, claimed that Bolshevik tactics were essentially the same as those of anarchists, and welcomed the dictatorship and tough policies of the Bolsheviks as necessary to success. When Takabatake Motoyuki asked him whether the dictatorship was not against the anarchist creed, Ōsugi replied that "among early anarchists there were those who insisted on dictatorship, too."[29] Ōsugi was not immune to the elitist view shared by both Marxists and syndicalists that the unenlightened masses needed strong leadership to guide their thoughts and actions. He believed that the Bolshevik dictatorship eventually would give birth to "freedom." Moreover, according to Yamakawa's memoirs, during Ōsugi's visit to Yamakawa's house in the summer of 1919, Ōsugi commented that "the soviets' regional autonomy is good. But, when [the soviets] created the central government, they killed the revolution." He qualified this statement, however, by speculating that "if we had been in Russia at that time, if we had been in their shoes, we would probably have done the same thing."[30]

In October 1919, Ōsugi and his followers, with the help of Sakai Toshihiko and Yamakawa Hitoshi, established the Organization of the Workers' Movement (Rōdō undōsha), and a newspaper, *Rōdō shinbun*. To raise funds for his organization, Ōsugi toured western Japan during the Rice Riots. Historians have argued that the Tokyo socialists largely ignored the peasant riots as inconsequential to the industrial proletariat's revolutionary struggle, but this is not entirely accurate.[31] Ōsugi, for one, considered the riots a manifestation of general revolutionary fervor in Japan: "The second Russian Revolution made an enormously deep impression on the masses. The dispatches that appeared in the daily newspapers were read avidly and with great interest. However, the capitalists and the government were confident that revolution was a foreign, not Japanese, thing. Then suddenly, but occurring naturally, there erupted the Rice Riots of the summer of '18 two years ago."[32] Moreover, the feminist anarchist Itō Noe, Ōsugi's partner and comrade, also placed high hopes on the rural areas, idealizing village communities and considering them to be a model of broader social organization.[33] Nevertheless, before Ōsugi made contact with Russian revolutionaries, he shared the opinion of other Japanese socialists that a socialist revolution would happen in Japan only after the rest of the advanced capitalist world accomplished its revolutions, rather than with a peasant uprising at home.

Meanwhile, Ōsugi and his fellow socialists and anarchists engaged in a flurry of organizational activities. In 1919, Ōsugi was among the organizers of a syndicalist study group, Hokufūkai (North Wind Society), which attracted many students and workers, including twenty-four-year-old Takao Heibē. In 1920, the syndicalist movement saw a significant influx of activists, students, and labor unions, who had become disillusioned with the universal suffrage movement after it was halted by Prime Minister Hara Takashi and with the liberal-democratic movement in general, and who now placed their hopes on expanding the union movement. The biggest labor union, Yūaikai, was renamed the Sōdōmei (Japan Federation of Labor) in 1921, which took a more radical, anarcho-syndicalist position. In December 1920, Yamakawa, Sakai, Ōsugi, Takabatake, and others organized the Shakaishugi Dōmei (Socialist League), which was ordered to disband, by which time membership had grown from 1,033 to 6,000–7,000 members.[34] In June 1921, the seventh issue of their magazine, *Shakaishugi,* published the Comintern Declaration, which was sent to Japan from Moscow by Katayama Sen, but the issue was banned.[35] The Shakaishugi Dōmei's membership was eclectic, ranging from anarchists to Marxists and unionists. Many Chinese and Korean residents of Japan also joined the league, including Li Dazhao, one of the founders of the Chinese Communist Party—a diversity that reflected the internationalist mood of the time.[36] There was no adopted program or unity in the objectives of the league, but the overall goal was to unite the socialist and labor union movements. The ban on the league, a legal socialist organization, later in 1921 was devastating and convinced many of its younger members that only illegal activity was possible, pushing them to work toward the creation of an illegal communist party.

Many Korean and Chinese anarchists found refuge in Tokyo, which was in the early 1920s safer than Seoul and Shanghai. In November 1921, under the sponsorship of the anarchists Ōsugi Sakae and Iwasa Sakutarō (1879–1967), and socialists Sakai Toshihiko and Takatsu Seidō (1893–1974), the Korean anarchist group Kokutōkai (The Black Wave Society) was established in Tokyo. Its editor in chief was the Korean anarchist Bak Yeol (1902–1974), who was arrested with his Japanese partner Kaneko Fumiko (1903–1926) in the wake of the 1923 Kantō earthquake for their alleged plot to assassinate the Japanese emperor. In the first issue of its publication, the group issued a statement claiming that their goal was to fight Japanese and Korean nationalism and strive for a social revolution both in Korea and Japan, which they believed would result in the creation of a united world (*sekai yūgō*) beyond national borders.[37] Eventually, in many instances programs of international solidarity and mutual aid offered by Korean anarchists proved to be more radical and progressive than those of Japanese anarchists.

The real test of Japan's anarchist internationalism arrived from abroad. Port cities—Tokyo, Shanghai, Pusan, Shimonoseki, Kobe, Yokohama, Vladivostok, and even San Francisco—not only became the end points of extremely politicized travel routes but emerged as the centers of Asia-wide radical networks, from which people, texts, and ideas traveled inland. During 1919, the Far Eastern branch of the Comintern in Vladivostok sent Chinese and Korean radicals to initiate contact with Japanese socialists on behalf of the Comintern. They approached Yamakawa and Sakai first, and invited them to Moscow for the Second Comintern Congress, held in July–August 1920. But Sakai and Yamakawa, not trusting these messengers or the Comintern itself, and concerned that they might be charged with treason, declined the offer.[38] They were long blamed for this reluctance and labeled as cowards by Japanese Marxist historians. Yamakawa wrote in his autobiography: "In 1920, we heard that there was a Comintern person in East Asia, but we did not know who this person was, what his status was. That person was trying hard to make contact with us, it seems. But we were not familiar with the official institution of the Comintern in Shanghai; we could not just go there without an official invitation."[39] Yamakawa advised the Korean envoy, who came in August 1920, to approach Ōsugi, as he was sufficiently "reckless" to go to China and meet the Russians.

Ōsugi accepted the offer and went to Shanghai in October 1920.[40] He wanted to meet the Russian revolutionaries but was also attracted to the idea of meeting with Korean radicals in Shanghai. In April 1919, a Korean provisional government was established in Shanghai, which drew together Korean nationalists and communists. The elected prime minister at the time was Yi Tong-hwi (1873–1935), who in 1911 had immigrated to Vladivostok after the annexation of Korea and in 1918 had become one of the founders of the Korean People's Socialist Party in Khabarovsk. At the Conference of East Asian Socialists in Shanghai, Ōsugi befriended Yi Tong-hwi and was impressed by his ideas about military resistance to the Japanese empire. (Dissatisfied with the provisional government's lack of action, Yi Tong-hwi returned to Manchuria after the conference to resume his armed guerrilla struggle against the Japanese interventionist forces.) Ōsugi also met with Yo Un-hyung (1885–1947), the cofounder of the provisional government, who in 1945 became one of the founders of the Korean People's Republic; Chen Duxiu (1879–1942), who in 1921 cofounded the Chinese Communist Party and served as its first general secretary until 1927; and the Comintern agent Grigory Voitinsky.

According to Ōsugi's account of the trip in *Nihon dasshutsu ki* (Account of an escape from Japan, 1923; in English, *My Escapes from Japan*, 2014), Chinese and Korean radicals in Shanghai were not communists and were at times annoyed by Voitinsky's intrusive directives. In fact, by 1920 Asian radicals had already developed an alternative to the Comintern plan—namely the creation of an Asia-wide "League of Far Eastern Communist Party"—which Ōsugi enthusiastically supported. They also agreed with Ōsugi's view that the socialist movements in Asian countries were each unique and ought to be independent of the Comintern. In 1920, however, Ōsugi's insistence on independence was probably less staunch than it was in 1923, when *Nihon dasshutsu ki* was published, because he accepted the hefty sum of 2,000 yen from Voitinsky and promised to work in close cooperation with the Comintern. On returning home, he revived his journal *Rōdō undō* (January–June 1921), which published both anarchist and communist articles and included most notably the communist Kondō Eizō, which suggests Ōsugi's commitment to communism and the Comintern's program.[41]

Ōsugi's first article after his return from Shanghai, the famous "Nihon no unmei" (Japan's destiny, January 1921), reflected his changed position after making contact with Asian and Russian communists. Most significantly, Ōsugi began to place the utmost importance on the activities of the Asian communist movement and the Comintern. The Asian and Russian revolutionaries, he argued, would instigate the struggle against the Japanese empire in the colonies, which would in turn shake to the core the political and social system in the metropole. Japanese imperialist actions in East Asia would disrupt Japanese society itself and bring all its contradictions out into the open in the most extreme way. Ōsugi thus sided with Lenin's prediction that "imperialism is the eve of the proletarian social revolution," and believed that a socialist revolution would come to Japan within a year, as a result of the new anti-imperialist revolutionary struggle in Asia. He pointed out that foreign intervention in Russia had failed, that Soviet Russia was regaining its power in East Asia, and that Japan was helpless to curb the Bolshevization of the Siberian, Mongolian, Chinese, and Korean radicals. In the near future, he warned, Japan would face a joint enemy in Russia, Korea, and China, which it would not be able to withstand. What would follow, Ōsugi continued, would be a civil war, similar to the ongoing Russian civil war. A "revolutionary war between old Japan and new Japan" would result in the emergence of a completely new Japan, and he urged Japanese radicals to be "prepared when a conflict erupts" to seize control of the country.[42] In his view, an upcoming revolutionary upheaval would be the result of a war and not depend on the level of development of labor or the socialist movement within Japan, the position he had held before his trip to Shanghai.

In the same year, he proclaimed: "Kropotkin is not my ideal. I passed this stage already. And I am not an anarchist; it is too limited." As the historian Asukai Masamichi pointed out, it would be incorrect at this point to label Ōsugi and his fellows as anarchists in a strict sense.[43] In his memoirs, the communist Kondō Eizō wrote that Ōsugi honestly wanted a united front with communists and envisioned a communist revolution in Japan in which he would play a central role. When a Korean envoy visited Japan in April 1921, Ōsugi sent Kondō to Shanghai to renew contacts with the Comintern and obtain the rest of the funds promised by Voitinsky to Ōsugi during his trip to Shanghai in October 1920. However, according to Beckmann and Stanley, Ōsugi increasingly began to suspect that the Japanese communists did not want the anarchists to be in contact with the Comintern and tried secretly to cut ties between him and the people in Shanghai.[44] The matter, of course, involved money: who would control the flow of the Comintern cash from Shanghai to Japan. According to Kondō, however, Yamakawa and his followers always wanted to have Ōsugi as a member of the JCP and kept urging him to join. In the end, as a result of a clash of personalities and quarrel over funds, from late 1921 Ōsugi distanced himself from the communist movement.

Beginning in this period, Ōsugi's support of Russian Bolshevism began to wane. All fifteen issues of *Rōdō undō* that appeared between December 1921 and July 1923 published articles critical of Russian Bolshevism. The Bolshevik government's repression of its own anarchists, of the Socialist Revolutionary Party, and of the Kronstadt Rebellion of March 1921 had a large impact on some Japanese radicals who, like Ōsugi, started to criticize the Russian Communist Party.[45] Moreover, Ōsugi's writings circulated via radical underground newspapers across Asia and influenced the Chinese anarchists' critique of Russian Bolshevism as well. Ōsugi translated into Japanese anti-Bolshevik reports by Emma Goldman, Alexander Berkman, and Pyotr Kropotkin, whose disillusionment with the Soviet Union played a significant part in the increasing critique of Bolshevism by anarchists worldwide. Echoing Emma Goldman's words, Ōsugi maintained that the Bolsheviks betrayed their own revolution by implementing the New Economic Policy (NEP), which permitted private trade and property.[46] So great was Ōsugi's disappointment that he began to claim that Russian workers had in fact little to do with the October Revolution and its success. The Russian Revolution was not a bottom-up social revolution, he argued, but instead a political coup through which a small group of people usurped power. Ōsugi wrote: "The October Revolution, which overthrew the democratic government of Kerensky, taught us how revolution must be done. However, the development of the Bolshevik revolution after October taught us how revolution must not be done."[47] Ōsugi's critique of Soviet Russia went so far that he began to support the Siberian Intervention by the Japanese interventionist forces in the hope that it would crush the Bolshevik regime. Later, he actively opposed the recognition of the USSR by Japan, a position he shared with nationalist right-wing groups.[48]

Ōsugi's critique of Russian Bolshevism launched what is known as the ana-boru debate (*ana-boru ronsō*).[49] The first public debate provoked by the Russian Revolution among Japanese socialists, the ana-boru debate spelled out new goals and strategies for the socialist movement.[50] It was during this debate, which lasted roughly from 1921 to 1924, that Japanese socialists began to identify themselves as anarchists or Bolsheviks based chiefly on differences of opinion concerning organization and tactics.[51] The formal separation between anarchists and Bolsheviks took place in September 1922 at a conference in Osaka, the goal of which was to establish a national labor union. Opinions split over the union's organization: anarchists insisted on a free alliance of small, local, self-governed unions having an absolute right to join or withdraw from the national union at any time, while Bolsheviks wanted a more disciplined centralized body in which a central committee would coordinate nationwide activities. The participants in the conference regarded the conflict as a power struggle between different factions—the labels "anarchist" and "Bolshevik" meant very little to them. At the close of the debate, radicals who were unwilling to condone centralized authority of any sort or a regulated organizational discipline withdrew and sabotaged the attempt to create a new national labor union.

However, the conflict at the Osaka conference, which ended in a physical brawl that required police intervention, exposed far more fundamental problems. The debate touched on a variety of important questions. Should the radical movement struggle to transform and liberate the individual first, or should its primary aim be to end class exploitation? This led radicals to the question of how revolutionary change ought to take place: through long-term social changes based on individual transformations or rapid political change enacted by a group of conscious revolutionaries? Socialism from below or socialism from above? Another variation on this problem was the question of whether the model of the Russian Revolution—that is, a highly centralized proletarian movement under the control of the vanguard party—was applicable to the Japanese case.

What especially alarmed Ōsugi was Lenin's vision of the relationship between socialist intellectuals and workers. Ōsugi and Yamakawa were well aware of their differences from the working class in terms of upbringing, education, and vocation yet refused to present themselves as "intellectuals," which they both regarded as a problematic category within the revolutionary program. Yamakawa was content with this difference, because he believed (as did Karl Kautsky) that labor and socialist movements, although separate, flow in the same direction and eventually merge.[52] It was Lenin, however, who most persuasively resolved the problem of working-class dependence on intellectuals. Unlike Kautsky, Lenin emphasized the necessary difference between the working class and intellectuals as a precondition for the former to realize socialist goals for itself:

> There could not yet be Social-Democratic consciousness among the workers. This consciousness could only be brought to them from without. The history of all countries shows that the working class, exclusively by its own effort, is able to develop only trade union consciousness. . . . The theory of socialism, however, grew out of philosophic, historical and economic theories elaborated by educated representatives of the propertied classes, by intellectuals. According to their social status, the founders of modern scientific socialism, Marx and Engels, themselves belonged to the bourgeois intelligentsia.[53]

By proposing that someone needs to occupy a position of leadership and arguing that the working class is unable to fill this role from within its own ranks, Lenin established the dominant position for the socialist intelligentsia, whose task was "to divert the labor movement from its spontaneous, trade unionist striving to go under the wing of the bourgeoisie, and to bring it under the wing of revolutionary Social-Democracy."[54]

Ōsugi, however, rejected the idea of a difference between socialist (bourgeois intelligentsia) and labor movements. Ōsugi criticized Lenin's idea of the socialist intellectual and firmly rejected Lenin's framework of socialist intellectuals leading the working masses. For Ōsugi, the dictatorship of the proletariat was, in reality, a dictatorship of communist party intellectuals.[55] Preoccupied with theoretical questions and concerned with holding on to power, these intellectuals distorted and harmed workers' movements. Ōsugi could not imagine the enforcement of uniform rules and discipline on a national level; his rejection of the difference between socialist (intellectual) and labor movements led him ultimately to abandon the Leninist notion of the dominant authority of one party. To prove his point, Ōsugi even moved into a workers' slum and started to dress and talk like a worker and to attack Yamakawa for his intellectualism and self-imposed distance from the revolutionary class. He criticized any self-proclaimed champions of the masses, whether liberal democrats, moderate unionist leaders, or Marxists.[56] The irony, of course, was that the workers did not accept Ōsugi as one of them (they saw him as an odd figure, an outsider in the slum surroundings); nor did those in other anarchist workers groups, such as Takao Heibē, because they thought him too preoccupied with debates and writings instead of action.

This problem lies at the core of the ana-boru debate. Should workers gradually and on their own grow into class and revolutionary consciousness, or should they be subjected to the supervision and leadership of the vanguard? Ōsugi insisted that a genuine social revolution starts with a transformation of consciousness, which would prevent the need for coercion when a revolution finally comes about. He insisted that the workers could not be forced into a more advanced state of political consciousness: this would need to be a process that developed gradually. Ōsugi maintained: "Within the old society, within the old state, a new society, a new state will be born naturally. The reconstruction of society and the reconstruction of the state will happen naturally."[57] The goal was not to create a new ruling class (for Ōsugi, exemplified by the new Bolshevik elite in Soviet Russia) but to abolish classes altogether, which would also eliminate the need for the state and politics. The dictatorship of one party would only reproduce the evils of the old society. The liberation of workers, he believed, begins with developing individuality (*jinkaku*), which becomes the guarantor of personal freedom from the state and capitalist system.[58]

Both anarchists and "Bolsheviks" focused on labor unions as the primary area for their work. Speaking for the "Bolsheviks," Yamakawa Hitoshi urged socialist intellectuals to merge with the unions—precisely because it was the centralized labor union movement, not the communist party, he insisted, that was the key to revolutionary change. The success of the revolution depended on the centralization and unification of labor unions into one national union governed by a central committee. This was why the debate with Ōsugi over the organization of nationwide labor unions became so important to Yamakawa, who considered the ana-boru debate decisive for the whole Japanese socialist movement.[59] Yamakawa thus attempted to merge the socialist and labor movements into one entity, under which labor unions would assume a political character and begin to function as a party. Socialist intellectuals would become labor activists, while labor unions would assume the character of the legal "vanguard party."[60] Japanese historians contend that cooperation between anarchists and Bolsheviks ended at the end of the Osaka conference, in September 1922.[61] However, on the level of political activities, there was more cooperation than division. Not only Ōsugi and Yamakawa were convinced that cooperation between the communists and anarchists was necessary for the Japanese revolution, but both also agreed that labor unions, not a vanguard party, must be their priority.

On the theoretical level, in contrast, anarchists and communists split widely. Ōsugi envisioned nonstate- and nonparty-centered concepts and practices, which would allow regional formation and adaptation. The main attraction of the Russian Revolution for him was its transnational, internationalist, and anti-imperialist perspective. The Comintern and Japanese Bolsheviks' insistence on the creation of a national communist labor union or party with centralized leadership betrayed his ideal, which prompted him ultimately to reject not simply cooperation with the JCP, but communism and Marxism all together. This was an unfortunate development for East Asian leftist radicalism, also keenly realized by the Comintern. Unconstrained by any Marxist doctrinal matters, anarchists were the most adept at launching Asia-wide anti-imperialist socialist activities. Unlike Japanese communists, anarchists managed for a while to remain aloof from national-chauvinist culturalism and embrace as equals Korean and Chinese radicals with different agendas.

Revolutionary violence was as much a feature of Japanese radicalism as it was elsewhere. Modern revolutionary terrorism was inaugurated in tsarist Russia, beginning in April 1866 with the first unsuccessful attempt on the life of Tsar Alexander II, through July 1918, when Lenin and his associates ordered the assassination of Tsar Nicholas II.[62] Compared to Russia, in Japan leftist political violence developed much later and was less frequent. In both cases, however, leftist militancy was a reaction to the state's denial of certain political rights: the demand for a constitution and the liberation of serfs in tsarist Russia, and for universal suffrage and rights for the working class in imperial Japan. Japanese leftists took note of Russian revolutionary terrorism as the more effective "propaganda of the deed." In this instance, Kemuyama Sentarō's *Kinsei musei-fushugi* (Modern anarchism, 1902), which introduced Russian political terrorism to Japan, was hugely influential among leftists. How influential the Russian path became is shown in the further radicalization of Japanese socialist émigrés in the United States. A Japanese anarchist group in Berkeley, California, published *Revolution* between late 1906 and early 1907, a magazine that openly advocated terrorism. "Our policy is toward the overthrow of Mikado, King," the first issue stated, "The sole means is the bomb. The means whereby the revolution can be funded too is the bomb. The means to destroy the bourgeois class is the bomb."[63] In November 7, 1907, on the birthday of Emperor Meiji, a leaflet was distributed in California titled *Terrorism* (Ansatsushugi), most probably composed by the Japanese anarchist émigré Iwasa Sakutarō (who on his arrival to Tokyo in 1919 joined Ōsugi's Rōdōsha group). The 1907 pamphlet asserted that it was necessary for socialists to progress from propaganda to assassination. It pointed to the terrorist attacks which had been made on state officials in Russia and France and vowed that Japanese terrorists would base themselves on the rich experience of those countries.[64]

The post–World War I period saw the upsurge of anarchist and labor union militancy, attracting more and more people—petty workers, students, and even yakuza. One of these new anarchists was a young worker from Nagasaki, Takao Heibē (1895–1923). His peak activities lasted a mere four or five years, but his case amply represents the attraction Bolshevik tactics had for Japanese anarchists. His name became nationally known after his murder in June 1923 by the leader of a nationalist gang, which almost coincided with the murder of Ōsugi by military police some three months later. For socialists, these murders exemplified the authoritarian nature of the imperial state and the advent of popular fascism in Japan, backed by the conservative government. But Takao's short life was no less significant, as he was one of dozens of Japanese leftists who carried out subversive activities in Siberia and one of the very few who met Vladimir Lenin himself. He exemplified the current within Japanese anarchism that was strongly attracted to Bolshevism—its success, tactics, resoluteness, and militancy. This current continued in the cooperation between the anarchist Zenkoku Rōdō Kumiai Jiyū Rengōkai, or Zenkoku Jiren (All-Japan Libertarian Federation of Labor Unions, established in 1926) and the Profintern (Red Trade Union International), a branch of the Comintern, in 1926–27. Nevertheless, for Takao, as well as for many other young men, communism and its party, with its perspective on the future and strong stress on centralized and coordinated organization, remained fundamentally alien. At the same time, the JCP was not able to accommodate and restrain these hot-headed militant activists, many of whom left its ranks to embark on independent activities. Situated here and now, rather than in the coming communist "tomorrow," Takao resorted to independent actions with his small anarchist band. This tendency for noncentralized—and ultimately uncoordinated and chaotic—activities of disparate anarchist groups eventually proved to be one of the reasons for the demise of the whole anarchist movement in interwar Japan.

From early 1918 on, anarchist ideas grew in popularity among workers, especially in the Kansai area centered around Osaka. Anarchist periodicals such as *Rōdō undō, Jiyū rengō, Kōsakunin,* and *Kokushoku seinen* appeared one after another and contributed to the spread of anarchist ideas. That is how the restless Takao heard about Ōsugi Sakae and anarchist activities in Tokyo while doing certain small jobs in Osaka. In 1918, he finally decided to move to Tokyo to take part in Ōsugi's activities. He joined the Hokufūkai, which was established by Sakai, Wada Kyūtarō, and others and was the main socialist gathering of the day, with a strong anarchist agenda. Sakai Toshihiko and Yamakawa Hitoshi also frequented the gatherings for a short time before they moved on to work on establishing a communist party in Japan. Even among rowdy members of the anarchist group, Takao stood out for his deliberately uninhibited and radical stance. At one meeting, for example, Takao attacked a student from the prestigious Waseda University, saying that he studied the science of bourgeois exploitation and therefore could not understand the plight of the workers. At another meeting, he called for a discussion about not when a revolution would occur, but when and how they ought to make it happen.[65] He adopted this arrogant attitude to quell the concerns of other members that he was a police spy. It was common police practice to infiltrate leftist organizations with agents provocateurs or to buy off existing members, which was not that difficult because the socialist and labor movements attracted a great many drifters, people without any particular profession, and adventurers.

The quarrels that Takao initiated were not isolated incidents but denoted a larger problem in the growing misunderstanding between new working-class members of anarchist circles and veteran socialist anarchists (who had a solid theoretical and literary background), together with elite university students who were attracted to new socialist and anarchist theories. Quite soon, Takao would turn against his teacher Ōsugi. In March 1921, Takao organized the Rōdōsha group (not to be mistaken for the Rōdōsha group organized by Ōsugi), which actively participated in the resurgent Ashio mine strikes that since 1907 had been a battleground between government and big business, on one hand, and mine workers and their socialist supporters, on the other.[66] Takao called Ōsugi and his followers to join his battles on the ground instead of meeting in coffee shops and town halls. In a personal attack, in the first issue (April 1921) of the group's newspaper *Rōdōsha,* Takao chastised Ōsugi for his habitual drinking and gambling and notorious love affairs—which, Takao argued, diverted Ōsugi's attention from important revolutionary matters.[67] Takao also criticized Ōsugi for taking what he saw as an intellectual approach to the workers' question. Instead of writing articles, Takao insisted, Ōsugi ought to take the fight to the streets. Of course, it was ironic that Takao charged Ōsugi with intellectualism at the same time that Ōsugi criticized the Russian communists for their elitist approach.[68]

Takao's first run-in with the police and experience with right-wing agitation came about during his involvement in the famous Morito Incident in 1921. A junior economics professor at Tokyo Imperial University, Morito Tatsuo, published an article on "Kropotkin's Anarchist Communism as a Social Ideal" (Kuropotokin no shakai shisō no kenkyū, January 1920), analyzing Kropotkin's critique of both the monarchy as an institution and parliamentary government. Morito praised Kropotkin's vision of an anarcho-communist society but rejected illegal means to achieve it. Articles on Kropotkin and other socialist thinkers had routinely appeared in numerous publications before and after Morito's article. In March and May 1920, the magazine Kaizō published twelve articles on Kropotkin, and none of these issues was banned. The publication of Morito's article was inflated into a major incident through the agitation of the Brotherhood for National Support (Kōkoku Dōshikai), a group of right-wing students organized by the conservative professor Uesugi Shinkichi. The brotherhood and Uesugi were successful in blowing the incident out of proportion, attracting nationwide attention. The Morito Incident became one of the first episodes in the growing confrontation between the emerging, and increasingly militant, left-wing and right-wing groups.

The Justice and Home ministries seized on the Morito scandal to mount a show trial condemning foreign ideologies that might "sow misgivings among the general public regarding the sovereignty of our state or promote a tendency to hold the property rights of the individual in contempt."[69] The courts sentenced Professor Morito to three months in prison for disturbing public order under the Newspaper Law (passed in 1909), and he simultaneously lost his teaching post.[70] The Morito Incident was significant because it was the first state crackdown on oppositional thought, even though there was no evidence of riots, strikes, or other crimes being perpetrated under the article's influence. The incident was symptomatic of the growing concern over domestic instability and the undermining of national morals by the infiltration of foreign modes of thought. In a way, the conservative bureaucracy and pundits were correct in holding that foreign ideologies did "sow misgivings"; because angered by the reactionary bureaucracy, Takao challenged them with his individual actions. Acting on his own, Takao printed Morito's article together with Kropotkin's Law and Authority and distributed them on the streets of Tokyo, for which he was arrested and served a five-month prison sentence. During one of the court hearings, Takao famously took off his clothes and remained naked in protest, an incident that earned him fame in certain circles.[71]

Very soon after his release, Takao was drawn into the international revolution-ary activities emanating from the Comintern. As a counterresponse to the Wash-ington Naval Conference (1921–22), to which Soviet Russia was not invited, the Comintern organized its own Congress of Far Eastern People. The Comintern's executive committee declared that it would convene at Irkutsk a "simultaneous conference of representatives of Eastern Revolutionary movements and thus indicate the strength of eastern opposition to imperialist plans in the East."[72] Apparently, the response of the toilers of the east was so great that the site of the congress was moved to Moscow and Petrograd, where the conference was held in January–February 1922. Japan occupied a central role in the Comintern's policy in East Asia. The Comintern agent Grigory Voitinsky sent his envoy—a young Chinese professor and one of the founders of the Chinese Communist Party, Zhang Tailei (1898–1927)—to Japan to persuade the various left-wing groups to send delegates to the congress. All seven Japanese representatives, including three anarchist members of the printing workers' union, were more or less sup-porters of anarcho-syndicalist tactics—that is, labor strikes and labor education as the main forms of political activity. In Moscow, they were joined by five Japa-nese radicals from the United States. During the several days of the congress, Soviet leaders (such as the head of the Comintern Grigory Zinoviev, Georgy Safa-rov, Nikolai Bukharin, and Bela Kun) tried to persuade the Japanese delegation to abandon the "infantile sickness of anarcho-syndicalism" and join forces in establishing a communist party in Japan. They did persuade some, as one of the Japanese delegates remained in Moscow as a student of the Communist Univer-sity of Toilers of the East to study Marxism-Leninism, and several of those who returned declared themselves to be followers of communism.

Takao Heibē was among the original seven representatives who departed Japan in the winter of 1921. However, Takao did not reach Moscow because in Shanghai he met with Voitinsky, who persuaded him to return to Japan with Comintern funds for organizational expenses. These funds were first used to sway public opinion to the Soviet side by organizing a pro-Soviet movement in Japan.[73] The Comintern reckoned that broad public movements were a good opportunity for spreading Bolshevik ideas and gaining emotional sympathy for Russia. Takao and his eighteen anarchist friends initiated drives to aid hunger relief in Russia, which became part of a worldwide campaign. In response to a widespread and severe famine in war-torn Soviet Russia, the Comintern founded the Interna-tional Workers' Aid Society, which proved to be quite successful at drawing sym-pathy and support from many noncommunist intellectuals and workers. Takao also brought radicals together to participate in the movement to repeal the "three evil Laws" (the Extreme Socialists Control Law, Labor Unions Law, and Concilia-tion of Tenant Farmers Dispute Law). Takao Heibē's group also cooperated with the labor union Sōdōmei, the international socialist Cosmo club (Cosmopolitan Club), and some Korean socialist and anarchist organizations.

Takao was able to unite socialist activists around himself, and they proved to be particularly useful in transregional leftist undertakings. In March 1922, at the urging of the Comintern, Takao and other members of his Rōdōsha group entered Siberia with the aim of establishing a printing press to produce propaganda leaflets for the Japanese army stationed there. Takao brought with him workers from the Japan Printers' Union, who established a printing press in Chita and for the next six months produced propaganda leaflets for soldiers stationed in Vladivostok, as well as pamphlets for distribution in Japan. The printing press was obtained by the wife of another of Takao's fellow travelers, Yoshihara Tarō, a Japanese radical émigré from the United States. Yoshihara's wife was a geisha in Manchuria. She purchased and brought the printing press to Manchuli, where Takao picked it up.[74]

Yoshihara was a curious figure. He had been trusted as an operative, extensively traveling between Russia and Japan on the Comintern's instructions and funds. During 1922, he was sent by Profintern to organize unions but mysteriously lost the diamonds he had received on his way, and thus he arrived without organizational funds. In December 1922, he accompanied the anarchist Arahata Kanson to Beijing to meet Adolf Ioffe. There, at the request of the nationalist Kokuryūkai, he tried to negotiate the purchase of North Sakhalin from Russia, a topic that Ioffe flatly refused to discuss. Incidentally, Arahata was not aware of Yoshihara's secret mission on behalf on Japanese nationalists. On his return to Japan, Yoshihara began to associate increasingly with right-wing groups. Arahata later claimed that when he was in jail in 1937, Yoshihara was brought in drunk and boasted that he had been a Comintern agent disguised as a right winger.[75] Besides Yoshihara, the Soviet side was particularly interested in another friend of Takao, the ex-military man Nagayama Naoatsu, who converted to socialism during his service in the Japanese interventionist forces in Siberia. They tried to persuade him to stay in Russia and become a member of the Russian Communist Party, but Nagayama declined.

Russian Bolsheviks' efforts to win over anarchists bore fruit when Takao adopted communist tactics. Interested in winning over Japanese anarchists, the Comintern central committee invited Takao to Moscow in the summer of 1922, where he met, among other notable figures, Vladimir Lenin. Takao's several meetings with Zinoviev, Bukharin, and most importantly Lenin left a permanent mark on him, which he always acknowledged.[76] After his experience in Russia, Takao penned the pamphlet "Revolution or Death," which his fellows tried to smuggle into Japan, but it was seized by the police at the port of Nagasaki in September 1922.[77] The pamphlet preached violent revolution according to the

Russian model. It projected that a violent revolution would erupt in the fall of 1924 because the economic situation was grave and unemployment was rising. The first steps toward this revolution, the pamphlet suggests, are organizing a nationwide general strike and destroying the machines. After this, revolutionaries could arrest politicians and the rich, disband the army, and establish soviets, revolutionary committees, and the Red Army. The new society would abandon private property under the slogans of communism, establish total administration by revolutionary committee, manage industry with the help of local soviets, and build a dictatorship of the proletariat.[78]

Takao's piece very much resembled Ōsugi's "Japan's Destiny": both were written in the wake of the authors' direct contact with the Russian Bolsheviks. The two pamphlets reflect how loose and flexible the positions of Taishō anarchists were, at times indistinguishable from the tenets of Leninist communism. But what was novel for socialist discourse in Japan, and what these thinkers owed to the Comintern theoreticians, was a new observation that another world war was coming, and that that war would originate in the Pacific region. The eventual world war between the United States and Japan would draw in all surrounding countries, creating a revolutionary situation, which Japanese and other Asian socialists must exploit to the maximum. As the head of the Comintern Zinoviev announced at the Congress of the Toilers of the Far East in 1922:

> The war [in the Pacific Ocean] is inevitable. As sure as morning follows night, so will the first imperialist war, which ended in 1918, be followed by a second war which will center around the Far East and the problem of the Pacific. This can be avoided only by a victory of the proletarian revolution. It is not possible to say whether this war will break out in 1925 or 1928, a year earlier or later, but it is inevitable. It can no more be avoided than fate. It will be possible to avoid this war only if the young working class of Japan rapidly becomes sufficiently strong to seize the Japanese bourgeoisie by the throat, and parallel with that there will be a victorious revolutionary movement in America.[79]

Zinoviev continued in his speech to say that there was no issue in East Asia that did not involve the Japanese empire, and that the Japanese proletariat held "the key to the solution of the Far Eastern question," and would decide the fate of several hundred million people living in China, Korea, and Mongolia.[80] The task of the Japanese socialists thus was to prevent the war by creating an anti-imperialist front. Simultaneously, socialists in Japan and in the rest of Asia must anticipate that the coming war in Asia would become a catalyst and once-in-a-lifetime opportunity for toppling the existing regime and social order—the opportunity that the Bolsheviks successfully exploited in Russia during the last world war in Europe.

Ōsugi and Takao openly approved of not only direct action but a militant takeover in the manner of the Bolshevik Revolution. In his 1922 letter from Lyon, France, Ōsugi wrote, "I am still unable to decide whether I should work with the masses or carry on the purest anarchist movement we have now."[81] While Ōsugi pondered if anarchists should merge with the labor movement or act as an independent, "pure" group, some of his comrades resolved this by actions. In the summer of 1921, a member of Ōsugi's clique planned the assassination of Prime Minister Hara Takashi—who was, however, killed by a rightist man in November 1921. In 1922, anarchists were planning to assassinate the English prince of Wales, the future King Edward VIII, during his visit to Japan. When this plan was foiled, they set their sights on Crown Prince Hirohito, the next emperor Showa. It was a lone shooter, Nanba Daisuke, inspired by Kōtoku and Russian populists, who finally made an attempt on Hirohito's life. It was against "hotheads" like Ōsugi, Takao, and their followers that Yamakawa Hitoshi wrote his celebrated article "A Change in Course for the Proletarian Movement" (Musan kaikyū undō no hōkō tenkan), published in the July–August 1922 issue of Zen'ei, which criticized the idea of a militant struggle in favor of a gradual approach to social revolution.[82] For Yamakawa, one of the most important tasks of the day was to fight the "infantile malady of the anarcho-syndicalist ideology," which had won over the most active and influential subgroups of industrial workers. He tried to convince his fellows that the anarcho-syndicalist position of rejecting political activity in favor of individual terrorist acts was childish, old-fashioned, and nonproletarian. The urgent task was to go back "To the Masses!" and work on educating the workers and infiltrating the unions.

Agreeing in principle with the Bolsheviks' militant tactics and their insistence on an anti-imperialist front, Ōsugi saw gross inconsistencies in how the Bolsheviks were organizing their state and society—the terror against their opponents, NEP, and the bureaucratization of the Bolshevik Party. He also came to despise the way the JCP attempted to centralize leftist activities in the country. Takao, however, seemed to have no qualms about Bolshevik state building. On his return to Japan in the fall of 1922, Takao became an active member of the JCP. Takao subsequently addressed an open letter to Ōsugi in Rōdō undō, written during his one-month stay in Shanghai after returning from Moscow, "Why Do You Not Support the Russian Revolution?" (Naze shinkōchū no kakumei o yōgo shinainoka). In the letter, Takao wondered why Ōsugi did not support worker-peasant Russia when any real friend of the proletariat was obligated to support the ongoing revolution there. He disagreed with the whole ana-boru debate because it weakened the proletarian movement and empowered the enemy. Takao even went so far as to compare Ōsugi to Takabatake Motoyuki, who left the socialist group in 1919 to start a national socialist movement. The whole debate seemed to him too intellectual, and he was sure that Ōsugi and the Japanese anarchists misunderstood the premises of Marxism.

> I believe that before arriving at an anarchist society, we must pass through the same [communist] revolutionary process that Soviet Russia is going through now. It is impossible for the present inadequate productive forces to jump into a heavenly future in one leap. Of course, the workings of the present Soviet government are not all ideal, but they are struggling with many difficulties and are nevertheless engaged in constructive work. The destruction of the old forces is not yet finished in Russia.[83]

In September 1922, Ōsugi answered in "Why I Do Not Support the Ongoing Revolution" (Naze shinkōchū no kakumei o yōgo shinainoka): "I also doubt one can ascend to Heaven in one bound. But the argument that, to reach anarchist society, it is necessary to pass through socialism or Bolshevism, is invented by the enemies of anarchism ... In any case, I will make clear that I believe in the immediate realization of anarchism."[84] Instead of the statist conception of socialism introduced from above, Ōsugi insisted that society's revolutionary transformation had to come from below in order to be the product of the workers' self-activity and self-organization at the point of production. Ōsugi accused Takao of taking up the side of the enemy of anarchism, Bolshevism, and thus Takao could not be called a true anarchist. Be that as it may, Takao did indeed champion the cause of Soviet Russia in Japan, by bringing Lenin's message of Russia's nonaggressive plans for Asia to Gotō Shinpei through his good acquaintance, the nationalist politician Nakano Seigō, and organizing various pro-Soviet movements.

Both Ōsugi and Takao, however, very soon found themselves critically targeted by their communist comrades. Although the ana-boru debate began with the anarchists' attack on the Bolsheviks, the debate was initiated from the Bolshevik side and directed not at anarchists in general but at those in the labor unions and the JCP. The polemics against the anarchists, which sought to expose deficiencies in the anarchist creed, were intended primarily as a campaign for ideological purification within the party and the unions. One reason for this "purification" seemed to be trivial: money. Because anarchists were initially the ones who traveled to China and Russia to obtain funds, they became the target of scrutiny at home, focused on how these funds were spent. After the JCP was established as a branch of the Comintern, it had to submit receipts and account records regularly to Moscow. Some historians have speculated that Sakai Toshihiko probably decided to cleanse the party of individuals suspected of "improper" use of general funds. Both Sakai and Arahata, in their letters and reports to the Comintern, sounded very scrupulous and ashamed about the inappropriate behavior of their countrymen. Moreover, the Japanese Bolsheviks accused anarchists of accepting bribery from the Japanese government and profligacy with Comintern funds.[85] The accusations, which were to some extent true, were directed primarily against Ōsugi, Takao Heibē, and a few others.[86]

After returning from the Fourth Congress of the Comintern (November–December 1922), Takase Kiyoshi (Sakai's son-in-law) created a committee to investigate how Takao had spent Comintern funds. For example, people remembered that Takao helped a Japanese prostitute return home by giving her money but questioned his motives. Offended by the investigation, Takao withdrew from the JCP. Ōsugi was another easy and obvious target because of his very public, at times scandalous lifestyle. Blame from his fellows for spending Comintern money insulted Ōsugi as well: "Eventually I realized, albeit late, that cooperation with the Communists in real life and in theory is impossible. More than that, I understood that the Communist party is similar to the capitalist parties and is the most disconcerting enemy of us, the anarchists."[87] JCP members claimed that the Comintern funds were never intended for personal use, contrary to what Ōsugi understood when he met Voitinsky in Shanghai. Ōsugi was accused of not discriminating among his financial sources, even to the point of requesting and receiving money from Gotō Shinpei. In other words, he was receiving support from the very people against whom the whole socialist movement was struggling.

After Ōsugi and Takao distanced themselves from the communist movement at the end of 1922, they engaged in separate activities. Ōsugi decided to bring Japanese anarchism into the international anarchist network. With this aim, he left Japan for Europe in December 1922 to participate in the International Anarchist Conference that was to be held in Berlin the following January or February. Unable to obtain a visa for Germany, Ōsugi stayed in France for several months. In France, he became fascinated with Nestor Makhno, a self-proclaimed Ukrainian anarchist who fought simultaneously against the communists, the counterrevolutionary army, and the interventionists. Ōsugi found in him a true revolutionary, the only leader who embodied the true meaning of the Russian Revolution by supporting autonomous and self-ruling communities.[88] Ōsugi also studied the Rolland-Barbusse debate, in which Romaine Rolland criticized the Soviet Communist Party's dictatorship, violence, arrogance, and intention to universalize the Soviet model to include non-Russian societies. Just before his death, Ōsugi published two pieces on Mikhail Bakunin: the article "Marx to Bakunin: Socialism and Anarchism" (January 1923, in *Kaizō*) and the book *Two Revolutionaries: Marx and Bakunin* (1922). Why had Ōsugi become interested in Bakunin at that juncture? In the preface to the book, he wrote that he had read Bakunin for the first time some twenty years earlier but quickly moved on to Pyotr Kropotkin. However, he continued, he recently found himself attracted again to Bakunin as a man of the time of destruction (*ranse*), as a man of action. Bakunin was the perfect inspiration for his turn toward criticizing Marxist socialism. Ōsugi even went so far as to write that "Marxism will never allow the people to create their own destiny."[89] Ōsugi was especially drawn to Bakunin's critique of Marxism as essentially statist and therefore authoritarian doctrine. It was in large part due to popular disillusionment with the Russian Revolution that interest in terrorism, Russian populism, and Bakunin experienced a resurgence in Japan.

Ōsugi returned to Japan shortly before the Great Kantō earthquake in September 1923. In its aftermath, on September 16, Ōsugi, the anarchist-feminist Itō Noe (his partner), and his six-year-old nephew were murdered by the military police captain Amakasu Masahiko. Amakasu did not act alone; the Tokyo police and government officials were implicated in the murders of leftists and Asian migrants. Specifically, Minister of Justice Hiranuma Kiichirō encouraged rumors that the Koreans, aided by Japanese anarchists, "were burning houses, killing people, and stealing money and property." He also provided funds to rightist organizers of anti-Korean violence, who staged acts of arson all over Tokyo. As a result, over the next few days about six thousand Korean residents in Japan, as well as several Japanese socialists and anarchists, were massacred. Even after his death, Ōsugi was not left alone. The rightist organization Taikakai stole his ashes from the funeral home. Amakasu, after three years in prison, went on to have a solid career in Manchukuo, while members of the Taikakai were never prosecuted. The ashes of Ōsugi were never recovered.

Takao's fate was no less tragic. As he distanced himself from the communist organization, Takao immersed himself in labor activities. He did not engage, however, in organizational matters but became the labor unions' fighting arm.[90] Since 1919, there had been a proliferation of political violence simultaneously from the Left and the Right. As the militancy of anarchists' and labor unions' strikes increased, the Right mobilized as well, sweeping in the lower orders and middle strata. Drawing from the disaffected and disoriented, rightist organizations disseminated pamphlets and newspapers and organized rallies in the name of defending the emperor and national community against the foreign threat and its internal agents. The primary activity of nationalist organizations was to contain labor unrest, intimidate labor unions, and threaten their political opponents: socialists and others of a leftist orientation, as well as leaders of the universal suffrage movement. These groups espoused various ideas—from reverence for the emperor to aggressive imperialism—but they all shared a reactionary desire to crush leftist activism inspired by the Russian Revolution.

Most notorious were the Kokusuikai (est. 1919), the Yamato Minrōkai (Japanese People's Labor Society, est. 1921), and the Sekka Bōshidan (est. 1922).[91] Among them, the Kokusuikai was the most numerous, and its fistfighters were involved in crushing famous strikes—including those at Yahata Ironworks (1920), the Singer Sewing Machine Company (1925), and Noda Shōyu (1927–28). In one well-known incident in 1923, more than one thousand members of the

Kokusuikai fought for three days in the streets of Nara city against more than one thousand supporters of the Suiheisha (est. 1922), a prosocialist organization struggling against discrimination against the Burakumin outcast community. The Kokusuikai justified the violence as expressions of loyalty to the imperial house, prevention of corruption of national morals, and promotion of harmony between labor and capital.[92] Hundreds of the Suiheisha members were brought to trial, while the Kokusuikai members were hardly punished, because they enjoyed the patronage of the Home and Justice ministries.

In 1922–23, street fights between leftists and rightists seemed to become a new norm. Both sides formed combat squads and in this, the streets of Japan's industrial cities resembled those of Europe, where political violence had been escalating since the end of the Great War. In the last year of his life, Takao dedicated his energy to combating the violence perpetrated by right-wing groups by organizing Sensen dōmei (Front League), with his loyal ex-military friend from the Siberian Intervention, Nagayama Naoatsu, and the anarchist Yoshida Ichi. After engaging in several street fights with rightist gangs, Takao decided to confront the leader of the Sekka Bōshidan, Yonemura Kaichirō. In a confrontation between the two men that occurred on June 26, Takao was shot and killed by Yonemura, who received only a suspended sentence.[93]

State repression—whether conducted through its military and thought police (Akamasu's murder of Ōsugi and Itō), rightist organizations (the Sekka Bōshidan's murder of Takao), or laws (the Peace Preservation Law)—undoubtedly contributed to the demise of the anarchist movement in interwar Japan. But the group's internal intellectual and political trajectory was no less detrimental. The anarchists' rejection of Soviet communism and anything that reminded them of it (centralized organization, movement, or party—anathema to anarchists' ears) backfired strongly. Anarchism in Japan thus evolved into either "propagation by the individual deed"—that is, terrorism—or rejection of the labor movement as another form of class-based organization. Both trajectories isolated and greatly weakened anarchism. Japan's interwar anarchist evolution is reminiscent of the evolution of the Russian radical movement of the late nineteenth century, which went through a similar development. After the "going to the people" movement failed in 1874, the populist organization Zemlya i volya (Land and Freedom) split into rival factions: the elitists of Narodnaya volya (The People's Will), who embraced terrorism, and the gradualists of Cherny peredel (The Black Repartition of the Land), who opposed terrorism and stuck to propaganda among the workers. The People's Will spent the next several years in a campaign of terror that culminated in the assassination of Alexander II in 1881.

The targeted murders of anarchists and indiscriminate slaughter of Asian migrants during the summer and fall of 1923, combined with the state's tacit approval of the violence, sent shock waves throughout the Left. The repressive government was reminiscent of the tsarist tyranny, and as happened in Russia, its attacks called for an equal retribution. Japanese anarchists, harking back to their own history of militant resistance, set out on the path of terrorism to avenge the deaths of their leaders.[94] Wada Kyūtarō, Muraki Genjirō, and a few others from the Girochinsha attempted to murder Fukuda Masatarō (the former commander under martial law) in September 1924 and to blow up a police station and a prison in Osaka; they also succeeded in setting off a bomb in a Ginza-area train. The whole group (five people in Tokyo, sixteen in Kyoto and Osaka) was captured and tried in 1925; most of them died in prison.[95] Yet another self-professed anarchist terrorist, Nanba Daisuke, attempted to murder the emperor (the Toranomon Incident). The Korean anarchist Bak Yeol and his Japanese partner, Kaneko Fumiko, were arrested in 1923 and convicted for an alleged plot to assassinate the prince regent Hirohito (the Bak Yeol Incident). The anarchist Mukumoto Un'yū, who kept Kaneko Fumiko's ashes after her suicide in prison in 1926, together with Korean anarchists attempted the assassination of the Japanese consul-general in 1933 in Shanghai. Finally, in the so-called Sakuradamon Incident of January 1932, the Korean anarchist Lee Bong-chang made an unsuccessful attempt to assassinate Emperor Showa. Anarchist terrorism culminated in the activities of the Nihon Museifu Kyōsantō (Anarchist Communist Party of Japan, established in January 1934). Paranoia over police infiltration reached its height as one of the party members murdered another out of suspicion. After a series of bank robberies, the party was crushed by the police in 1936. Looking back at these events, the anarchist Yamaguchi Kensuke's verdict was not far from the truth: "The Party . . . due as much to its elitist heroics and self-righteousness as to its adventurism, which was completely isolated from the masses, delivered the final blow to an army already on the brink of defeat."[96]

Notwithstanding the terrorism, anarchists attempted to organize. Two nationwide popular anarchist organizations were established in 1926: the Kokushoku Seinen Renmei, or Kokuren (Black Youth League) and the Zenkoku Jiren. The two were extremely close, with the Kokuren (a tighter and more militant organization) often acting as muscle for the Zenkoku Jiren. When unions affiliated to Zenkoku Jiren became involved in industrial disputes, it was often Kokuren militants who took on the most dangerous forms of direct action, such as battling with the police and firebombing the bosses' houses.[97] Yet unity was short lived. The advocates of "pure anarchism" from the Kokuren (a pejorative term coined by their anarcho-syndicalist opponents), most notably Iwasa Sakutarō (the author of the pamphlet "Terrorism," published in Berkeley in 1907) and Hatta Shūzō, came to reject the principles of anarcho-syndicalism and, remarkably, the whole labor movement.

"Pure" anarchism stood on the same old anarchist rejection of the Russian Revolution and Russian communism. Most importantly, the "pure" anarchists now doubted not simply the communist principle of centralized organization but the very concept of class struggle conducted by means of union organization. In what is known as his "labor union mountain bandit theory," Iwasa argued that the labor union movement was a minority of urban, male workers who occupied a relatively advantageous position within the working class. As the historian John Crump explained, "just as whoever might seize the leadership of a gang of mountain bandits would have no influence on their pillaging relationship with the surrounding villages, so whichever side emerged victorious from the class struggle between the capitalists and the 'labor movement' would leave the basically exploitative nature of society unaffected."[98] As happened with the Soviet dictatorship of the proletariat, the labor leadership in Japan would maintain its privileged position, while the working masses would see little improvement in their lives. "Pure" anarchists claimed that Japanese society could not be reduced to a schematic class structure of workers versus capitalists. Instead, Iwasa proposed to abandon labor union organization in favor of a wider mass workers' movement. Not class struggle, but a classless, mass movement was in order.[99] Exactly how the mass workers' movement would be coordinated was, however, unclear.

Initially, in 1926 it seemed as if the anarchist movement was about to be brought into the communist fold. The main cause of this was the new aggressive course in China that the Japanese government, under the premiership of General Tanaka Gi'ichi beginning in April 1927, resolved to take. Since 1925, the Chinese Revolution had been gaining momentum with anti-Japanese strikes in Shanghai (the May Thirtieth Movement) and anti-British strikes and boycotts in Canton and Hong Kong. In May 1927, Tanaka initiated the Shandong Expedition that would "separate Manchuria and Mongolia," and confirm Japan's special position in both areas. The immediate goal was to stop the Chinese Northern Expeditionary forces, led by the Guomindang, and prevent the Chinese Revolution from spreading to Manchuria.[100] Japan's militarism in China greatly alarmed both Japanese socialists and the Soviet leaders. The Profintern, run by the Comintern and the leaders of the Soviet Communist Party, stepped up its activities, organizing the Pan-Pacific Trade Union Conference, held in Hankow on May 20–26, 1927.[101] The Profintern's general objective was to accomplish international unity among trade unions and gradually win them over, not simply to the communist cause but to the creation of an anti-imperialist united front that would simultaneously defend the Soviet Union. Greatly focused on Asia, the Profintern actively sought the inclusion of Japanese unions.[102]

Concerned not only with the increasing state crackdown on labor activities within Japan but also with the deployment of the state military machine to crush the Chinese Revolution run by labor unions, the Zenkoku Jiren sought ways to establish contacts with international unions in order to coordinate a united opposition to escalating Japanese imperialism. The Zenkoku Jiren accepted the Profintern's invitation to the Pan-Pacific Trade Union Conference in 1927. One of the conference's declared themes was "Preventing a Pacific War." It appealed to the workers of Japan and China, warning them of an upcoming war in the Pacific: "The struggle between the imperialist powers, particularly between England, Japan and the United States, for hegemony in the Pacific grows every day and inevitably leads to a new imperialist world war."[103] The final resolution stated: "The only way to prevent a new world war is to transform the threatening imperialist war of races and nations into a war of classes, a war of exploited against the exploiters. To accomplish this, it is necessary to draw into the trade unions millions of workers; to imbue the masses with the spirit of class consciousness and of class war."[104]

As with Ōsugi and Takao a few years earlier, the Japanese anarchists were warned that because of Japanese imperialism, the East Asian region was on the brink of a war that would eventually develop into a world war. For that reason, Japanese socialists, anarchists, and unions held an enormous responsibility to wage a class struggle within their nation and to unite with their counterparts in China, Korea, and elsewhere in anti-imperialist efforts. Initially, Ōsugi and Takao in 1920–22, and then the Zenkoku Jiren delegates in 1927, became attracted to the anti-imperialist agenda of Soviet communism because they recognized Japanese imperialism as the main evil on the destruction of which both social revolution at home and peace in the region essentially depended.

Unfortunately, none of these plans materialized, because Japanese anarchism once again distanced itself from the communist-led international movement in favor of a nation-focused struggle. The faction of "pure" anarchists in the Kokuren attacked the returning delegates for their betrayal in siding with the treacherous Russian Bolsheviks and denounced the conference and the proposal for collaboration as evidence of Bolshevik intrigue. Remarkably, the "pure" anarchists' reasoning found wide support among the two anarchist federations. They were able to expel those remaining activists who still tried to strengthen the movement through domestic and international networks of labor unions. Insistence that the reform of Japanese society could not be reduced to a class-based struggle, as the "purist" Iwasa Sakutarō proclaimed, but instead should unite all segments of national society was a slippery argument. By the late 1920s, the anarchists' anti-authoritarian quest and continuous striving for communality and totality evolved into support of the national polity (*kokutai*) for Ishikawa Sanshirō or the idea of local/national community (*kyōdōtai*) for Hatta Shuzō.[105] Finally, in February 1937, Iwasa published an essay titled "Outline of the Theory of the State" (Kokka ron taikō), where he stated: "Isn't it only our unique Great Japanese Empire which is a naturally generated state and the others which are all artificially constructed states, no matter whether monarchical or democratic?"[106]

Japanese anarchism seemed to come full circle. For the Taishō anarchists, Kōtoku's assault on the imperial state and its head marked the beginning of their movement. After disappointment with the Russian Revolution set in, they revived the tradition of direct assault on the head of the imperial and imperialist state. In this sense, the historian Asukai Masamichi's claim that anarchists were the most revolutionary radicals holds true, because only anarchists confronted the emperor and the police state face to face. Early Taishō anarchists were creative and proactive in terms of casting a critical eye on the Russian Revolution in Japan and, above all, establishing contacts with Russian and Asian revolutionaries. The anarchist origins of many Japanese Marxists and communists influenced how they became Marxists and shaped certain features of the Japanese Left that diverged from the Leninist interpretation of Marxism that they formally espoused.

Nevertheless, as I have argued, because of their fundamental disagreement with the premises and the course of the Russian Revolution, Japanese anarchism developed in a seemingly dead-end direction. Moreover, with the deaths of Takao and Ōsugi, Taishō anarchism's orientation toward an international movement also vanished, together with its organized cooperation with Chinese, Korean, and Russian radicals and its confidence in the workers' movement.[107] After 1923, Japan-based Korean anarchists moved en masse to China, bringing to the national liberation movement the transnational and internationalist appeal of Japanese anarchism. Tokyo, and Japan in general, ceased to be the hub of East Asian anarchism. Anarchism in Japan was inherently anti-authoritarian and came from a longing for individualism. Suspicious of any centralization and witnessing the "degeneration" of the Russian Revolution, anarchism in Japan ended in individual acts of terror. Undertaken out of selfless idealism and sincere revolutionary convictions, anarchists' terrorist campaigns hardly shook the foundation of the political regime. As anarchist groups acted largely independently and did not unify into a coordinated movement, the imperial government was able to suppress them effectively. By the 1930s, many anarchists began to differentiate between the state and the nation on historical terms, arguing that the latter, moral and egalitarian, preceded the former, artificial and repressive. The nation thus was identified as a national community, for the sake of which the anarchist struggle for liberation of the people from capitalist productive relations must be accomplished.

THE JAPANESE COMMUNIST PARTY
AND THE COMINTERN

It is there, in the West, that the chains of imperialism which were forged in Europe, and which have been strangling the world, must first be broken. . . . And yet the East must not be forgotten by us even for a moment. It must not be forgotten for the reason that it provides inexhaustible reserves and is the most reliable rear base for world imperialism.

—Joseph Stalin, "Do Not Forget the East," *Zhizn' natsional'nostei*, November 24, 1918

The Japanese Communist Party (JCP) was born in the summer of 1922 as a Comintern branch in the midst of Japan's Siberian Intervention, Japan's assistance to the White counterrevolutionary forces, and the Japanese imperialist advance in China. The Comintern expected the new Japanese communist movement to initiate an anti-intervention effort and reinforce opposition to imperialism among the Japanese. This prompted early Japanese communists to confront the issue of the relationship between international and national proletarian movements, and ultimately between nation, empire, and colonies. Furthermore, the Marxist unilineal historical framework, popularized by Russian revolutionaries and Japanese Marxists, was responsible for the new understanding among Japanese leftists that they were part of global, world-historical social changes. As part of the revolutionary strategy, Japanese leftists had to question where Japan stood in the Marxist scale of world-historical development and interpret the history of Japanese political and economic development in accordance with Marxist doctrine. Quite remarkably, despite their admiration for the Russian Revolution, early Japanese communists concluded that the Russian model of socialist revolution was not applicable to Japan's conditions. Instead, they came up with their own vision for the Japanese revolution, one that was quite divergent from the expectations of the Comintern for the role of the JCP in the Asia-wide anti-imperialist struggle.

This chapter examines the initial contacts between the Comintern and the JCP, and their differing views on revolutionary strategy in Japan, by looking at the writings of the socialist Yamakawa Hitoshi (1880–1958). By 1922, Yamakawa emerged as the main theoretician of the Japanese Left, authoring the first JCP program that determined the trajectory of the Japanese Left for the next decade. His program for the JCP was faithful (maybe pedantically so) to the principles of Marxist orthodoxy, but his immediate and urgent task was to formulate a political program that would unite the various disparate trends of the Japanese socialist movement: anarchists, syndicalists, social democrats, and communists. However, Yamakawa also actively disagreed with the creation of a party of professional revolutionaries, insisting instead on a mass proletarian party. He also opposed the Comintern's suggestions for JCP tactics, which he rightly suspected were tailored for China. Through a close reading of Russian Comintern archives and the writings of Yamakawa Hitoshi, including his reports to the Comintern, this chapter reveals that throughout the 1920s, the JCP retained a degree of independence from the Comintern.[1] At the same time, Comintern officials in Moscow often acknowledged that they had little information about Japan, and up until 1928 they delegated the coordination—theoretical and practical—of the JCP to either the Comintern's eastern branch in Shanghai, headed by Grigory Voitinsky (1893–1956), or more often to the Japanese communists themselves.[2]

In the 1920s, Japanese communists still had the self-confidence to question the decisions of the Comintern. Contrary to the prevalent assumption in Western and Japanese historiography that the JCP was an obedient subsidiary of the Comintern, I demonstrate, first, that the Comintern wielded far less influence and control over Japanese communists and socialists than has hitherto been presumed; and second, that the JCP's assessment of Japanese social and capitalist development had far-reaching implications for its revolutionary strategy at home and in the Japanese colonies.[3]

The Comintern established two transnational routes to connect with Japanese socialists: a "western route" (Amsterdam—New York—Mexico City) and an "eastern route" (Irkutsk—Vladivostok—Shanghai).[4] The "western route" was managed by the old socialist Katayama Sen (1859–1933), the "eastern route" by Grigory Voitinsky. In the initial period between 1919 and 1922, it was Katayama Sen and fellow Japanese immigrants in the United States, such as Kondō Eizō, Takahashi Kamekichi, Taguchi Unzō, Yoshihara Tarō, Maniwa Suekichi, Ishigaki Eitarō, Suzuki Mosaburō, and Inomata Tsunao, who were the most important links between Russian Bolsheviks and Japanese socialists.[5] They translated socialist and Comintern literature from English into Japanese and obtained crucial collaboration from sailors and other people engaged in trans-Pacific literature-smuggling operations. They also translated Japanese reports on domestic socialist and labor movements into English and dispatched them via Amsterdam to Moscow.[6] Katayama himself radicalized after meeting Leon Trotsky, Nikolai Bukharin, Vladimir Volodarsky, and Alexandra Kollontai in New York in the spring of 1917.

In 1919, he established the Association of Japanese Socialists in New York, and joined the newly formed Communist Party of America. At his urging, Yoshihara Tarō, a Japanese émigré living in the United States, attended the Congress of the Peoples of the East—held in Baku, Azerbaijan, in September 1920—as the only representative of Japan.[7] After helping establish a network of Japanese immigrants on the East and West Coasts, as well as in Hawaii and Mexico, Katayama departed for Moscow in 1921 to serve as chairman of the Far Eastern People's Congress. He stayed there until his death in 1933, serving as the representative of the Japanese communist movement at the presidium of the Comintern.

The "eastern route" of the Comintern's advance into the Japanese socialist scene was managed from Shanghai by Grigory Voitinsky, who became a central figure in the history of the JCP and the Chinese Communist Party (CCP) and had a big influence on Lenin's East Asian policies and, subsequently, Stalin's East Asian policies.[8] Voitinsky had lived in the United States (1913–18) and then returned to Russia, where he joined the Bolshevik Party. During the Civil War, he worked for the party in the Russian Far East, was arrested by the White forces in 1919 in Vladivostok and sentenced to a life of hard labor in Sakhalin, where he led a convict revolt and managed to escape. In Vladivostok, he started working in the apparatus of the Comintern, and in April 1920, at the age of twenty-seven, he was sent to China as the leader of a small group of communist comrades tasked with the mission to reorganize the various Marxist groups in Japan, China, and Korea into communist parties amenable to Comintern directions. While there, he assisted in the early development of the Chinese communist movement, both financially and in the training of young cadres. Until 1927, Voitinsky worked as one of the Comintern's experts on China and Japan, drafting directives for the Comintern's executive committee as well as for the CCP and JCP, and writing on the revolutionary movement in Japan and China for the *Communist International* and the *International Press Correspondence (Inprecor)*.[9]

As far back as 1920, the Comintern branches in Irkutsk, Vladivostok, and Shanghai had been sending Korean and Chinese radicals to Japan to establish contacts with Japanese socialists and encourage them to create a communist party as a branch of the Comintern. In 1921–22, the arrival of Asian continental radicals with questionable affiliations, vast sums of money, and persistent invitations to travel to Moscow through the Siberian war zone and carefully watched military police outposts in Shimonoseki and Shanghai, disconcerted the Japanese socialists. Not sure what to make of the Third International, Sakai voiced his doubts about the Comintern in *Shinshakai hyōron*, in July 1920:

> A new international Communist party has arisen with its headquarters in Russia, and it is called the Third International. It is important to know from the start whether we will oppose it or support it. How

these two varieties of international socialism [i.e., the Second and Third Internationals] will oppose one another and how they will unite is truly a major topic of interest.[10]

Sakai and Yamakawa were familiar with and committed to the Second International and therefore had some hesitation about throwing in their lot with the still unfamiliar Third Communist International. Yamakawa would recollect in his memoirs that the creation of the Comintern transformed the Japanese radical movement: "Everyone interested in socialist thought was influenced by the Russian Revolution. At one brief moment, we all as one supported the revolution. There was such a period. But this was before the Comintern was created. After that, everything settled, and opinions gradually split."[11] In the end, it was anarchists and Japanese émigrés from the United States who initially agreed to work with the Comintern.[12]

Despite his later critique of the Comintern, in 1921 Yamakawa was quickly persuaded that Japanese socialists ought to establish a communist party in Japan and therefore join the global communist movement. Under pressure from one of the "Katayama boys"—Kondō Eizō (1883–1965), who returned from the United States to Japan in 1919—and after meeting another Korean Bolshevik envoy in April 1921, Sakai, Yamakawa, and others set up the Preparatory Committee of the JCP. In the same month, Yamakawa drafted the Manifesto of the Preparatory Committee, which Kondō took to Shanghai in May. The manifesto was then passed on to Moscow, where it was published in September and October of that year as the Charter and Manifesto of the Japanese Communist Party. It seems that Yamakawa, Sakai, and other members of the Preparatory Committee were making plans to visit Soviet Russia, but they were thwarted by the arrest of Kondō Eizō. In Shanghai, Kondō received from Voitinsky an enormous (by contemporary standards) sum of 6,500 yen for organizational expenses but was arrested as soon as he returned to Japan, sparking antisocialist legislation within the home bureaucracy.[13] Due to tightened security, the planned visit of Japanese socialists to Moscow was foiled. Only Japanese immigrants from the United States, Taguchi Unzō and Yoshihara Tarō, attended the Third Comintern Congress in the summer of 1921, where they claimed to be members of the (nonexistent) Japanese Communist Party and showed Lenin Yamakawa's manifesto as a proof of their affiliation.

Despite these setbacks, the Japanese socialists were determined to establish a Japanese communist party as a Comintern branch. This time the major push came from two other sojourners to Moscow, Takase Kiyoshi and Tokuda Kyūichi, who were enthralled by the Russian Bolsheviks at the Conference of the Far Eastern Revolutionary Organizations, held in Moscow in the winter of 1922. The official date of the establishment of the first JCP is considered to be July 15, 1922, and its creation was announced at the Fourth Congress of the Comintern in November 1922.[14] The general secretary was Arahata Kanson, and the secretary of the International Sector was Sakai Toshihiko. At its founding, the JCP had fourteen cells and fifty-eight members.[15]

Communist parties in East Asia were formed in the following order: Korea (May 1921, in Irkutsk and Shanghai), China (July 1921), and Japan (July 1922). The activities of the Comintern in East Asia constituted the only crucial factor in their creation. But because the JCP was forged in the context of the Siberian Intervention and Japan's imperialist advance in China, the Comintern anticipated that, as "the best organized and strongest force" in Eastern countries, the Japanese proletariat would strike "the first decisive blow against foreign and predatory imperialism and imperialist coercion."[16] At the Congress of Toilers of the Far East (January 1922), Zinoviev, the head of the Comintern, especially emphasized the importance of bringing the Japanese socialist movement into the communist fold:

> The Japanese bourgeoisie rule over and oppress many millions of people in the Far East, holding in its hands the fate of all that sector of the world. Therefore, the defeat of the Japanese bourgeoisie and the final victory of the revolution in Japan can alone solve the Far Eastern question.... This makes the responsibility of the young Japanese proletariat particularly great.... The fate of the Japanese revolutionary movement is acquiring an enormous international importance.[17]

In the eyes of the Comintern, the ultimate objective of the JCP was to reinforce the peoples' and workers' opposition to Japanese imperialism. Japanese socialists bore a heavy responsibility: peace in the East Asian region depended on their actions.

As mentioned before, in April 1921 Yamakawa wrote the Manifesto of the Preparatory Committee of the JCP, based on the program of the British Communist Party. The document was written in English, as was the Program of the Communist Party of Japan, which Yamakawa wrote in September 1922 for the National Convention of the Communist Party of Japan. Yamakawa's program was sent to Moscow for the Fourth Congress of the Comintern (November–December 1922) as proof of the formal establishment of the JCP.[18] It remained the only program of the JCP throughout the 1920s, even after the party was reorganized in 1926, after which Yamakawa left it. Given the lack of access to Russian archives, it was traditionally presumed that the JCP program was written by the Russian Bolshevik Nikolai Bukharin during the Fourth Comintern Congress, the so-called Bukharin Theses of 1922. As will be discussed later in more detail, what are known as the Bukharin Theses of 1922 were written in 1924 and became known in Japan only in 1928. Hence, Yamakawa's program from 1922 was the only communist program of the first JCP known to the Japanese.

The program unequivocally recognized the JCP as a branch of the Comintern. As an illegal proletarian party, the objectives of the JCP were "the overthrow of the Capitalist regime through the establishment of the Dictatorship of the Proletariat based on Soviet Power."[19] Yamakawa then established that Japan was "the most powerful of the capitalist nations of the Orient," and therefore "The Communist Party takes upon itself the task of organizing these proletarian masses into a powerful fighting body, leading them on to the Proletarian Revolution—the seizure of political power and system of production in the hands of the proletariat."[20] In other words, the JCP program considered Japan to be an advanced capitalist country on a par with Western countries and therefore in need of an immediate proletarian, not a bourgeois, revolution, which would "establish the Proletarian Dictatorship based on the Soviet of the workers, peasants and soldiers."[21]

In the 1921 manifesto of the JCP, Yamakawa had already proclaimed that the Meiji Revolution of 1868 was a bourgeois-democratic revolution, and that it had laid the foundation for capitalist development in Japan. Therefore,

> The progress of capitalism in Japan . . . gave impetus to the proletarian movement. The sharp growth of the workers' movement in 1918 and, later on, the innumerable strikes and workers' protests, the rapid awakening and development of class consciousness of the workers, the powerful, unstoppable spread of socialist doctrine throughout the country—all of this is the fruit of the economic development of Japan.[22]

Yamakawa's claim that the Meiji Revolution was in fact a bourgeois revolution marked the beginning of a decade-long debate about the nature of the Meiji Revolution, which culminated in the late 1920s in a series of seminal debates over Japanese capitalism (*Nihon shihonshugi ronsō*). Yamakawa supported the idea that Japan's economy during the Tokugawa period paved the way for its rapid capitalist development in the modern period, rejecting therefore the idea that after the Meiji Revolution foreign capitalism merged with Japanese feudalism to produce a highly contradictory socioeconomic and political system. Yamakawa was confident that Japan was moving steadily toward greater democratization and that after World War I, as Japanese industry and trade grew steadily, the new generation of the bourgeoisie began to demand more political rights and break with existing bureaucratic-military political structures. In the aftermath of the war, Yamakawa argued, a modern capitalist state was finally coming into existence in Japan, bringing with it the completion of the Meiji bourgeois democratic revolution. The rise of the first commoner, Hara Takashi, to the premiership and the dominance of party politics were proof for Yamakawa that bourgeois democratic political power was firmly established in Japan.[23] This new development, he thought, put Japan on a level with advanced Western countries.

Since the JCP considered the Japanese proletariat to be advanced and therefore an independent political force, the issue arose of whether socialists should support the universal suffrage movement championed by the progressive bourgeoisie. Some JCP members agreed that the party, and socialists of all persuasions, must support the universal suffrage movement and strive for workers' rights through a legal proletarian party. However, Yamakawa, Sakai Toshihiko, Arahata Kanson, and other leaders of the JCP rejected any cooperation and a united front with liberal democratic forces. Yamakawa specifically refused to create a legal proletarian party, which would, he feared, be drawn into bourgeois politics in the Diet. Yamakawa expected that the JCP would organize "proletarian political action outside the Diet, to help accelerate the 'progress of Democracy,'" while "exposing the hypocrisy and futility of bourgeois democracy, and demonstrating to the proletariat the necessity of creating their own machinery of Government."[24] He firmly believed that Japan, as an advanced capitalist country with a long history of a socialist movement had to establish an autonomous labor movement based on the industrial working class in order to achieve a suitable vehicle for the propagation of socialism.[25]

In fact, in 1919–22, Yamakawa made a name for himself as a critic of the Taishō democratic movement, which he insisted was championed by the capitalist and imperialist petite bourgeoisie. He insisted that in the age of imperialist expansion, the bourgeoisie would always and a priori remain antagonistic to the proletariat. He recalled Lenin's analysis that the imminent and inevitable collapse of capitalism (of which imperialism is the last stage) caused an increased need among the capitalists to secure their assets by manipulating nationalist circles against the revolutionary working class. Only in this way, Lenin argued, could the capitalist bourgeoisie safeguard its interests and profits achieved through expansion and war. Yamakawa suspected that the Japanese bourgeoisie was using the universal suffrage movement to advance its own interests against the old conservative authority, big capital, and landowners.[26] He argued that even the well-meaning leaders of the universal suffrage movement—Yoshino Sakuzō and Ōyama Ikuo, who claimed to represent the interests of the whole nation—did not understand the antagonistic class nature of society: the continuous oppression of one class by the other. In his view, the cooperation (kyōdō) of national interests, on which Yoshino placed his hopes, really meant the interests of only one class—the bourgeoisie.

Similarly, Yamakawa justified the Bolsheviks' terror against their opponents as necessary for dealing with the Russian petite bourgeoisie, which still tended to

side with the old reactionary forces and, Yamakawa believed, was solely responsible for the political violence in the country.[27] He held a view common among
non-Russian communists during the Russian Civil War: that the persecution
of the opposition in Soviet Russia, the concentration of power in the hands of
the party's political bureau, and the party's total control of the economy, the
state, and the justice system were unavoidable but temporary. Once the whole of
society had proletarianized, Yamakawa was confident that the dictatorship and
bureaucratism of the soviets would disappear.[28]

Yamakawa therefore declared the true enemy of the people to be the bourgeoisie, rather than the old feudal absolutist forces (the emperor, the military, and the
landlord aristocracy).[29] The Japanese proletariat, he believed, must nurture its
own class consciousness and reject collaboration with the progressive bourgeoisie. Right until the Kantō earthquake in September 1923, Yamakawa and other
socialists following his lead were calling on workers to abstain from voting, as
their participation in the electoral process would only further empower bourgeois democracy and its institutions.[30] In this way, the JCP initially rejected the
option of a legal proletarian party and insisted instead on illegal activities. One
outcome of Yamakawa's position was that democratic mass movements that had
the potential to address or curb authoritarian state power began to be looked
down on by socialist intellectuals and other political activists as historically backward. The historian Itō Akira has even argued that Japanese socialists were partly
responsible for the fact that popular fascism failed to develop in Japan: fascism
in Europe attacked democracy, which in Japan had been crushed by the socialists
before it could gain a wider audience.[31]

What was the Comintern's position on this issue? Despite its hopes that
the Japanese proletarian movement would initiate a successful battle against
its own country's capitalism and imperialism, China was what preoccupied
the Bolshevik leaders the most. After the communists' defeats in Europe, they
turned their attention and high hopes to Asia, considering now that the revolutionary upheaval in China would ensure the subsequent success of proletarian
revolutions in the West. The Bolsheviks' Asian policy was based on the ideas
developed by Lenin during World War I. Lenin recognized the great revolutionary potential of nationalism in Asia and thus recommended to the "toilers of
the East" that they fight "not against capital but against medieval remnants,"
not against bourgeois but against feudal exploiters. In fact, the nascent proletariat and peasants in colonial and semicolonial Asia were to join hands with
the national bourgeoisie to end Western imperialist dominance. Revolutionary Asia thus had to overthrow simultaneously both native feudalism and foreign imperialism.[32] When Lenin came up with his revolutionary program for
Asia, however, he had in mind Persia, Central Asia, India, and China in their

struggles against the British Empire. Neither Japan's proletariat nor its imperialism was ever included in his considerations.

The first time that Bolshevik leaders paid special attention to the Japanese case was at the Fourth Comintern Congress (November 1922). In response to instructions from Lenin, who relied on reports by the Siberian communist Boris Shumyatsky and Grigory Voitinsky from Siberia and China, respectively, a special recommendation for the young JCP was written during the congress.[33] And yet the Comintern's recommended revolutionary strategy for Japan was similar to its recommendations for India and China. In the Comintern assessment, like China, imperial Japan was a semifeudal country, whereas Japanese imperialism was a product of the military, big landowners, and semifeudal Asiatic absolutism. The Comintern declared that Japan had not yet achieved the stage of bourgeois democracy, and thus the provisional objective must be the full democratization of the political regime and establishment of bourgeois democratic rule. In the eyes of the Bolshevik leaders, therefore, Japan's modernity was incomplete. The immediate task of the JCP was therefore to form a united front with the bourgeoisie, which would constitute the first stage of the two-stage revolution.[34] The future bourgeois-democratic revolution, brought about by the united front of proletariat, peasants, and national bourgeoisie, would eliminate the vestiges of feudalism. Only after that revolution was complete would the proletarian revolution follow in Japan.

The Soviet leaders themselves, however, were not convinced. Even so, lacking sufficient knowledge and theoretical analysis of Japan's modern development, they remained ambivalent about what to make of Japan. As E. H. Carr noted, for the Soviets, "Japan was both the Britain and the Germany of the Far East."[35] In the proceedings of the Fourth Comintern Congress, Japan was curiously included in both the sections on Western imperialist countries and the colonial and semicolonial world. Traditionally Asian, with its large agrarian sector and imperial institution, Japan was also industrially developed, never colonized, and the biggest imperialist threat to the Soviet Union. Voitinsky, for example, observed that the Japanese state was strong and progressive in its own way: it included bourgeois parties in the Diet, it was highly modernized, and it had an advanced industry and a developed proletariat.[36] Despite Voitinsky's assessment and the obvious fact that Japan was an industrialized empire threatening the existence of the Soviet Union, the Comintern concluded in the Fourth Congress that in Japan "remnants of feudal relationships are manifested in the structure of the state, which is controlled by a bloc of commercial and industrial capitalists and big landlords." At the same time, the emperor was perceived less as the country's supreme political figure than as the grandest of its "semi-feudal big landlords," in accordance with Marx's description of the Asiatic despot.[37]

Thus, in Lenin's developmental scale of revolutionary progression, Japan was slotted into the semicolonial category and therefore afforded only a secondary place in the coming world revolution. Despite bringing Asia's revolutionary struggle to the forefront of communist discussions, Lenin retained the old Marxist belief that the West would be the chief battleground of the world revolution, and that Asia's freedom was a part of the white man's burden.[38] Revolutions in the colonized and semicolonized world, including Japan, would play only a supplementary role in the grand scheme of things: they would disrupt global capitalism and help trigger revolution in Europe. Only after the European revolutions succeeded, not least by dismantling the system of Western imperialism and colonialism, would the liberation of colonial Asia, including Japan, be possible. Not until then would Japan be ready for the second stage—the proletarian revolution.[39]

This leads us to the issue of the "Asiatic despot"—what was, then, the imperial institution in modern Japan? Remarkably, in the early 1920s, neither the Comintern nor the JCP considered the abolition of the monarchy to be a central issue. In the case of the early JCP, the issue in theory was resolved fairly easily. Because Japan was an industrialized capitalist country, the monarch (*kunshu*) was simply a remnant of the feudal past. As Japan's capitalist development was unstoppable and sure, the monarchy was destined to disappear soon, to be succeeded by a democratic "constitutional system" (*rikkensei*).[40] It was believed unnecessary to make the imperial institution the focal point of the communist struggle because capitalist development would, in the natural course of things, sweep it away as a feudal remnant of the past.

Historians have traditionally assumed not only that the JCP program was written down in the Bukharin Theses of 1922 (or, the 1922 Comintern Theses on Japan), but also that the focal point of the theses was the abolition of the imperial system (*kunshusei haishi*). Bukharin, it was claimed, declared the preeminent objective of the JCP to be the establishment of "proletarian dictatorship and the replacement of the military-plutocratic monarchy with the authority of the Soviets."[41] According to official JCP history and historians of Japanese communism, on receiving the Bukharin Theses on Japan, the JCP immediately called a special meeting at Shakujii, a Tokyo district, on March 15, 1923, and adopted them as its official program.[42]

However, based on his extensive research at the Comintern archives in Moscow, Katō Tetsurō has shown that the 1922 Comintern Theses did not call for the abolition of the imperial institution! In fact, Katō persuasively argued that the official JCP story—that it prioritized the struggle against the monarchy from the beginning—has been largely misrepresented by post–World War II Japanese historians with Marxist leanings. The story was originally made up by the communist party member Tokuda Kyūichi during his police interrogations in 1929.[43] According to Katō, there was no such thing as the Bukharin Theses in 1922. It is more likely that what was discussed by Japanese communists at the special meeting at Shakujii in March 1923 was Bukharin's proposal for the Comintern's general program, not the Comintern's program for Japan.[44] The Comintern general program, obviously, did not contain any specific details about Japan.

Indeed, if we examine the day-to-day proceedings of the Fourth Congress, it is evident that Bukharin presented his general proposal at the start of the congress, on November 18.[45] Believing that the victory of the world socialist revolution was just a few years away, Bukharin disapproved of the new Comintern policy of a united front with noncommunists—a policy largely influenced by the diplomatic and political needs of the struggling Soviet state—and instead pressed for the more radical program of an offensive on the "capitalist world." Bukharin was famous among early Bolsheviks for his radical position. He justified, for example, the Soviet invasion of Poland in 1921 and, invoking the French Revolution, declared that Soviet Russia had the right to use military offensives to initiate proletarian revolutions in other countries. Nevertheless, nowhere in his speech does he mention Japan. His proposal was opposed by the majority of the attendees and paralyzed the work of the congress, at which point Lenin (already seriously ill), Trotsky, Karl Radek, and Grigory Zinoviev had to intervene. Their joint resolution rejected Bukharin's proposition and became the resolution of the congress; it asserted the necessity of the transitional demands of the united front and the adoption of tactics suitable for the peculiar context of each country. Zinoviev offered to lead the way in creating programs for each individual communist party, basing them on the draft of the general Comintern program.[46] Therefore, the delegates at the Fourth Congress adopted neither a program put forward by the JCP nor a general program of the Comintern.

In 1922–23, the JCP was preoccupied less with the monarchy than with the revolutionary strategy for Japan. The Shakujii report, written in English (the original is in the Comintern archives in Russia), reveals that JCP members were engrossed in discussing where imperial Japan fit into the Marxist-Leninist historical framework. The debate raged over whether the JCP should agree with the Comintern proposal of the two-stage revolution and the creation of a legal proletarian party and, in general, whether the JCP ought to follow the Comintern's orders at all, as they seemed not to be based on actual knowledge of Japanese conditions.[47] The monarchy issue seemed to be secondary to the more urgent and important one of Japan's place in world history (at least in the Marxist-Leninist version). Moreover, Katō also points out that in the police interrogations of JCP members after the 1923 arrests, there was no mention of the emperor issue. The only two concerns of the police were confirming that the JCP was in fact established as a Comintern branch and clarifying what the theory of the two-stage revolution entailed.[48]

If the Comintern considered Japan's task to be fighting against feudalism, why was the abolition of the monarchy omitted in its recommendations? Here it seems one ought to consider again Soviet foreign affairs. In 1921–22, the Soviet regime still struggled for its own survival. It was of the utmost urgency for the Soviet leaders to negotiate the withdrawal of Japanese troops from Russian territory and to establish diplomatic relations with Japan. It was understood in Moscow that the radical program of the JCP to abolish the imperial system and immediately implement a socialist revolution could endanger diplomatic relations between Soviet Russia and Japan. The needs of the new government took priority over the revolutionary agenda of the Comintern, and the latter conceded. While continuing to recommend the strategy of a united front of the proletariat and national bourgeoisie against Japanese imperialism, the Comintern avoided direct confrontation with the Japanese imperial institution.

Russian Bolsheviks, of course, realized the centrality of the monarchy for Japanese imperialism. The Bukharin Theses, in fact, did exist and did state the need to replace the "military-plutocratic monarchy." But they were not written in 1922 and did not become the Comintern's official recommendation for the JCP. What were later to become known as the Bukharin Theses were originally written in German, in late 1923 and 1924, for the publication of *Materialien zur Frage des Programms der Kommunistische Internationale* (Collection of the programs of the Communist International) in Hamburg, Germany, in 1924. The German edition of the theses included a section on "a proletarian dictatorship," which declared that "the replacement of the military-plutocratic monarchy with the power of the Soviets" was "the goal of the Communist Party."[49]

However, the radicalization of the Comintern position in 1924 had less to do with the Japanese monarchy than with the internal struggle within the Russian Communist Party. The "turn to the left" was initiated by Stalin, who was making his way to power as Lenin was dying. After the abortive German revolution in October 1923, Stalin used the opportunity to defeat his internal rivals, Trotsky and Radek, putting the blame for the failed revolution on their shoulders. Stalin denounced Trotsky-supported united front tactics and took a deliberately radical position, which included a seemingly uncompromising fight against Japan's imperial institution. The *Collection of Programs* for foreign communist parties, including the Bukharin Theses on Japan, served as the guideline for the Comintern's new radical policy.[50] The catch was that no one in Japan—neither the JCP nor the police and government—was aware of the new Comintern demand to abolish the monarchy. The Japanese translation of the theses was published in Japan only in 1928. Yamakawa mentioned that there were rumors of the existence of the Bukharin Theses, but very few people had read the document. Yamakawa therefore was unaware of the monarchy issue because he himself read the

Bukharin Theses in French translation only in 1928.[51] It is probably not coincidental that the revision of the Peace Preservation Law was undertaken in 1928, the year when the issue of the abolition of the monarchy turned up in Japan for the first time.

By refusing to work on the establishment of a legal proletarian party, the early JCP intended to reproduce the tactics of the then illegal Russian Communist Party prior to 1917.[52] In June 1923, at the Third Plenum of the Enlarged Congress of the Comintern Committee (ECCI), Arahata spoke openly against Zinoviev's proposal to establish a legal proletarian party, arguing that such a party would further alienate militant and anarcho-syndicalist elements of the working class.

> Must we form a party and risk losing the support of the active elements in the working class? The syndicalist workers have been against the communist movement for the very reason that the latter became involved in politics. If we form a [legal] party we shall suffer defeat. . . . It is important [first] to educate the workers in politics before we organize them into a political party.[53]

The JCP, and Yamakawa specifically, always insisted that their ultimate goal was the capture of political power, establishment of the dictatorship of the proletariat, and creation of a soviet government. In the meantime, the JCP must create the system of proletarian political education; support the Suiheisha movement; infiltrate and radicalize unions, peasant organizations, and even, remarkably, the army and the navy by organizing clandestine "cells" in order to guide these groups to a socialist revolution.[54]

Yamakawa regarded Japanese labor unions as the closest approximation in Japan to Russian soviets in terms of organization and paradoxically considered labor unions, rather than the vanguard communist party, as the main revolutionary force in the country. In his estimation, it would be organized workers, acting through unions, who would eventually overthrow capitalism, accomplish a socialist revolution, and take control of the country with absolute mass support. In his understanding, the JCP as a party of socialist intellectuals would eventually merge with the bigger labor union movement. Until then, however, the success of the revolution depended on the centralization and unification of labor unions into one national union governed by a central committee. Yamakawa specifically stipulated that the primary task of the JCP was to attract the majority of the working class into the unions. It was within the unions that the emancipation and maturation of the political and individual consciousness of the workers would occur—the necessary precondition for a socialist revolution.[55] Yamakawa thus attempted to merge the socialist and labor movements into one, whereby the labor unions would assume a political character and begin to function as a party.

Yamakawa was inspired by the impact that labor unions were having on domestic and foreign politics. One of the most visible success stories was the anti-interventionist movement initiated by the procommunist labor union Sōdōmei, whose actions were inspired by British labor unions. In 1919, British labor unions and left-wing organizations organized a Hands off Russia Committee, which was fairly successful in turning the British public and workers against the government's intervention in Russia. In July 1920, a delegation sent by the British Labour Party published its report on the situation there; the report had an enormous impact on the public's outlook on the Russian question.[56] The British also sent a report titled "Japanese in Siberia" to the Sōdōmei. The report revealed atrocities committed by the Japanese army in Siberia. The British committee warned that it would make sure that workers around the world boycotted Japanese goods unless the Japanese government changed its aggressive policy in the Russian East. In May and November 1921, the Sōdōmei lodged its protest against the intervention with the Japanese government and voiced opposition to a renewal of the Anglo-Japanese alliance. Moreover, in the May First celebrations of 1921, under the Sōdōmei's influence labor unions in Tokyo began for the first time to demand recognition of the USSR.[57] At the 1922 Sōdōmei national convention, demands were passed for the recognition of the Soviet Union by Japan, the restoration of economic relations with Russia, and the immediate withdrawal of Japanese troops from Siberia. The resolutions of the national convention were written by Akamatsu Katsumaro and Nosaka Sanzō, both members of the JCP, together with Nishio Suehiro, a prominent labor activist. The very public and highly effective political activities of the labor unions were in stark contrast to the socialists' individual attempts to criticize Japanese state actions at home and abroad.[58] Finally, the soviets in Russia and, corresponding to them, the labor unions in Japan, came to be regarded as the makers of the revolution, not the vanguard party of socialist intellectuals.

By 1917, Japanese socialists already had been reckoning with Japanese imperialism for some time, and it was nothing new for them when the Comintern declared that the domestic revolutionary struggle of the Japanese socialists would need to go hand in hand with their struggle against Japanese imperialism in Korea and China.[59] In theory, Japanese communists considered Japanese imperialism as a stage in the development of capitalism in Japan, which resulted in Japan's aggressive expansion and exploitation of backward economic regions in Asia. Capitalism at home was thus the cause of imperialism abroad. The JCP Program of 1922 closed with a section titled "Korean, Chinese, and Siberian Questions." The full text of this section reads as follows:

> The Communist Party of Japan is resolutely opposed to every species of Imperialist policy. It is opposed to the intervention, open and secret,

in China and Siberia, the interference with the governments of these countries, the "Sphere of Influence" and "Vested Interests" in China, Manchuria, and Mongolia, and all other attempts and practices of a similar nature.

The most infamous of all the crimes of Japanese Imperialism has been the annexation of Korea and the enslavement of the Korean People. The Communist Party of Japan not only condemns this act but is taking every available step for the emancipation of Korea. The majority of the Korean patriots, fighting for the Independence of Korea, is not free from the bourgeois ideology and nationalist prejudices. It is necessary that we act in cooperation with them—necessary not only for the victory of the Korean Revolution but also for winning them over to our Communist principles. The Korean Revolution will bring with it a national crisis in Japan and the fate of both the Korean and Japanese proletariat will depend on the success or failure of the fight carried on by the united effort of the Communist Parties of the two countries.

The three principal nations in the Far East, China, Korea, and Japan, are most closely related to one another in their political, social, and economic life, and thus bound to march together toward the goal of Communism. The international solidarity of the proletariat and particularly of these three countries is indispensable to the Victory and Emancipation of the Proletariat, not only of the respective countries but of the whole world.[60]

The JCP recognized the intertwined revolutionary destiny of Japan, Korea, and China, which were "bound to march together toward the goal of Communism." Nowhere were the Western countries and Soviet Russia mentioned, so Japanese communists did not consider Soviet Russia and socialist revolutions in the West to be the indispensable precondition for revolutionary change in Asia. Workers of Asia—Japan, Korea, China, Taiwan—were the makers of their own liberation. In this, the JCP's position diverged from Marx's and Lenin's view that proletarian victory of the Western workers would free the "backward" East.

Non-European communists strongly disagreed with the Comintern's view that the liberation of the non-West "can be victorious only in conjunction with the proletarian revolution in the advanced countries."[61] The early JCP agreed with the Indian revolutionary Manabendra Roy, founder of the Communist Party of India, who first mounted a critique of the Eurocentric orientation of the Bolshevik Party at the Second Congress of the Comintern (in the summer of 1920). Roy argued that the victory of socialism in Russia had saved all backward countries from the historical necessity of passing through a capitalist stage. With the aid of local communist parties, workers of India, China, and elsewhere can take a shortcut to communism. Thus, he rejected Lenin's prescription to subordinate the communist movement of the urban working class to the national bourgeoisie in the non-European countries. He maintained that at the very start of the revolution the communist vanguard ought to seize leadership and not allow it to remain in the hands of the bourgeoisie. Roy's conclusion was that the colonized would initiate their own revolution, regardless of the outcomes of the proletarian struggle in Europe. Moreover, Roy and other Asian communists insisted that the proletarian revolution must triumph in Asia in order for the communist movement in Europe to succeed.[62] Similarly, Yamakawa and the early JCP members believed that the proletarian struggle in Japan must be independent from, and not subsidiary to, the revolution in either the Western advanced countries or Soviet Russia.

Moreover, the early JCP argued that the Japanese revolution must not depend on the Asian colonies—that is, Korea and China—because they were in a different stage of historical development compared to Japan. In the JCP program, Yamakawa made a critical remark that the Korean and Chinese revolutionary movements were still not free from "nationalist prejudices," wrongly prioritizing the slogan of independence from Japanese imperialism over the slogan of independence from capitalism, both Japanese and domestic. Yamakawa and most other Japanese communists regarded Korean and Chinese leftist movements as nationalist rather than truly proletarian in nature.[63] Yamakawa was highly suspicious of what he perceived as virulent Korean nationalism, which he felt was out of step with internationalist and modern socialist movements. In his view, in Asia it was only the Japanese industrial proletariat that had attained an advanced level of proletarian and internationalist class consciousness, and it alone was capable of leading and representing other colonial workers. Yamakawa maintained that the Korean national independence movement should abandon its national liberation aims and instead rise up against its own capitalist class under the guidance of the more progressive Japanese socialist movement.[64] The far-reaching conclusions for the JCP were to brush off the Korean national liberation movement as historically backward; deny the priority of an anti-imperialist struggle, which would require prioritizing the struggle in the colonies and misguided cooperation with the bourgeoisie; and separate the Japanese leftist movement from those of Korea and China.

How and whether to collaborate with Korean colonial workers, and what kind of revolutionary strategy to implement, were the main questions that occupied the Japanese Left in the first half of the 1920s. Only from the mid-1920s forward did Japanese leftists become seriously interested in the Chinese revolutionary movement. Yamakawa's first writings on China appeared only in 1926. In them, he continued to hold the same position—that without the destruction of the imperial government at home, in the Japanese metropole, by means of a socialist revolution, there could be no destruction of Japanese imperialism and therefore no Chinese revolution.[65] Yamakawa did not see himself or the Japanese people as aggressors against Korea and China, since he did not identify the Japanese masses with the imperial state. Ultimately, his "economist" thinking made him somewhat indifferent to the question of imperialism and the role of Japan's empire in Asia. Despite the Comintern's early call to prioritize the anti-imperialist struggle in Japan and East Asia, under Yamakawa's guidance Japanese socialists insisted on the priority of the domestic national struggle against domestic capitalism, which they believed would eventually benefit the whole colonial world in Asia.

Early JCP activities were seriously hampered by the police crackdown and internal turmoil. In June 1923, the police arrested more than one hundred socialists and members of the JCP. Thirty party members, including Yamakawa in 1924, were brought to trial under the Public Order and Police Law. Yamakawa was acquitted and released due to lack of evidence; the others received sentences ranging from eight to ten months of imprisonment. Four prominent communists—Sanō Manabu, Kondō Eizō, Takatsu Seidō, and Yamamoto Kenzō—managed to escape to Vladivostok, where they were joined by Arahata, who was attending the Third Plenum of the Comintern, as well as by Wada Kiichirō, Yamazaki Kazuo, and Maniwa Suekichi from Moscow, and Tsujii Taminosuke from Chita. In March 1924, they established the foreign bureau of the Japanese Communist Party in Vladivostok, which acted as an intermediary between Moscow and the remaining Japanese communists in Japan.[66]

The JCP and the bureau in Vladivostok, however, went through hard financial times, exacerbated by a series of embarrassing incidents for the JCP. In early 1923, the communist Yoshihara Tarō disappeared en route from Moscow to Tokyo with a large sum of money and diamonds he had received from the Comintern to finance communist activities in Japan. In 1925, a member of the bureau, Tatsuo Kitahara, traveled to Shanghai, where he received the enormous sum of 10,000 yen from the Comintern, then disappeared with the money somewhere in Japan, paralyzing the activities of the bureau and the remaining Japanese communists at home.[67] There were other incidents of abuse of funds, and in the eyes of outsiders they cast a dubious light on the whole communist group. There is no doubt that rumors about "easy" Comintern money attracted opportunists, rogues, and pretenders, and that some of them were recruited by the police to spy on the leftist radicals.

But it was a natural disaster and its aftermath that completely crushed the early JCP. On September 1, 1923, a massive earthquake hit Tokyo, killing around 120,000 people. In the ensuing chaos, about six thousand Korean residents were killed in a kind of pogrom, and a number of known leftists, including Ōsugi, were murdered by the military police. Demoralized by the arrests, murders, and general devastation of the city, at the JCP meeting on October 22, 1923, the remaining members decided to disband the party.[68] Post–World War II Japanese Marxist historians explained the collapse of the first JCP by referring to Japan's initial lack of independent Marxist theorists and experienced domestic agitators. This, they argued, led to the JCP's dependency on Comintern instructions, which were not based on adequate knowledge of Japanese society and history. Consequently, the communist movement failed to develop indigenous roots, remained alien to Japanese society, and did not succeed in organizing significant resistance to the authoritarian state. This opinion was echoed by Soviet scholars, who used to point out that given the low level of societal development and paucity of socialist thought in Japan, the first JCP may have been a premature creation.[69] Western scholars have also described the creation of the JCP as a case of forced importation of revolution from Soviet Russia, with the JCP functioning as an obedient subsidiary of the Comintern.[70] Robert Scalapino has argued that the ideological heterogeneity and immaturity of JCP members in terms of their growth as "true Marxist-Leninists," combined with ignorance among Soviet and Comintern authorities regarding the situation in Japan, resulted in the collapse of Japan's communist movement.

Archival evidence suggests, however, that it was not the Marxist theoretical "immaturity" of JCP members that brought about the dissolution of the JCP. Rather, the main cause was lack of conviction among its founders about the necessity of the party's very existence. The composition of the first JCP was diverse. Many Japanese intellectuals were emotionally and intellectually attracted to Marxism and were potential communist adherents or sympathizers. Numerous activists joined the JCP, united by a shared concern over growing poverty and social displacement, and agitated for the democratization of the political system. Thus, although the party was "communist" in name, most of its members were not communists properly speaking. But most importantly for Yamakawa, the dilemma of how to organize the work of the illegal communist party in different organizations and settings, and how best to set up the relationship between the party and labor unions, was never resolved. The murders of Asian immigrants by working-class mobs shook Yamakawa's faith in the maturity and revolutionary potential of Japanese workers. The Kantō earthquake and its aftermath thus became the turning point for the early communists, prompting many of them to turn from illegal to legal revolutionary activities.

In late 1923, after the earthquake, Yamakawa announced for the first time the need to create a legal mass proletarian party. He and other members of the socialist circle began to insist on participating in the universal suffrage movement and abandoned the tactic of abstaining from voting. Yamakawa realized that the unions had limited appeal for the working masses, but that a legal prole-tarian party could become a conduit for workers' interests in the Diet and create conditions that would allow the workers' movement and class consciousness to grow. This, Yamakawa now insisted, was the only revolutionary path available to Japan in its present condition.[71] Yamakawa finally agreed with the Comintern's earlier assessment that Japan's modernity was incomplete, its working class was not ready for a proletarian revolution, and cooperation with the liberal bourgeoi-sie in parliamentary institutions was desirable.

At this point, however, the Comintern did not have a unified view on Japan. At the Fifth Comintern Congress in July 1924, no resolution was reached regarding the situation in Japan due to lack of sufficient information and the absence of delegates from Japan.[72] The Comintern headquarters relegated the responsibility for dealing with the situation in Japan to its agent in Shanghai, Grigory Voitinsky, who authored the so-called Shanghai Theses of 1925. Voitinsky had always main-tained that Japan and China had very little in common. He strongly believed that the Comintern's commitment to the alliance of the Chinese communists with the bourgeois anti-imperialist Guomindang nationalists should not be replicated in Japan. The time for such an alliance had passed, he argued, opposing the new course of Japanese socialists to unite with progressive liberal forces. In the post-earthquake situation, Voitinsky urged, the imperialist state went on an offensive against the proletariat at home, as well as in Korea and China, and coopera-tion with the bourgeoisie or even the social democrats was no longer possible. Voitinsky had some criticism for the Comintern's headquarters in Moscow, too. He urged the Comintern decision makers to distinguish between conditions in China and Japan and modify their recommendations accordingly. He declared that Japanese capitalism had reached its highest stage and its emerging crisis would soon establish the preconditions for a proletarian revolution.[73] The rees-tablishment of the JCP was in order.

When Sakai and Yamakawa received the Shanghai Theses in Tokyo in Feb-ruary 1925, they categorically disagreed with the proposition to reestablish the JCP. Sakai argued that the communist movement could not develop with the illegal party at its head. Yamakawa refused to participate in the reorganization of the JCP, asserting that the theses ignored the uniqueness of Japan's position and demonstrated a lack of understanding of the country's socioeconomic and his-torical development.[74] At this stage, Yamakawa argued, Japanese socialists should work through a legal proletarian party, unions, and intellectual societies. The existence of an illegal party would hamper such activities, isolating the vanguard from the masses and subjecting it to useless and unnecessary persecution.[75]

The Comintern in Moscow also hesitated and in fact never endorsed the mil-itant Shanghai Theses. Quite to the contrary, the party leadership in Moscow seemed to agree with Yamakawa's and Sakai's resistance to Voitinsky's plans. In the summer of 1925, after the recognition of the USSR by Japan, the Soviet trade mission was opened in Tokyo. Karlis Yanson (1882–1939), an old revolutionary who helped create the American Communist Party together with John Reed and Katayama Sen in 1919, as well as the Canadian Communist Party and the Workers Party of Canada in 1921–22, became head of the embassy. Yanson became the first Russian revolutionary in Japan who could give a firsthand account of the Japanese communist movement. He was in close contact with Japanese communists, lending them money and helping to organize their activities, even after his transfer to Shanghai in 1927 to replace Voitinsky. In Japan, Yanson was able to assess the situation on the ground, and he agreed with Yamakawa's position that the creation of a communist party was premature, as there seemed to be no mass support for it. In fact, Adolf Ioffe made similar comments in his reports from Tokyo to Moscow in the spring of 1923 that Japan was not ready for a communist movement. Yanson reported to Moscow that strengthening labor unions and creating a mass labor party on the model of the British Labour Party must be the priority.[76] In his December 1926 report, in which he notified the Comintern of the reorganization of the JCP, Yanson maintained that the creation of a legal mass proletarian movement was of utmost importance, even more so as conservative and radical right-wing groups were becoming a dominant force in big politics and military circles. Both Yanson and Yamakawa maintained that transition to a new social order was possible only by means of a legal proletarian party, which would (at least initially) struggle for a social democratic order within the bourgeois-democratic political system.

In his reports to Zinoviev, Yanson urged that the Comintern assist with publishing Japanese translations of Russian communist thinkers such as Lenin and Stalin—who were in high demand in Japan and whose works could be disseminated legally—as well as attend to the publication of Russian translations of Japanese leftist authors. Yanson pointed out that Russia still lacked adequate knowledge about Japan, especially its modern history, and that it was of the utmost urgency to initiate academic studies of the country.[77] Zinoviev repeated Yanson's recommendations concerning Japan at the Comintern meeting in September 1925 and ordered an immediate translation of Lenin's works into Japanese. Zinoviev was the head of the Comintern between 1919 and 1926, and in formulating his position on Japan—which was therefore the official Comintern position—he adopted not Voitinsky's argument to reestablish an illegal JCP but Yanson's moderate one. Zinoviev endorsed the creation of a legal party in Japan, maintaining that it was a strategic mistake to create an illegal party on the model of the prerevolutionary Social Democratic Party in Russia. Other matters, the Japanese radicals would have to decide for themselves:

We have not studied Japan enough, and we know very little about its development. We must not make hasty decisions, even about organizational matters. . . . Those who will go from our organization to Japan or who already work there must first of all study the country. We must find someone who will write a study about the situation in Japan, as comrade Roy did about India. We need to have such a book.[78]

The Comintern did not arrive at any firm conclusions about how to proceed, and Zinoviev finally entrusted the eastern branches of the Comintern, in Vladivostok and Shanghai, with the task of proposing a course of action for the JCP. He specifically asked the Japanese communists and the Comintern's agents in Vladivostok and Shanghai to produce economic and political analyses of the situation in Japan.

Japanese communists were well aware of the Comintern's ambivalence and factionalism. Yamakawa, for example, disagreed not with the Comintern headquarters in Moscow (which, as we have seen, was indecisive and in general supported the creation of a legal proletarian party), but with those who were pushing for the reestablishment of the JCP, namely Voitinsky and local Japanese communists. Yamakawa was aware that the Comintern was not a monolithic organization but rather combined several "nerve centers" at different localities, which defined its local policies. His disagreements were thus not with the Comintern itself but with its agents in China, who were pushing their own local agenda.

As long as the Comintern endorsed Yamakawa's plan to work through a legal organization, the cooperation between Russian and Japanese communists continued. Comintern documents reveal that Yamakawa was in close contact with Yanson and submitted several reports to the Comintern until 1927.[79] During this period, Yamakawa and other communists worked on infiltrating several leftist organizations, of which he duly notified the Comintern. Japanese communists had a strong influence in the militant Nihon Nōmin Kumiai (Japan Farmers' Union, established in 1922), which by 1925 had a membership of more than seventy thousand.[80] Communists also infiltrated the Seiji Kenkyūkai (Political Research Association, established in December 1923), which was devoted to educating the masses and assisting in forming a proletarian party. The association experienced amazing growth, and by 1925 included some four thousand workers, peasants, students, white-collar workers, and professionals in over fifty branches throughout the country. Communists also dominated the Nihon Rōdō Kumiai Hyōgikai (Japan Labor Union Council), which, by the end of 1925 and only a few months after its formation, consisted of fifty-nine unions with a membership of thirty-five thousand workers. The Hyōgikai soon became affiliated with the Pan-Pacific Trade Unions Secretariat, a creation of Profintern. Through these organizations, the communist group influenced the country's first legal proletarian party, the Rōdōsha Nōmintō (Worker-Farmer Party, established in March 1926).[81] The enactment of universal manhood suffrage in 1925 raised Yamakawa's hopes that the workers' legal struggle was becoming possible, although his expectation was counterbalanced by the enactment of the Peace Preservation Law in the same year.

Yamakawa's final break with the Comintern and Soviet communism happened because of the Comintern Theses on Japan, authored by Nikolai Bukharin, in 1927. What caused the break was that Yamakawa finally realized that for the Russians, China and the Chinese Revolution would always take precedence over Japan and its socialist movement. Publication of the Comintern Theses on Japan was itself a reaction to events in China. To be fair, the original request came from members of the reorganized JCP (1926), who resided at the time in Moscow. Whether they were asked to write the request by their Russian comrades or it was a genuine concern is unclear and not important. Concerned with the Shandong Expedition of April–May 1927, and Japanese military participation in the suppression of the Chinese Revolution, in June 1927 the JCP requested that the Comintern write up a thesis on Japan, citing as the main reason the growing importance of the China question for the world revolution.[82] The main impact on the theses, however, came from the massacre of Chinese communists by the Guomindang nationalists in April 1927. Since 1922, Stalin and Bukharin had promoted the alliance of the Chinese communists with Guomindang nationalists, a policy about which Trotsky and Zinoviev had reservations. After the 1927 disaster, Stalin and Bukharin shifted their policy 180 degrees and blamed Trotsky and Zinoviev for the Comintern's failure in China. Stalin and Bukharin now advocated for restructuring and restrengthening militant communist parties around the world; no alliances with "treacherous," "social fascist" nationalist and social democratic groups were allowed.

The Comintern Theses on Japan, written by Bukharin and adopted on July 15, 1927, reflected the new radical position of the Comintern. Bukharin focused on two issues: Japanese imperialism and the nature of the Japanese state. In regard to Japanese imperialism, Yamakawa agreed with Bukharin's assessment that it had a peculiar characteristic that made it different from the more familiar Western version. Since the early 1920s, Yamakawa had pointed to mass nationalism as responsible for the unhindered development of the Japanese Empire.[83] Japanese imperialism, Bukharin argued, was getting stronger and more aggressive largely due to wide support by the Japanese masses, who were being "duped" by the government's promises of opportunities for them in mainland China. Noting especially the entanglement of capitalism, imperialism, and militarism, both Yamakawa and Bukharin pointed out that it was the mixture of nationalism and patriotism, carefully orchestrated by the military, that enabled Japanese capitalist imperialism to carry on with the silent support of the masses.

But if Yamakawa saw redemption in the gradual maturation of Japanese workers' class consciousness, for Bukharin Japan could be "saved" only by outside influence. He concluded that only the Chinese Revolution and the crumbling of the Japanese Empire would change Japan's domestic situation; therefore, the future of the revolution in Japan must be discussed in relation to the Chinese Revolution. If the Japanese Empire could be brought down in the colonies, the Chinese Revolution would rapidly gain strength and its success would inspire socialist movements worldwide, including in Japan. The socialist movement in Japan would be aided by the success of the CCP's struggle on the mainland. In the text of the 1927 Theses, the first four tasks listed concerned Japanese imperialism, while only the fifth task pertained to the dissolution of the Diet, followed by the abolition of the monarchy.[84] Therefore, Bukharin proclaimed, the most important tasks for the JCP were the struggle against Japanese imperialism in China, on the one hand, and against Japan's preparation for war against the USSR, on the other.

The second issue raised by Bukharin was the stage of Japanese capitalist development, which directly related to his insistence on the need for an independent communist party in Japan. Bukharin perceived that the recent rapid growth of capitalism and imperialism had propelled Japan's capitalist bourgeoisie to power, and that the country's feudal absolutism had developed into a bourgeois monarchy. He acknowledged that the previous Comintern strategy of a united front for China and Japan was wrong. Japan had all the conditions in place for a social coup and the dictatorship of the proletariat. Japanese communists should therefore be aware of their vanguard task in leading the coming revolution. Bukharin drew attention to Yamakawa's misguided belief that the communist party could be replaced by a legal proletarian party or leftist labor unions. The new JCP, Bukharin argued, must be "steel-like, ideologically mature, Leninist, disciplined, centralized, and a mass communist party."[85] Moreover, the communist party must undertake the task of defeating the social democrats because of "their spreading of parliamentary illusions, and their role as helpmates and camp followers of the pseudo-liberal bourgeoisie."[86]

The Comintern's insistence that the illegal JCP work to ensure the survival of the Chinese Revolution at the expense of domestic socialist development finally broke the relationship between Yamakawa and his supporters with the Comintern. Yamakawa, Arahata Kanson, Sakai Toshihiko, Inomata Tsunao, and others, exited the JCP and established their own faction, Rōnō-ha (Labor-Farmer Faction), named after their journal Rōnō (Labor farmer). Witnessing the upsurge of proletarian parties, Yamakawa and the Rōnō-ha became really concerned that the illegal JCP would endanger the whole proletarian movement and jeopardize the few gains they had made so far.[87] In February 1928, the followers of the Rōnō-ha were formally expelled from the JCP by order of the Comintern.

There was a strong tendency among European and Japanese communists to draw a distinction between an orthodox Marxism, applicable to conditions in the advanced countries of Western Europe and Japan, and a separate Leninism rooted in the realities of backward peasant Russia. Concerns about the predominance of Soviet state interests over the national revolutionary requirements of the communist parties took a critical turn after 1924. Despite the popularity of the Russian Revolution, the dominant view of Japanese leftists in the 1920s was that Japan's revolutionary path should emulate that of advanced West European countries, where the role of the communist party was minimalized. In general, Yamakawa and the Japanese Left in the 1920s maintained that with the inevitable collapse of world capitalism and the growth of legal labor movements, a true socialist democratic society would be established in Japan. Yamakawa was never at ease with the Bolshevik vision of militant and violent revolutionary progression to socialism, or with the Leninist theory of the vanguard party. Nor did he agree with the Comintern's assessment of Japan's social and capitalist development.

This chapter has shown that in the postrevolutionary years, the Comintern did not exercise as much intellectual and practical control over Japanese communists as more orthodox interpretations have argued. Often Comintern agents (Grigory Voitinsky in Shanghai, Karlis Yanson in Tokyo), as well as Japanese communists themselves, acted independently of Moscow's instructions, and Moscow in turn gave them a lot of leeway. Until the late 1920s, Japanese and other foreign communists, while accepting guidance from Bolshevik experts, still had the confidence and critical capabilities to judge what kinds of revolutionary actions were possible in their own local settings. Thus, although by the end of 1927 the JCP had "bolshevized," it still disregarded Comintern instructions on some crucial matters. For example, despite the Comintern's campaign against "fascist social democrats," Japanese communists actively worked on creating a united front with the centrist Nihon Rōnōtō (Japan Labor-Farmer Party), Rōdō Nōmintō (the Labor-Farmer Party), and the Shakai Minshūtō (Socialist Mass Party).[88] Nor were the Comintern's demands as radical as had hitherto been assumed. The Comintern did not demand that the JCP topple the imperial institution either in 1922 or in 1927; it agreed that a legal, noncommunist party was a better solution for the time being; and agreed with Yamakawa that Japan was an industrially advanced country rather than a semifeudal one.

The only consistent point of disagreement between Russian and Japanese communists remained the question of the place of the JCP in the regionwide anti-imperialist struggle, and specifically the JCP's relation with the Chinese Revolution. At the core of this disagreement were two different visions of revolution. Russian communists believed that because it was so successful their revolution was the only correct one, and that they had the right and responsibility to prescribe the course of actions for foreign communist parties, even if they were ignorant of the local conditions. Yamakawa and his followers, for their part, in the Rōnō-ha faction believed in the unilinear schema of historical development, according to which, they thought, Russia was behind Japan, and therefore the Russian Revolution was not applicable to modern Japan. Consequently, the Japanese communists of the 1920s accepted the Comintern's recommendations for how to accomplish a revolution with justifiable reservations.

Now, Yamakawa and the Rōnō-ha faction did not represent the whole Japanese interwar Left and, in fact, since the late 1920s their critical view of the Comintern had not been the dominant one. After the Rōnō-ha's exit, the remaining JCP members accepted the 1927 Theses, and thus the Comintern's insistence on the priority of the Chinese Revolution for the Japanese leftist agenda. Several factors weighed on the JCP's acceptance of this new course. First, starting in the mid-1920s, and due to the extremely complex situation within the Soviet Union's leadership, the Comintern began increasingly to demand that its members conform ideologically and organizationally to the ruling party of Russia.[89] The Comintern's increased centralization and bureaucratization left little space for Japanese and other foreign communists to voice their opposition. The historian Sandra Wilson has argued that since that point the core members of the JCP were "by definition loyal to the Comintern."[90] It is true that, due to Yamakawa's departure and the centralization of the Comintern, the critical impulse within Japanese communism diminished.

However, the Comintern alone could not have forced Japanese leftists to suddenly accept its instructions and, by extension, the Russian revolutionary model as the only correct one. The JCP's acceptance of the Comintern party line was due, I argue, to the escalating imperialist actions of the Japanese government in China.[91] In April 1927, the new prime minister, General Tanaka Gi'ichi, initiated an aggressive course in China that would "separate Manchuria and Mongolia," confirm Japan's special position in both areas, and prevent the Chinese Revolution from spreading to Manchuria. In May 1928, Japanese and Chinese forces clashed at Jinan (the so-called Jinan Incident), and in June 1928 officers of the Kwantung army assassinated Chang Tso-lin, the warlord of Northeast China, paving the way for the future takeover of the whole of Manchuria by Japanese forces. In 1931, the Japanese seized all of Manchuria; in January 1932, Japan virtually annexed parts of Shanghai; in March 1932, the Japanese puppet-state Manchukuo was established. These were the first steps in the Sino-Japanese struggle that, in 1937, led to a full-scale Japanese invasion of China. The subsequent intense pressure on the leftist opposition at home by the police and the government, the proliferation of radical and conservative right-wing organizations, and the changing economic and political structures at home dictated by the demands of Japan's intervention in China, made it obvious to the JCP that the futures of China and Japan had become intertwined.

The Left's preoccupation with Japanese aggression in China and its repercussions at home, however, ended the debates over the meaning of the Russian Revolution. Being a communist in Japan in the 1930s was different than being a communist in the early 1920s. The motives for joining and the goals of the struggle were distinct. While the early JCP fought to expand the political and social rights of the Japanese people, Japanese communists of the 1930s set their sights on curbing Japanese imperialism abroad. Since 1928, the majority of the Left found in the Chinese Revolution and the defense of the Soviet state the only way in which the Japanese proletarian revolution could ever be achieved. The JCP itself became committed to the Comintern more than ever, as it came to believe that only the Comintern, and the Russian revolutionary model, could provide a framework for international cooperation and struggle.

NATIONAL SOCIALISM AND SOVIET COMMUNISM

> **All their [Lenin's and Trotsky's] actions are centered on the establishment of political authority. But there is not much difference between the Russian Bolshevik government and the Western gentlemen's clique governments. Both rest on strong authority. Both are class governments. The main difference is that the strong authority in Russia is not in the hands of the gentlemen's clique but in the hands of workers.**
>
> —Takabatake Motoyuki, "Political and Economic Movements from the New Point of View," *Shinshakai*, May 1918

Parallel to the early JCP's critical engagement with the Comintern-imposed revolutionary framework, another group of Japanese socialists prompted by the Russian Revolution embarked on a "revision of socialism" from the national point of view. In 1919, the socialist Takabatake Motoyuki (1886–1928) declared that national socialism (*kokka shakaishugi*) was an improved version of Marxism more suitable for post–World War I realities. Like classical Marxism, Japanese national socialism, Takabatake proclaimed, continued to strive for an anticapitalist and social revolution, which would, however, strengthen the role of the state and address the needs of the national community. The Russian Revolution, he continued, was none other than the first of the national socialist revolutions to come in the world.

The emergence of statist and nationalist doctrines on the Left and the Right was a global phenomenon during and after World War I.[1] They were, however, not simply a reaction to the collapse of empires and the appearance of various nation-states. National and statist ideas had come to fruition by the end of the 1910s as a rejection of liberalism (and associated with it, capitalism), parliamentary politics, and internationalist Marxism. Japan's national socialist doctrines therefore resembled radical ideas about the relationship between the state, society, and the individual, emerging simultaneously most notably in Germany and Italy. Japanese national socialism, however, could be best described as what Zeev Sternhell called the interwar "non-conformist Left."[2] In their pursuit of a social revolution and revision of Marxism, the interwar generation of socialists in Europe and Japan abandoned the idea of the working class as the prime revolutionary force and instead replaced it with the nation as a whole. This gave birth to a new concept of the state, which was to organize, direct, and defend the national community, as well as reflect the wishes and aspirations of the newly "awakened" masses rather than those of the old political and economic elites. This desire to go beyond Marxism and find in the nation and the state the true revolutionary force was, as Sternhell argued, "one of the main routes for going from left to right and from the extreme left to the extreme right."[3]

Takabatake and his followers, however, never became an internal part of the Japanese interwar radical Right, despite collaborating closely with extreme rightist groups.[4] Japanese national socialists stubbornly and publicly identified themselves as Marxists and saw the Soviet Union as their aspiration and the model of the proletarian state. Nevertheless, preoccupied first and foremost with social and economic tensions, Takabatake and his followers found in nationalism, rather than in class struggle and international proletarian brotherhood, the means to awaken the masses to their revolutionary potential and to radically reorganize state and society. The end goal for the national socialists was the destruction of the capitalist order, so that ultimately, in their thinking, anticapitalism replaced socialism. Consequently, Takabatake's influential interpretation of the Russian Revolution as a national, statist, and anticapitalist revolution made those who were not necessarily on the Left—politicians, reform bureaucrats (*kakushin kanryō*), and even some among the military—look favorably at the Soviet communist project. Searching for ways to reorganize the social order in the post-Depression period, the bureaucratic and military elite in the 1930s took notice of the national socialist program. Taking advantage of the interest and believing that a revolution was to be made by a "conscious" elite, not the working class, many national socialists (and their ideas) found their way into the highest echelons of power in wartime Japan.

As this chapter demonstrates, the most important moment in the development of Taishō national socialism was Takabatake's early engagement with the Russian Revolution. Addressing his fellow socialists, he insisted that the Russian Revolution was done in the name of and for the Russian nation, not its working class. By arguing this, Takabatake aspired to transform the Japanese socialist movement into a national socialist one and develop it into a potent political party. In this way, the Russian Revolution was utilized by national socialists to win over the Japanese Left to their radical vision of social and political organization. The curious case of Japanese interwar national socialism is that despite the fact that the turbulent social and political shifts of the 1920s seemed like the most opportune time for national socialism, its adherents had never succeeded in organizing an independent political movement, neither on the Left nor on the Right. On one hand, national socialists failed to convince the Japanese Left to abandon the proletariat and the notion of class struggle as its revolutionary concern in favor of the nation; on the other hand, the existing state, despite its internal fractures, managed to keep its monopoly on power. Specifically, reform bureaucrats and the military elite, not least stimulated by leftist and rightist agitation from below as well as their programs, eventually came up with their own conception of a new order by the late 1930s.[5]

Taishō national socialism differed from its counterparts in Germany and Italy in one major way: it arose in the context of the growing Japanese Empire, which had to compete intensely not only with the European powers and the United States but also with another emerging superpower in East Asia, the Soviet Union. Germany and Italy lost the Great War, the aftermath of which prompted the rise of the anticommunist fascist movement from below. Japan, in contrast, as one of the Allies, technically won, acquiring a more preeminent position in Asia. As an empire with expansionist aspirations, Japan benefited greatly from World War I and in the aftermath of the war developed ambitious plans for economic and political expansion in China, which was increasingly challenged by communist Russia. While admiring Soviet state building in principle, Takabatake and his followers developed the most virulent anticommunist critique, which was rivaled only by the anarchists' attack on Russian communists. But, as this chapter demonstrates, national socialists' anticommunism stemmed from the same old insecurities and perception that the northern neighbor was the perpetual threat to the Japanese nation. In fact, the old insecurities were superseded in the interwar period by fears of an even more aggressive Soviet imperialism, which additionally buttressed the idea of the primacy of the national community above social classes. Like the conservative bureaucracy, national socialists considered communism and its central doctrine of class struggle to be a tool of the Soviet Union to destabilize the Japanese national community by targeting its most vulnerable segments of society. Taishō national socialism thus was shaped within the imperial context in which the perceived need to forestall Soviet expansionism contributed to its conception of the state and the nation. The explosive mixture of national socialists' convictions—preeminence of the state, nationalism, elitism, and most importantly, anticommunism/anti-Sovietism—ultimately resulted in their support of Japan's imperial expansion.

Takabatake Motoyuki's path to socialism followed the common pattern of his generation of socialists—dismayed at the poverty of the people and at the corruption and elitism of contemporary politics, Takabatake, baptized Christian in his youth (something that he renounced later), found in socialism a moral and theoretical vindication.[6] But it was the Russo-Japanese War of 1904–5 that shaped Takabatake's political attitude. The war became the crucible for early Japanese socialism, which confronted its followers with the choice of either "the motherland" or "international solidarity." Appalled at the hardships caused by mobilization for the war, in 1903 the socialists Kōtoku Shūsui and Sakai Toshi- hiko established the Heiminsha (Commoners' Society). The society organized antiwar protest meetings and public forums; produced radical antiwar and antigovernment publications that sold well; published works by Marx, Engels, Lassalle, Bebel, Kropotkin, and Tolstoy; and established contacts with the inter- national movement, including with the then-unknown Vladimir Lenin. The antiwar socialist faction was, however, in the minority. Most Japanese leftists supported the war, which they regarded as a war of progress, just and neces- sary to combat Russian autocracy and imperialism. Still a student, Takabatake strongly disagreed with Kōtoku's condemnation of patriotism and militarism and instead considered them virtues necessary for the survival and strength of the Japanese state in the face of Russian expansionism. The Russo-Japanese War and the debates over national versus international loyalties left a long and divi- sive legacy in the Japanese Left and foreshadowed similar debates in the Second International in the wake of World War I.

Takabatake's enthusiasm for the Russo-Japanese War was influenced by the prominent public figure Yamaji Aizan (1864–1917), who regarded the war as paramount to the interests of the Japanese state.[7] Besides the issue of war, Yamaji's version of state socialism also had a formative influence on Takabatake. In August 1905, Yamaji, by that time the leader of the "right-wing socialists," announced the establishment of the National Social Party (Kokka shakaitō), which declared its aim to be the reestablishment of socialist practices that Yamaji claimed had already existed in ancient Japan. In his view, ancient Japan possessed a just social order, with a benevolent monarchy presiding over its obedient sub- jects. To bring back that type of socialism, Yamaji called for restrictions on liberal capitalism, advocated a social-reformist state socialism, and declared the coming twentieth century to be the age of nationalism. Yamaji was strongly criticized by Sakai Toshihiko for his nationalist ideology that concealed the class nature of Japanese society.[8] What Yamaji did for Takabatake was that he "eternalized" socialism as an aspiration for a just social order—separating it from capitalist antagonisms, historical context, and social realities, and thus from the working class itself. In its rudimentary form, Takabatake's national socialist ideas were shaped during 1904–5 through his support of the imperialist war against Russia and Yamaji Aizan's version of "ethical" socialism for the sake of the nation.

Despite his disagreement with the antiwar position of Kōtoku Shūsui, Tak- abatake joined Kōtoku's anarcho-syndicalist group in Tokyo in early 1907, attracted by its militancy and direct-action tactics.[9] The militant phase did not last long, however. Eager to quell opposition to Japan's annexation of Korea in 1910, the Japanese government acted swiftly and indicted Kōtoku Shūsui and twenty-four other anarchists for plotting to assassinate the emperor. Like the rest of the nation, Takabatake was shocked by the public trial and execution of his former comrades, yet he continued to associate with the shrunken socialist group. Despite the mass desertions from socialist circles, Takabatake stuck with his socialist convictions and worked at Sakai Toshihiko's publishing office, Baibunsha, as the editor of the international column in their publication *Shinshakai*.

The Russian Revolution, and the unprecedented policies of the new Soviet regime (dictatorship of the Bolshevik Party, war communism, NEP, militarization of labor unions, etc.), confronted Japanese socialists with challenges for which their education in the West European socialist tradition had not prepared them. The process of the Russian Revolution eventually split the previously unified Left into anarchists, the early communists, and those who soon began to call themselves *kokka shakaishugisha*, or national socialists. Takabatake needed, however, to go through an intense intellectual engagement with the Russian Revolution before he could launch his own movement. In fact, over the course of 1918 he emerged in the socialist scene as the most effective defender of the Soviet regime. The first public socialist debate, about the nature of the Russian Revolution and consequently the goals and strategies of the Japanese radical movement, was conducted by the two leftist theoreticians, Takabatake and Yamakawa Hitoshi, who would eventually tear the Left apart. Yamakawa, following the Marxist scheme, argued that the Bolshevik Revolution was a social revolution in which the Russian proletarian class toppled the capitalist system.[10] In contrast, Takabatake insisted that the October Revolution was not a social revolution from below—in other words, a workers' mass uprising—but rather a political revolution from above, accomplished by the Bolshevik Party that was made up of the vanguard of Russian socialist intellectuals.

Having confronted the paradox that plagued many socialist thinkers in 1917— why did the world's first socialist revolution happen in backward Russia, against all the predictions of Marxist theory?—Takabatake's answer was that Marx was wrong and Lenin was right. Following Lenin, he pointed to the inconsistency of the Marxist belief that a socialist revolution, although an outcome of social and economic contradictions, could be accomplished by a small vanguard of "professional" revolutionaries.[11] Takabatake believed that Russia offered a model for Japan. Although Japan's proletariat was meager and immature by comparison, the Russian example had convinced him that there could be a version of socialism in which backwardness and the existence of the imperial institution were not hindrances but advantages. A small group of revolutionaries could implement changes from above without waiting for the class consciousness of the workers to mature and without dismantling the imperial institution—a move that, he feared, might lead to civil war, as was happening in Russia at the time. Yamaji

Aizan's version of socialism—devoid of any historical, social, and economic context—certainly prepared Takabatake to accept the Russian Revolution's "unexpected" timing. Consequently, the first lesson Takabatake retained from his engagement with the Russian Revolution was that the proletariat was, after all, irrelevant for a successful revolution.

As the Bolshevik leaders were consolidating their power in 1919–20, Takabatake confronted another dilemma in Marxist theory—the withering away of the state. Marxists around the world were grappling with the fact that, contrary to Marx's prophecy that the workers' revolution would result in the end of the state as a mode of governance, the Bolshevik leadership in Russia was devoting its energy to building an even stronger state than the one it had toppled (despite Lenin's insistence on the transitory character of the new Soviet regime).[12] Takabatake argued that the reality of the Soviet state, and especially its dictatorial character, revealed that Lenin did not follow or support Marx's state theory. In the Russian Revolution, he explained, the Bolsheviks seized state power and, acting *as the state socialist authority*, united the masses to fight capitalists and resist foreign intervention in order to gain national unity and strength: "First, through the implementation of public ownership [*kōyūshugi*], the power of the state concentrated in the hands of the Bolshevik leadership; second, the Bolsheviks abandoned the social-reformist program promoted by labor union movements and legislation; third, they ignored the democratic element of the socialist program, and at times even opposed it."[13]

In addition to the elitism and statism of Leninism, Takabatake also approved of its nondemocratic style of governance. Hastening to defend the Bolshevik regime against its critics, Takabatake pointed out that "democracy" was an intellectual product of Western capitalist liberal ideology and had nothing to do with the active participation of the people in politics and civic life. In this sense, Bolshevism was indeed antidemocratic and anti-Western. Takabatake argued that even though the October Revolution was a takeover pulled off by a small group of individuals rather than a mass uprising, it had been carried out in the name of and for the benefit of all the people of Russia. Hence, he claimed, the proletarian dictatorship and its violent means for achieving an equitable and prosperous nation-state were justified.[14]

Takabatake pointed out that the reality of the Soviet state and its dictatorial character revealed that Lenin did not follow or support Marx's state theory. In reality, Russian Marxists approved the state and used it, first to capture power and then to build a socialist economy.[15] The Bolsheviks thus merely revealed the shortcomings of Marx's state theory and exposed the indispensability of the nation-state. Takabatake blamed Japanese socialists for not clarifying socialism's core doctrine as it was determined by the Russian Revolution—that is, centralized production, state ownership, and nationalization of industries. Instead, they allowed Japanese anarchists to take center stage and claim that true socialism was the abolition of the state. Takabatake called for socialists to discredit and distance themselves from the anarchists, whose utopian visions were damaging the socialist movement in Japan.[16] Judging from the Bolshevik success, the Japanese Left must realize, Takabatake insisted, the paramount importance of politics and the state in the reorganization of society.

Moved by the Russian and German revolutions to take action, Takabatake grew increasingly impatient to start a mass movement and organize a political party, despite Sakai's wariness. He assembled around himself a group of young men—Kitahara Tatsuo, Endō Tomoshirō, Mogi Kyūhei, and Ozaki Shirō—who came from the universal suffrage movement but, inspired by the Russian Revolution and frustrated at the passivity of the "masses" (*minshū*), sought out Takabatake in hopes of participating in more radical actions. Ozaki Shirō wrote in 1918: "A new era needs new people. New people must practice a new politics under a new system and new forms of organization. We must destroy the old system first in order to welcome a new era."[17] In the November 1918 issue of *Shinshakai*, Endō Tomoshirō announced: "Even in the radical Russia before the revolution, anarchism and non-statism were dominant, but the revolution created a new government and is building a new nation-state. In other words, anarcho-communism destroyed the old system but is building a new society on the basis of national socialism [*kokka shakaishugi*] and collectivism. This should become for us a condition to achieve success in the present world."[18] In early 1919, Takabatake and his followers broke from the old socialist group and created a small vanguard group, *kokka shakaishugi*. Takabatake's ambition was to develop it into a potent movement, but the group struggled financially, falling apart in a few months. Nevertheless, the successful socialist revolution in backward Russia inspired these young men in the belief that they could replicate it at home. Captivated by the Leninist vanguard group and ignoring the role of the working class, Takabatake was ready to venture outside the social-democratic system to search for more radical solutions to Japan's problems.

Kokka is an ambiguous term that entered common usage in the early Meiji period. It denotes both the nation as a group of people and the state as an institution of government. The double meaning of *kokka* as "nation" and "state" served Takabatake's purposes, for it enabled him to imply that (a) the ethnically homogenous Japanese masses (*kokumin*) constitute the nation; (b) the Japanese nation is coterminous with the state; and (c) socialism provides economic equality for all members of the nation-state, thus ensuring its unity and stability. In his founding statement, Takabatake explained:

Strictly speaking, *kokka shakaishugi* must be translated as state socialism, because national socialism is translated as *kokuminteki shakaishugi*.
However, we translate into English our theory of *kokka shakaishugi*
as *National Socialism* [*sic*]. In the West, state socialism denotes social
reformism, and thus although it has "socialism" in its name, in fact, in
its essence social reformism is against socialism. *National Socialism* is
almost not used, except by the famous English social democrat [Henry
Mayers] Hyndman, who named his party the National Socialist Party.
There are also few socialist parties in the world that use "national" in
their name. But if you think about it, the majority of socialist parties
in the world are national socialist. Those who laugh at our theory of
national socialism, claiming that nationalism [*kokkashugi*] and socialism [*shakaishugi*] are like water and oil, are in fact ignorant of the global
trend of socialism.[19]

It was not the case, Takabatake believed, that the state is a necessary step to
achieving socialism; rather, socialism is needed to guarantee the well-being of
the nation-state. The state, using its economic and political power, was responsible for implementing social reforms and establishing a welfare system to eliminate economic inequality. As Takabatake put it, "national socialism is a hybrid
of socialism and statism, and therefore best described as state socialism [*kokka
shakaishugi*], rather than national socialism [*kokumin shakaishugi*]." The blend
of nationalism, statism, socialism, and anticapitalism was, Takabatake pointed
out, the present trend in global Marxism.[20] And this global socialist trend of
national interests trumping international ones, he argued, was exemplified by
none better than the new Bolshevik regime.

By 1919, Takabatake had sensed that classical Marxism had already become
anachronistic in the reality of the post–World War I world. Contrary to Marx's
belief that "the working men have no country" (*The Communist Manifesto*, 1848),
that liberation of the workers hinged on their internationalist solidarity, it was
apparent to post–World War I socialists that revolutionaries did have a country. Marx and Engels believed that capitalism was causing national differences
and antagonisms to disappear and dismissed nationalism as a political sentiment produced and disseminated by the bourgeoisie. Takabatake joined many
other foreign Marxists who grappled with the idea of an alternative association
to class. Social class, they argued now, was not responsible for shaping human
consciousness, beliefs, and commitments.[21] Revisions of Marx's view of history
had already begun with Friedrich Engels, who pointed out that long before the
rise of economic classes, humans associated with each other in families, tribes,
and kinship systems. This suggested that Marx's claim that "the history of all

hitherto existing society is the history of class struggles" could not be true without important qualifications.[22]

Ultimately, Takabatake's belief that the masses had two fundamental desires—national unity and economic equality—led him to abandon the Marxist concept of workers' international solidarity, as well as the notion of "class" itself. Socialism, Takabatake believed, was not about the working class but about the whole nation. Takabatake observed that workers experienced ethnic and racial or historical and cultural bonds, rather than a sense of belonging to a *class*. Therefore, not only worker unionism but the whole of society ought to be based on a sense of belonging to one ethnic nation (*minzoku*) with a shared language, culture, and history. Given post–World War I reality, in which the world was being cut up into nation-states, Takabatake believed that nationalism (*kokkashugi*) was the best path to creating and organizing workers' unity.[23] As particular measures, Takabatake offered the slogan, "Japanese proletariat, unite," in place of "Proletariat of the whole world, unite," and advocated the establishment of a Labor Day specifically for Japan, which would be celebrated instead of International Labor Day on May 1.[24]

Viewed from this perspective, the genealogy of Taishō national socialism was different from the version for which Germaine Hoston has previously argued. For Hoston, Marxism was appropriated in the early 1920s in order to respond to "Japan's domestic ills during the Taishō era," but "the addition of a nationalist or statist element to Marxism was a rational response to the changed, threatening conditions of its international context."[25] Hoston then argues that this sense of crisis and external threat culminated in a mass "ideological conversion" (*tenkō*) of Japanese communists in the 1930s that united both Left and Right in support of Japan's expansion into Asia in the 1930s and 1940s. Furthermore, Hoston finds the cause of nationalism in the Taishō period to lie in the "indigenous patterns of thought on the *kokutai* (national polity)," nationalistic attachment to which Takabatake, as well as other leftists who were committed to *tenkō*, could not overcome. Interwar socialists, Hoston concluded, abandoned Marx's internationalism and ended up as nationalists, "advocat[ing] values traditionally identified with the Japanese *kokutai*—harmony between ruler and ruled, collectivism, and ethnic unity personified in the emperor."[26]

The roots of Taishō national socialism, however, were neither in the "indigenous" nationalist attachment to the land and the monarchy nor in the "hostile" international context of the day. It is true that the national socialists, like other rightist groups, embraced the doctrine of imperial sovereignty. This, however, was more of a tactical move. For the national socialists, when mass politics were not yet developed and when recognition from the political establishment was crucial, the allegiance to imperial sovereignty and the constitutional order granted by the emperor was a necessary political strategy. Despite their call for "revolution" (*kakumei*), "renovation" (*kakushin*), or "reconstruction" (*kaizō*) of the state and economy, national socialism never appealed to violence or the overthrow of the current political regime by military means, as did the Russian Bolsheviks or Italian Fascists. Rather, Japanese national socialists strategically embraced traditional principles of legitimacy.

Takabatake's support of the imperial system and his "respect for *kokutai*" were quite different from the thinking of the conservative Right. He did not support the *kokusuishugi* (national essentialism) critique of the apparently "mindless adulation" of Western ideas and goods. Neither did he approve of *kazokushugi* (familism), which stressed "the beautiful custom" of mutual respect between superior and subordinate, nor of *nōhonshugi*'s (agrarianism's) spiritual and economic revitalization of the countryside. None of these conservative movements understood the principles of Japanese polity, according to him.[27] The rightist suspicions of Takabatake's view on the imperial institution made their way into a public attack launched by the monarchist poet Fukushi Kōjirō (1889–1946) in 1927. Fukushi published a series of open letters to Takabatake in *Yomiuri shinbun* in December 1927–January 1928, criticizing Takabatake for his subversive Marxism and for his "disrespect of the imperial institution" based on his abstract, Hegelian-type concept of the nation-state. In his reply, Takabatake tied the veneration of the imperial institution to the force of tradition. Belief in the "unbroken imperial line" (*bansei ikkei*) was based on historical memory, he argued, and should not be taken uncritically as a religious doctrine: "The emperor was the ruler of the country for centuries, so people naturally deify him and worship him."[28] The only function of the monarchy as the locus of cultural and historical memory was to unite the people and rally them to defend the nation, as happened during the Meiji Revolution of 1868.

To rebuke his rightist critics, Takabatake clarified that his national socialist revolutionary program did not call for the abolition of the monarchy—a measure that was neither necessary nor desirable.[29] National socialists also acknowledged respect for ancestral achievements—after all, they pointed out, Japan's imperial family had founded the nation more than two thousand years ago. Imperial sovereignty ensured Japan's survival in the modern era, national socialists reckoned, and it was the Meiji emperor, not the people, who granted the constitution. Furthermore, Takabatake pointed out that the Japanese state originated with the founding of the imperial house and therefore would continue to exist only as a monarchy. National socialists thus professed a more secular approach to the Japanese monarchy and were close to the official interpretation of the monarchy offered by Minobe Tatsukichi (1873–1948), a scholar of constitutional law, who regarded the emperor as an organ of the state and the repository of sovereignty, but who was still a constituent part of the larger entity, the state. This paradigm was overturned in the late 1930s by the conservatives, who established the new orthodoxy of the divinity of the emperor.

Takabatake seemed to be influenced by Gustave Le Bon (1841–1931), a French sociologist whose bestseller, *The Crowd: A Study of the Popular Mind* (1895)—valued very highly by Mussolini, Hitler, and Georges Sorel—was translated in 1915 by Ōyama Ikuo and Maeda Nagatarō as *Minzoku shinri oyobi gunshū shinri* (National psychology and mass psychology). Takabatake was especially taken by Le Bon's suggestion that, for the modern individual, only authority from above and outside the masses could unite him with his countrymen, lead them, and thus assuage his loneliness. Following Le Bon's crowd theory, Takabatake saw behind the support of the imperial system the masses' desire for a hero, yearning to belong, and denial of their own powerlessness. The imperial institution instills the myth of membership by arousing mass faith and stimulating the masses to action. Through and by the emperor, the masses and therefore the nation unite and acquire power and will.[30] Takabatake saw the same basic desire in the thinking and actions of Japanese socialists who, however, chose the Russian Bolsheviks as their new heroes.[31] Hence, Takabatake urged that, if the *instinctive* loyalty of the people were left alone and not nurtured, directed, and managed by the state, with time, *kokutai* would be conquered and destroyed either by Western capitalism or Soviet "internationalism."[32]

The rise of radical programs after World War I was informed not by nationalist attachment but rather by a long-running dissatisfaction with and rejection of capitalism as an economic system and liberalism as its political form. Anticapitalism—or rejection of the principles of private property and private profit at the expense of community—was Takabatake's guiding principle, which brought him into the socialist movement in the first place and which he never abandoned. By the end of World War I, Takabatake declared, the state in Japan was near collapse because it had been hijacked by capitalists, who usurped and manipulated political power for their own selfish interests.[33] Importantly, Takabatake opposed capitalism because it established the malicious exploitation of one class over another instead of the "pure domination" of the neutral state and confused people into thinking that the state itself was an "evil" institution. Takabatake argued that the main sin of capitalism is that because of its pursuit of profit and exploitative nature, it constantly reproduces class struggle, transforming the nation from the end to the means. Capitalism in principle is not able to produce a unified nation-state and sustain its citizens' loyalty. His group's task, therefore, was to advance the rescue of "the Japanese state and people from the poison of capitalism" by advocating a radical economic measure: the nationalization of land, big industry, and business.[34] If the capitalist system were abolished and a "patriotic economic organization" established to oversee the economy, conflict between capital and labor would disappear. A true state would stop being an exploitative organ, win back the loyalty of its people, and establish unity between itself and the national community.[35]

Ultimately, however, the key to social and economic equality and development became who managed the state and politics and how. In this regard, Takabatake was influenced by people like Robert Michels (1876–1936), a German-Italian sociologist who developed the theory of elites and evolved from a Marxist to a Fascist. Like Michels, Takabatake asserted that the state should be managed by its best minds, which would constitute a new ruling elite. Thus, in his scheme, forms of political organization—be it democracy or autocracy—became irrelevant. Takabatake wrote that democracy as popular self-rule was merely a myth created to satisfy the crowd. Even if it were implemented as a style of government, it would only bring disintegration and chaos. Only the state as a transcending power was capable of quelling class conflict.[36] Takabatake thus did away with the traditional Marxist distinction between the primacy of productive forces and the state's political superstructure. The political authority, or the elite, can permanently alter the social structure (not the other way around), and the state acquires its own dynamic, independent of the mode of production. The ruling elite and the state can then impose their will on the masses—which become, in this scheme, classless and homogeneous. Hence, the state stops being the "executive organ" of society and acquires an authoritarian character.

As a political ideologue, Takabatake tended to stress basic values, offering almost no details on the economic structure of the new state, nor did he explain by what means his economic and political vision should be implemented. But this vagueness was also intentional, because it enabled him to attract ideological support from groups with different belief systems. In 1919, Takabatake and his group found support among the famous group of nationalist pan-Asianists—Mitsukawa Kametarō, Ōkawa Shūmei, and Kanokogi Kazunobu. Through Mitsukawa, Takabatake met Kita Ikki, whose national socialist program closely resembled Takabatake's ideas. However, they never became friends or collaborators, never mentioned each other in their writings, and their paths seemed never to cross again, most probably because of Kita Ikki's sinister reputation and his eccentric and gangster-like behavior.[37] In contrast, Takabatake was emerging as a respectable theoretician, being contracted in 1919 by a publishing company to translate Marx's *Das Kapital*.[38] Invited by Mitsukawa Kametarō to a meeting of the Rōsōkai group to give lectures on socialism, Takabatake attracted a great deal of attention from the military officers in attendance.[39] Mitsukawa recalled that senior army officers were surprised to learn from Takabatake's lectures that socialism, and particularly its anticapitalist message, corresponded to their own vision of how to reconstruct the Japanese state.[40]

Takabatake explored different ways of popularizing his vision, and the post–World War I period, when there still was extreme fluidity among groups with different political and ideological leanings, afforded him many opportunities to mingle with the right kind of people. The Pan-Asianist Mitsukawa proved to be particularly useful. Through their friendship, Takabatake relied on many of Mitsukawa's extensive contacts among the media and upper echelons of the intellectual and military world. In 1921, Mitsukawa arranged a meeting between Takabatake and Home Minister Tokonami Takejirō (1866–1935) and the head of the Home Ministry Police Affairs Bureau. At the meeting, Takabatake asked for permission to establish a national social party, but the authorities refused. However, he was successful in gaining the home minister's approval to publish and distribute his translation of Marx's *Das Kapital*, which proved to be Takabatake's life achievement.

Takabatake's connections, however, proved insufficient to launch a mass movement, because his national socialist group was deemed too radical and was constantly harassed by the police, forcing it finally to disband in 1920.[41] The police deemed the group's critique of the state as the political instrument of big capital to be a direct assault on the national body politic. Thus, even though the national socialist group professed loyalty to the Japanese state, the authorities did not tolerate its overtly radical anticapitalist rhetoric. The failure of the national socialist group in the early 1920s suggests that their conflation of statism and anticapitalism did not yet have sufficient political appeal for the military and bureaucracy, a goal the group would achieve in the 1930s.

To initiate a mass movement, national socialists needed to appeal to nationalistic sentiment. Nationalists are usually most successful when they can mobilize support against an alleged threat to the nation. The real or imagined threat might come from a variety of directions and could be utilized simultaneously or separately. The threat might come from a political or ethnic minority: in imperial Japan it was the Japanese communist group and the Koreans; from an internationalist political movement like Soviet communism; and from the persecution of a country's nationals abroad, as exemplified by the 1924 anti-Japanese Immigration Act in the United States. In his feverish attempts to gain the support of the Japanese public, as well as leftists, by appealing to nationalism, Takabatake used all the rhetorical techniques at his disposal.

How far to the right Takabatake's thinking leaned can be gleaned from his reaction to the mob massacre of almost six thousand Korean and Chinese residents, as well as a dozen Japanese labor activists, socialists, and anarchists, in the aftermath of the great Kantō earthquake of September 1, 1923. Takabatake responded to the massacre with an article titled "Taishū no shinri" (Psychology of the masses), which was published on the front page of the magazine *Shūkan Nihon*, the organ of the right-wing organization Taikakai (Taika Reform Association). He speculated that the Koreans might have been doing what they were accused of (looting, raping, murdering), but he also pointed out that the murderous behavior of the Japanese working-class mob was normal. He declared that the basic feature of mass mentality was its irrational "instinct" (*honnō*), with its two coexisting elements—patriotism (*aikokushugi*), which manifests itself at times of national distress, and victim mentality (*higaisha tarubeki shinri*), which refers to the people's self-perception as victims of unjust economic and social circumstances.[42] For Takabatake, this mob patriotism should be vindicated, cherished, and indulged. He welcomed the outburst of "patriotic" spirit among the masses and derided Japanese communists for their naïve belief in the "internationalist" spirit of the workers. Similarly, Takabatake tried to rally people to his national socialist cause in his discussion of the 1924 Immigration Act, which virtually banned Japanese immigration to the United States. In an attempt at racialized writing, Takabatake attacked the United States' decision but pointed out that historical development was governed by the conflict between white and nonwhite races, rather than social classes.[43]

But it was the Soviet Union and its Japanese communist agents that Takabatake singled out as the foreign threat in the face of which the nation must arise and unite, and Japanese socialists should embrace his leadership. Despite the Soviet Union being the inspiration for Takabatake's ideal "proletarian state," he changed his position dramatically after the Japanese Communist Party (JCP) was established in 1922. What most bothered Takabatake was that the JCP was created as a Comintern branch, with Comintern money and under its firm guidance. In fact, replacing capitalists with communists as public enemy number one, national socialists joined the government's crackdown on communists and anarchists. When the police and public learned about the existence of a Japanese communist cell after the arrest of Kondō Eizō in May 1921, Takabatake was outraged. He saw the Comintern's actions as Russia's direct meddling in Japanese domestic politics. When as the consequence of the communists' arrest the government introduced the Anti-Radical Bill in 1922, Takabatake threw his support behind the proposed legislation. In his public attack he declared that the bill was fair, necessary, and even urgent, and his support of it marks the first instance in which he openly went against his former comrades.[44]

By the mid-1920s, Takabatake did little to hide his loathing of Japanese communists, whom he regarded as Soviet agents conspiring to destabilize domestic politics. When the first Japanese proletarian party, Nōmin Rōdōtō, was banned by the government in 1925, Takabatake cheered the decision by declaring the whole proletarian movement to be a cover for Comintern activities in Japan. He also welcomed the 1925 Peace Preservation Law, which targeted leftist radicals and criminalized the expression of any ideas that aimed to alter the *kokutai*. He called on the government and police to continue even further in persecuting Japanese communists as traitors to the nation, working for the benefit of the Soviet Union.[45] The more public Takabatake's contempt for Soviet communism became, the more distance grew between him and his former socialist friends. When Takabatake threw a big celebration on completing his translation of *Das Kapital* in 1926, no one from the socialist group accepted his invitation. At this point, the socialists were openly calling him a fascist.[46]

Because for Takabatake socialism was first and foremost a means to increase the country's strength, he fundamentally distrusted the internationalist slogans of Russian Bolsheviks. Takabatake rebelled against the Comintern's policy of protecting the Russian Revolution and could not accept "proletarian internationalism," in which defense of the USSR against imperialist powers was a more important priority than the domestic interests of workers in their home country. In the end, Takabatake declared that the Japanese needed to reject communist internationalism and capitalist democracy alike.

> Capitalists shout "brothers and sisters" while exploiting workers; socialists sing "internationalism" while offering their fellow socialists as human bullets. In words, they are internationalist; in their hearts, they burn with nationalism. Unless as a country and as a nation we become strong, unless we achieve equal strength with the West in wealth, science, military power, social organization, and revolution, we can give up on internationalism as the topic of Westerners. The utmost goal for the Japanese now is to achieve strength as the Japanese.[47]

Takabatake declared that Western Marxists treated their Asian fellows as servants and deep in their hearts wanted to enslave them for the advancement of their own capitalism and socialism. More importantly, rather than treat Soviet communism as an alternative socioeconomic and political order, Takabatake began to operate within the racialized East-West framework, in which the Soviet Union and Russian communists were firmly placed within the white "West," with all the negative attributes it implied. Takabatake, for example, insisted that Russian socialists despised nonwhite people. For the Japanese to become equal with the West, they needed to reject communist internationalism and democracy alike.

The turnabout, given his previous defense of the Russian Revolution, was dramatic. Concerned about the expansion of Soviet influence in Japan and East Asia, Takabatake warned that, like other Western powers, the Soviet Union aimed at colonial expansionism. Soviet Russia's foreign policy seemed aimed at territorial expansion in a manner reminiscent of tsarist Russia's, which in Takabatake's view demonstrated that Soviet Russia was using the concept of the world socialist revolution to achieve world domination. Takabatake pointed out that by 1924, the USSR had regained the old tsarist territories Russia had lost after the revolution. Now Soviet Russia was restored to the same size and inclination toward territorial expansion of its former imperial state.[48] The Soviet Union was in fact more dangerous than other Western countries because it manipulated people's discontent with their domestic social and economic system: "Communism is imperialism that uses socialism as its weapon. It is easier to fight a military threat, but here they target the social system. *To fight it, we need to carry out a fundamental reconstruction of our social system* [italics mine]. Proletarian imperialism is more dangerous than tsarist imperialism. Japan must watch out for Russia."[49]

With the passage of the Peace Preservation Law, an emerging police state did an effective job in suppressing the internal enemies of the nation. The JCP also disbanded in late 1923. Since there was no menace to nationalism at home that might have aroused a sense of danger and compelled masses of people to join their movement, national socialists turned to portraying the Soviet Union as an obstacle to Japan's aspirations for empire in Asia. In 1927, Takabatake's most important article on the issue of Soviet expansionism, "Rōnō teikokushugi no kyokutō shinshutsu" (Proletarian imperialism's advancement to the Far East) dealt with the case of Outer and Inner Mongolia.[50] After having some success in creating "Soviet colonies" in Central Asia, Soviet Russia "colonized" Outer Mongolia, making it an outpost for spreading Bolshevism throughout Asia. Takabatake described in detail the formation of the Mongolian People's Party in 1921 under the leadership of the Comintern and the establishment of the Mongolian People's Republic in 1924. Takabatake took great pains to demonstrate that Soviet expansion violated the interests of the Mongolian people, arguing that Comintern agents had murdered Mongolian nationalists and opposition members and manipulated Chinese revolutionary forces, including the nationalist leader Sun Yat-sen, into allowing Mongolia to become a Soviet satellite-state.[51] Takabatake expressed concern that the Soviets planned to annex Inner Mongolia, which together with South Manchuria was in Japan's sphere of interest, and turn a united Outer and Inner Mongolia into an outpost for spreading Bolshevism throughout Asia, particularly in China. He was especially alarmed at the news that Red Army officers were being sent to China to create and head military academies. Takabatake warned that the danger of Soviet internationalism lay in its special ability to capture the hearts of colonial people with socialist and anti-imperialist rhetoric. By relying on the help of the Comintern to achieve national liberation, the Mongols and Chinese had stepped on a sure path to becoming Soviet colonies.

Accusing the USSR of imperialist intentions, Takabatake obviously could not avoid addressing Japanese imperialism on the continent. His view was that Soviet expansionism was a symptom of the imperialist drive at the heart of every state, whether proletarian or capitalist. Indeed, in one of his few articles on Japanese colonialism, Takabatake argued that Japan's imperial project was the result of a *natural* drive for territorial expansion rooted in the nature of any state.[52] Moreover, Takabatake justified Japanese imperialism as a reaction to Western imperialism, as if this were an unavoidable requirement of international politics.

Nonetheless, imperialism per se and natural impulses for expansion, Takabatake continued, must be contained. Like Kita Ikki, Takabatake criticized Japan's imperialist advance in China, insisting that Japan must respect and aid China's efforts to build an independent national state. Independent nation-states working in mutual respect—that was his vision of the international order.[53] Unlike Japanese pan-Asianists, he did not think domestic reconstruction depended on Japanese expansion in Asia. Takabatake's attitude toward China wavered between concern with the growing strength of Chinese communists, presumably under the Soviet spell, and his desire to see an independent Chinese nation-state, for which cooperation with the communists was necessary. Takabatake urged Chinese radicals, both nationalist and communist, to make a more unified effort at building a strong Chinese nation-state that could resist foreign encroachment—by which he meant the Soviet Union rather than Japan. To achieve this, he believed, the Chinese must learn to emulate the original patriotic spirit of Vladimir Lenin, the "true Russian nationalist," who managed to strengthen a devastated Russia and unite it under a single-party regime. Takabatake concluded that if China did not succeed in producing its own Lenin, Mussolini, or Kemal Atatürk, even though it might free itself from the bonds of imperialist powers, its destiny was to become "food for proletarian imperialism." Witnessing the growing strength of Chinese communists within the Guomindang, Takabatake concluded that Chinese nationalist forces were hopelessly "contaminated" by communists and "Russian agents." However, he was highly critical of the Chinese nationalists' purge of communists in April 1927, because he believed it weakened the Chinese independence movement. He argued that the purge was necessary but premature and ought to have followed the establishment of a strong independent Chinese nation-state.

Ultimately, Takabatake sided with his pan-Asianist friends in categorizing the Japanese Empire as nonimperialist and even benevolent, and representing it as a defensive measure against Western (including Soviet) imperialist advances. The difference was that pan-Asianists thought of the Anglo-American powers as the greatest evil to combat, making cooperation with the Soviet Union necessary. Contrary to that, Takabatake, together with the army, insisted that Soviet imperialism represented the greatest danger. As we have seen, fear of the Soviet Union's advance in northeast Asia was paramount in Takabatake's transformation into an anticommunist but also in his decision to support the Japanese Empire, whose role was to defend Japan's interests and liberate all of Asia from capitalist and proletarian imperialism. He feared that after Mongolia, Manchuria would be the next place to become a potential "Soviet colony," and thus it was Japan's mission to defend the Asian borders. For Takabatake, the Japanese Empire was the only force capable of stopping the Bolshevik advance in East Asia and liberating Asia from Soviet imperialism; and therefore the Chinese government would have to acknowledge Japan's supreme role on the continent and yield to its dominance. Although Takabatake died before the Japanese government started hostilities in China, he and his later followers regarded Japanese imperialism as a moral crusade to save Asia from the Russian/Soviet imperialist encroachment. In the 1930s, however, Takabatake's followers abandoned his anti-Soviet sentiments. National socialists became so concerned with the rise of the Chinese Communist Party and the threat it represented for the Japanese Empire that they began to advocate an alliance with the Soviet Union as a means to contain and control the activities of the CCP.[54]

After Takabatake's initial national socialist group failed to gain the approval of the authorities, he made another bid to initiate a political movement by teaming up with the respected conservative professor of law Uesugi Shinkichi (1878–1929). Uesugi, as discussed in Chapter 5, gained notoriety from his involvement in the Morito Incident in 1921, when the junior professor Morito was expelled from Tokyo Imperial University for his article on Kropotkin's anarchism. In January 1923, Takabatake and Uesugi established the Keirin Gakumei (Statecraft Study Association)—which, together with the Gen'yōsha and the Kokuryūkai, was considered by contemporary commentators to be the main progenitor of all important nationalist organizations.[55] Takabatake hoped that Uesugi would provide finances to establish a political party through his higher-up connections. The immediate incentive for the establishment of the association was the victory of the Italian Fascist Party in October 1922. Takabatake, however, was more impressed with Mussolini's political success than the content of his Fascist program. According to a bizarre anecdote, when Takabatake heard of Mussolini's victory, he became very upset at his own failures and, in a fit of rage, repeatedly punched a wall with his fist until it started bleeding, after which he was unable to hold a pen for a month.[56]

The main tenets of the Keirin Gakumei group were total social mobilization and militarization, struggle against capitalism and the contemporary political system, and opposition to communism and the Soviet Union in particular. The Keirin Gakumei oath succinctly expressed the group's allegiances and ambitions:

"We pledge our total devotion to the emperor [*tennō*], to revealing to the world the genius and abilities of the Japanese nation [*Nihon minzoku*], to the domestic preservation of the true spirit of the Japanese nation, and to groundbreaking new work on opening a new era in world history." Moreover, Uesugi's statements regarding the objectives of the association might be easily characterized as fascist: "The goal of the association is, by educating the spirit and the body, to nurture future statesmen who will display steel-like strength of spirit and body. Who but us can create warriors [*bushi*] to promote the glory of our national polity?"[57]

Takabatake, however, drew inspiration from the Soviet experiments. He was apparently inspired by Leon Trotsky, the founder of the Soviet Red Army, and his tactics for the militarization of labor unions. During the Russian Civil War, Trotsky used labor unions to draft workers into the Red Army, thus transforming them into official arms of the Bolshevik regime. Trotsky described the "militarization of labor" as "the inevitable basic method for the organization of our labor force."[58] Approving the militarized nature of the proletarian state, Takabatake began to advocate universal conscription, substantial increases in military spending, and compulsory military education in schools and workplaces.[59] Takabatake envisioned a nation of soldiers—be they workers, women, or children—so that when the time came, everyone could contribute to the war effort. In the end, for Takabatake the proletarian state would have to be led by a single party, economically and politically centralized, militarized, and with unlimited control over society.[60]

The creation of the Keirin Gakumei group greatly alarmed Japanese intellectuals, activists, and bureaucrats from the Ministry of Justice, who sensed in this alliance the beginning of the new Radical Right and saw the association as the first fascist organization in Japan in the manner of Mussolini's Fascist Party.[61] In March 1923, the leftist magazine *Kaizō* ran a special issue under the heading "Shinkō aikoku dantai hihan" (Critique of the new patriotic organizations), in reaction to the formation of the Keirin Gakumei. Commentators did not fail to notice parallels between it and Italian Fascism and remarked on Takabatake's ambition to become the Japanese Mussolini. The association, and Takabatake's public attacks on Japanese communists from 1922 onward, resulted in the irreparable breakup of the previously united socialist movement.

Tellingly, Takabatake vehemently denied allegations of fascism on the grounds that the Italian Fascist Party was a party of political opportunists and bullies whose power was based on their association with modern Italian finance and industrial capitalism. Takabatake was so bothered by these allegations that in 1928 he felt compelled to write his last book, *Mussorini to sono shisō* (Mussolini and his thought), to clarify the differences between national socialism and fascism. Insisting that he was Marxist and anticapitalist, Takabatake essentially adhered to the Comintern definition of fascism, which treated it as a middle-class reaction sponsored by oppressive government, big business, and the police and working against labor, socialist, and communist movements.[62] Uesugi repeated Takabatake's arguments, adding that Italian Fascism was a reaction against both communism and socialism. Since communism would never take hold among the patriotic Japanese masses and the Japanese socialist movement was inconsequential, fascism could not emerge in Japan. The Comintern debates in 1922–23 over the nature of Italian Fascism were the first theoretical attempts to explain the new phenomenon, and they were appropriated in Japan not only by leftists but—via people like Takabatake—by the radical rightists and conservatives as well.

There were doubters of Takabatake's turn to fascism in Japan, as well as in the Soviet Union. In fact, Takabatake's ideas had already drawn the attention of Soviet scholars in 1933. The Soviet scholars O. Tanin and E. Yohan introduced national socialism in their infamous book *Militarism and Fascism in Japan* (1933). This study was originally intended for internal use in the Soviet intelligence service, but it immediately caught the attention of Stalin. Stalin ordered it to be published in English in 1934 for wider public circulation as part of his campaign against "Japanese fascism and militarism" in the wake of the establishment of Manchukuo in 1932. Not only did Tanin and Yohan note the direct correlation between the rise of Taishō national socialism and the ensuing belligerence of Japanese imperialism, they also identified the broad social support for national socialist ideas (itself an outcome of the expansion of mass political participation). Interestingly, the Soviet scholars did not consider Japan a fascist but rather a militarist state, nor did they think a fascist dictatorship was possible in Japan. They warned, however, that the new nationalist organizations might be used by the army to widen social support for the monarchy, curb big business, and prepare the country for an imperialist war on the continent, which would be aimed primarily against the Soviet Union.[63]

The Keirin Gakumei dissolved within a few years of its formation, mainly due to personality clashes, but its significance rests on its establishment of a theoretical precedent that validated nationalism within the socialist movement and socialism within radical nationalist thought. Both Takabatake and Uesugi used their experience with Keirin Gakumei to work on other rightist projects.[64] Takabatake became especially close to the notorious group Taikakai. The founder of the group, Iwata Fumio (1891–1943), was a *tairiku rōnin* (continental adventurer) in China, where in Shanghai he befriended the radical social nationalist Kita Ikki. At Kita's urging, and most likely acting as an informant for the Japanese army, Iwata traveled to Siberia twice for intelligence gathering but was captured by Soviet counterintelligence and spent six months in prison in the small Siberian town of Chita. On his return in 1923, he founded Taikakai, which consisted mainly of rogue elements, with the aim of eliminating "old slave thoughts" and slave-like imitation of foreign revolutionary ideologies and to recover the Japanese military spirit. Iwata saw himself as a follower of Takabatake's national socialism and as his confidant. With Taikakai's financial help, Takabatake published his journal *Kyūshin* (The radical), which was devoted above all to the introduction of Western Marxism to Japanese audiences.[65] Taikakai also acted as the muscle for promulgating Takabatake's ideas. In May 1923, at Takabatake's urging, Taikakai gangs attempted to disrupt the welcoming party for the Soviet diplomat Adolf Ioffe, who had come to Japan to negotiate the recognition of the USSR.[66] The most notorious incident perpetrated by the Taikakai gang to which Takabatake's name was linked, albeit without proof, was the theft of the remains of the slain anarchist Ōsugi Sakae after his murder by the military police in the aftermath of the Kantō earthquake, with the result that the funeral had to be conducted without the body.[67] The irony is that the anarchist Ōsugi was famous for being an outspoken anticommunist: he had supported Japan's Siberian Intervention and later denounced the Japanese government for its negotiations over the recognition of the USSR. But while Ōsugi rejected communism as an ideological and institutional suppression of human freedom, Takabatake was concerned that recognition would ease Russian access to the Japanese interior. Shocking his former socialist friends, Takabatake, who had always intensely disliked Ōsugi, approved of Iwata's scandalous theft of the remains and declared such measures to be just punishment for "traitors who supported the cause of red imperialism."

In addition to his involvement with the Taikakai, Takabatake became an adviser and inspiration to a number of right-wing terrorist organizations, such as Dai Nippon Kokka Shakaitō (the National Socialist Party of Great Japan), founded by Ishikawa Junjūrō, and the Aikoku Kinrōtō) (Patriotic Labor Party), created by Tsukui Tatsuo, whose views and organizational structure closely resembled those of the Nazi Party. Takabatake was also connected to the Kenkokukai (National Creation Society), created in 1926 by the former socialists Akao Bin, Tsukui Tatsuo, and Atsumi Masaru. Hiranuma Kiichirō, head of the Privy Council and the House of Peers, personally patronized the organization. It was the same Hiranuma Kiichirō who pushed for the promulgation of the Peace Preservation Law in 1925, and who sponsored pogroms against Korean and Chinese migrant workers in the aftermath of the Kantō earthquake. Through the Kenkokukai, national socialists linked up with powerful conservative bureaucrats and the military.

Throughout the 1920s, numerous rightist organizations and smaller groups used violent political tactics to struggle against perceived enemies of the national community—be they businessmen, outcasts, Koreans, feminists, labor activists, or communists. But most of them lacked a clear political program and therefore gravitated to national socialism, which by comparison had a coherent agenda—that is, a highly interventionist state, anticapitalism, a state socialist economy in the manner of the Soviet Union, nationalism, anti-Sovietism, and expansion in Asia. Yet the national socialists also had to seek elite patrons for themselves. Witnessing the success of the Russian Bolsheviks in mobilizing the masses, Takabatake hoped to replicate it in Japan. But the reality was that despite the social, political, and economic unrest of the early 1920s, the Japanese state was stable and mass politics still nascent. For political success, national socialists needed not mass mobilization (which would require many years to achieve) but elite manipulation through private contacts and publications and, in the 1930s, assassinations.

Witnessing the success of legal proletarian parties in the wake of the promulgation of universal suffrage, Takabatake ventured on another attempt to create a political party but with the backing of some of the most influential figures of the day. Teaming up with the leaders of the Shakai Taishūtō (Social Mass Party), Asō Hisashi and Akamatsu Katsumaro, in 1926 Takabatake announced the new political program. At a public lecture titled "Musan aikokutō no kichō" (The necessity of the proletarian patriotic party), Takabatake clarified: "There is a tendency among the right-wing groups to act as tools of bureaucracy and parties, while the left, including social democrats, act as tools of foreign (Russian) powers. Neither the right nor the left are patriots. But we are, because there is no power or authority behind our back. We are independent spirits."[68] Takabatake envisioned a radically new proletarian patriotic party working outside the democratic framework of existing political parties. Takabatake believed that the new party must, in fact, transcend the opposition between Left and Right, thus enabling it to circumvent and trump the political establishment. Takabatake claimed that national socialism professed radical patriotism. The radicalism lay in advocating revolutionary policies to abolish capitalism, as well as to combat communism, while the patriotism of the new party would be expressed in activities that attempted to fulfill the demands of the nation as a whole.

Through the connection of his old friend, the pan-Asianist Ōkawa Shūmei, Takabatake approached General Ugaki Kazushige (1868–1956), who served as army minister in 1924–27 and again in 1929–31, with a request for funding and political support for Takabatake's new party. That Takabatake approached the military instead of powerful politicians suggests that the military was becoming a new independent political player. Ugaki's statement from 1925—that political parties could not play the central role of achieving national unity because "the assumption of party politics is the existence of opposition parties," and that therefore this role must be assumed by the army, "because it is very impartial and has close contact with the people through conscription"—came close to

Takabatake's thinking.[69] There were rumors, however, that Japan's Prime Minister Tanaka Gi'ichi was behind Takabatake's and Asō's plans to create a new mass progovernment party to counterbalance procommunist parties. In any case, Takabatake's plans found support among the highest echelons of power: Army Minister Ugaki, Prime Minister Tanaka Gi'ichi, Minister of Imperial Railways Ogawa Heikichi, and a few members of the powerful Seiyūkai Party expressed their approval.[70] Anticapitalist rhetoric did not scare them away anymore. By the end of the 1920s, in the wake of the Great Depression and its disastrous effects on the Japanese economy, the eagerness of state authorities to defend capitalism had waned. According to police manuals of the time, acts attempting to change or deny the private property system by peaceful means were to be permitted and even supported.[71] National socialism, which promised relief from social and economic problems by means of total control of the economy by a centralized state, social mobilization, and national and bloc self-sufficiency, finally found great resonance among the military (which had long been interested in such a measure), as well as among right-leaning politicians and bureaucrats.[72]

Takabatake died unexpectedly in December 1928 at the age of forty-two from cancer, just as his political career was taking off. Takabatake's national socialist group was neither very successful nor influential during the 1920s, but it took off at the end of the decade, when society and the political world began to be destabilized by the repercussions of the Great Depression. Although the developments of the 1930s are outside the scope of this study, we can point to a remarkable continuity between Takabatake's thought and the trajectory of social thought in the following decade. Takabatake's ideas found great resonance among those at the top of the political world in the post-Depression period of the 1930s. Under the leadership of Tsukui Tatsuo (1901–1989) and retired colonel Ishikawa Junjūrō (1899–1980), the national socialist group continued Takabatake's plans to form an alliance with the army, reform bureaucrats, and proletarian political parties, and seek different possibilities and support groups to implement what they thought were necessary political and social changes.[73] Reform bureaucrats (kakushin kanryō) of the 1930s, for example, greatly sympathized with leftist anticapitalist aspirations and with the national socialists' belief in the technocratic rule of the few.[74] The national socialists also actively cooperated with social democratic and proletarian parties and groups in the 1930s, working on bringing to power right-wing national socialist factions within those parties. At the Congress of the Shakai Taishūtō in January 1932, three resolutions directly inspired by Takabatake's national socialism were accepted: anticommunism, anticapitalism, and antifascism.[75] Social democrats (shakai minshūshugi ha) drew on a national socialist program of anticommunism and statism to tackle the Shōwa Depression and even formulated the concept of a "Far Eastern International," which would eventuate socialism at home and ensure solidarity among Asian people. It was envisioned by the members of the newly established Shakai Taishūtō that the relationship between Japan and the Far Eastern International would be identical to that between the Soviet Union and the Third International.[76]

National socialists' manipulation of the elite continued through personal contacts and publications. In 1931, in the wake of the Manchurian Incident, Tsukui Tatsuo and Ishikawa Junjūrō teamed up with Ōkawa Shūmei and established the Nihon Shakaishugi Kenkyūjō (Research Institute of Japanese Socialism), with its monthly publication *Nihon Shakaishugi*, later renamed *Kokka Shakaishugi*. In Ōkawa, national socialists found another powerful patron, who was at that time the head of the Research Institute of the SMRC and taught at a small private academy on the grounds of the imperial palace.[77] The Research Institute of Japanese Socialism declared its aim to build a new Japan based on the principles of state socialism, with the goal of strengthening Japanese ethnic communal spirit.[78] In its publications, national socialists criticized laissez-faire capitalism, advocated a centralized planned economy, and sought the elimination of the class struggle between labor and capital. They also glorified Japanese imperialism, viewing international relations as a war between nationalities (*minzoku tōsō*), in which the Japanese nation had the natural right to fight against Anglo-American white imperialism.

What is important for us is that national socialists of the 1930s never sought to contest the objectives of the Russian Revolution, which they understood in their own way. Like Takabatake, they continued to aspire for a Soviet-type single-party regime structured around revolutionary principles, lauding Stalin's Five-Year Plan and publishing extensive research articles on Soviet industrialization efforts. In this they combined forces with the Ōkawa-run Research Institute of the SMRC, which was also keenly interested in Soviet industrialization. They extensively covered the struggle between Stalin and Trotsky, unequivocally supporting Stalin. National socialists saw Stalin as the true heir to Lenin and lauded the "socialism in one country" doctrine proposed by Stalin and Bukharin. Remarkably, national socialists identified themselves as orthodox Stalinists and criticized Japanese communists as Trotskyists. National socialists dismissed Trotsky's "permanent revolution" doctrine, according to which the Russian Revolution was the first among world proletarian revolutions, on the success of which its survival depended. In a fascinating twist of rhetoric, national socialists disparaged the JCP as Trotskyists because the JCP followed the orders of the Comintern, instead of formulating an independent national socialist program, and relied on Russian communists to build socialism in Japan. National socialists called themselves Stalinists because they agreed with his doctrine of "socialism in one country," which placed priority on the national community over the international one, and they were confident that socialism could be built within a nation without reliance on the revolutionary transformation of the rest of the world.[79]

One of the organizations in which national socialist theory found acceptance was the Shōwa kenkyūkai (Shōwa Research Association), a brain trust for Prince Konoe Fumimaro, the most popular politician of the day. Intellectuals, politicians, and bureaucrats of the association, such as the economist Shintarō Ryū, the political scientist Masamichi Rōyama, the philosopher Miki Kiyoshi, and the economist Takahashi Kamekichi, relied heavily on Marxism for their analysis of society and rejected the principles of capitalism and liberalism in favor of the nationalization of industries, a single-party regime, and a state-regulated economy. Not coincidentally, many of the members of the Shōwa Research Association were former socialists and communists.[80]

Most of the members of the association participated in the Imperial Rule Assistance Association (IRAA), created by Konoe in 1936 to provide an institutional backing for his vision of national political unity. The IRAA geared up for nationwide popular participation, which "could mobilize the total energy of the state and enable all national subjects to act as one in assisting imperial rule in wartime Japan."[81] The IRAA was part of a larger movement, the New Order in East Asia, which declared cooperation among Japan, Manchukuo, and China as the foundation of peace and justice in East Asia, ensuring a joint defense against the communist Soviet Union, an economic alliance, and the creation of a new "culture." Nevertheless, the IRAA and the New Order movement were criticized by conservatives and some rightists for being too communistic, and there were allegations that communist elements had infiltrated the association and were using it as a base for their propaganda activities. Konoe acknowledged at a press conference that it was influenced by communist ideology and admitted that left-wing people joined it. But he effectively justified the situation by comparing the New Order movement to a huge drum: "Beat it hard, it sounds strong; beat it lightly, it sounds soft. At times it may sound Nazi, and at other times it may sound Marxist, but its true sound is rooted in Japan's *kokutai*."[82] In a way, he summarized the whole trajectory of national socialism in interwar Japan.

Takabatake perceived the period after World War I as a time of great transformation in which the Western liberal capitalist and imperialist order was destined to be supplanted by new models. As Japanese society and politics stood at a crossroads in the post–World War I period, the Bolsheviks embarked on their own revolutionary experiment under the leadership of Vladimir Lenin, and as such the new Soviet Russia became the inspiration and model for post–World War I political thinking in Japan, as elsewhere. Remarkably, despite all his anti-Soviet and anticommunist agitation, until his death Takabatake regarded himself as a true Marxist, while the Soviet regime remained for him an ideal proletarian state. Takabatake's analysis of the Russian Revolution and his attempts to formulate an alternative to Soviet communism attracted those on the Left and the undecided who doubted the universal applicability of the Russian Revolution and had trouble with the notion of "class struggle," fearing it would emasculate the national collectivity. Appropriating many features of Soviet communism, Takabatake engaged in formulating a political program that would fit, he believed, the needs of the Japanese nation-state and its people.

Takabatake's bid to lead a "reformed" socialist movement in Japan in the early 1920s had important consequences. His theory of national socialism implied the elimination of all political competition—left, right, and center; the supraclass elite's dictatorship; total control of all institutions, including economic ones; and higher collective purposes. His split from the socialists and his formulation of a nation-centric socialism divided and weakened the Japanese Left; his public attacks on the Soviet Union and international communism discredited the spirit of internationalism and justified Japanese imperialism; his writings inspired and legitimized attacks by rightist gangs against his former fellow anarchists and socialists; his doubts about workers' political potential undermined the nascent labor movement; and his statism sanctioned the government's dictatorial politics. In his drive to overcome the tensions and contradictions of modern mass society and capitalist industrial development without making Japan a communist state Takabatake formulated political thought that offered at its core a totalitarian state model.

Conclusion

IMPERIAL JAPAN AND SOVIET COMMUNISM IN THE 1930s

> JOSEPH STALIN: **"The European problem can be solved in a natural way if Japan and the Soviets cooperate."**
> MATSUOKA YŌSUKE: **"Not only the European problem! Asia also can be solved!"**
> JOSEPH STALIN: **"The whole world can be settled!"**
>
> —Joseph Stalin and Matsuoka Yōsuke at the Moscow Yaroslavsky railway station, April 13, 1941

Who were the Bolsheviks? What did they want and what would they settle for? Could they be trusted? The shifting balance of power in the aftermath of World War I, the new opportunities for enrichment, the increased interdependence of nations (coupled with real or imagined external threats), as well as domestic agitation for political reforms, were decisive in the way that the Japanese state and public answered these questions. This book shows that there was no agreement in the 1920s, either among factions of the government and bureaucracy, or among members of socialist and rightist movements, about the significance of the Russian Revolution and what to make of Soviet Russia. Each of these groups was pursuing its own agenda, and Soviet Russia and communism ultimately became instruments in their mutual competition to shape the future of the nation and empire.

This is not to say that communism was not perceived as a genuine threat. There were extensive debates in the mainstream media, academic publications, rightist gatherings, university halls, and corridors of power about whether communist propaganda might harm the Japanese national community, state, and empire by influencing the "unstable minds" of Japanese imperial subjects. Although generally focused on the protection of the ephemeral *kokutai*, anticommunism in interwar Japan was, however, multifaceted. In this book I have identified two strands: a liberal-conservative anticommunist alliance preoccupied with the coherence of domestic society, and the anticommunism of the army absorbed with the defense of the empire. If the former was inadvertently responsible for the emergence of a police state in the 1930s to the 1940s, the latter became the driving force behind the army's imperialist expansion into Asia.

Liberals and conservatives outside and inside the government and bureaucracy were united in their concern over the threat of communist ideology. If one has to discern the main tenet of communism that propelled the ideological reaction to it, it would be the Marxist notion of class struggle. The sudden political activity of rioting peasants, striking workers, rebellious students, outcasts, feminists, homegrown socialists, and other previously marginalized groups in the post–World War I period unnerved the political, economic, and intellectual establishment as the sign of the coming of class conflict to Japanese shores. Both liberal and conservative commentators realized that Meiji imperial orthodoxy was no longer capable of dealing with the requirements of the post–World War I age—namely, the demand for a more egalitarian mass politics and the rise of nationalism in the metropole, colonies, and in the whole East Asian region. They agitated for a reworking of state ideology, offering various programs ranging from liberal paternalistic to traditionalist conservative to fascist. However, it is important to note that communism always had been considered as foreign and alien thought, the movement of which could be prevented or regulated by the state and police apparatus. Despite the many voices inside and outside the government that doubted the necessity of such regulation and the state's ability to do so, they were unable to limit the institutional development of the police state.

It was, however, the anticommunism of the army that had a direct impact on Japan's foreign policy in the 1930s. The components of it are complex and multilayered. I have traced the emergence of the army's anticommunism to the direct clash of the Russian Bolsheviks, the Japanese army, and the Korean and Chinese national liberation fighters during the Siberian Intervention. The concern of the army was, however, less with communist ideology (which they initially did not take seriously) but more with the geopolitical reconfiguration of the area after the end of the Great War. The disappearance of imperial Russia, rise of Chinese nationalism, arrival of US business interests in Asia, and the new opportunities to solidify the political and economic power of Japan in the region—all were factors that greatly complicated the outlook of East Asian geopolitics in 1917–19. Finally, as the Soviet regime emerged victorious from the Russian Civil War and claimed the old tsarist possessions in Outer Mongolia and northern Manchuria (the CER), the long-standing competition with imperial Japan for its sphere of influence on the Asian continent was renewed. In this sense, anticommunist sentiments developed in the army during the Siberian Intervention as the result of brutal fighting with the communists, mixed with old anxieties over the northern neighbor, which dated back to the late nineteenth century.

The army's anti-Bolshevik sentiments were driven by ideological matters once communism became a political force in colonial Korea and China—even more so as the military understood that the revolutionary upheavals in Korea and China were spurred by the anti-imperialist message of the Russian Revolution and disseminated in the region by Comintern agents. Therefore, the "red scare" for the Army was the danger Bolshevism presented to the stability and unity of Japan's empire in Asia. Russian communism threatened not only the Japanese national community but more importantly Korea and China, on which (according to the military) the survival of that national community depended. The events that presented the military with constant, unabating concern were the Russian-backed Korean anti-Japanese guerilla fighting, Korean communist parties, the communist-led provisional government of independent Korea (1920), the establishment of the Mongolian People's Republic in 1924, the Sino-Soviet agreements and subsequent Soviet control of the CER (also in 1924), Soviet active interference in Chinese domestic affairs, the strengthening of the Chinese Communist Party, and finally the outbreak of the Chinese Revolution in 1925.

The army's fears were shared by some members of the Foreign Ministry corps, the South Manchurian Railway (SMR), and some members of the Seiyūkai party. Matsuoka Yōsuke, then a director of the SMR (in office between 1921 and 1926), warned of the communist threat to Japan's interests and promoted the notion of special relations between Japan and China. The SMR, the Foreign Ministry, and finally the cabinet under the Kiyoura Keigo premiership (1924) agreed with the General Staff's proposal that the only solution able to address the Soviet communist threat, as well as the threat of revolution in China, was to support the northern Chinese warlord Chang Tso-lin.[1] Driven by concern over the Bolshevization of China, by 1926 Japan's decision to support Chang became the most crucial factor in his ascendance to power in northern Manchuria. Few in Tokyo anticipated the disastrous consequences: considering Chang Tso-lin a liability, the Kwantung Army officers assassinated him in 1928, thus precipitating the takeover of Manchuria in 1931.[2] This assassination also marked the moment when the Foreign Ministry lost control over the Kwantung Army.

The army's plan to create a buffer zone against the Soviet Union and thus prevent the Bolshevization of China and Japan had been entertained since the mid-1920s. Two documents prepared by the General Staff were most revealing: "Situation of the Strong Advance of the Workers-Peasant Union in China" (Shina ni okeru rōnō reimei no seiryoku shinten no jyōkyō, November 1925), and "About Plans for the Bolshevization of Japan" (Nihon sekka keikaku ni kansuru ken, February 1926).[3] The Intelligence Bureau of the General Staff reported that the CER and the Soviet consulate in Harbin were the headquarters of Bolshevik operations. Moreover, Japanese intelligence indicated that the Chinese Revolution was the result of concerted efforts by the Soviet leadership, and Chinese and Russian communists' agitation on the ground. Soviet Russia sponsored not only Chinese communists and nationalists but also Japanese communists. The

Comintern, it was alleged, still hoped to bolshevize Japan and implement a proletarian revolution aimed at overturning the Japanese *kokutai*. This was in direct violation of the Japanese-Soviet Basic Treaty (article 5), and the General Staff urged the government to take measures to stop the Comintern's activities. Finally, taken together the two documents essentially argued that in order to protect Japan, the army's duty was to eliminate Soviet influence in China, specifically in northern Manchuria. Some of the detailed proposals included instigation of unrest among ethnic minorities in Asiatic Russia, Koreans, and white émigrés in Manchuria; sabotage on the Trans-Siberian Railway and of telecommunication lines; and the dispatch of intelligence agents disguised as Japanese fishermen.

To stop the Bolshevization of China, Minister of War Ugaki Kazushige (in office 1924–27) had already voiced plans for the takeover of Manchuria in 1926. Ugaki was especially indignant at the failure of his civilian colleagues to appreciate the scale of the communist danger in China and Japan. Russians, Ugaki warned in 1927, had a "habit of expansion" (*shinryaku kuse*), and were implementing "red imperialism" in northern Manchuria by converting the Chinese to communism. Japan must attack first and occupy the whole of Manchuria and Inner Mongolia.[4] This anticommunist cause was fully appropriated by the frontier Kwantung Army. In 1929, Ishiwara Kanji, a chief strategist of the Manchurian campaign, drafted a memorandum "A Kwantung Army Plan for the Occupation of Manchuria and Mongolia" (Kantōgun Man-Mō ryōyū keikaku). He claimed that as long as Russian power and influence existed in northern Manchuria, Japanese safety was threatened. To solve the "Manchuria problem," the Japanese must penetrate the whole of Manchuria, establishing there a self-defense zone. In the future, Ishiwara insisted, the whole Russian maritime region would have to come under Japanese influence.[5] While acting as minister of war (1932–34), General Araki Sadao, veteran of the Russo-Japanese War and the Siberian Intervention, member of the conservative Kokuhonsha organization, and probably the most hardened anticommunist in the military establishment, declared that as long as the USSR existed, all nations—and Japan in particular, as its cities were within bombing range of Vladivostok—were under threat of Bolshevization.[6]

The military's anticommunist thinking thus ranged from creating a buffer zone to a declaration of war on the Soviet Union. For the military and their supporters in the civilian political establishment, the existence of communist Russia left the entire East Asian region, including imperial Japan, vulnerable to the social disease of Marxism—an illness that threatened to weaken domestic society and the Asian community, exposing it to Soviet proletarian and/or Anglo-American capitalist imperialisms.

This anticommunism was, however, countered by the opposite trend within the establishment. There were political realists at the other end of the spectrum who recognized that Japan's interests in China could not be secured without cooperation with the Soviet Union. That was the same understanding that governed Japan's foreign relations with imperial Russia between 1905 and 1917 and forced it to recognize communist Russia in 1925. The navy, party politicians, and some members of the Foreign Ministry (Shidehara, Shiratori Toshio) were more concerned with the encroachment of Anglo-American white economic domination and the rise of Chinese nationalism, and advocated a Soviet-Japanese alliance. In some versions, China was included (e.g., Gotō Shinpei's advocacy and Prime Minister Tanaka Gi'ichi's support of a Sino-Soviet-Japanese alliance), while in later ones Nazi Germany also was considered as part of the Eurasian bloc. Matsuoka Yōsuke, who in the 1920s declared Soviet Russia as the main threat to Japan's empire, as foreign minister in 1940–41 proposed that the Soviet Union join the Tripartite Pact. Considerations about communist ideology were put aside in favor of a geopolitical Eurasian alliance against the North Atlantic alliance of Great Britain and the United States. Neither Stalin nor Hitler took this proposal seriously, but the fact remains that the Japanese political establishment was ready to overlook whatever ideological disagreements they might have had vis-à-vis Soviet communism.

Moreover, to combat Chinese nationalism, even the military was ready to cooperate with the Soviet Union, when necessary. In early 1929, Chang Hsüeh-liang, son of the slain Chang Tso-lin, tried to wrest control of the CER from the Soviets. In the ensuing Sino-Soviet military conflict in late 1929, the Japanese government signaled its approval of the Soviet Union's military actions in northern Manchuria and was more in sympathy with the Russians than the Chinese.[7] This incident indicated that the Japanese government, including the military (specifically, the so-called control faction, or *tōsei-ha*) was willing to accept the traditional division of the sphere of influence. In fact, whereas the Peace Preservation Law was revised in 1928 to make "alteration of the *kokutai*" punishable by death, foreign-policy makers did not shy away from striking a deal with Russian communists. Domestic and foreign policies diverged, in which the former's anticommunist stance did not alter the foreign policy focused on securing Japan's position in China by way of rapprochement with communist Russia.

The Manchurian Incident in 1931 greatly complicated the situation, mainly because there was no longer a buffer zone between the Soviet Union and the Japanese Empire. The focus of tension moved to the borders between Soviet Outer Mongolia and Manchukuo, where in 1935–39 there was a continuous series of minor frontier incidents. The Soviet government initially adopted an appeasement policy, unsuccessfully offering to conclude a nonaggression pact with the Japanese and selling the CER to Manchukuo in 1935. Simultaneously, the USSR hastened its buildup of military strength in the Far East, increasing the number of troops, double-tracking the Trans-Siberian Railway, and establishing the Pacific Fleet. The Soviet government also pressured the United States and the League of Nations for diplomatic recognition, which the United States gave in 1933. In September 1934, the USSR was accepted into the League of Nations. At the same time, the Soviet Comintern leadership also went into offensive mode, issuing the 1932 Theses on Japan—which, *for the first time*, called for the destruction of the absolutist state power exemplified by the figure of the emperor.

In November 1936, Japan concluded the Anti-Comintern Pact with Germany, which despite its name did not have much substance. The pact itself was anodyne and stated that the signatories would be on guard against the Comintern. Both the Foreign Ministry and the army were careful not to antagonize the Soviet Union. The Japanese government communicated with the Russians two days before publication of the pact, providing assurances that it was against the Comintern but not the Soviet Union![8] The Japanese inverted the traditional argument used by Soviet officials during the negotiations over the recognition of the USSR: that the Soviet Union had nothing to do with the Comintern, which was an international organization composed of many foreign communist parties. In fact, many understood that the Anti-Comintern Pact was anticommunist in form but anti-British in fact. It was a running joke that "Someday Stalin may join the Anti-Comintern Pact."[9]

Nevertheless, the Russians were offended and adopted a hard line over fisheries and various minor issues in Soviet-Japanese relations. After the outbreak of the Sino-Japanese War in 1937, the Soviets concluded a nonaggression pact with China and began to provide military aid to sink Japan deeper into its war with China. Recurring border disputes since 1933 increased in intensity after 1936 and resulted in two small wars. In 1938 in the Changkufeng Incident (known in Russia as the Lake Khasan Incident, at the convergence of the Soviet, Korean, and Manchukuo borders) and the Nomonhan War of 1939 (known in Russia as the Battle of Khalkhin Gol, on the Manchukuo–Outer Mongolian border), the Soviet Union defeated Japan.[10] The Japanese government chose not to provoke the Soviet Union any further and adopted a policy of "keeping peace and status quo" (*seihitsu hoji*).[11]

Since 1938, the New Order in East Asia movement advocated by then prime minister Konoe Fumimaro had aimed at preventing US, British, and French interference in Asian affairs. Importantly, it did not conceive of the Soviet Union as a force to be kept out of East Asia. Revolutionary Russia, it was understood, would support Japan's own "revolutionary" challenge to Anglo-American world dominance. In the spring of 1941, both the Soviet Union and Japan faced grave international challenges and thus more vigorously pursued mutually conciliatory relations. The Soviet-Japanese Neutrality Pact of April 1941 once again confirmed the traditional division of influence. The treaty stipulated that the Soviet Union would respect the territorial integrity and inviolability of Manchukuo, and the Japanese made an identical pledge with regard to the Mongolian People's Republic.[12] During negotiations in Moscow in March 1941, Matsuoka declared that it was Britain and the United States who tricked Japan into intervening in the Russian Revolution in Siberia in the summer of 1918. In doing so, they prevented Japan and the Soviet Union from becoming close partners, as they always should have been. Matsuoka further claimed that he was the true heir to the ideals of Gotō Shinpei and a true friend of the Russian communists.[13] This was not the first time that Matsuoka declared his friendly attitude. In November 1932, on his way to the League of Nations meeting over the Manchurian Incident, where the Japanese delegation famously walked out in protest, Matsuoka stopped in Moscow for five days. While never affirming the tenets of communism, Matsuoka praised the Soviet Union for "conducting a great experiment for human beings, whereas western civilization is in decline."[14]

In a way, the Russian Revolution ended in 1943, when Stalin dissolved the Comintern, publicly abandoning the program of world proletarian revolution. The Soviet-Japanese status quo, reminiscent of the division of the spheres of influence in East Asia between imperial Russia and imperial Japan before 1917, remained intact until the summer of 1945. The anti-imperialist and anti-Japanese declarations and actions of Russian and Asian communists determined the responses of the Japanese political, military, and bureaucratic establishment in domestic and foreign policies. However, apart from the radical anti-Soviet and anticommunist faction within the military (especially the Imperial Way faction under Araki Sadao), the government and military taking a pragmatic approach were confident that communism, while still an ideological threat, could be contained and that the domestic society and its unique nature, exemplified in the term *kokutai*, were secured by various institutional and ideological measures. More often than not, Japanese policy makers chose the path of peaceful coexistence with Soviet Russia because of the apparent advantages for the Japanese Empire and the whole East Asian region.

The Russian Revolution did not have the same meaning in Asia as it did in Europe or Russia itself. Moreover, it was understood differently in Japan than in the rest of Asia because Japan was not a colonized country but rather a colonizer. Asian revolutionaries outside Japan adopted the Leninist critique of capitalist imperialism and, as an alternative path to modernization, followed the communist program. But to contemporary Japanese commentators it was already obvious that although in colonial (Korea) and semicolonial (China) Asia the Russian Revolution merged with the goals of national independence and modernization, in Japan it had to answer to different goals. In Japan, the Russian Revolution overlapped with domestic agitation for reforms that aimed to extend political rights to outsider groups, rein in the exercise of arbitrary power, and find a solution to the colonial problem. The Russian Revolution happened at a time when the Japanese public began to question the historical foundations of their modernized imperial state and its future in the new post–World War I global context. The period between 1918 and 1924 was the most unstable and turbulent for the imperial government since the Meiji Revolution in 1868. The Meiji order, which had established an emperor-centered constitutional system, promoted a capitalist, industrializing economy, and recognized expansion in Asia as an essential part of "national defense and well-being," was being challenged by new political and social forces. The Russian Revolution provided a model for organization and tactics to achieve what Japanese nongovernmental groups and activists had always sought: participation in national politics in order to improve social and economic conditions. Viewed from this perspective, the arrival of communist ideas heralded the revival of a long-standing current in Japanese oppositional thinking, and the emergence of a new theoretical framework for resisting the increasingly authoritarian state.

Marxism had been known and studied in Japan since the late 1890s, but it was not until the Russian Revolution and subsequent domestic unrest—specifically the Rice Riots of 1918 and numerous labor strikes—that Marxism became the ideology of the Japanese revolutionary movement and the guiding principle of social science in Japan. These domestic and international upheavals validated for many in Japan the Marxist understanding of social structure based on social classes. They seemed to give credence to the notion that class conflict—which was fundamentally international in character and transcended state boundaries— was at once society's essential problem and the key to its liberation. The Japanese state took the threat of proletarian internationalism seriously and, beginning with the implementation of the Peace Preservation Law of 1925, devised a mechanism to bring leftists back to the national community. Class conflict was also an issue for the state, the police, and the conservative and radical Right; but distinctly in the Japanese case, anticapitalist rhetoric was largely tolerated and even shared by members of these groups.

The government, however, did not have to worry about domestic leftist opposition because Japanese communists in the 1920s came to regard the international anti-imperialist struggle as a secondary goal. As Japanese leftist intellectuals struggled to make sense of their world and their aspirations for their people and country, they devised a revolutionary program that diverged from the Russian model and the Comintern's recommendations. Japanese socialists produced three main interpretations of the Russian Revolution: national socialism, anarchism, and communism (of the early JCP variety), and all three of them failed to exclude the trappings of national rhetoric. Each had different motives for its preference of national causes over internationalist objectives but, as I have argued, at its root was their deep preoccupation with and "protest against the quality of political life," which ultimately resulted in their rejection of the universality of the Russian revolutionary model and Marxist-Leninist communism.[15] The breakup of the previously united Japanese socialist movement started with the departure of the newly established national socialist group. The emergence of this group revealed a larger pattern within Japanese leftist political thought: it was inspired in its anticapitalist critique by Marxism but ultimately driven by the interests of national and bloc self-sufficiency. Referring to the example of the Russian Revolution, national socialists concluded that the only agent of historical change was the nation as a whole, not a particular social class. In this way, they rejected internationalism in favor of nationalism as a means for ensuring the prosperity of the state and empire. On the political level, national socialists found it more befitting to side with fascists, the conservative Right, and the establishment, rather than with "traitorous" Japanese communists.

Taishō anarchism and early communism maintained their internationalist orientation because they had an institutional referent in the Comintern (this was true for anarchism until 1923). The Kōza-ha, the dominant school of Japanese communism in the 1930s, was blamed by post–World War II Japanese Marxist historians for taking for granted the exceptional character of the Japanese nation-state based on its distorted analysis of Japan's historical development. In contrast, the Rōnō-ha and its original leader, Yamakawa Hitoshi, were commended for regarding Japan as one of the capitalist powers rather than insisting on its exceptionalism.

But as I have argued, Japanese communists, regardless of what faction they belonged to, were not immune to the power of nationalism. While resisting the Russian Marxist framework of "advanced Europe and backward Asia," Yamakawa differentiated between "advanced Japan" and the rest of "backward Asia," prioritizing the former over the latter. If we look at how the Rōnō-ha treated Japan's proletarian engagement with the colonial struggle in Asia, it becomes obvious that they replicated the Orientalist outlook of Marxism-Leninism and inverted it. Yamakawa and the early JCP came to believe that the Japanese socialist movement, due to its more progressive character, occupied a superior position in relation to socialist movements in Korea and China. Caught between domestic social issues, on one hand, and the international anti-imperialist struggle, on the other, the Japanese Left ultimately chose the former as the more urgent of the two fronts. With its internationalist tendencies muted, the national communist movement in Japan was poorly equipped to withstand the pressure of the militarized state in the 1930s. When, in the late 1920s, Japanese communists placed their hopes in the Chinese Revolution and attempted to form a united anti-imperialist front with their Chinese counterparts, their efforts remained abortive. After the outbreak of war in China in 1927 and subsequent mass arrests of leftists, and especially after the invasion of Manchuria in 1931, there was far less room to mount a meaningful opposition to military expansion abroad.

Did leftist internationalism in interwar Japan have a chance to succeed? Most probably not. The reason for this is not that the state was too powerful, nor that police repression was too thorough, but that leftist thinking from the start included a fatal flaw that would prove to be its undoing—namely, the belief that Japan was exceptional and/or superior to the rest of Asia, and even to revolutionary Russia. Japanese leftists might not have been able to stop the war in China, but they might have altered the course of those tragic events had their response to the Russian Revolution's supranational vision been different.

Notes

INTRODUCTION

1. On the global impact of the Russian Revolution in the twentieth century, see Eric Hobsbawm, *The Age of Extremes: A History of the World, 1914–1991* (New York: Vintage, 1996).

2. The first Korean socialist party was formed in Khabarovsk in 1919, and Korean communists dominated the Korean Provisional Government in Shanghai, established in 1920. Communist parties were established in Persia, India, and Turkey in 1920; Palestine in 1922; and Vietnam, Malaya, Siam, Laos, and the Philippines in 1930.

3. To clarify, Korean and Chinese activists obviously struggled against Japanese imperialism, while the Mongol national liberation struggle was directed against Republican China, the heir to the Qing Empire.

4. Quoted from Boris Nicolaevsky, "Russia, Japan, and the Pan-Asiatic Movement to 1925," *Far Eastern Quarterly* 8, no. 3 (1949): 285.

5. Tadashi Anno, *National Identity and Great-Power Status in Russia and Japan: Non-Western Challengers to the Liberal International Order* (New York: Routledge, 2018).

6. Quoted from Allen S. Whiting, *Soviet Policies in China, 1917–1924* (New York: Columbia University Press, 1954), 25.

7. Exceptions to this general trend were studies done by historians of Japanese-Russian relations: George Lensen, *Japanese Recognition of the USSR* (Tokyo: Sophia University, 1970); Joseph Ferguson, *Japanese-Russian Relations, 1907–2007* (London: Routledge, 2008); and Peter Berton, *Russo-Japanese Relations, 1905–1917: From Enemies to Allies* (London: Routledge, 2012; originally published as a PhD dissertation, "The Secret Russo-Japanese Alliance of 1916," Michigan University, 1956). In Japanese scholarship imperial Russia and the Soviet Union have occupied much more prominent positions. See, for example, Yoshimura Michio, *Nihon to Roshia: Nichiro sengo kara Roshia kakumei made* (Tokyo: Hara Shobō, 1968); Tomita Takeshi, *Senkanki no Nisso kankei: 1917–1937* (Tokyo: Iwanami Shoten, 2010); and recently Asada Masafumi, *Nichiro kindaishi: Sensō to heiwa no hyakunen* (Tokyo: Kodansha, 2018). In Russian, see especially Petr Podalko, *Iaponiia v sud'bakh rossiian: Ocherki istorii tsarskoi diplomatii i rossiiskoi diaspory v Iaponii* (Moscow: Institut vostokovedeniia Rossiiskoi akademii nauk, 2004); and Vasilii Molodiakov, *Rossiia i Iaponiia: V poiskakh soglasiia, 1905–1945* (Moscow: AIRO, 2012).

8. Yamakawa Hitoshi, *Yamakawa Hitoshi jiden*, ed. Yamakawa Kikue and Sakisaka Itsurō (Tokyo: Iwanami Shoten, 1961), 370.

9. For a recent study of the Japanese Left, see Kurokawa Iori, *Teikoku ni kōsuru shakai undō: Daiichiji Nihon Kyōsantō no shisō to undō* (Tokyo: Yūshisha, 2014).

10. Akira Iriye's book, *After Imperialism*, is an exception in singling out the importance of the Soviet moment in East Asia, but it deals more with international politics. See Akira Iriye, *After Imperialism* (Cambridge, MA: Harvard University Press, 1965). Soviet scholarship on the impact of communism in interwar Japan was overtly ideological, while contemporary Russian scholarship on Japan has not yet addressed this topic, largely due to the present general confusion in Russia about how to approach the Soviet past historically.

11. I did not venture into exploring the relationship between the state and communist organizations in the 1930s; neither did I incorporate the Japanese Marxist

debate of the 1930s on Japanese capitalism (*Nihon shihonshugi ronsō*) put forward by the two major Marxist schools, the Kōza-ha (Lectures Faction) and the Rōnō-ha (Worker-Farmer Faction). For that, see Germaine Hoston, *Marxism and the Crisis of Development in Prewar Japan* (Princeton, NJ: Princeton University Press, 1986). Neither did I engage extensively with Japanese communist sojourners' experiences within the Soviet Union, and their often tragic lives during the height of the Stalinist terror. For the latter issue, see Katō Tetsurō, *Mosukuwa de shukuseisareta Nihonjin: 30-nendai Kyōsantō to Kunisaki Teidō, Yamamoto Kenzō no higeki* (Tokyo: Aoki Shoten, 1994).

12. Sheila Fitzpatrick, *The Russian Revolution* (Oxford: Oxford University Press, 2008), 1–4.

CHAPTER 1. BEFORE 1917

1. For a detailed account of early Russo-Japanese relations, see George A. Lensen, *The Russian Push toward Japan* (Princeton, NJ: Princeton University Press, 1959); and Lensen, "Early Russo-Japanese Relations," *Far Eastern Quarterly* 10 (November 1950—August 1951): 2–37. For early modern Japanese views of Russia, see Bob T. Wakabayashi, *Anti-Foreignism and Western Learning in Early-Modern Japan: The New Theses of 1825* (Cambridge, MA: Council on East Asian Studies, 1986), 58–99.

2. Peter Berton, Paul F. Langer, and Rodger Swearingen, *Japanese Training and Research in the Russian Field* (Los Angeles: University of Southern California Press, 1956), 6.

3. Adding to this new Japanese interest in Russia, a study based on the interrogation notes of the Russian explorer Vasily Golovnin, who was captured by the Japanese in 1811 and held as a prisoner for two and a half years in Hokkaido, was published in Japanese a few years after his release. Japanese officials also used Golovnin to train their first Russian experts and expand their area studies material. See Vasily Golovnin, *Memoirs of a Captivity in Japan, 1811–1813* (Oxford: Oxford University Press, 1973). Incidentally, Golovnin's memoirs were the first extensive description of Japan by a Russian. Within a decade, they were translated into Japanese and several European languages.

4. Berton, Langer, and Swearingen, *Japanese Training and Research in the Russian Field*, 2–4.

5. It is suggestive that the Qing Empire had had similar anxieties about the Mongol population vis-à-vis the expanding Russian Empire. See Jonathan Schlesinger, *A World Trimmed with Fur: Wild Things, Pristine Places, and the Natural Fringes of Qing Rule* (Stanford, CA: Stanford University Press, 2017).

6. Tessa Morris-Suzuki, "Lines in the Snow: Imagining the Russo-Japanese Frontier," *Pacific Affairs* 72, no. 1 (Spring 1999): 69.

7. Kurosawa Fumitaka, "Edo, Meiji ki no Nichiro kankei: Roshia imēji wo chūshin ni," *Nihon rekishi* 802, no. 3 (2015): 53–72.

8. Lensen, *Russian Push toward Japan*, 442–46; Key-Hiuk Kim, *The Last Phase of the East Asian World Order: Korea, Japan, and the Chinese Empire, 1860–1882* (Berkeley: University of California Press, 1980), 218–19.

9. Wada Haruki, "Japanese-Russian Relations and the United States, 1855–1930," in *A Hidden Fire: Russian and Japanese Cultural Encounters, 1868–1926*, ed. Thomas J. Rimer (Stanford, CA: Stanford Univerity Press, 1995), 205.

10. Shinichi Fumoto, "Russia's Expansion to the Far East and Its Impact on Early Meiji Japan's Korea Policy," in *Russia and Its Northeast Asian Neighbors: China, Japan, and Korea, 1858–1945*, ed. Kimitaka Matsuzato (Lanham, MD: Lexington Books, 2018), 2–3.

11. Kurono Taeru, *Teikoku kokubō hōshin no kenkyū: Riku-Kaigun kokubō shisō no tenkai to tokuchō* (Tokyo: Sōwasha, 2000), 22.

12. England, France, the Netherlands, and the United States (later joined by Austria, Prussia, Denmark, and Sweden) belonged to the highest category of "civilized countries" (*bunmei no kuni*). After the second category, the list descends as follows: China, India, Turkey, Persia, and the African nations north of the Sahara were classified as "semi-enlightened countries" (*hankai no kuni*), while the nomadic tribes in Siberia, Central Asia, Arabia, and Africa were classified as "countries of uncivilized manners and customs" (*izoku no kuni*). Last were the "barbarians" (*yaban*): the American Indians and the natives of Africa and Australia. See Togawa Tsuguo, "The Japanese View of Russia before and after the Meiji Restoration," in *Hidden Fire*, 215.

13. Asada Masafumi, *Nichiro kindaishi: Sensō to heiwa no hyakunen* (Tokyo: Kodansha, 2018), 31–33.

14. For the list of books published on Russia by the sojourners from the army, the navy, and the Foreign Ministry, see Berton, Langer, and Swearingen, *Japanese Training and Research in the Russian Field*, 18.

15. Enomoto Takeaki, *Shiberia nikki*, 3 vols. (Tokyo: Kaigun yūshūkai, 1935).

16. Sven Saaler, "Fukushima Yasumasa's Travels in Central Asia and Siberia: Silk Road Romanticism, Military Reconnaissance, or Modern Exploration," in *Japan on the Silk Road*, ed. Selçuk Esenbel (Leiden: Brill, 2017), 69–86.

17. John J. Stephan, *The Russian Far East: A History* (Stanford, CA: Stanford University Press, 1994), 77.

18. Igor Saveliev and Yuri Pestushko, "Dangerous Rapprochement: Russia and Japan in the First World War, 1914–1916," *Acta Slavica Iaponica* 18 (2001): 31.

19. Yamamuro Shin'ichi, *Nichiro sensō no seiki: Rensa shiten kara miru Nihon to sekai* (Tokyo: Iwanami Shoten, 2005), 32–33.

20. George A. Lensen, "Japan and Tsarist Russia—The Changing Relationships, 1875–1917," *Jahrbücher für Geschichte Osteuropas* 10, no. 3 (October 1962): 340.

21. Yoshimura Akira, *Nikorai sōnan* (Tokyo: Iwanami Shoten, 1993).

22. Robert T. Tierney, *Monster of the Twentieth Century: Kōtoku Shūsui and Japan's First Anti-Imperialist Movement* (Berkeley: University of California Press, 2015), 84.

23. Okamoto Shumpei, *The Japanese Oligarchy and the Russo-Japanese War* (New York: Columbia University Press, 1970), 63–67.

24. Ian Nish, *The Origins of the Russo-Japanese War* (London: Routledge, 1985), 154.

25. Hosoya Chihiro, "Japan's Foreign Policy toward Russia," in *Japan's Foreign Policy, 1868–1941: A Research Guide*, ed. James W. Morley and James B. Crowley (New York: Columbia University Press, 1974), 371–72. Tanaka served in Manchuria, rising to the rank of lieutenant colonel as an aide to General Kodama.

26. Okamoto, *Japanese Oligarchy and the Russo-Japanese War*, 63–67.

27. Sandra Wilson, "The Russo-Japanese War and Japan: Politics, Nationalism, and Historical Memory," in *The Russo-Japanese War in Cultural Perspective*, ed. David Wells and Sandra Wilson (London: Palgrave Macmillian, 1999), 175.

28. The historian Andrew Malozemoff has argued, however, that the worsening of relations was not predetermined. It was left to Nicholas II to decide to intervene in 1895, as the Russian government was split on this question. However, it was up to Emperor Meiji to make the decision to conclude the anti-Russian Anglo-Japanese alliance in 1902 because the pro-Russian faction was quite strong and the Japanese counsels were divided to the last about whether to work with or against the Russians (*Russian Far Eastern Policy, 1881–1904* [New York: Octagon Books, 1977]).

29. Seki Shizuo, *"Taishō" saikō: Kibō to fuan no jidai* (Kyoto: Mineruva Shobō, 2007), 107–28.

30. Tomoko Aoyama, "Japanese Literary Responses to the Russo-Japanese War," in *Russo-Japanese War in Cultural Perspective*, 73.

31. David Schimmelpenninck van der Oye, *Toward the Rising Sun: Russian Ideologies of Empire and the Path to War with Japan* (DeKalb: Northern Illinois University Press, 2001). On the discourse of the "yellow race," see Lensen, "Japan and Tsarist Russia"; and Rosamund Bartlett, "Japonisme and Japanophobia: The Russo-Japanese War in Russian Cultural Consciousness," *Russian Review* 67, no. 1 (2008): 8–33.

32. Asukai Masamichi, *Kindai bunka to shakaishugi* (Tokyo: Shōbunsha, 1970), 95–96.

33. William G. Beasley, *Japanese Imperialism, 1894–1945* (Oxford: Oxford University Press, 1991), 90–100; Alvin D. Coox, *Nomonhan: Japan against Russia, 1939* (Stanford, CA: Stanford University Press, 1985), 1–16.

34. Beasley, *Japanese Imperialism*, 97–98.

35. The association organized diplomatic meetings, encouraged development of trade between the two countries, provided a trade inquiry service and lectures in the Russian field, served as an information center for the Russian press, and sponsored research on the Russian economy.

36. Hara Teruyuki "Nichiro sensōgo no Roshia kyokutō—chiiki seisaku to kokusai kankyō," *Roshia shi kenkyū* 72 (2003): 6–22; Vasilii Molodiakov, *Rossiia i Iaponiia: Zolotoi vek (1905–1916)* (Moscow: Prosveshchenie, 2008).

37. Hosoya, "Japan's Foreign Policy toward Russia," 373.

38. Saveliev and Pestushko, "Dangerous Rapprochement," 20.

39. Hosoya, "Japan's Foreign Policy toward Russia," 376–77.

40. Saveliev and Pestushko, "Dangerous Rapprochement," 21.

41. Yaroslav Shulatov, "Chōsen mondai wo meguru Nichiro kankei (1905–1907)," *Surabu kenkyū* 54 (2007): 183–205.

42. Ivan Sablin and Alexander Kuchinsky, "Making the Korean Nation in the Russian Far East, 1863–1926," *Nationalities Papers* 45, no. 5 (2017): 798–814.

43. Wada Haruki, "Koreans in the Soviet Far East, 1917–1937," in *Koreans in the Soviet Union*, ed. Dae-Sook Suh (Honolulu: University of Hawaii Press, 1987), 32; Boris Pak, *Koreitsy v Rossiiskoi imperii* (Moscow: Moskovskii gosudarstvennyi universitet, 1993).

44. Igor Saveliev, "Militant Diaspora: Korean Immigrants and Guerrillas in Early Twentieth Century Russia," *Forum of International Development Studies* 26 (2004): 147–62.

45. Saveliev and Pestushko, "Dangerous Rapprochement," 35.

46. Hara Teruyuki, "The Korean Movement in the Russian Maritime Province, 1905–1922," in *Koreans in the Soviet Union*, 1–23.

47. Saveliev and Pestushko, "Dangerous Rapprochement," 38.

48. Teramoto Yasutoshi, *Nichiro sensō igo no Nihon gaikō: Pawā poritikusu no naka no Man-Kan mondai* (Tokyo: Shinzansha, 1999); Sakamoto Masako, *Zaibatsu to teikokushugi: Mitsui Bussan to Chūgoku* (Kyoto: Mineruva Shobō, 2003).

49. Beasley, *Japanese Imperialism*, 119.

50. On the recent assessment of Russo-Japanese relations in this period, see Kurosawa Fumitaka, "Meiji sue, Taishō shoki no Nichiro kankei: Teki ka mikata ka, hatamata tomo ka?" *Journal of the Diplomatic Archives* 30, no. 3 (2017): 57–74.

51. Eduard Baryshev, *Nichiro dōmei no jidai, 1914–1917: "Reigaitekina yūkō" no shinsō* (Fukuoka: Hanashōin, 2007); Peter Berton, *Russo-Japanese Relations, 1905–1917.*

52. Sho Konishi, *Anarchist Modernity Cooperatism and Japanese-Russian Intellectual Relations in Modern Japan* (Cambridge, MA: Harvard University Asia Center, 2013), 5.

53. Nobori Shomu and Akamatsu Katsumaro, *The Russian Impact on Japan: Literature and Social Thought: Two Essays* (Los Angeles: University of Southern California Press, 1981), 113.

54. Berton, Langer, and Swearingen, *Japanese Training and Research in the Russian Field*, 51–54.

55. Konishi, *Anarchist Modernity*, 93–141.

56. Tetsuo Mochizuki, "Japanese Perceptions of Russian Literature in the Meiji and Taisho Eras," in *Hidden Fire*, 17–21.

57. Miki Kiyoshi, "Shesutofuteki fuan ni tsuite," *Kaizō* (September 1934): 392–405.

58. Paul Anderer, "Kobayashi and Dostoevsky," in *Hidden Fire*, 45.

59. Asada, *Nichiro kindaishi*, 58–62.

60. Wada, "Japanese-Russian Relations and the United States," 206.

61. Chushichi Tsuzuki, "Kotoku, Osugi, and Japanese Anarchism," *Hitotsubashi Journal of Social Studies* 3, no. 1 (1966): 30.

62. Asukai Masamichi, "Roshia Daiichiji Kakumei to Kōtoku Shūsui," *Shisō* 520 (1967): 1–21.

63. Takeuchi Yoshimi, *Nihon to Ajia* (Tokyo: Chikuma Shobō, 1993), 343.

64. Wada, "Japanese-Russian Relations and the United States," 208.

65. Ogino Fujio, *Shoki shakaishugi shisōron* (Tokyo: Fuji Shuppan, 1993); Matsuzawa Hiroaki, *Nihon shakaishugi no shisō* (Tokyo: Chikuma Shobō, 1973).

66. See, for example, Kōtoku Shūsui's *Shakaishugi shinzui* (The Essence of Socialism, 1903); and Matsuzawa, *Nihon shakaishugi no shisō*, 17–22.

67. Hyman Kublin, "The Origins of the Japanese Socialist Tradition," *Journal of Politics* 14, no. 2 (May 1952): 262.

68. In its first year, *Heimin shinbun* sold an impressive two hundred thousand copies, in addition to numerous copies distributed through socialist networks. The Heimin association organized 120 socialist meetings in 1904, including 13 women's socialist association meetings, and established socialist organizations in over 20 cities and towns across Japan. It helped finance the Ashio copper mine riots in Hokkaido and organize the resettlement of those involved (Konishi, *Anarchist Modernity*, 189; Wilson, "Russo-Japanese War and Japan," 174–75).

69. Vera Mackie, "Motherhood and Pacifism in Japan, 1900–1937," *Hecate* 14, no. 2 (1988): 28–49; Nobuya Bamba, *Pacifism in Japan: The Christian and Socialist Tradition* (Kyoto: Minerva Press, 1980).

70. George T. Shea, *Leftwing Literature in Japan* (Tokyo: The Hosei University Press, 1964), 15.

71. Shea, *Leftwing Literature in Japan*, 16.

72. Hyman Kublin, "Japanese Socialists and the Russo-Japanese War," *Journal of Modern History* 22 (1950): 322–23.

73. Asukai, *Kindai bunka to shakaishugi*, 195–231.

74. There were ninety thousand Russian POWs scattered in twenty-eight camps across Japan, but the most numerous one was in Nagasaki, where the POWs intersected with a Jewish émigré community (Konishi, *Anarchist Modernity*, 197–203).

75. While the Japanese police suppressed the publication of *Heimin shinbun* and harassed Kōtoku and his fellows, they deliberately overlooked Russo-Japanese socialist cooperation in regard to socialist propaganda among prisoners of war. The Japanese authorities hoped that Russian revolutionary activities would weaken and undermine the Russian imperial state.

76. For more detailed discussion, see Vladimir Tikhonov, "A Russian Radical and East Asia in the Early Twentieth Century: Sudzilovsky, China, and Japan," *Cross-Currents: East Asian History and Culture Review* 18 (2016): 51.

77. Rebecca E. Karl, "Creating Asia: China in the World at the Beginning of the Twentieth Century," *American Historical Review* 103, no. 4 (1998): 1113.

CHAPTER 2. REVOLUTION AND INTERVENTION

1. Hara Takashi, *Hara Takashi nikki*, ed. Hara Kei'ichirō (Tokyo: Kangensha edition, 1950–51), 7:142. The first commoner and leader of a majority party in the lower house of

the Japanese Diet to become prime minister, Hara Takashi served from September 1918 to November 1921. He was assassinated on November 4, 1921, by a disgruntled nationalist angry at the Hara Cabinet's approval of the reduction of the army budget, another consequence of the Siberian Intervention.

2. The Julian calendar (old style), which is thirteen days behind the Gregorian calendar (new style) of the West, was in use in Russia until 1918. From here on, new style dates will be used.

3. Ronald G. Suny, *The Soviet Experiment: Russia, the USSR, and the Successor States* (Oxford: Oxford University Press, 1998), 35–44.

4. Harima Narakichi, "Rōnō kakumei jikkenki," *Jiji shinpō*, March 31, 1917. For more information, see Kikuchi Masanori, *Roshia kakumei to Nihonjin* (Tokyo: Chikuma Shobō, 1973), 8–11.

5. Suny, *Soviet Experiment*, 42.

6. Asukai Masamichi, "Roshia kakumei to Nikō jiken," in *Taishōki no kyūshinteki jiyūshugi: Tōyō keizai shinpō wo chūshin toshite*, ed. Inoue Kiyoshi and Watanabe Tōru (Tokyo: Tōyō Keizai Shinpō, 1972), 269.

7. Kikuchi, *Roshia kakumei*, 21.

8. Tomita Takeshi, *Senkanki no Nisso kankei* (Tokyo: Iwanami Shoten, 2010), 13.

9. Kikuchi, *Roshia kakumei*, 27.

10. Tomita, *Senkanki no Nisso kankei*, 14.

11. Kikuchi, *Roshia kakumei*, 37–48; Hara Teruyuki, *Shiberia shuppei: Kakumei to kanshō* (Tokyo: Chikuma Shobō, 1989), 125.

12. Asukai, "Roshia kakumei to Nikō jiken," 299.

13. Mitsukawa Kametarō, *Sangoku kanshō igo* (Tokyo: Ronsōsha, 2004), 150–51. Waseda University became the hotbed of communist activities in Japan, accommodating early student communist groups and communist professors, among whom Sano Manabu, leader of the JCP, was the most famous.

14. Quoted from Sharon Nolte, *Liberalism in Modern Japan: Ishibashi Tanzan and His Teachers, 1905–1960* (Berkeley: University of California Press, 1986), 152. Terauchi was forced to step down in September 1918 after the Rice Riots and was succeeded by Hara Takashi.

15. Kikuchi, *Roshia kakumei*, 14.

16. Mitsukawa, *Sangoku kanshō igo*, 149.

17. Peter Berton and Paul F. Langer, "Nobori Shomu: A Pioneer in Russo-Japanese Cultural Relations," in *The Russian Impact on Japan: Literature and Social Thought: Two Essays*, ed. Nobori Shomu et al. (Los Angeles: University of Southern California Press, 1981), 13–20.

18. Takabatake Motoyuki, "Kakumei kachū no rodoku," *Shinshakai* (May 1917).

19. Sheila Fitzpatrick, *The Russian Revolution* (Oxford: Oxford University Press, 2008), 64–66.

20. Suny, *Soviet Experiment*, 56–64.

21. Allen S. Whiting, *Soviet Policies in China, 1917–1924* (New York: Columbia University Press, 1954), 30.

22. John J. Stephan, *The Russian Far East: A History* (Stanford, CA: Stanford University Press, 1994), 114–16.

23. Jamie Bisher, *White Terror: Cossack Warlords of the Trans-Siberian* (London: Routledge, 2005).

24. Gaimushō Hyakunenshi Hensan Iinkai, ed., *Gaimushō no hyakunen* (Tokyo: Hara Shobō, 1969), 1:673.

25. Tomita Takeshi, "Roshia Kakumei to Nihonjin," *Shisō* 1119 (July 2017): 101.

26. Hara, *Shiberia shuppei*, 121.

27. Hara, *Shiberia shuppei*, 121.

28. Kikuchi, *Roshia kakumei*, 48–53. The Japanese newspapers relied heavily on British Reuters and uncritically accepted the negative British position toward the October Revolution. See also Mitsukawa Kametarō on the general hysteria in Japanese newspapers about the October Revolution, Lenin, and the advance of Germany (Mitsukawa, *Sangoku kanshō igo*, 153–55).

29. Hosoya Chihiro, *Shiberia shuppei no shiteki kenkyū* (Tokyo: Iwanami Shoten, 2005 [1955]), 10.

30. Hosoya, *Shiberia shuppei no shiteki kenkyū*, 12.

31. Tomita, *Senkanki no Nisso kankei*, 14.

32. *Gaimushō no hyakunen*, 1:675.

33. *Gaimushō no hyakunen*, 1:677.

34. Tomita, *Senkanki no Nisso kankei*, 14.

35. Izao Tomio, "Shiberia shuppei kōzō no henyō: Terauchi naikaku oyobi gaikō chōsakai wo chūshin ni shite," *Hōsei Kenkyū* 66, no. 4 (2000): 173n31.

36. Tomita, *Senkanki no Nisso kankei*, 16.

37. *Gaimushō no hyakunen*, 1:681.

38. *Gaimushō no hyakunen*, 1:687.

39. Hara, *Shiberia shuppei*, 292, 378–81.

40. Kitaoka Shin'ichi, *Gotō Shinpei: Gaikō to bijon* (Tokyo: Chūō Kōronsha, 1988), 179.

41. Izao Tomio, "Shiberia shuppei ron no kōzō to haikei," *Kyūdai Hōgaku* 78 (1999): 332.

42. *Gaimushō no hyakunen*, 1:678.

43. Uchida Kōsai, *Uchida Kōsai kankei shiryō shūsei*, ed. Michihiko Kobayashi (Tokyo: Kashiwa Shobō, 2012), 3:213.

44. Uehara Yūsaku, *Uehara Yūsaku nikki* (Tokyo: Shōyū Kurabu, 2011), 70–75.

45. Leonard A. Humphreys, *The Way of the Heavenly Sword: The Japanese Army in the 1920s* (Stanford, CA: Stanford University Press, 1995), 26.

46. *Gaimushō no hyakunen*, 1:674; Hosoya, *Shiberia shuppei no shiteki kenkyū*, 14.

47. David Wolff, "Open Jaw: A Harbin-Centered View of the Siberian-Manchurian Intervention 1917–1922," *Russian History* 36, no. 3 (2009): 339–59.

48. Concessions included the construction of a railway line for military purposes between Harbin and Chanchung, and construction in Harbin of a telephone line for the military (Tomita, *Senkanki no Nisso kankei*, 17–21). Araki did not trust the general because of his preference for US and British help and instead actively supported Ataman Semenov.

49. For Japanese expansion into Chinese politics in 1918, see Itō Masanori, "Shiberia shuppei go no Tōshin tetsudō mondai (1924–1928): Nisso kankei no ichi sokumen," *Sophia Historical Studies* 36 (1991): 29–50; and Guoqi Xu, *China and the Great War: China's Pursuit of a New National Identity and Internationalization* (New York: Cambridge University Press, 2004), 235–36.

50. For more detailed discussion of the Siberian Intervention, see James Morley, *The Japanese Thrust into Siberia, 1918* (New York: Columbia University Press, 1958); and Paul Dunscomb, *Japan's Siberian Intervention, 1918–1922: "A Great Disobedience against the People"* (Lanham, MD: Lexington Books, 2011). In Japanese, Hosoya Chihiro's *Shiberia shuppei no shiteki kenkyū* and Hara Teruyuki's *Shiberia shuppei* are still the most authoritative studies. In Japanese scholarship interest has surged in the Siberian Intervention as the precursor to Japanese expansionism in China in the 1930s. See Asada Masafumi, *Shiberia shuppei: Kindai Nihon no wasurerareta shichinen sensō* (Tokyo: Chūō Kōron Shinsha, 2016).

51. George Kennan, *Soviet-American Relations, 1917–1920* (Princeton, NJ: Princeton University Press, 1956), 484.

52. Four great powers were involved—Britain, France, Japan, and the United States. Britain and the United States intervened also in Murmansk and Arkhangelsk, the northwestern part of Russia, in March and August 1918, respectively, to protect military supply matériel, believed to be threatened by German-supported Finnish forces. Although there was some fighting with the Bolsheviks, the northern front was not that important for the outcome of the Civil War. Britain also dispatched troops to Central Asia, fearing the Turks' advance through Afghanistan to India. The French in Ukraine withdrew their forces in early 1919, without any fighting. Thus, the only important danger for the new Bolshevik government was the Japanese army in Siberia and the Russian Far East.

53. Izao Tomio, *Shoki Shiberia shuppei no kenkyū: "Atarashiki kyūseigun" kōsō no tōjō to tenkai* (Fukuoka: Kyūshū Daigaku Shuppankai, 2003), 34–35.

54. Izao, *Shoki Shiberia shuppei no kenkyū*, 143–46; Shibata Yoshimasa, "Shiberia shuppeiki tairo bōeki gyōsha shiensaku to Nichiro jitsugyō kabushiki gaisha no katsudō," *Tōyō kenkyū* 195, no. 1 (2015): 1–45.

55. *Gaimushō no hyakunen*, 1:688. The Japanese government initiated a Japanese yen economic zone in northeast Asia by issuing and circulating banknotes of the Bank of Chosen (the central bank of Japanese colonial Korea), or gold-backed Japanese military notes in Manchuria, Siberia, and the Russian Far East. The bank had nine branches and offices in Siberia, and its currency was favored by the locals over the discredited Russian currency. It was used for tax payments in the Far Eastern Republic and subsequently in Soviet Russia. Around 4 percent of the banknotes issued were to be found in Siberia by the end of 1921, 17 percent of the bank's total lending was in Manchuria and Siberia by the end of 1924. The Vladivostok branch of the bank operated until 1930. Eighty percent of the trade that passed through the port of Vladivostok was handled by Japanese trading firms. See Keishi Ono, "The Siberian Intervention and Japanese Society," in *Japan and the Great War*, ed. Oliviero Frattolillo and Antony Best (London: Palgrave Macmillan, 2015), 103–4.

56. Matsuoka's proposal for the removal of restrictions on the rights of foreigners to hold land, mine and explore mineral deposits, harvest the forest, navigate inland waters, and engage in coastal trade in Siberia, and open Vladivostok as a free port were rejected by Uchida and Shidehara. See David J. Lu, *Agony of Choice: Matsuoka Yōsuke and the Rise and Fall of the Japanese Empire, 1880–1946* (Lanham, MD: Lexington Books, 2002), 32–34.

57. Wolff, "Open Jaw," 357.

58. There were numerous reports that Japanese soldiers and officers did not pay in shops and would often beat shop owners with rifle butts if confronted. There were also reports about the rape of local women.

59. Hara, *Shiberia shuppei*, 390.

60. Uchida, *Uchida Kōsai kankei shiryō shūsei*, 3:250–51.

61. Hosoya Chihiro, "Nihon to Koruchāku seiken shōnin mondai," *Hitotsubashi Daigaku Hōgaku Kenkyū*, no. 3 (1961): 13–135; *Gaimushō no hyakunen*, 1:685–90.

62. See also Elena Varneck and Harold Fisher, eds., *Testimony of Kolchak and Other Siberian Materials* (Stanford, CA: Stanford University Press, 1935), 107–30. Semenov was captured by the Red Army in Harbin in 1945 and executed after trial in Moscow in 1946.

63. George Lensen, *Japanese Recognition of the USSR: Soviet-Japanese Relations, 1921–1930* (Tokyo: Sophia University, 1970), 9–48.

64. Hara Teruyuki, "Nikō jiken no shomondai," *Roshia shi kenkyū* 23 (1975), 2–17. For Japanese official and semi-official statements, see Varneck and Fisher, *Testimony of Kolchak*, 359–65.

65. Kobayashi Yukio, *Nisso seiji gaikōshi: Roshia kakumei to Chian ijihō* (Tokyo: Yūhikaku, 1985), 225.

66. Hara Teruyuki, "Japan Moves North: The Japanese Occupation of Northern Sakhalin (1920s)," in *Rediscovering Russia in Asia: Siberia and the Russian Far East*, ed. Stephen Kotkin and David Wolff (New York: M. E. Sharpe, 1995), 55–67.

67. Elena Varneck and Harold Fisher, eds., *Testimony of Kolchak*, 334.

68. On the "Korean factor" of Japan's intervention in Siberia, see Kan Dokusan, "Nihon teikokushugi no Chōsen shihai to Roshia kakumei," *Rekishigaku kenkyū* 329 (1969), 37–76; and Hara Teruyuki, "Kyokutō Roshia ni okeru Chōsen dokuritsu undō to Nihon," *Sanzenri*, no. 17 (February 1979): 47–53; Kobayashi, *Nisso seiji gaikō shi*, 213–24.

69. Chong-Sik Lee, *Revolutionary Struggle in Manchuria: Chinese Communism and Soviet Interest 1922–1945* (Berkeley: University of California Press, 1983), 26–35.

70. Erik W. Esselstrom, "Rethinking the Colonial Conquest of Manchuria: The Japanese Consular Police in Jiandao, 1909–1937," *Modern Asian Studies* 39, no. 1 (2005): 39–75.

71. Nikita A. Popov, *Oni s nami srazalis' za vlast' sovetov: Kitaiskie dobrovol'tsy na frontakh grazhdanskoi voiny v Rossii (1918–1922)* (Leningrad: Lenizdat, 1959), 127.

72. Popov, *Oni s nami srazilis'*, 141.

73. Lensen, *Japanese Recognition of the USSR*, 13–14, note c.

74. The catchphrase "Korea lies like a dagger ever pointed toward the very heart of Japan" was first popularized in the 1880s and reflected modern Japan's strategic anxieties and predatory interests in Korea. See Peter Duus, *The Abacus and the Sword: The Japanese Penetration of Korea, 1895–1910* (Berkeley: University of California Press, 1995).

75. Erik Esselstrom, *Crossing Empire's Edge: Foreign Ministry Police and Japanese Expansionism in Northeast Asia* (Honolulu: University of Hawaii Press, 2009), 73.

76. Lensen, *Japanese Recognition of the USSR*, 13–14, note c.

77. Esselstrom, "Rethinking the Colonial Conquest of Manchuria," 46–50.

78. John W. Young, "The Hara Cabinet and Chang," *Monumenta Nipponica* 27, no. 2 (1972): 140.

79. Esselstrom, *Crossing Empire's Edge*, 78–85.

80. Japanese fishermen were most in contact with the Russians and were thus often subjected to communist propaganda. "The propaganda was disseminated by pistol-packing Japanese and Korean Communists, who came to the Japanese fishing sheds allegedly under the protection of the Soviet secret police, made speeches, and distributed printed material" (Lensen, *Japanese Recognition of the USSR*, 349).

81. Lee, *Revolutionary Struggle in Manchuria*, 11–13.

82. Humphreys, *Way of the Heavenly Sword*, 45–46.

83. Petr Podalko, *Iaponiia v sud'bakh rossiian: Ocherki istorii tsarskoi diplomatii i rossiiskoi diaspory v Iaponii* (Moscow: Institut vostokovedeniia Rossiiskoi akademii nauk, 2004), 118–69.

CHAPTER 3. THE ANTI-WESTERN REVOLUTION

1. Fuke Takahiro, *Mitsukawa Kametarō: Kōgai no kokorozashi nao sonsu* (Tokyo: Mineruva Shobō, 2016), 152–54.

2. Sven Saaler, "Pan-Asianism in Modern Japanese History: Overcoming the Nation, Creating a Region, Forging an Empire," in *Pan-Asianism in Modern Japanese History*, ed. Sven Saaler and Victor Koschmann (London: Routledge, 2007), 2. In Japanese, see Matsuura Masataka, *"Dai Tōa Sensō" wa naze okita no ka: Han Ajiashugi no seiji keizaishi* (Nagoya: Nagoya Daigaku Shuppankai, 2010).

3. Christopher Szpilman, "Between Pan-Asianism and Nationalism: Mitsukawa Kametarō and His Campaign to Reform Japan and Liberate Asia," in *Pan-Asianism in Modern Japanese History*, ed. Sven Saaler and Victor Koschmann, 91.

4. Marius Jansen, *The Japanese and Sun Yat-Sen* (Cambridge, MA: Harvard University Press, 1954).

5. Mitsukawa remains largely unknown in Anglophone historiography. See Christopher Szpilman, "Mitsukawa Kametarō: A Brief Biographical Sketch," in *Mitsukawa Kametarō: Chiiki, chikyū jijō no keimōsha,* ed. Christopher Szpilman (Tokyo: Takushoku Daigaku Shuppankyoku, 2001), 512–20; and Szpilman, "Between Pan-Asianism and Nationalism." In Japanese, see Fuke, *Mitsukawa Kametarō.*

6. Tetsuya Sakai, "The Soviet Factor in Japanese Foreign Policy, 1923–1937," *Acta Slavica Iaponica* 6 (1988): 28.

7. The language of Asian solidarity gained new momentum after the Russo-Japanese War, as Indian, Chinese, and Vietnamese anticolonial nationalists flocked to Japan. It was, however, Mitsukawa's encounter with the Indian sojourners and anticolonial activists in exile in Japan (which by 1941 reached one thousand people) that proved to be formative for his subsequent political activities and outlook. See Mitsukawa Kametarō, *Sangoku kanshō igo,* ed. Hasegawa Yūichi (Tokyo: Ronsōsha, 2004), 128–32.

8. Ōkawa Shūmei held a doctoral degree from Tokyo Imperial University in Indian philosophy, but by 1916 he had emerged as a leading advocate in Japan for India's independence from British colonial rule because of the publication of his first major work on India, *The Origin and the Present State of the Nationalist Movement in India* (Indo ni okeru kokumin undō no genjō oyobi yurai, 1916). Ōkawa is credited as one of the first to use the term "Pan-Asianism" in 1917, which encompassed not only the traditional East Asian region (China, Korea, Japan) but also the South and West Asian regions. Ōkawa was prosecuted at the Tokyo Tribunal as a Class A war criminal but was acquitted as mentally unfit after he knocked the former prime minister, Tōjō Hideki, on the head during the trial. See Christopher Szpilman, "The Dream of One Asia: Ōkawa Shūmei and Japanese Pan-Asianism," in *The Japanese Empire in East Asia and Its Postwar Legacy,* ed. Harald Fuess (Munich: Ludicium, 1998), 49–63.

9. Christopher Szpilman, "Kaidai," in *Mitsukawa Kametarō,* ed. Szpilman, 1:459.

10. Ōkawa Shūmei, "Sovieto renpō no taigai seisaku," *Ōkawa Shūmei zenshū* (Tokyo: Kankōkai, 1962), 4:534.

11. Quoted in George M. Wilson, *Radical Nationalist in Japan: Kita Ikki, 1883–1937* (Cambridge, MA: Harvard University Press, 1969), 68.

12. The pamphlet is included in Mitsukawa, *Sangoku kanshō igo,* 297–301.

13. Mitsukawa, "Naze ni Borushevizumu wo teki to nasu ka," in *Sangoku kanshō igo,* 297.

14. Mitsukawa, *Sangoku kanshō igo,* 156–57.

15. Matsumoto Ken'ichi, *Ōkawa Shūmei* (Tokyo: Iwanami Shoten, 2004), 162.

16. Matsumoto, *Ōkawa Shūmei,* 158. Although critical of the government's handling of the Rice Riots, Ōkawa, unlike Mitsukawa, never openly criticized the Siberian Intervention or Japan's Twenty-One Demands to China.

17. Itō Takashi, *Shōwa shoki seiji shi kenkyū* (Tokyo: Tokyo Daigaku Shuppankai, 1969); Gregory J. Kasza, "Fascism from Below? A Comparative Perspective on the Japanese Right, 1931–1936," *Journal of Contemporary History* 19, no. 4 (1984): 607–29.

18. Ōkawa Shūmei, "5/15 Jiken jinmon chōsho," in *Ōkawa Shūmei zenshū* (Tokyo: Kankōkai, 1962), 5:683–84.

19. Mitsukawa, *Sangoku kanshō igo,* 172. *Minshushugi* was represented by the rival of the Rōsōkai, the liberal Reimeikai, founded by Yoshino Sakuzō and Fukuda Tokuzō, discussed in the next chapter.

20. Szpilman, "Kaidai," 460.

21. For example, Kanokogi Kazunobu, a professor of philosophy at Tokyo Imperial University and a member of the Yūzonsha, wrote about a totalitarian state, mass mobilization and planned economy since 1918, with often references to the Soviet state-building. For more on Kanokogi, see Christopher Szpilman, "Kanokogi Kazunobu: Pioneer of Platonic Fascism and Imperial Pan-Asianism," *Monumenta Nipponica* 2, no. 2 (2013): 233–80.

22. Ōkawa Shūmei, "Kakumei Yōroppa to Fukkō Ajia," in *Fukkō Ajia no shomondai* (Tokyo: Meiji Shobō, 1939).

23. Boris Nicolaevsky, "Russia, Japan, and the Pan-Asiatic Movement to 1925," *Far Eastern Quarterly*, no. 3 (1949): 269.

24. The argument that Russia was part of Asia gained even more traction after the establishment of Manchukuo, which was envisioned as a union of the East and the West and had a sizable population of Russian Slavic and other Asian (Kalmyk, Buryat, Bashkir, Tatar, etc.) émigré communities, which the Japanese administrators sought to integrate into the new state. See Mitsukawa, "Ishin kanreki to kyōsen jūnen," in *Mitsukawa Kametarō*, ed. Szpilman, 1:239–49.

25. Yukiko Hama, "Russia from a Pan-Asianist View: Saburo Shimano and His Activities," *Ab Imperio*, no. 3 (2010): 227–43.

26. Mitsukawa, "Shingunkoku Roshia no shutsugen to Nihon," *Chūgai*, no. 1 (June 1921).

27. Ōkawa Shūmei, "Atarashiki sekai sen," *Kaihō* (May 1920).

28. Ōkawa, *Fukkō Ajia*, 7, 162–76, 170–85.

29. In fact, not only Mitsukawa but other pan-Asianists as well had friends among Japanese communists. Ōkawa assisted a colleague at Takushoku University who was persecuted as a communist and arrested. Kita Ikki also helped provide accommodation for his Korean communist friend, who was escaping police. See Matsumoto, *Ōkawa Shūmei*, 7.

30. Mitsukawa, "Taihō kensetsu no risō," *Shakai kyōiku kenkyūjo rīfuretto* 5 (Tokyo: Shakai Kyōiku Kenkyūjo, 1925), 7–8.

31. Mitsukawa, "Taihō kensetsu no risō," 7–8.

32. Mitsukawa, *Sangoku kanshō igo*, 187–90.

33. Matsuo Takayoshi, "Wasurerareta kakumeika Takao Heibē," *Shisō*, no. 577 (July 1972): 88–113.

34. Vasilii Molodiakov, ed., *Katsura Taro, Goto Simpei i Rossiia: Sbornik dokumentov 1907–1929* (Moscow: AIRO, 2005), Doc. 57, 122–23.

35. Thomas Stanley, *Ōsugi Sakae, Anarchist in Taishō Japan: The Creativity of the Ego* (Cambridge, MA: Council on East Asian Studies, 1982), 199n.42.

36. Mitani Taichirō, *Nihon seitō seiji no keisei: Hara Kei seiji shidō no tenkai* (Tokyo: Tokyō Daigaku Shuppankai, 1995), 97–103, 305.

37. Tanaka Sōgorō, *Kita Ikki: Nihonteki fashisuto no shōchō* (Tokyo: Miraisha, 1959), 250–51.

38. Molodiakov, *Katsura Taro, Goto Simpei i Rossiia*, Doc. 64, 183.

39. Mitsukawa, *Sekai gensei to Dai Nihon* (Tokyo: Kōchisha, 1926).

40. Among the examples of how socialism can destroy people's lives, Kita picked the idea of free love and the rejection of the institution of marriage. Kita cited the love triangle of Kōtoku Shūsui, Arahata Kanson, and Kano Suga, as well as the notorious private life of Ōsugi Sakae. See Kita Ikki's letter to Yamaga Taiji in Mitsukawa Kametarō, *Mitsukawa Kametarō shokanshū: Kita Ikki, Ōkawa Shumei, Nishida Mitsugi ra no shokan*, ed. Hasegawa Yuichi, Christopher W. Szpilman, and Imazu Toshiaki (Tokyo: Ronsōsha, 2012), 78–79. Yamaga Taiji (1892–1970) was an anarchist and a close friend of Ōsugi Sakae, on whose advice he moved to China to work with Chinese anarchists. He lived in Kita Ikki's house when he was young and was therefore viewed by Kita as his younger brother.

41. Kita Ikki's letter to Yamaga Taiji, in Mitsukawa, *Mitsukawa Kametarō shokanshū*, ed. Hasegawa, Szpilman, and Imazu, 73–80.

42. Christopher W. Szpilman, "Kita Ikki and the Politics of Coercion," *Modern Asian Studies* 36, no. 2 (2002): 467–90.

43. Wilson, *Radical Nationalist in Japan*, 104.

44. Xenia J. Eudin and Robert C. North, *Soviet Russia and the East, 1920–1927: A Documentary Survey* (Stanford, CA: Stanford University Press, 1957), 209.

45. Nicolaevsky, "Russia, Japan, and the Pan-Asiatic Movement to 1925," 266.

46. Gotō had, to a degree, been known as Russia's patron. As we may recall, Gotō was the first president of the SMRC between 1906 and 1908 and was the one who convinced Itō Hirobumi to go to Harbin in 1909 to meet with a Russian representative in Manchuria, where Itō was assassinated by a Korean nationalist. Gotō also obtained funds and the support of the government and the Kwantung Army to establish the Harbin Institute of Russian Studies (Harupin Gakuin) in 1920, whose graduates, it was hoped, would play as important a role in later Russo-Japanese relations as the students of Tōa Dōbun Shoin (East Asia Common Culture Academy) had done in Sino-Japanese trade and diplomacy. Gotō also served as a long-term president of the Russo-Japanese Society, an important venue for academic, business, and cultural relations.

47. Hosoya Chihiro, "Japan's Foreign Policy toward Russia," in *Japan's Foreign Policy, 1868–1941: A Research Guide*, ed. James W. Morley and James B. Crowley (New York: Columbia University Press, 1974), 392.

48. Gaimushō [Japanese Foreign Office], ed., *Nihon gaikō bunsho* (Tokyo: Nihon Kokusai Kyōkai, 1953–64), 1:759–61, 821–55. Lenin granted a concession to the US oil company Sinclair in Sakhalin during the intervention. George A. Lensen, *Japanese Recognition of the USSR* (Tokyo: Sophia University, 1979), 106.

49. Tsurumi Yūsuke, *Gotō Shinpei* (Tokyo: Fujiwara Shoten, 2004–6), 8:70–78.

50. Gotō's memorandum to the cabinet from February 1923. Quoted from Hosoya, "Japan's Foreign Policy toward Russia," 392.

51. Kitaoka Shin'ichi, *Gotō Shinpei: Gaikō to bijon* (Tokyo: Chūō Kōronsha, 2000), 224.

52. Lensen, *Japanese Recognition of the USSR*, 104–105.

53. Sakai Tetsuya, *Taishō demokurashī taisei no hōkai: Naisei to gaikō* (Tokyo: Tōkyō Daigaku Shuppankai, 1992), 154.

54. Sakai, *Taishō demokurashī taisei no hōkai*, 153–54.

55. Molodiakov, *Katsura Taro, Goto Simpei i Rossiia*, Doc. 57, 129.

56. Daba Hiroshi, "Gotō, Ioffe kōshō zengo no Gen'yōsha, Kokuryūkai," *Takushoku Daigaku Hyakunen Shi Kenkyū*, no. 6 (2001): 30–45.

57. Lensen, *Japanese Recognition of the USSR*, 89.

58. Tsurumi, *Gotō Shinpei*, 7:610.

59. Molodiakov, *Katsura Taro, Goto Simpei i Rossiia*, Doc. 57, 132.

60. Tsurumi, *Gotō Shinpei*, 7:611–12.

61. Kitaoka, *Gotō Shinpei*, 220.

62. Mitsukawa, *Mitsukawa Kametarō*, ed. Szpilman, 2:4.

63. Kitaoka, *Gotō Shinpei*, 220. For contemporary newspaper coverage of Trotsky's fall, see *Japan Weekly Chronicle* (March 8, 1928), 276–77.

64. Podalko, *Iaponiia v sud'bakh rossiian*, 133–34.

65. Sakai, *Taishō demokurashī taisei no hōkai*, 178n19.

66. Charles M. Beard, *Cross Currents in Europe Today* (Boston: Marshall Jones, 1922), 163–81.

67. Vasilii Molodiakov, *Goto Simpei i russko-iaponskie otnosheniia* (Moscow: AIRO, 2006), 143–45.

68. Quoted in Hosoya, "Japan's Foreign Policy toward Russia," 392.

69. Tsurumi, *Gotō Shinpei*, 7:611–12.

70. Lensen, *Japanese Recognition of the USSR*, 109.

71. Gotō's memorandum from February 1923. Quoted in Hosoya, "Japan's Foreign Policy toward Russia," 392.

72. Quoted in Lensen, *Japanese Recognition of the USSR*, 109.

73. Allen S. Whiting, *Soviet Policies in China, 1917–1924* (New York: Columbia University Press, 1954), 221–23.

74. Gaimushō Hyakunenshi Hensan Iinkai, ed., *Gaimushō no hyakunen* (Tokyo: Hara Shobō, 1969), 1:487.

75. Quoted in Hosoya, "Japan's Foreign Policy toward Russia," 393–94.

76. Erik Esselstrom, *Crossing Empire's Edge: Foreign Ministry Police and Japanese Expansionism in Northeast Asia* (Honolulu: University of Hawaii Press, 2009), 65–91.

77. Iriye, *After Imperialism*, 50–51.

78. Quoted in Iriye, *After Imperialism*, 51.

79. Hattori Ryūji, *Higashi Ajia kokusai kankyō no hendō to Nihon gaikō, 1918–1931* (Tokyo: Yūhikaku, 2001), 231.

80. Molodiakov, *Goto Simpei i russko-iaponskie otnosheniia*, 182.

81. Tsurumi, *Gotō Shinpei*, 8:119–26.

82. Interestingly, the Soviet deputy Ioffe in his reports from Tokyo in the spring of 1923 mentioned that, considering present stable capitalist relations in Japan and the insignificant number of Japan's industrial proletariat, no socialist or bourgeois revolution in Japan seemed to be possible (*Katsura Taro, Goto Simpei i Rossiia*, Doc. 57, 140).

83. *Katsura Taro, Goto Simpei i Rossiia*, Doc. 95, 269–70.

84. Molodiakov, *Goto Simpei i russko-iaponskie otnosheniia*, 182.

85. Lensen, *Japanese Recognition of the USSR*, 180.

86. Quoted in Lensen, *Japanese Recognition of the USSR*, 345.

87. Kobayashi Yukio, *Nisso seiji gaikōshi: Roshia kakumei to Chian ijihō* (Tokyo: Yūhikaku, 1985), 152–53.

88. *Pravda*, no. 18 (January 22, 1925), 3. Quoted in Eudin and North, *Soviet Russia and the East*, 321.

89. Chong-Sik Lee, *Revolutionary Struggle in Manchuria: Chinese Communism and Soviet Interest 1922–1945* (Berkeley: University of California Press, 1983), 62–94.

90. Tomita Takeshi, *Senkanki no nisso kankei: 1917–1937* (Tokyo: Iwanami Shoten, 2010), 53–55.

91. Nevertheless, economic gains were huge for Japan. Japanese businesses operated lumber, ore, and fur concessions, dominated banking and shipping in the Russian Far East, and controlled 90 percent of Far Eastern fisheries. Japanese fishery companies employed 22,600 Japanese in 1925 and 38,600 in 1930; in Kamchatka, seasonal Japanese workers outnumbered the local population. Smooth business operations were ensured by Japanese consulates in Khabarovsk, Blagoveshchensk, Petropavlovsk, and Aleksandrovsk (North Sakhalin). Basically, during the 1920s the Russian Far East was developed with Japanese money. See John J. Stephan, *The Russian Far East: A History* (Stanford, CA: Stanford University Press, 1994), 163–77.

92. Bruce A. Elleman, "The Soviet Union's Secret Diplomacy concerning the Chinese Eastern Railway, 1924–1925," *Journal of Asian Studies* 53, no. 2 (1994): 459–86.

93. Eudin and North, *Soviet Russia and the East*, 321–22.

94. Lensen, *Japanese Recognition of the USSR*, 365.

95. Quoted in Eudin and North, *Soviet Russia and the East*, 321–22.

96. Lensen, *Japanese Recognition of the USSR*, 196–202.

97. Szpilman, "Between Pan-Asianism and Nationalism," 92–93.

98. Mitsukawa Kametarō, "Tōyōdai ni kakuramutosu," in *Mitsukawa Kametarō*, ed. Szpilman, 160–63.

99. Eudin and North, *Soviet Russia and the East*, 321–22.

100. Molodiakov, *Goto Simpei i russko-iaponskie otnosheniia*, 160–61.

101. For how serious the Soviet leadership was in regard to the issue of Japanese immigration and the general policy of appeasement of Japan, see the strictly confidential

resolution "Voprosy nashei politiki v otnoshenii Kitaia i Iaponii" (April 1, 1926), in Grant M. Adibekov and Wada Haruki, eds., *VKP(b), Komintern i Iaponiia, 1917–1941* (Moscow: Rosspen, 2001), Doc. 9, 28–34. The resolution also mentions the possibility of a Soviet-Chinese-Japanese alliance.

102. Molodiakov, *Goto Simpei i russko-iaponskie otnosheniia*, 162–63.

103. Nakano Seigō, "Nichiro shinkō no shinkachi," *Warekan* (March 1925).

104. Nakano Seigō's statement is quoted in Arima Manabu, *"Kokusaika" no naka no teikoku Nihon, 1905–1924* (Tokyo: Chūō Kōronsha, 1999), 252.

105. *Katsura Taro, Goto Simpei i Rossiia*, Doc. 70, 201–4.

106. Hattori, *Higashi Ajia kokusai kankyō no hendō*, 79.

107. Hosoya, "Japan's Foreign Policy toward Russia," 379–80.

108. Quoted from Suda Teiichi, "Shihaisō ni okeru seiji rinri no keisha: Nisso kōshō shi wo chūshin toshite," *Shisō* 391 (January 1957), 75–87.

109. Janis Mimura, *Planning for Empire: Reform Bureaucrats and the Japanese Wartime State* (Ithaca, NY: Cornell University Press, 2011), 25.

110. Molodiakov, *Goto Simpei i russko-iaponskie otnosheniia*, 168–69.

111. *Japan Weekly Chronicle* (October 27, 1927), 443.

112. Kurono Taeru, *Teikoku kokubō hōshin no kenkyū: Riku-Kaigun kokubō shisō no tenkai to tokuchō* (Tokyo: Sōwasha, 2000), 109.

113. Molodiakov, *Goto Simpei i russko-iaponskie otnosheniia*, 183–87.

114. Mitsukawa Kametarō, "Kakumeiteki Daiteikoku," in *Mitsukawa Kametarō*, ed. Szpilman, 478–79.

115. Kitaoka, *Gotō Shinpei*, 221.

116. Kitaoka, *Gotō Shinpei*, 221.

117. Mitsukawa, "Ishin kanreki," 245–246.

118. Mitsukawa, "Tōyōdai ni kakuramutosu," 160–63.

119. Li Narangoa, "Japanese Geopolitics and the Mongol Lands, 1915–1945," *European Journal of East Asian Studies* 3, no. 1 (2004): 45–67.

120. Szpilman, "Kaidai," 460. See also Mitsukawa, "Ishin kanreki," 249.

121. Ronald G. Suny, *The Soviet Experiment: Russia, the USSR, and the Successor States* (Oxford: Oxford University Press, 1998), 152.

122. Quoted in Nicolaevsky, "Russia, Japan, and the Pan-Asiatic Movement to 1925," 285.

123. Nicolaevsky, "Russia, Japan, and the Pan-Asiatic Movement to 1925," 263.

124. Eudin and North, *Soviet Russia and the East*, 43–44.

125. Nicolaevsky, "Russia, Japan, and the Pan-Asiatic Movement to 1925," 283.

126. *Nichi nichi* was one of Japan's leading newspapers, with a circulation of about two million. The Russian text of Fuse's interview with Stalin was first published in *Pravda*, Moscow, July 4, 1925 (Eudin and North, *Soviet Russia and the East*, 335–37).

127. Sakai, *Taishō demokurashī taisei no hōkai*, 152.

128. Wada Haruki, "Japanese-Russian Relations and the United States, 1855–1930," in *A Hidden Fire: Russian and Japanese Cultural Encounters, 1868–1926*, ed. Thomas J. Rimer (Stanford, CA: Stanford Univerity Press, 1995), 213.

129. Quoted in Eudin and North, *Soviet Russia and the East*, 336.

130. See Stalin's statement in his "Political Report for the Central Committee of the Communist Party of the Soviet Union" at the Fourteenth Congress of the CPSU on December 19, 1925. Quoted in Lee, *Revolutionary Struggle in Manchuria*, 88. Stalin's statement was carefully discussed and prepared at the China Commission (Kitaiskaia kommissiia) meeting of the Ministry of Foreign Affairs on December 3, 1925. See Adibekov and Wada, *VKP(b), Komintern i Iaponiia*, Doc. 7, 27.

CHAPTER 4. ANTICOMMUNISM WITHIN

1. Matsuo Takayoshi, "Daiichiji taisengo no fusen undō," in *Taishōki no seiji to shakai*, ed. Inoue Kiyoshi (Tokyo: Iwanami Shoten, 1969), 159–204.

2. Peter Duus, "Liberal Intellectuals and Social Conflict in Taishō Japan," in *Conflict in Modern Japanese History*, ed. Tetsuo Najita and Victor J. Koschmann (Princeton, NJ: Princeton University Press, 1982), 412–40; Peter Duus and Irwin Scheiner, "Socialism, Liberalism, and Marxism, 1901–1931," in *The Cambridge History of Japan*, ed. Peter Duus (Cambridge: Cambridge University Press, 1989), 654–710.

3. Yoshino Sakuzō, "Roshia no kakumei," *Chūō Kōron* (April 1917).

4. Yoshino Sakuzō, "Minponshugi, shakaishugi, kagekishugi," *Chūō Kōron* (June 1919), 26–34. "Orthodox" socialism came to be understood in terms of Karl Kautsky's doctrinal interpretation of Marx's and Engels' ideas and became universally accepted. As scientific socialism, it promoted the evolutionist, determinist, and scientific form of Marxism. See Leszek Kolakowski, *Main Currents of Marxism* (Oxford: Oxford University Press, 1978), 2:31–60.

5. Murobuse Kōshin, "Kokka shakaishugi no hihyō," *Hihyō* (July 1919); Ōyama Ikuo, "Rokoku kagekiha no jisseiryoku ni taisuru kashōshi to kono seiji shisō no kachi ni taisuru kadaishi," *Chūō Kōron* (May 1918). Ōyama would become a Marxist in 1922 and later a leader of a proletarian party movement. Murobuse Kōshin, in contrast, while frequently changing his position, ended up supporting Japanese imperialist expansion in South Asia.

6. Peter Duus, "Ōyama Ikuo and the Search for Democracy," in *Dilemmas of Growth in Prewar Japan* (Princeton, NJ: Princeton University Press, 1971), ed. James William Morley, 434.

7. Quoted in Jung-Sun N. Han, "Envisioning a Liberal Empire in East Asia: Yoshino Sakuzō in Taishō Japan," *Journal of Japanese Studies* 33, no. 2 (2007): 376.

8. Leonard A. Humphreys, *The Way of the Heavenly Sword: The Japanese Army in the 1920s* (Stanford, CA: Stanford University Press, 1995), 51–52. For example, in "One Lesson of the World War" (*Tokyo nichi nichi shinbun*, January 4, 1918), an army general promoted universal suffrage as it would aid state and military mobilization. See Mitani Taichirō, *Nihon seitō seiji no keisei: Hara Kei seijishidō no tenkai* (Tokyo: Tokyo Daigaku Shuppankai, 1995), 97–103, 305.

9. Kokuryūkai's magazine *Ajia jiron* published extensively on the army's issues. See Hara Teruyuki, *Shiberia shuppei: Kakumei to kanshō 1917–1922* (Tokyo: Chikuma Shobō, 1989), 421. For more on the soldiers' insubordination during the Siberian Intervention, see Fujiwara Akira, "Nihon guntai ni okeru kakumei to hankakumei," *Hitotsubashi University, Departmental Bulletin*, no. 10 (March 31, 1969): 85–123. Among the most famous records of the Siberian expedition are the diaries of Kuroshima Denji (*Guntai Nikki*) and Matsuo Katsuzō (*Shiberia shuppei nikki*).

10. Yoshino Sakuzō, "Seinen shōkō no mitaru Shiberia shuppei gun no jitsujō," *Chūō kōron* (May 1922).

11. Hara, *Shiberia shuppei*, 424.

12. Hara, *Shiberia shuppei*, 570–71.

13. Uehara Yūsaku, *Uehara Yūsaku nikki* (Tokyo: Shōyū Kurabu, 2011), 79–81. We don't know what they talked about. The diary entry mentions Fukuda's name and time allocated for the meetings, usually the whole morning.

14. For more about Fukuda, see Inoue Takutoshi and Yagi Kiichiro, "Two Inquiries on the Divide: Tokuzō Fukuda and Hajime Kawakami," in *Economic Thought and Modernization in Japan*, ed. Sugihara Shiro and Tanaka Toshihiro (Cheltenham: Edward Elgar, 1998), 60–77. In Korea, Fukuda is known almost exclusively as the author of the original stagnation theory that would become one of the perennial ideological props of Japanese

colonial rule on the peninsula (Owen Miller, "The Idea of Stagnation in Korean Historiography," *Korean Histories* 2, no. 1 [2010]: 3–12). On Fukuda's influence on Chinese Marxists see Ishikawa Yoshihiro, "Chinese Marxism in the Early 20th Century and Japan," *Sino-Japanese Studies* 14 (April 2002): 24–34.

15. Fukuda Tokuzō, "Nihon ni shakaishugi okoru naki ya," *Kyokutō jihō* (October 14, 1917).

16. Fukuda Tokuzō, "Tadashiki rikai wo yōsu," *Roshia hihyō* (July 1919), in *Taishō daizasshi* (Tokyo: Ryūdō Shuppan, 1978), 132–33.

17. Fukuda, "Tadashiki rikai wo yōsu," 132–33.

18. Fukuda Tokuzō, *Reimeiroku* (Tokyo: Daitōkaku, 1920), 1039.

19. Itō Narihiko, "Nihon shakaishugi undō to Rōsa Rukusenburugu," *Shisō* 568 (October 1971): 39–55.

20. Fukuda, *Reimeiroku*, 870–77.

21. Fukuda, *Reimeiroku*, 1039.

22. Aoki Seiichi, "Shakai seikatsu no kekkan ni yotte," *Roshia hihyō* (July 1919), in *Taishō daizasshi*, 134–35. *The Protocols of the Elders of Zion* was introduced to Japan during the Siberian Intervention, first by an early graduate of the Russian Orthodox Nikolai Seminary in Tokyo and the Theological Seminary in Saint Petersburg, Higuchi Tsuyanosuke (1870–1931), who was a professor of the Russian language in the army during the intervention. In 1921, Higuchi published his collected lectures under the title *Yudayaka* (The Jewish peril), thus coining the Japanese term. Shiōten Nobutaka, a member of the military staff in Vladivostok during the intervention, was the first Japanese-language translator of the *Protocols*. See David G. Goodman and Masanori Miyazawa, *Jews in the Japanese Mind: The History and Uses of a Cultural Stereotype* (Lanham, MD: Lexington Books, 2000), 81.

23. Murobose Kōshin, "Kageki shisō to Nihon," *Roshia hihyō*, in *Taishō daizasshi*, 138–39.

24. Ōba Kakō, "Kagekihashugi to minshūshugi," *Roshia hihyō*, in *Taishō daizasshi*, 136–37. Ōba's fate, however, was tragic. In late 1921, he went to Russia as a journalist but was arrested in Chita on suspicion of being a Japanese spy. Very little is known about what happened to him, but he was most likely executed around 1924 in Siberia. See Kume Shigeru, *Kieta shinbun kisha* (Tokyo: Yuki Shobō, 1968).

25. Kemuyama Sentarō, "Raido wo itashimeyo," *Roshia hihyō*, in *Taishō daizasshi*, 135.

26. Kayahara Kazan, "Konton yori konton he," *Roshia hihyō*, in *Taishō daizasshi*, 137–38.

27. Fukuda, *Reimeiroku*, 1054–55.

28. Yoshino Sakuzō, "Tandoku kōwa ni yotte Rokoku wa nanimono wo toran tosuru," *Chūō Kōron* (January 1918); "Kageki shisō taisaku," *Chūō Kōronsha* (May 1919).

29. Fukuda, *Reimeiroku*, 1039.

30. Sheldon Garon writes about the new mood of pragmatic reform and even democratic idealism among the Home Ministry's junior and middle-level officials, most of whom studied in Europe during the 1910s (*The State and Labor in Modern Japan* [Berkeley: University of California Press, 1987], 89–98). Ōyama Ikuo pointed out that the bureaucracy realized that traditional politics no longer worked. Its democratic concessions were a strategy to adapt to the world trend for its own profit and to use party politics as a tool.

31. Elise Tipton, *The Japanese Police State: The Tokkō in Interwar Japan* (Honolulu: University of Hawaii Press, 1990), 19.

32. Umemori Naoyuki, "The Historical Context of the High Treason Incident: Govermentality and Colonialism," in *Japan and the High Treason Incident*, ed. Masako Gavin and Ben Middleton (London: Routledge, 2013), 52–63.

33. Accounts of this arrest are not all clear. Japanese communists blamed Kondō for weakness of character, while Kondō denied the circumstances of his arrest, claiming that the police were expecting a Japanese Comintern envoy and easily tracked him down.

34. Inumaru Gi'ichi, *Daiichiji kyōsantō shi no kenkyū: Zōho Nihon kyōsantō no sōritsu* (Tokyo: Aoki Shoten, 1993), 16; Kondō Eizō, *Komuminterun no misshi* (Tokyo: Bunka hyōronsha, 1949), 275.

35. Ōyama Ikuo exemplified the route of many frustrated members of the liberal intelligentsia who chose to join the proletarian party movement in 1924–25 (Duus, "Ōyama Ikuo," 442–58). Beginning in 1920, the socialist Yamakawa Hitoshi appealed to the labor movement to abandon its support of the universal suffrage movement.

36. Richard H. Mitchell, "Japan's Peace Preservation Law of 1925: Its Origins and Significance," *Monumenta Nipponica* 28, no. 3 (1973): 329.

37. Okudaira Yasuhiro, ed., *Gendaishi shiryō 45: Chian ijihō* (Tokyo: Misuzu Shobō, 1973), 65.

38. Max Ward, "The Problem of 'Thought': Crisis, National Essence and the Interwar Japanese State" (PhD diss., New York University, 2011), 52.

39. George A. Lensen, *Japanese Recognition of the USSR* (Tokyo: Sophia University, 1979), 125.

40. George M. Beckmann and Okubo Genji, *The Japanese Communist Party, 1922–1945* (Stanford, CA: Stanford University Press, 1969), 68.

41. Mitchell, "Japan's Peace Preservation Law of 1925," 331.

42. Christopher W. Szpilman, "The Politics of Cultural Conservatism: The National Foundation Society in the Struggle Against Foreign Ideas in Prewar Japan, 1918–1936" (PhD diss., Yale University, 1993), 88–89.

43. Szpilman, "Politics of Cultural Conservatism," 114.

44. Akiyama Kiyoshi, *Nihon no hangyaku shisō* (Tokyo: Gendai Shichōsha, 1968), 148–52.

45. Mitchell, "Japan's Peace Preservation Law of 1925," 333. In a twist of irony, it was Itō Hirobumi who gave the gun to Nanba Daisuke's grandfather.

46. Kobayashi Yukio, *Nisso seiji gaikōshi: Roshia kakumei to Chian ijihō* (Tokyo: Yūhikaku, 1985), 320.

47. Kobayashi, *Nisso seiji gaikōshi,* 334–36.

48. Kobayashi, *Nisso seiji gaikōshi,* 186, 334.

49. Ward, "Problem of 'Thought,'" 78–79.

50. Quoted in Mitchell, "Japan's Peace Preservation Law of 1925," 339.

51. *Kokutai* had been used officially twice before: in the 1873 Newspaper Ordinance, signifying something akin to national prestige (*kokui*); and in the Imperial Rescript on Education of 1890 (*kokutai no seika*) as an ethical index of the Confucian morals of filial piety and loyalty (Ward, "Problem of 'Thought,'" 62n51).

52. Mitchell, "Japan's Peace Preservation Law of 1925," 343.

53. Ward, "Problem of 'Thought,'" 30.

54. Ward, "Problem of 'Thought,'" 32.

55. Mitchell, "Japan's Peace Preservation Law of 1925," 341.

56. Kobayashi, *Nisso seiji gaikōshi,* 330–31.

57. Kobayashi, *Nisso seiji gaikōshi,* 331. On opposition to the Peace Preservation Law, see Oguri Katsuya, "Chian ijihō hantai ron no shosō," *Hōgaku kenkyū* 68, no. 1 (1995): 509–37.

58. The Universal Manhood Suffrage Act (*Futsūsenkyohō*) was passed in May 1925, one month after the Peace Preservation Law was issued. On the Universal Manhood Suffrage Bill and the later 1928 general election, see Thomas R. H. Havens, "Japan's Enigmatic Election of 1928," *Modern Asian Studies* 11, no. 4 (1977): 543–55.

59. Mitchell, "Japan's Peace Preservation Law of 1925," 342.

60. See Kobayashi, *Nisso seiji gaikōshi*.

61. Cited in Okudaira, *Gendaishi shiryō 45*, 52.

62. Mitchell, "Japan's Peace Preservation Law of 1925," 341.

63. Richard H. Mitchell, *Janus-Faced Justice: Political Criminals in Imperial Japan* (Honolulu: University of Hawaii Press, 1992), 78.

64. Ward, "Problem of 'Thought,'" 67.

65. *Japan Weekly Chronicle*, March 1, 1928, 246.

66. Tipton, *Japanese Police State*, 20–24.

67. Quoted in Rodger Swearingen and Paul Langer, *Red Flag in Japan: International Communism in Action, 1919–1951* (New York: Greenwood Press, 1968), 31.

68. Tipton, *Japanese Police State*, 29.

69. Okudaira, *Gendaishi shiryō 45*, 120.

70. Ward, "Problem of 'Thought,'" 122.

71. Ward, "Problem of 'Thought,'" 77.

72. Byron K. Marshall, *Capitalism and Nationalism in Prewar Japan: Ideology of the Business Elite, 1868–1941* (Stanford, CA: Stanford University Press, 1967).

73. Ward, "Problem of 'Thought,'" 106–7.

74. Most suspects passed the "thought conversion" test and were released before being brought to trial, while only about 15 percent were placed within the prison or parole system (Ward, "Problem of 'Thought,'" 91n109).

CHAPTER 5. ANARCHISM AGAINST BOLSHEVISM

1. During the same period, anarchist ideas were also the main ideology of Chinese radicalism, due largely to the influence of Japanese radicals. See Arif Dirlik, *Anarchism in the Chinese Revolution* (Berkeley: University of California Press, 1991). For the popularity of anarchism in global radicalism, see Ilham Khuri-Makdisi, *The Eastern Mediterranean and the Making of Global Radicalism, 1860–1914* (Berkeley: University of California Press, 2010).

2. The labor history of the Taishō period is relatively well studied in English. See, for example, Stephen S. Large, *Organized Workers and Socialist Politics in Interwar Japan* (Cambridge: Cambridge University Press, 1981); and Andrew Gordon, *Labor and Imperial Democracy in Prewar Japan* (Berkeley: University of California Press, 1991).

3. Ogino Fujio, *Shoki shakaishugi shisōron* (Tokyo: Fuji Shuppan, 1993); Matsuzawa Hiroaki, *Nihon shakaishugi no shisō* (Tokyo: Chikuma Shobō, 1973).

4. Dirlik, *Anarchism in the Chinese Revolution*, 3–4.

5. For the only comprehensive study of Kōtoku Shūsui in English, see F. G. Notehelfer, *Kōtoku Shūsui: Portrait of a Japanese Radical* (Cambridge: Cambridge University Press, 1971). See also Hyman Kublin, "The Origins of the Japanese Socialist Tradition," *Journal of Politics* 14, no. 2 (1952): 257–80; and Hyman Kublin, "Japanese Socialists and the Russo-Japanese War," *Journal of Modern History* 22, 4 (1950): 322–39. For the early anti-imperialist movement in Japan, see Robert T. Tierney, *Monster of the Twentieth Century: Kōtoku Shūsui and Japan's First Anti-Imperialist Movement* (Berkeley: University of California Press, 2016).

6. Chushichi Tsuzuki, "Kotoku, Osugi, and Japanese Anarchism," *Hitotsubashi Journal of Social Studies* 3, no. 1 (3) (1966): 35.

7. Tsuzuki, "Kotoku, Osugi, and Japanese Anarchism," 35.

8. Tsuzuki, "Kotoku, Osugi, and Japanese Anarchism," 34.

9. Miyashita Takichi, one of the dozen socialists executed in 1911, said during the trial: "when the emperor is attacked by a bomb and injured, he will bleed like us. I believed that this was the best way to destroy the superstition that the emperor Meiji

was a descendent of *kami*" (quoted from Asukai Masamichi, "Roshia dai ichi ji kakumei to Kōtoku Shūsui," in *Taishōki no kyūshinteki jiyūshugi: Tōyō keizai shinpō wo chūshin toshite*, ed. Inoue Kiyoshi and Watanabe Tōru (Tokyo: Tōyō Keizai Shinpō, 1972), 263.

10. The Akahata Incident refers to an incident in which, after a party to celebrate a fellow activist's release from jail, a group of Kōtoku's followers staged a demonstration by waving two flags inscribed with the words "anarchism" and "anarchism-communism."

11. Umemori Naoyuki, "The Historical Context of the High Treason Incident: Governmentality and Colonialism," in *Japan and the High Treason Incident*, ed. Masako Gavin and Ben Middleton (London: Routledge, 2013), 52–63.

12. F. G. Notehelfer, *Kōtoku Shūsui*, 203.

13. Mitsukawa Kametarō, "Kakumei jidai no tōrai," *Sankoku kanshō igo*, ed. Yūichi Hasegawa (Tokyo: Ronsōsha, 2004), 104–7.

14. Arahata Kanson's short story from 1913, "Defectors" (Tōhisha), reflects the atmosphere after the High Treason Incident.

15. It is quite remarkable that in the same period the Fraternal Society of Korean Students in Tokyo (Zai Nihon Tōkyō Chōsen ryūgakusei gakuyūkai) was able to publish (beginning in April 1914) the periodical *Hak ji gwang* (The light of learning), which advocated direct action by agrarian tenants as a way out of their poverty and hardship. It also published anarchism-inspired articles on mutual aid, transformation of the self, and women's liberation. See Dongyoun Hwang, "Beyond Independence: The Korean Anarchist Press in China and Japan in the 1920s and 1930s," *Asian Studies Review* 31, no. 1 (2007): 22n6.

16. Quoted in George M. Beckmann and Okubo Genji, *The Japanese Communist Party* (Stanford, CA: Stanford University Press, 1969), 12.

17. For introductions to Lenin and the Bolshevik group in Japan, see Yamanouchi Akito, "Borisheviki bunken to shoki shakaishugi, Sakai, Takabatake, Yamakawa," *Shoki shakaishugi kenkyū* 10 (September 1997): 101–15. As the prominent socialist Arahata Kanson wrote in his memoir: "I did not know about the character of the Russian Revolution or the Soviet organizations or parties that formed the new government. I knew the difference between the Socialist Revolutionary party and the Social Democratic party. But no one had heard about the Mensheviks and Bolsheviks. There was almost no one who knew the names of Kerensky, Lenin, or Trotsky. The leaders of the Russian Social Democratic proletarian party whom we knew were Plekhanov, Zasulich, Deich, but strangely there was no information about Lenin's party. Thus it is no wonder we were absolutely in a fog" (*Arahata Kanson jiden* [Tokyo: Iwanami Shoten, 1975], 228). For the contemporary reaction to the February uprising, see Yamakawa Hitoshi, "Jihyō," *Shinshakai* (April 1917).

18. For example, the same May 1917 *Shinshakai* issue featured an article about one of the founders of the Russian social revolutionary party, a former anarchist herself, Ekaterina Breshko-Breshkovskaya, "Grandmother of the Revolution" (Kakumei no obāsan), and about the famous Russian female narodnik Vera Figner, "Contemporary Woman Revolutionary Like a Beautiful Flower" (Senkenka no gotoki tonen no kakumei fujin). In August, Arahata Kanson published a poem dedicated to the narodniki.

19. Ronald G. Suny, *The Soviet Experiment: Russia, the USSR, and the Successor States* (Oxford: Oxford University Press, 1998), 49–51.

20. Wada Haruki, *Nikorai Raseru* (Tokyo: Chūō Kōronsha, 1973), 2:307.

21. Grant M. Adibekov and Wada Haruki, eds., *VKP(b), Komintern i Iaponiia, 1917–1941* (Moscow: Rosspen, 2001), Doc. 270, 249–50.

22. The letter and resolution were published on August 14, 1918, in the newspaper *CentroSibir* and on September 27, 1918, in *Pravda*. See Adibekov and Wada, eds., *VKP(b), Komintern i Iaponiia, 1917–1941*, Doc. 270. For the activities of the Japanese socialists in 1917–1918, see Yamabe Kentarō and Takemura Eisuke, "Jūgatsu kakumei wa Nihon ni

ataeta eikyō," *Zen'ei*, no. 135 (December 1957): 124–48; and Yamanouchi Akito, *Shoki Kominterun to zaigai Nihonjin shakai shugisha: Ekkyōsuru nettowāku* (Kyoto: Mineruva Shobō, 2009).

23. Matsuzawa Hiroaki, *Nihon shakaishugi no shisō* (Tokyo: Chikuma Shobō, 1973), 148. In 1922, someone sent a letter to the wealthy residents of Kanagawa, Osaka, and Hyōgo prefectures titled "Declaration of Death Sentence" (Shikei wo senkoku suru), threatening the rich with the death penalty for their "exploitation of the proletariat." See the full text in Kindai Nihon Shiryō Kenkyūkai, eds., *Tokubetsu yōshisatsujin jōsei ippan: Zoku 2* (Tokyo: Meiji Bunken Shiryō Kankōkai, 1957), 156–57.

24. Kobayashi Hideo and Sasaki Rūji, "Fuyu no jidai kara no dakkyo: Jūgatsu kakumei to Nihon," *Rekishigaku kenkyū*, no. 515 (April 1983): 35–38.

25. Umeda Toshihide, *Shakai undō to shuppan bunka* (Tokyo: Ochanomizu Shobō, 1998).

26. For the list of new unions in 1919, see Akiyama Kiyoshi, *Nihon no hangyaku shisō* (Tokyo: Gendai Shichōsha, 1968), 78.

27. See Sakai Toshihiko's articles in the May, June, and July 1917 issues of *Shinshakai*. In October, Sakai published his translation of Lenin's "Russian Revolution," based on Lenin's lecture in Zurich, "The Task of Russian Social-Democratic Party in the Russian Revolution" (March 1917). Sakai's translation, however, did not include the notion of the dictatorship of the proletariat.

28. Ōsugi Sakae, "Museifushugisha no mita Roshia kakumei," in *Ōsugi Sakae zenshū. Roshia kakumei ron* (Tokyo: Gendai Shichōsha, 1963), 7:3–4. Originally published in *Rōdō undō* (December 1922). Thomas Stanley argues that Ōsugi did not make a connection between World War I and the possibility of revolution and thus did not engage in any antiwar revolutionary activities. The Russian Revolution of 1917 was a surprise for him (Stanley, *Ōsugi Sakae: Anarchist in Taishō Japan: The Creativity of the Ego* [Cambridge, MA: Council on East Asian Studies, Harvard University, 1982], 196n8).

29. Kondō Kenji, *Ichi museifushugisha no kaisō* (Tokyo: Heibonsha, 1965), 79.

30. Kondō Kenji, *Ichi museifushugisha*, 17–18; Yamakawa Hitoshi, *Yamakawa Hitoshi jiden*, ed. Yamakawa Kikue and Yamakawa Shinsaku (Tokyo: Iwanami Shoten, 1961), 371; Ōsugi, "Dokusai to kakumei," in *Ōsugi Sakae zenshū*, 7:59–66. Originally published in *Rōdō undō* (October 1922).

31. It is true that socialists and anarchists were largely preoccupied with industrial workers, a trend that originated in Kōtoku's time. For example, in 1931 Sakae Toshihiko published *A History of the Japanese Socialist Movement* (Nihon shakaishugi undō shi), in which he did not mention the Rice Riots.

32. Ōsugi, "Nihon ni okeru saikin no rōdō undō to shakaishugi undō," quoted from Stanley, *Ōsugi Sakae*, 130.

33. Itō Noe, "Museifu no jijitsu," in *Itō Noe zenshū* (Tokyo: Gakugei Shorin, 2000), 2:464.

34. Fujii Tadashi, *Nihon shakaishugi dōmei no rekishiteki igi* (Tokyo: Ōtsuki Shoten, 1978).

35. Yamanouchi Akito, "Katayama Sen: Zaibei Nihonjin shakaishugidan to shoki Kominterun," *Ōhara Shakai Mondai Kenkyūjo Zasshi*, no. 544 (March 2004): 49.

36. Fujii, "Nihon shakaishugi dōmei," 48–55.

37. Hwang, "Beyond Independence," 12–13.

38. Yoshihiro Ishikawa, *The Formation of the Chinese Communist Party* (New York: Columbia University Press, 2013).

39. Yamakawa, *Yamakawa Hitoshi jiden*, 389.

40. There is still little research on Ōsugi's contacts with the Comintern. See Yamaizumi Susumu, "Ōsugi Sakae, Kominterunu ni sōgūsu," *Shoki shakaishugi kenkyū*, no. 15 (2002): 86–121; and Yamanouchi, *Shoki Kominterun*.

41. Quoted from Kurokawa Iori, *Teikoku ni kōsuru shakai undō: Daiichiji Nihon Kyosantō no shisō to undō* (Tokyo: Yūshisha, 2014), 155–57.

42. Ōsugi Sakae, "Nihon no unmei," *Ōsugi Sakae shū: Kindai Nihon shisō taikei* 20 (Tokyo: Chikuma Shobō, 1974), 256–57.

43. Asukai, "Roshia kakumei to Ōsugi Sakae," *Gendai Riron* 4, no. 10 (1967): 34–42.

44. Stanley, *Ōsugi Sakae*, 137.

45. On Ōsugi's reaction to the Kronstadt Rebellion, see Ōsugi, "Rōnō seifu wo toose," *Seishin* (April 1921). The Kronstadt Rebellion of March 1921 was an anti-Bolshevik uprising of radical sailors and soldiers at the naval fortress of Kronstadt, who were dissatisfied with the economic policies of the Bolshevik government. After twelve days of fighting between the rebels and the Red Army, the uprising was crushed, leaving thousands dead. The Kronstadt Rebellion, it is said, prompted Lenin to initiate the NEP that relaxed state economic control.

46. Ōsugi Sakae, "Sovietto seifu, museifushugisha wo jūsatsu su," in *Ōsugi Sakae zenshū*, 7:22–28.

47. Ōsugi Sakae, "Museifu shugisha no mita Roshia kakumei," *Ōsugi Sakae zenshū*, 7:3–4.

48. Ōsugi Sakae, "Sonna koto wa dō date ii mondai janai ka. Rōnō Roshia shōnin mondai hihan," *Ōsugi Sakae zenshū*, 7:75–77.

49. On the women's *ana-boru ronsō*, see Patricia E. Tsurumi, "Feminism and Anarchism in Japan: Takamure Itsue, 1894–1964," *Bulletin of Concerned Asian Scholars* 17, no. 2 (April–June 1985): 9–12. The Korean Black Wave Society also broke into anarchist and Bolshevik groups in December 1922. In July 1923, Bak criticized the Bolsheviks as a "new privileged class" exploiting and ruling the masses, rejected centralized union-led activities, and supported direct action strategy (Dongyoun Hwang, *Anarchism in Korea: Independence, Transnationalism, and the Question of National Development, 1919–1984* [New York: State University of New York Press, 2016], chap. 3). The Suiheisha (a political organization fighting discrimination against outcasts) also had an ana-boru debate; for them, the question was: should they join the socialist movement and rely on its political activity or should outcasts liberate themselves?

50. The end of the syndicalist phase is usually attributed to the annual meeting of Sōdōmei in 1924, when the union took the new direction of "realistic socialism." It took, however, until 1927 for the labor movement to decide on a course of action. In 1927–28, the left wing of the labor movement assumed leadership of the illegal Japanese Communist Party, while the right wing moved toward parliamentary political action and the strategy of accommodating the institutions of capital and the state (Matsuzawa, *Nihon shakaishugi*, 174; Gordon, *Labour and Imperial Democracy*, 183–84).

51. Already by 1922, many prominent anarchists had proclaimed the syndicalist tactics of industrial struggle to be a dead end. The most famous example was Arahata Kanson, the leader of the Kansai anarchist group who, after the failure of Italian strikes in 1921, shifted his support to communism. See Arahata Kanson, "Shindikarizumu no hatan," *Nihon rōdō shinbun*, February 10, 1921.

52. For more on this, see Suman Gupta, *Marxism, History, and Intellectuals: Toward a Reconceptualized Transformative Socialism* (Madison, NJ: Fairleigh Dickinson University Press, 2000).

53. Vladimir I. Lenin, "What Is to Be Done," in *Essential Works of Lenin* (New York: Dover Publications, 2012), 74.

54. Lenin, "What Is to Be Done," 82–83.

55. Ōsugi Sakae, "Naze shinkochu no kakumei o yōgo shinai no ka," in *Ōsugi Sakae zenshū*, 7:67–74.

56. Ōsugi Sakae, "Chishiki kaikyū ni atau," *Rōdō undō* (January 1920).

57. Ōsugi Sakae, "Tettei shakai seisaku," *Rōdō undō* (November 1919).

58. Ōsugi, "Rōdō undō no seishin," *Rōdō undō* (October 1919).

59. Yamakawa Hitoshi, "Tōmen no mondai," *Yamakawa Hitoshi zenshū*, ed. Yamakawa Kikue and Yamakawa Shinsaku (Tokyo: Keisō Shobō, 1966), 4:408–416.

60. Yamakawa Hitoshi, "Kaizō Nihon to musan kaikyū undō," in *Yamakawa Hitoshi zenshū*, 5:77–82.

61. Inumaru Gi'ichi, *Daiichiji Kyōsantō shi no kenkyū* (Tokyo: Aoki Shoten, 1993).

62. Anna Geifman, *Thou Shalt Kill: Revolutionary Terrorism in Russia, 1894–1917* (Princeton, NJ: Princeton University Press, 1996), 3.

63. Socialists had tried to smuggle the magazine into Japan, but the police seized it (John Crump, *The Origins of Socialist Thought in Japan* [London: St. Martin's, 1983], 203).

64. Crump, *Origins of Socialist Thought in Japan*, 202–5.

65. Hagiwara Shintarō, *Takao Heibē: Eikyū kakumei he no kishi* (Tokyo: Riberutēru no Kai, 1972), 45–49.

66. Robert Stolz, *Bad Water: Nature, Pollution, and Politics in Japan, 1870–1950* (Durham, NC: Duke University Press, 2014).

67. In 1915, Ōsugi was married to Sakai Toshihiko's sister-in-law and had two lovers simultaneously. The next year, his wife left him, and one of his lovers stabbed him. Ōsugi stayed with his second lover, Itō Noe, until their death in 1923. There were also allegations that he had made off with the wife of another prominent anarchist, Tsuji Jun (Stanley, *Ōsugi Sakae*, chap. 7).

68. Hagiwara, *Takao Heibē*, 74–75.

69. Gregory James Kasza, *The State and the Mass Media in Japan, 1918–1945* (Berkeley: University of California Press, 1993), 40n19.

70. For more on the Morito Incident and the outrage it caused among university students and in the intellectual community as a whole, see Henry D. Smith, *Japan's First Student Radicals* (Cambridge, MA: Harvard University Press, 1973), 63–65; and Richard H. Mitchell, "Japan's Peace Preservation Law of 1925: Its Origins and Significance," *Monumenta Nipponica* 28, no. 3 (1973): 324–25.

71. Hagiwara, *Takao Heibē*, 74–75.

72. Quoted in Beckmann and Okubo, *Japanese Communist Party*, 38.

73. Takao went from Shanghai via Pusan, where he met a Japanese prostitute from Harbin, who was gravely ill and wanted to travel back to Japan but had no money. Takao paid for her ticket and a doctor out of the Comintern's funds, but on arrival at Tsushima she died (Hagiwara, *Takao Heibē*, 97–100).

74. Matsuo Takayoshi, "Wasurerareta kakumeika: Takao Heibē," *Shisō*, no. 577 (1972): 96; Kurokawa, *Teikoku ni kōsuru shakai undō*, 173–77. The Comintern was very keen on establishing a printing shop in Chita and enrolling Asian radicals in the Communist University of Toilers of the East in Moscow (Adibekov and Wada, *VKP(b), Komintern i Iaponiia*, Doc. 272, 254).

75. Beckmann and Okubo, *Japanese Communist Party*, 39.

76. Matsuo, "Takao Heibē," 98–99.

77. Matsuo, "Takao Heibē," 96–97.

78. Takao Heibē, "Kakumei ka shi ka," in *Tokubetsu Yōshisatsu Jōsei Ippan*, 155–56.

79. "Zinoviev's Analysis of the Eastern Situation and of the Tasks in the East (Second Sessions of the Congress of the Toilers of the Far East, January 23, 1922)," in *Soviet Russia and the East, 1920–1927: A Documentary Survey*, ed. Xenia J. Eudin and Robert C. North (Stanford, CA: Stanford University Press, 1964), 224–25. From East Asia, twelve Japanese, fifty Koreans, and thirty Chinese participated in the Congress.

80. "Zinoviev's Analysis of the Eastern Situation."

81. Tsuzuki, "Kotoku, Osugi and Japanese Anarchism," 42.

82. Yamakawa Hitoshi, "Musan kaikyū undō no hōkō tenkan," in *Yamakawa Hitoshi zenshū*, 4:336–45.

83. Hagiwara, *Takao Heibē*, 126. For the full text, see Takao, "Naze shinkōchū no kakumei wo yōgo shinainoka," in *Ōsugi Sakae zenshū*, 7:67–71.

84. Ōsugi Sakae, "Seishisei ni kotaeru," in *Ōsugi Sakae zenshū*, 7:71–74.

85. For Ōsugi's reply to the accusations, see "Borushebiki yonju hachi teura omote," *Ōsugi Sakae zenshū*, 6:115–26; and "Kumiai teikokushugi," *Ōsugi Sakae zenshū*, 6:127–40.

86. Matsuo, "Takao Heibē," 106–8.

87. Ōsugi Sakae, *Nihon dasshutsuki* (Tokyo: Iwanami Shoten, 1971), 312.

88. Ōsugi Sakae, "Museifushugi shōgun: Nesutoro Mafuno," in *Ōsugi Sakae zenshū*, 7:154–75.

89. Ōsugi, "Museifushugi shōgun," 164.

90. Militancy increased on the leftist side as well. See Sheldon Garon, *The State and Labor in Modern Japan* (Berkeley: University of California Press, 1987), 42, 71; and Gordon, *Labor and Imperial Democracy*, 144–48.

91. By 1930, Kokusuikai membership was estimated to be around 200,000, with branches all around the country; by 1932, Seigidan had 70,000 members; Yamato Minrōkai had 20,000; the Kinno Renmei had 3,000; and the Dai Nippon Sekka Bōshidan had 2,000. See Eiko Maruko Siniawer, *Ruffians, Yakuza, Nationalists: The Violent Politics of Modern Japan, 1860–1960* (Ithaca, NY: Cornell University Press, 2008), 108–38.

92. Eiko Maruko Siniawer, "Liberalism Undone: Discourses on Political Violence in Interwar Japan," *Modern Asian Studies* 45, no. 4 (2011): 981.

93. Among the activities of Sekka Bōshidan were disputes with anarchists, militant dispersal of labor strikes, public showings of the movie *The Misery of Red Russia* (which they borrowed from the Home Ministry), and demonstrations against the visit of the Soviet diplomat Ioffe. After the murder of Takao, the organization gradually disbanded. See Matsuo, "Takao Heibē," 112.

94. Interestingly, contrary to the conventional view of yakuza as fervent nationalists, according to some memoirs, anarchist groups and some Japanese gangs grew very close in this period. Many Japanese criminal gangs, especially in the Kansai area, sympathized with the anarchists and assisted them in avenging Ōsugi's and Takao's murders.

95. Akiyama, *Nihon no hangyaku shisō*, 148–52.

96. Quoted from John Crump, *Hatta Shūzō and Pure Anarchism in Interwar Japan* (New York: Palgrave Macmillan, 2014), 186.

97. Crump, *Hatta Shūzō and Pure Anarchism*, 75–83.

98. John Crump, "Anarchist Communism and Leadership: The Case of Iwasa Sakutarō," in *Leaders and Leadership in Japan*, ed. Ian Neary (London: Routledge, 1996), 166.

99. Crump, *Hatta Shūzō and Pure Anarchism*, 111–17.

100. Ikuhiko Hata and Alvin D. Coox, "Continental Expansion, 1905–1941," in *The Cambridge History of Japan*, vol. 6, ed. Peter Duus (Cambridge: Cambridge University Press, 1989), 287.

101. The first global conference organized by the Profintern was the Conference of the Transport Workers of the Pacific, held in Canton in 1924 (Eudin and North, *Soviet Russia and the East*, 268).

102. Chairman Lozovsky's speech in November 26, 1926 included the following: "we must pay particular attention at present to Japan; we must see that the workers' movement of this highly developed capitalist country does not remain outside the world union movement" (Eudin and North, *Soviet Russia and the East*, 269).

103. Eudin and North, *Soviet Russia and the East*, 269–70.

104. Eudin and North, *Soviet Russia and the East*, 270.

105. Takamure Itsue, an anarchist and pathbreaking feminist historian, glorified Japanese expansion overseas and wrote extensively on imperial history. As Eiji Oguma pointed out, Takamure believed that ancient Japan offered examples of women's liberation, nature

unrestricted by artificial morals, and open freedom, and that the war meant the revival of these ideals. Ishikawa Sanshirō, another prominent anarchist and a close friend of Kōtoku Shūsui, admired *The Record of Ancient Matters* (Kojiki, compiled in 712) and the Kiki myths, which claimed that the founder of the imperial family had descended from the heavens in 660 BC. For more information, see Eiji Oguma, *A Genealogy of "Japanese" Self-Images* (Melbourne, VIC: Trans Pacific, 2002), introduction, chap. 10 (Ishikawa Sanshirō), chap. 11 (Takamure Itsue).

106. Crump, "Anarchist Communism and Leadership," 168.

107. Kurokawa, *Teikoku ni kōsuru shakai undō*, 122–51.

CHAPTER 6. THE JAPANESE COMMUNIST PARTY AND THE COMINTERN

1. Because the JCP was an illegal organization, historical sources are very scarce. The main primary sources in Japan are the interrogation reports from the 1930s, but not all of them have been made public. See Yamabe Kentarō, ed., *Gendaishi shiryō*, vol. 19–20 (Tokyo: Misuzu Shobō, 1967–68). Most of the documents concerning the prewar JCP are in the Comintern archives in the Russian State Archive of Socio-Political History (RGASPI) in Moscow, which until the early 1990s were classified. The only sources available to Japanese and English historians have been memoirs and police interrogations. Murata Yōichi, ed., *Shiryōshū Kominterun to Nihon* (Tokyo: Ōtsuki Shoten, 1986–88); and Murata Yōichi, ed., *Shiryōshū shoki Nihon Kyōsantō to Kominterun* (Tokyo: Ōtsuki Shoten, 1993) were the most important collections on the JCP, but they contained very few archival documents. The major breakthrough was the publication in 2001 of the newly declassified Comintern documents by Grant M. Adibekov and Wada Haruki, eds., *VKP(b), Komintern i Iaponiia, 1917–1941* (Moscow: Rosspen, 2001). This chapter is based on this collection of primary documents. The Japanese translation of the Comintern documents was published as Tomita Takeshi and Wada Haruki, eds., *Shiryōshū Kominterun to Nihon kyōsantō* (Tokyo: Iwanami Shoten, 2014).

2. Recent studies of Comintern activities in Europe and China reveal that there, too, until 1927–28 foreign communists enjoyed a great degree of independence in decision making and retained critical perspectives on Comintern directives. See Kevin McDermot, "The History of the Comintern in Light of New Documents," in *International Communism and the Communist International, 1919–43*, ed. Tim Rees and Andrew Thorpe (Manchester: Manchester University Press, 1998), 31–40.

3. The classic studies on the establishment of the early JCP are Iwamura Toshio, *Kominterun to Nihon kyōsantō no seiritsu* (Tokyo: San'ichi Shobō, 1977); and Inumaru Gi'ichi, *Daiichiji Kyōsantō shi no kenkyū* (Tokyo: Aoki Shoten, 1993). The historian Itō Akira points out that Japanese historians of the Japanese communist movement mainly focus on how correctly the party members understood Marxism-Leninism. These historical studies are biased and judgmental, and therefore somewhat limited in their usefulness. Moreover, they largely rely on state police archives, which described the Japanese communists as a small, isolated group. This bias in the primary sources led historians to miss the broader significance of communism and communists in prewar Japanese society (Itō Akira, *Tennōsei to shakaishugi* [Tokyo: Keisō Shobō, 1988]).

4. Yamanouchi Akito, *The Early Comintern and Japanese Socialists Residing Abroad: A Transnational Network* (Kyoto: Mineruva Shobō, 2007).

5. I agree with the official history of the Japanese Communist Party that Katayama was solely responsible for the transmission of communist thought and movement via the United States to Japan, and that he had a decisive impact on the creation of the first JCP in 1922. See the memoirs of Watanabe Haruo, *Katayama Sen to tomo ni* (Tokyo: Wakōsha, 1955); and Kondō Eizō, *Komuminterun no misshi* (Tokyo: Bunka Hyōron-sha, 1949). For the most recent study, see Yamanouchi Akito, "Katayama Sen: Zaibei

Nihonjin shakaishugidan to shoki Kominterun," *Ōhara Shakai Mondai Kenkyūjo Zasshi* 544 (March 2004): 38–68. In English, see Hyman Kublin, *Asian Revolutionary: The Life of Sen Katayama* (Princeton, NJ: Princeton University Press, 1964). The historian Asukai Masamichi, however, points out that Katayama did not have any influence on Japanese socialism and the Japanese communist movement and was in fact disliked by Japanese radicals because of his immigration to the United States in 1914 in the aftermath of the High Treason Incident, which they considered a dishonorable escape. Arahata Kanson was especially disappointed at Katayama's flight to the United States. See Asukai Masamichi, "Roshia Kakumei to Ōsugi Sakae," *Gendai riron* 4, no. 10 (1967): 36. During the 1920s, Japanese communists consistently warned the Comintern not to trust Katayama's recommendations and assessments, which they argued were driven by his concern for his career within the Comintern organization in Moscow. See, for example, Docs. 305 and 299 in *VKP(b), Komintern i Iaponiia*.

6. Yamanouchi Akito, "The Early Comintern in Amsterdam, New York and Mexico City," *Shien* (March 2010): 99–139. Japanese communists in the United States managed to smuggle massive amounts of propaganda literature into Japan well into the 1940s. See Rodger Swearingen and Paul Langer, *Red Flag in Japan: International Communism in Action, 1919–1951* (New York: Greenwood Press, 1968), 59–66.

7. The Baku Congress formalized the Bolshevik commitment to the liberation of colonial peoples and marked the shift in the Comintern's attention to the East. Acknowledging the importance of a national liberation struggle in the colonial world, the congress declared a revised slogan of the *Communist Manifesto*: "Proletarians and *oppressed peoples* of the world unite!" (John Riddell, ed., *To See the Dawn: Baku, 1920—First Congress of the Peoples of the East* [New York: Pathfinder, 1993]).

8. On Grigory Voitinsky, see Tony Saich, *The Origins of the First United Front in China* (Leiden: Brill, 1991). So successful was the Comintern Far Eastern Bureau in Shanghai as the "communications hub" of Asian revolutionaries, that it was dubbed the center of "a series of high-grade spy rings around the world" in the late 1920s and 1930s (Frederic Wakeman Jr., *Policing Shanghai 1927–1937* [Berkeley: University of California Press, 1994], 146)

9. Martin C. Wilbur and Julie L. How, *Missionaries of Revolution: Soviet Advisors and Nationalist China, 1920–1927* (Cambridge, MA: Harvard University Press, 1989), 6–7; Heng-yu Kuo and M. L. Titarenko, eds., *VKP(b), Komintern i Kitai*, vol. 1 (Moscow: Buklet, 1994).

10. Quoted from Ishikawa Yoshihiro, *The Formation of the Chinese Communist Party* (New York: Columbia University Press, 2013), 76.

11. Yamakawa Hitoshi, *Yamakawa Hitoshi jiden*, ed. Yamakawa Kikue and Yamakawa Shinsaku (Tokyo: Iwanami Shoten, 1961), 370.

12. Yamakawa and Sakai would later be blamed for their reluctant "unrevolutionary" attitude and labeled as cowards by Japanese Marxist historians. See, for example, Iwamura, *Kominterun to Nihon kyōsantō no seiritsu*, 78–105.

13. After his release, Kondō established the Enlightened People's Communist Party (Gyōmin Kyōsantō) in August 1921 but was arrested again three months later, together with other members of his party and a Comintern agent by the name of B. Grey, who had just arrived in Japan from Shanghai with more funds. Sakai and Yamakawa were also arrested but were released soon after. Another Comintern envoy, a Chinese communist in Tokyo, was deported to Shanghai in December (Inumaru, *Daiichiji Kyōsantō shi no kenkyū*, 16; Kondō, *Komintern no misshi*, 275).

14. Coined by judicial authorities in the investigations following the mass arrests of March 1928 and April 1929, the term "first JCP" distinguished the earlier party from the reconstructed party of 1926 onward, but it was also adopted by the defendants themselves

and has remained in common use. See Inumaru Gi'ichi, *Daiichiji Kyōsantō shi no kenkyū*, 501; and Sandra Wilson, "The Comintern and the Japanese Communist Party," in *International Communism and the Communist International, 1919–43*, ed. Tim Rees and Andrew Thorpe (Manchester: Manchester University Press, 1998), 305n27.

15. Matsuo Takayoshi, "Sōritsuki Nihon kyōsantō no tame no oboegaki," *Kyoto Daigaku Bungakubu Kenkyū kiyō*, no. 19 (March 1979): 132–33.

16. "The Interrelation between the National Revolutionary Movement and the Revolutionary Proletarian Movement" (Safarov's Statement at the Tenth Session of the Congress of the Toilers of the Far East, 27 January 1922), in *Soviet Russia and the East, 1920–1927: A Documentary Survey*, ed. Xenia J. Eudin and Robert C. North (Stanford, CA: Stanford University Press, 1964), 229.

17. "Zinoviev's Analysis of the Eastern Situation and of the Tasks in the East (Second Sessions of the Congress of the Toilers of the Far East, January 23, 1922)," in *Soviet Russia and the East*, 224–25. From East Asia, twelve Japanese, fifty Koreans, and thirty Chinese participated in the congress.

18. The original manifesto and program were discovered by the historian Katō Tetsurō in the Comintern archives in Moscow after the collapse of the USSR. Doc. 284, in *VKP(b), Komintern i Iaponiia*. The document was signed by Arahata and Sakai, but Katō has persuasively argued that the draft was written by Yamakawa. It is unknown how the Comintern reacted to this document.

19. Katō Tetsurō, "1922-nen 9-gatsu no Nihon kyōsantō kōryō (ue)," in *Ōhara Shakai Mondai Kenkyū zasshi*, no. 481 (1998): 45.

20. Katō, "1922-nen 9-gatsu no Nihon kyōsantō kōryō (ue)," 45.

21. Katō, "1922-nen 9-gatsu no Nihon kyōsantō kōryō (ue)," 45.

22. The Russian version of the manifesto is published in Docs. 254 and 274, *VKP(b), Komintern i Iaponiia*, 254–61.

23. Yamakawa Hitoshi, "Hara naikaku no rōdō seisaku," in *Yamakawa Hitoshi zenshū*, ed. Yamakawa Kikue and Yamakawa Shinsaku (Tokyo: Keisō Shobō), 1966, 2:159.

24. Yamakawa Hitoshi, "Futsū senkyō to musan kaikyū no senjutsu," in *Yamakawa Hitoshi zenshū*, ed. Yamakawa Kikue and Yamakawa Shinsaku (Tokyo: Keisō Shobō), 1967, 4:211–18.

25. Hence the striking absence of the peasantry question in the writings of Japanese socialists. Arahata Kanson later remarked that Meiji-era Japanese socialists were largely unfamiliar with the peasants' problems.

26. Yamakawa, "Futsū senkyō to musan kaikyū no senjutsu."

27. Yamakawa Hitoshi, "Marukusu to Marukusushugi," in *Yamakawa Hitoshi zenshū*, 2:216–24. Yamakawa Kikue expressed her support of the Soviet dictatorship in "Gendai seiji no byōhei," *Shakaishugi*, no. 4 (January 1921).

28. Yamakawa Hitoshi, "Shakaishugi kokka to rōdō kumiai," in *Yamakawa Hitoshi zenshū*, ed. Yamakawa Kikue and Yamakawa Shinsaku (Tokyo: Keisō Shobō, 1967), 3:188–99. One should remember that the Japanese knew nothing of the conspiratorial traditions of the prerevolutionary Bolshevik Party and Lenin's natural authoritarianism. Besides, the transformation of the Bolshevik Party (not until 1922 were factions in the Russian Communist Party forbidden) and its subsequent policy and form of rule were still to come due to the ongoing Russian Civil War.

29. Yamakawa Hitoshi, "Nihon ni okeru demokurashī no hattatsu to musan kaikyū no seiji undō," in *Yamakawa Hitoshi zenshū*, ed. Yamakawa Kikue and Yamakawa Shinsaku (Tokyo: Keisō Shobō, 1968), 5:357–90.

30. Yamakawa Hitoshi, *Shakaishugi no tachiba kara: Demokurashii no hanmon* (Tokyo: Mita Shobō, 1919); Itō Akira, *Tennōsei to shakaishugi*, 115.

31. Itō Akira, *Tennōsei to shakaishugi*, 117; Yasukuni Ishiko, "Naze fashizumu ni yabureta ka, Yamakawa Hitoshi wo yomu," *Kagakuteki shakaishugi*, no. 173 (September 2012): 88–93.

32. Conrad Brandt, "Lenin and Asian Nationalism: Sources of an Alliance," in his *Stalin's Failure in China, 1924–1927* (Cambridge, MA: Harvard University Press, 1958), 1–17.

33. The Fourth Congress was able to report some progress in non-Western countries: strikes in India in 1919–21, directed against the British; the formation of the Chinese Communist Party in 1921 and strikes in the newly created Chinese trade unions; the birth of the Indonesian Communist Party in 1920; attempts to establish a soviet government in the Gilan province of Persia; the Kemalist national revolution in Turkey; the growing anti-Japanese movement in Korea; unrest against the British in Egypt; and finally the revolutionary movement in Mongolia and the establishment of the Mongolian People's Republic in 1921. See Eudin and North, *Soviet Russia and the East*, 148.

34. Moreover, Katayama Sen urged the JCP to support the universal suffrage movement and fight bureaucratism and militarism. See "The Program of the JCP by Katayama Sen," Doc. 276, in *VKP(b), Komintern i Iaponiia*, 262–69. In "The Class War in Japan" (*Communist Review* 3, no. 8 [December 1922]), Voitinsky also called for a legal proletarian party and universal suffrage. He was concerned with the powerful anarchist movement in Japan which, he urged, must be won over. The full text is available at the Marxist Internet Archive (http://www.marxist.org). See also Doc. 282, in *VKP(b), Komintern i Iaponiia*, 278–80.

35. E. H. Carr, *A History of Soviet Russia: The Bolshevik Revolution 1917–1923* (Harmondsworth: Penguin Books, 1966), 3:486.

36. Voitinsky, "Class War in Japan."

37. Germaine A. Hoston, *The State, Identity, and the National Question in China and Japan* (Princeton, NJ: Princeton University Press, 1994), 254. For a discussion of how Soviet experts have treated modern Japanese history, see Yulia Mikhailova, "Soviet-Japanese Studies on the Problem of the Meiji ishin and the Development of Capitalism in Japan," in *War, Revolution and Japan*, ed. Ian Neary (London: Routledge, 2005), 33–38.

38. V. Lenin, "Backward Europe and Advanced Asia," *Pravda*, May 18, 1913. The full text is available at the Marxist Internet Archive (http://www.marxist.org).

39. "Tasks of the Japanese Communists," Doc. 278, in *VKP(b), Komintern i Iaponiia*, 271–75.

40. Carol Gluck, *Japan's Modern Myths: Ideology in the Late Meiji Period* (Princeton, NJ: Princeton University Press, 1985).

41. On traditional historiography, see Germaine Hoston, *Marxism and the Crisis of Development in Prewar Japan* (Princeton, NJ: Princeton University Press, 1986), 55–75.

42. "Report of the Executive Committee of the JCP about the Situation of the JCP" (March 25, 1923), Doc. 286, in *VKP(b), Komintern i Iaponiia*, 289–92; and "Report about the Emergency Meeting of the JCP," Doc. 287, in *VKP(b), Komintern i Iaponiia*, 292–95.

43. Katō Tetsurō, "1922-nen 9-gatsu no Nihon kyōsantō kōryō (shita)," *Ōhara Shakai Mondai Kenkyū zasshi*, no. 482 (1998): 40.

44. Katō mentions the possibility that the JCP might not even have received Bukharin's general address. In the police interrogations of Sakai Toshihiko after his arrest in May 1923, Sakai mentioned that he read the Bukharin address only in the *Inprecor* issue from November 1922. This, however, could have been an effort on Sakai's part to conceal evidence of any direct contact between the JCP and the Comintern. Sakai, in fact, denied the existence of the JCP to the police and claimed that the socialists' meetings were conducted to establish a legal proletarian party (Katō, "1922-nen 9-gatsu no Nihon kyōsantō kōryō (shita)," 49–51).

45. Here I consulted Aleksandr Iu. Vatlin's discussion of the Congress in *Komintern: Idei, resheniia, sud'by* (Moscow: Rosspen, 2009), 210–13.

46. Zinoviev said, "At first parties must be created, and only then their programs" (quoted in Vatlin, *Komintern*, 213).

47. Docs. 286 and 287, in *VKP(b), Komintern i Iaponiia*, 292–95.

48. Katō, "1922-nen 9-gatsu no Nihon kyōsantō kōryō (shita)," 51.

49. Katō, "1922-nen 9-gatsu no Nihon kyōsantō kōryō (shita)," 51.

50. Bukharin may have consulted Grigory Voitinsky's opinion as well. In December 1923, under the impact of the bloody aftermath of the great Kantō earthquake in September, Voitinsky published "Bourgeoisie and the Remnants of Feudalism in Japan" (Burzhuaziia i ostatki feodalizma v Iaponii, *Novyi Vostok*, no. 4, 1925), in which he stated that priority must be given to the struggle for abolishing the imperial system, which was, he argued, the root cause of Japanese nationalistic and imperialistic aggression. The publication of his article coincided with Bukharin's preparation of his theses on Japan, published the next year in Germany. The Comintern headquarters in Moscow did not react to Voitinsky's article.

51. Aono Suekichi, "Shinsai zengō nijū san," *Shakai kagaku* (October 1928). For more information, see Katō, "1922-nen 9-gatsu no Nihon kyōsantō kōryō (shita)," 52.

52. Yamakawa Hitoshi, "Kaizō Nihon to musan kaikyū undō," in *Yamakawa Hitoshi zenshū*, 5:77–82.

53. Eudin and North, *Soviet Russia and the East*, 273.

54. Starting in 1919, Sakai, Arahata, and Yamakawa ran the Labor Union Study Group (Rōdō Kumiai Kenkyūkai), aimed at educating labor activists and progressive workers, although the authorities often shut it down. Also in 1919, Tokyo socialists opened Heimin University (People's University), in which predominantly provincial students attended lectures on socialism and visited famous activists, professors, and artists. Heimin University was quite popular and created a nationwide network for socialist sympathizers, which would become the basis for the Socialist League in 1920–21. Arahata, Yamakawa, and Sakai wrote and published articles in workers' newspapers and gave public lectures at factories around the country, which sometimes attracted up to five thousand people. See Watanabe, "Roshia Kakumei to Nihon rōdō undō," *Gendai no riron* 4, no. 10 (1967), 21–33.

55. Yamakawa Hitoshi, "Sōrengō no ketsuretsu," in *Yamakawa Hitoshi zenshū*, 4:399–407; Yamakawa Hitoshi, "Musan kaikyū undō no hōko tenkan," in *Yamakawa Hitoshi zenshū*, 4:336–45.

56. On the British anti-intervention movement, see John Saville, "Ernest Bevin and the Defense of the Russian Revolution," in *The Politics of Continuity: British Foreign Policy and the Labour Government, 1945–46* (London: Verso Books, 1993), 218–22.

57. There were three slogans: immediate implementation of an eight-hour workday, recognition of Russia, and establishment of civil rights. See Yamabe Kentarō and Takemura Eisuke, "Jūgatsu kakumei wa Nihon ni ataeta eikyō," *Zen'ei*, no. 135 (December 1957): 147.

58. In 1918 and 1919, Takabatake Motoyuki and Yamakawa tried to publish their anti-intervention articles but were censored, and all the issues were confiscated. Yamakawa Hitoshi, "Tairo kanshō wo yameyo," in *Yamakawa Hitoshi zenshū*, 2:339–48. The only public expression of socialist opposition to the Siberian Intervention was Sakai Toshihiko's article from 1920. See Sakai Toshihiko, "Shiberia teppei no yōkyū," *Shinshakai hyōron* (June 1920); and Sakai Toshihiko, "L. F. kai no kūki," *Shinshakai hyōron* (July–August 1920). Sakai described how unions and anarchists were against the Siberian Intervention.

59. Robert T. Tierney, *Monster of the Twentieth Century: Kōtoku Shūsui and Japan's First Anti-Imperialist Movement* (Berkeley: University of California Press, 2015).

60. "Program of the JCP," Doc. 284, in *VKP(b), Komintern i Iaponiia*, 282–85. For the original English text see http://netizen.html.xdomain.jp/22program.html.

61. "Theses of the Fourth Congress of the Communist International on the Eastern Problem," in Eudin and North, *Soviet Russia and the East*, 235–36.

62. Eudin and North, *Soviet Russia and the East*, 39–41. See also Joseph Mcquade, "The New Asia of Rash Behari Bose: India, Japan, and the Limits of the International, 1912–1945," *Journal of World History* 27, no. 4 (2016): 641–67.

63. Nomura Kōichi, "Tairiku mondai no imēji to jittai," in *Kindai Nihon seiji shisōshi*, ed. Matsumoto Sannosuke and Hashikawa Bunzō (Tokyo: Yūhikaku, 1970), 4:52–108; Okamoto Hiroshi, "Taishō shakaishugi no kokusai ninshiki to gaikō hihan. Yamakawa Hitoshi no baai," in *Nihon gaikō no kokusai ninshiki: Sono shiteki tenkai*, no. 51 (1974): 87–108.

64. Yamakawa Hitoshi, "Kōryō no mondai," in *Yamakawa Hitoshi zenshū*, 6:250–69. In the same fashion, Yamakawa called on the anarchist-leaning Suiheisha outcasts movement to abandon its "instinctive" approach and create instead a centralized organization ("Musan kaikyū no seiji undō no shuppatsuten," in *Yamakawa Hitoshi zenshū* 5:83–89).

65. See Yamakawa's first publication on China "Shina no rōdōsha wa nan no tame ni tatakatte iruka," in *Yamakawa Hitoshi zenshū*, 1976, 6:174–78.

66. Voitinsky notified the Comintern about the disbandment of the JCP in his letter of May 1, 1924, from Shanghai. His report was based on his conversations with Arahata Kanson. See Doc. 303, in *VKP(b), Komintern i Iaponiia*, 333–41.

67. Doc. 305, in *VKP(b), Komintern i Iaponiia*, 342–43.

68. Defections from the first JCP due to disagreements with the Bolsheviks' policy of dictatorship happened even prior to October 1922. For example, Hashiura Tokio, an old Meiji socialist and friend of Kōtoku Shūsui, could not accept the centralized organization of the JCP and, despite being one of its founders, very quickly quit the group. See Hashiura Tokio, *Hashiura Tokio nikki* (Tokyo: Ganshisha, 1983).

69. Rostislav Ul'ianovskii, *Komintern i Vostok: Bor'ba za leninskuiu strategiiu i taktiku v natsional'no-osvoboditel'nom dvizhenii* (Moscow: Nauka, 1969).

70. Swearingen and Langer, *Red Flag in Japan*; Robert A. Scalapino, *The Japanese Communist Movement, 1920–1966* (Berkeley: University of California Press, 1968).

71. Yamakawa Hitoshi, "Nihon ni okeru demokurashii no hattatsu to musan kaikyū no seiji undō" in *Yamakawa Hitoshi zenshū*, 5:357–90.

72. At the Fifth Congress, Katayama Sen also criticized the actions of the Japanese old socialists and refused to acknowledge the legitimacy of their decision. See also Sano Manabu's letter to Voitinsky, in which he criticizes Katayama for his lack of understanding of Japanese conditions. Sano in his letter strongly urged Voitinsky to ignore Katayama's suggestions. For these documents, see Docs. 299, 302, and 305, in *VKP(b), Komintern i Iaponiia*.

73. The authors of the Shanghai Theses were Voitinsky, Sanō Manabu, and other members of the Japanese Communist Bureau in Vladivostok. See Doc. 303, in *VKP(b), Komintern i Iaponiia*, 333–341. Katō Tetsurō argues that the Japanese were not included in the writing of the theses, and Voitinsky was the sole author. For the text, see George M. Beckmann and Genji Okubo, *The Japanese Communist Party, 1922–1945* (Stanford, CA: Stanford University Press, 1969), 283–92.

74. Doc. 307, in *VKP(b), Komintern i Iaponiia*, 345–48.

75. Scalapino, *Japanese Communist Movement*, 21.

76. Yanson's report to the Eastern Bureau of the Comintern, "Our Following Organizational Steps in Japan" (July 3, 1925), Doc. 311, in *VKP(b), Komintern i Iaponiia*, 355–60. The report was written in Russian and sent to Zinoviev via Voitinsky. The report had an accompanying confidential letter to Voitinsky, in which Yanson confided that an illegal JCP would surely end in fiasco and that legal, not overtly communist activities should be prioritized. Yanson was transferred to Shanghai in 1927 to replace Voitinsky. According to

Japanese police reports, Yanson continued to sponsor Japanese labor union radicals even after his transfer. See Doc. 310, in *VKP(b), Komintern i Iaponiia*, 354–55.

77. Doc. 311, in *VKP(b), Komintern i Iaponiia*, 355–60.

78. Zinoviev's speech about the Japanese question at the ECCI presidium meeting from September 8, 1925, is Doc. 313, in *VKP(b), Komintern i Iaponiia*, 361–63. Original in German.

79. Yamakawa's report to the ECCI, "Present Stage of Development of Our Movement" (March 1927), which he passed via Yanson, is Doc. 327, in *VKP(b), Komintern i Iaponiia*, 394–406. The report was written in Japanese and translated into English in June 1927.

80. Ann Waswo, "The Transformation of Rural Society, 1900–1950," in *The Cambridge History of Japan*, vol. 6, ed. Peter Duus (Cambridge: Cambridge University Press, 1989), 593–605.

81. Beckmann and Okubo, *Japanese Communist Party*, 79–105.

82. Letter from the Japanese communists to N. I. Bukharin: "Dear Comrade Bukharin! Knowing well that you are very busy with many important matters to attend, nevertheless we on the behalf of the CP of Japan kindly ask you to write the Political Theses on the Japanese question. We make this comradely request because the Theses must lay down the very foundation upon which the CP of Japan shall be established. And, second, because the Japanese question is not only very complicated but also closely related to the Chinese question. With communist greetings, Moscow, June 10, 1927. Sen Katayama, Seki, Y. Kawasaki, Asano, Akita, Chiba, Mori, Kuroki, Yamane." See Doc. 333, in *VKP(b), Komintern i Iaponiia*, 435.

83. Yamakawa pointed out that Japanese workers' nationalism and prejudices against Korean workers enabled Japanese colonialism in Korea. He appealed to Japanese workers to abandon their prejudices and nationalism and embrace the Koreans as their brothers, because Japanese, Korean, and Chinese masses were all victims of the Japanese capitalist imperialist state. At the same time, however, he appealed to Korean workers in Japan to join the JCP as a more progressive political organization. See Kurokawa Iori, *Teikoku ni kōsuru shakai undō: Daiichiji Nihon Kyosantō no shisō to undō* (Tokyo: Yūshisha, 2014), 130.

84. "Theses of the ECCI on Japan." Adopted on July 15, 1927. The theses were written in Russian (see Doc. 338, in *VKP[b], Komintern i Iaponiia*, 450–61) but were published in a faulty English translation in *International Press Correspondence* (no. 2, 1928). See also Beckmann and Okubo, *Japanese Communist Party*, 119–25.

85. "Bukharin's Report at the Meeting of the Presidium of the ECCI on Japan Question," Moscow, July 15, 1927, Doc. 335, in *VKP(b), Komintern i Iaponiia*, 436–48. The text is in German.

86. "Bukharin's Report at the Meeting of the Presidium of the ECCI on Japan Question."

87. In the 1930s, Yamakawa consciously distanced himself from the JCP. In his "Waga kuni ni okeru Marukushizumu no hattatsu" (*Kaizō*, March 1933), he described the economists Kawakami Hajime and Kushida Tamizō as the central figures of Japanese Marxism until 1924, without even mentioning the early JCP. In his postwar memoirs, Yamakawa maintained that he had minimal connections with the first JCP and no contact with the Comintern after the party's dissolution in 1924. These statements, especially Yamakawa's claim that he never participated in the activities of the first JCP, angered Arahata, who rebuked Yamakawa in his own memoirs (*Arahata Kanson jiden* [Tokyo: Iwanami Shoten, 1975], 2:137–41).

88. The 1927 Theses stated, for example, that the Shakai minshūtō tries "to poison the masses with opportunism, nationalism, and imperialism" (Beckmann and Okubo, *Japanese Communist Party*, 303).

89. Kevin McDermott and Jeremy Agnew, *The Comintern: A History of International Communism from Lenin to Stalin* (Basingstoke: Macmillan, 1996), 41–80.

90. Wilson, "Comintern and the Japanese Communist Party," 285–86, 290.

91. Tatiana Linkhoeva, "New Revolutionary Agenda: The Interwar Japanese Left on the 'Chinese Revolution,'" *Cross-Currents* 6, no. 2 (2017): 83–104.

CHAPTER 7. NATIONAL SOCIALISM AND SOVIET COMMUNISM

1. Reto Hofmann, *The Fascist Effect: Japan and Italy, 1915–1952* (Ithaca, NY: Cornell University Press, 2015).

2. Zeev Sternhell, "The 'Anti-Materialist' Revision of Marxism as an Aspect of the Rise of Fascist Ideology," *Journal of Contemporary History* 22, no. 3 (1987): 379–400.

3. Sternhell, "'Anti-Materialist' Revision of Marxism," 382.

4. Gregory Kasza, "Fascism from Below?: A Comparative Perspective on the Japanese Right, 1931–1936," *Journal of Contemporary History* 19, no. 4 (1984): 607–30.

5. Gregory J. Kasza, *The State and the Mass Media in Japan, 1918–1945* (Berkeley: University of California Press, 1993); Janis Mimura, *Planning for Empire: Reform Bureaucrats and the Japanese Wartime State* (Ithaca, NY: Cornell University Press, 2011).

6. The most authoritative study on Takabatake is Tanaka Masato's *Takabatake Motoyuki: Nihon no kokka shakaishugi* (Tokyo: Gendai Hyōronsha, 1978). See also, Hashikawa Bunzō, "Kokka shakaishugi no hassō yōshiki: Kita Ikki, Takabatake Motoyuki wo chūshin ni," in *Nihon seiji gakkai nenpō seijigaku* (December 1968), 104–38; Satō Masaru, *Takabatake Motoyuki no bōrei: aru kokka shakaishugisha no kikenna shisō* (Tokyo: Shinchōsha, 2018). In English, see Germaine A. Hoston, "Marxism and National Socialism in Taishō Japan: The Thought of Takabatake Motoyuki," *Journal of Asian Studies* 44, no. 1 (1984): 43–64.

7. For Yamaji, the task of modern socialism was to ensure a strong, fair state in which "government officials take care of morals and food for the people," and the values of community and equality would be upheld. Yamaji was a widely known public historian, a good friend of the socialist Sakai Toshihiko, and a self-proclaimed socialist. See Peter Duus, "Whig History, Japanese Style: The Min'yūsha Historians and the Meiji Restoration," *Journal of Asian Studies* 33, no. 3 (1974): 415–36.

8. Yushi Ito, *Yamaji Aizan and His Time: Nationalism and Debating Japanese History* (Leiden: Brill, 2007), 124–34.

9. Takabatake's militant position got him into trouble; a year later, he was imprisoned for two months for participating in an anarchist demonstration.

10. Yamakawa Hitoshi, "Bōfū no mae," *Shinshakai* (December 1917).

11. Takabatake Motoyuki, "Tachiba no tachiba kara no seiji undō to keizai undō," *Shinshakai* (May 1918).

12. In "State and Revolution," written in the summer of 1917, Lenin emphasized that a proletarian semistate would serve as a short-term transition between the collapse of capitalism and the onset of communism.

13. Takabatake Motoyuki, "Kagekishugi no tachiba wo ronzu," *Kokka shakaishugi*, no. 4 (August 1919).

14. Tanaka, *Takabatake Motoyuki*, 158.

15. Takabatake Motoyuki, "Kagekiha no tachiba wo ronzu," *Kokka shakaishugi*, no. 4 (August 1919).

16. Takabatake Motoyuki, "Kokka shakaishugi de yuku," *Kaizō* (March 1923).

17. Arima Manabu, "Takabatake Motoyuki to kokka shakaishugi ha no dōkō," *Shigaku zasshi* 83, no. 10 (1974): 9–12.

18. Tanaka, *Takabatake Motoyuki*, 131.

19. Takabatake, "Kokka shakaishugi no irowake," *Kokka shakaishugi* (April 1, 1919). Henry M. Hyndman (1842–1921) was a leading figure of British socialism, one of the founders of the Social Democratic Federation in 1884 and the British Socialist Party in 1911. In 1916, he formed the National Socialist Party, which placed the interests of British workers above those of the international proletariat, supported British involvement in World War I, and opposed labor unions. After the October Revolution, Hyndman supported the Foreign Intervention, arguing that Russia was not ready for socialism and that attempts to build a socialist system in a vast, backward empire would result in failure and reactionism. See Henry Hyndman, *The Evolution of Revolution* (London: Hyndman Literary Trust, 1920), chap. 23, "Bolshevism and the Russian Revolution."

20. Their journal was also named *Kokka shakaishugi*, and the title was translated into English as *The National Socialism*. See Takabatake Motoyuki, "Shakaishugi kenkyū mondai," *Kokka shakaishugi* (June 1919).

21. James Gregor, *Marxism, Fascism, and Totalitarianism: Chapters in the Intellectual History of Radicalism* (Stanford, CA: Stanford University Press, 2009), 161–88.

22. Gregor, *Marxism, Fascism, and Totalitarianism*, 162–63.

23. Takabatake Motoyuki, "Shōhisha hon'i no taishū undō," *Genmetsusha no shakaikan* (Tokyo: Daitōkaku, 1923).

24. Arima, "Takabatake Motoyuki to kokka shakaishugi ha no dōkō."

25. Germaine A. Hoston, "Tenkō: Marxism & the National Question in Prewar Japan," *Polity* 16, no. 1 (1983): 58.

26. Hoston, "Marxism and National Socialism in Taishō Japan," 46.

27. See Takabatake Motoyuki, "Nihon no kazoku seidō," and "Gendai shisōkai no keikō," both in his *Jiko wo kataru* (Tokyo: Jinbunkai Shuppanbu, 1928), 12–34, and 35–47, respectively.

28. Takabatake Motoyuki, *Nihon shakaishugi taigi* (Tokyo: Nihon Shakaishugi Kenkyūjō, 1932), 282.

29. Takabatake Motoyuki, "Marukusu mujun to Kawakami Hajime no mujun," *Kaihō* (November 1921).

30. Takabatake Motoyuki, "Mussorini wa hi 'kōshitsu chūshin shugisha," *Yomiuri shinbun* (December 1927). For a more detailed discussion, see Fuke Takahiro, *Nihon Fashizumu ronsō: Taisen zen'ya no shisōkatachi* (Tokyo: Kawade Shobō, 2012), 228–39.

31. Itō Akira, *Tennōseishugi to shakaishugi* (Tokyo: Keisō Shobō, 1988), 57–62.

32. Takabatake Motoyuki, "Kenkoku sai," in *Jiko wo kataru*, 139–141.

33. As an example of Japan's manipulation by big business, Takabatake referred to the humiliating Treaty of Versailles (1919) and the Washington Naval Treaty (1922), which were signed (as the rightist commentators claimed) for the benefit of Anglo-American imperialism.

34. Takabatake Motoyuki, "Kokka shakaishugi no seisaku," in his *Hihan Marukusushugi* (Tokyo: Nihon Hyōronsha, 1929), 213–26.

35. Takabatake Motoyuki, "Rōdōsha ni kokka arashimeyo," *Kokka shakaishugi*, no. 1 (April 1919).

36. Takabatake, "Demokurashi shinri," in *Jiko wo kataru*, 169–70.

37. Hashikawa Bunzō, "Kokka shakaishugi no hassō yōshiki; Kita Ikki, Takabatake Motoyuki wo chūshin ni"; Christopher W. Szpilman, "Kita Ikki and the Politics of Coercion," *Modern Asian Studies* 36, no. 2 (2002): 467–90.

38. Takabatake's *Marukusu shihon ron kaisetsu*, which was considered an accurate introduction to the first volume of Marx's Das *Kapital*, was published in May 1919. The first printing of twenty thousand copies quickly sold out. Takabatake's translation of *Das Kapital*'s volume 1 was completed by 1924. In 1925–26, a new edition came out, followed by another edition in 1927–28 by the Kaizōsha publishing company. The 1928 edition was twelve times cheaper than the first edition. In total, over ten printings were issued

(Tanaka, *Takabatake Motoyuki*, 169). In addition, Takabatake published extensively on Marxist theory: he contributed to the famous *Lectures on Social Problems* (Shakai mondai kōza, 1927), authored *12 Lectures on Marxism* (Marukusu jūni kō, 1926) and *Dictionary of Social Problems* (Shakai mondai jiten, 1925), and coauthored the *New Introduction to Social Philosophy* (Shakai tetsugaku shingakusetsu taikei, 1928), to name a few (Tanaka, *Takabatake Motoyuki*, 236–37).

39. The Rōsōkai group lacked a clear program but attracted to its meetings a wide range of influential people—from the nationalist writer Ōzaki Shirō, the socialist feminist Yamakawa Kikue (wife of Yamakawa Hitoshi), and Sakai Toshihiko to military officers, members of parliament, and university students and professors. See Takabatake Motoyuki, "Rōsōkai to Reimeikai," *Shinshakai* (February 1919); and Fuke Takahiro, *Senkanki Nihon no shakai shisō: "Chōkokka" he no furontia* (Kyoto: Jinbun Shoin, 2010), chapter 4, "Rōsōkai no 'kyōdō.'"

40. Mitsukawa Kametarō, *Sangoku kanshō igo* (Tokyo: Ronsōsha, 2004), 175–78.

41. Under the provisions of antisocialist legislation, almost every issue of *National Socialism* was banned by the police, and Takabatake's public lectures were often cancelled. One meeting disbanded when a student from the audience asked why he was supposed to be proud of the Japanese eternal imperial line when in fact he did not believe in it (Tanaka, *Takabatake Motoyuki*, 161).

42. Takabatake Motoyuki, "Musan aikoku tō no kichō," in *Hihan marukusushugi*, 309–10; Takabatake Motoyuki, "Taishū no shinri," in *Hihan marukusushugi*, 153–62.

43. Takabatake Motoyuki, "Nichibei mondai hihan," *Shūkan Nihon* 6 (April 1924).

44. Takabatake Motoyuki, "Kageki undō torishimari hōan: Seitō katsu yūkō," *Kaihō* (April 1922).

45. Takabatake, "Kageki undō torishimari hōan." In 1927, General Tanaka Gi'ichi's cabinet revised the Peace Preservation Law and established the death penalty as punishment for subversive activities. Over the years, nearly seventy thousand people were arrested under this law.

46. Mizuno Masao, "Keikenteki genjitsushugi no fashizumu he no keikō," *Marukusushugi* (November 1926), was the first article to call Takabatake a fascist. Interestingly, the conservative scholar Uesugi Shinkichi, the liberal Yoshino Sakuzō, and the anarchists gladly attended the celebration (Tanaka, *Takabatake Motoyuki*, 235–36).

47. Takabatake Motoyuki, "Henkenteki intānashonarizumu," in *Hihan marukusushugi*, 246–47.

48. The reactions of Western observers were similar to those of the Japanese. The American scholar Gerard Friters wrote in 1927: "Soviet Imperialism has achieved a disguised annexation of Mongolia.... The imperialistic genius of Soviet Russia has certainly shown a greater ability in the treatment of the Mongols than Tsarist Russia." Quoted in Peter S. H. Tang, *Russian and Soviet Policy in Manchuria and Outer Mongolia, 1911–1931* (Durham, NC: Duke University Press, 1959), 371.

49. Takabatake Motoyuki, "Musan seitō kinshi yodan" (1925), in *Jiko wo kataru*, 90–101.

50. Takabatake Motoyuki, "Rōnō teikokushugi no kyokutō shinshutsu," *Kaizō* (April 1927).

51. Takabatake mentioned Sun Yat-sen's assistant, Liao Zhongkai, who had intimate connections with the Comintern and met the Soviet diplomat Adolf Ioffe while he was at the Japanese resort at Atami. Takabatake suggested that, on the Comintern's orders, Liao worked on infiltrating the Guomindang with communists.

52. Takabatake Motoyuki, "Teikokushugi no shinkyu," *Shunjū* (December 1927).

53. Takabatake Motoyuki, "Teikokushugi no hatten," in *Hihan marukusushugi*, 261–80. For Kita Ikki's position, see George M. Wilson, *Radical Nationalist in Japan: Kita Ikki, 1883–1937* (Cambridge, MA: Harvard University Press, 1969), 53–57.

54. Oikawa Eijiro, "The Relation between National Socialism and Social Democracy in the Formation of the International Policy of the Shakai Taishūtō," in *Nationalism and Internationalism in Imperial Japan: Autonomy, Asian Brotherhood, or World Citizenship?*, ed. Dick Stegewerns (London: Routledge, 2003), 213.

55. Tanaka, *Takabatake Motoyuki*, 199–204. See the *Kaizō* special issue of March 1923 on the Keirin Gakumei. Few historians in English have mentioned the organization, as they have tended to see it as an unnatural alliance doomed from the start. See, for example, Richard Storry, *The Double Patriots: A Study of Japanese Nationalism* (Boston: Houghton Mifflin, 1957), 320–21; and Ivan Morris, *Nationalism and the Right Wing in Japan: A Study of Post-War Trends* (Westport, CT: Greenwood Press, 1974).

56. Fuke, *Senkanki Nihon no shakai shisō*, 197.

57. Uesugi Shinkichi, "Kokutai no seika wo hatsuyo," *Kaizō* (March 1923).

58. Cited in Kasza, *State and the Mass Media in Japan*, 20.

59. Takabatake, "Kokka shakaishugi no seisaku." Ideas of total mobilization were already in the air by that time. The mass mobilization in Japan started during the Russo-Japanese War, when over one million men were drafted, followed by the establishment of the Imperial Military Reservist Association in 1910. Although army officials urged civil mobilization in Japan after observing World War I in Europe, little was done during the 1920s.

60. Takabatake, "Kokka shakaishugi de yuku."

61. Walter Skya, *Japan's Holy War: The Ideology of Radical Shinto Ultranationalism* (Durham, NC: Duke University Press, 2009), 161–62.

62. The first Japanese Marxist analysis of Japanese fascism was written by Sakai Toshihiko and Arahata Kanson as "Fascism in Japan" in the Profintern organ *Krasnyi internatsional profsoiuzov* in July 1923. For more information, see Fuke Takahiro, "Sen kyūhyaku nijū nen shoki Nihon ni okeru Itaria fashizumu kan no kōsatsu," *Bunmei Kōzō ron*, no. 3 (Kyoto University, 2007), 8. See also Yoshimi Yoshiaki, "Senzen ni okeru Nihon fashizumu kan no hensen," *Rekishigaku kenkyū*, no. 451 (December 1977), 20–32.

63. O. Tanin (real name O. S. Tarkhanov) and E. Yohan (E. Yolk), *Militarism and Fascism in Japan* (New York: International Publishers, 1934), 99–106, 272–73. Both were purged at the end of the 1930s and died in prison.

64. Uesugi went on to create the Shichishō (Seven Lives Society) in 1925 to combat liberal-democratic thought. Some of its members later joined the Ketsumeidan terrorist association, which murdered former Minister of Finance Inoue Junnosuke in February 1932, and the director of the Mitsui holding company Dan Takuma in March 1932.

65. Mogi Kyūhei, Takabatake's former disciple, became the chief editor and manager of the Taikakai publishing organ before following the Japanese army to China after the invasion of 1927. See Fuke Takahiro, "Sen kyūhyaku nijū nendai kōki ni okeru Takabatake Motoyuki no Itaria fashizumu ron ni tsuite," in *Kirisutokyō shakai mondai kenkyū*, no. 56 (2008), 70.

66. Tanaka, *Takabatake Motoyuki*, 204.

67. Fuke, *Senkanki Nihon no shakai shisō*, 216.

68. Takabatake Motoyuki, "Musan aikoku tō no kichō," in *Hihan marukusushugi*, 303–14.

69. Yoshihisa Nakamura and Ryōichi Tobe, "The Imperial Japanese Army and Politics," *Armed Forces and Society* 14, no. 4 (1988): 520.

70. Tanaka, *Takabatake Motoyuki*, 242–78; William D. Wray, "Asō Hisashi and the Search for Renovation in the 1930s," in *Papers on Japan*, vol. 5 (Cambridge, MA: East Asia Research Center, Harvard University, 1970).

71. Elise K. Tipton, *The Japanese Police State: The Tokkō in Interwar Japan* (Honolulu: University of Hawaii Press, 1990), 129.

72. Yonetani Masafumi, "Senjiki Nihon no shakai shisō: Gendaika to senji henkaku," *Shisō* 882 (December 1997), 69–120.

73. Oikawa, "Relation between National Socialism and Social Democracy," 200. On the activities of the national socialist group in the 1930s, see Fuke Takahiro, "Sen kyūhyaku sanjū nendai shoki Nihon ni okeru kokka shakaishugi undō: sono Nachi tōron to 'fashizumu' ron ni shōten wo atete," *Shigaku zasshi*, no. 118 (August 2009): 1485–508.

74. Mimura, *Planning for Empire*.

75. Tanaka, *Takabatake Motoyuki*, 285.

76. Oikawa, "Relation between National Socialism and Social Democracy," 201–2.

77. Wilson, *Radical Nationalist in Japan*, 104.

78. Tanaka, *Takabatake Motoyuki*, 283.

79. See, for example, *Kokka shakaishugi*, October 1931 and January 1933.

80. William Miles Fletcher, *Search for a New Order : Intellectuals and Fascism in Prewar Japan* (Chapel Hill: University of North Carolina Press, 1982).

81. Yoshitake Oka, *Konoe Fumimaro: A Political Biography* (Tokyo: University of Tokyo Press, 1983), 107.

82. Oka, *Konoe Fumimaro*, 114. The communist-inspired notion of planned economy was ultimately used by the military and reform bureaucrats during the war mobilization of the 1930s–40s (Bai Gao, *Economic Ideology and Japanese Industrial Policy: Developmentalism from 1931 to 1965* [Cambridge: Cambridge University Press, 1997]).

CONCLUSION

1. Hattori Ryūji, *Higashi Ajia kokusai kankyō no hendō to Nihon gaikō, 1918–1931* (Tokyo: Yūhikaku, 2001), 149–52; David J. Lu, *Agony of Choice: Matsuoka Yōsuke and the Rise and Fall of the Japanese Empire, 1880–1946* (Lanham, MD: Lexington Books, 2002), 46–49.

2. Edward J. Drea, *Japan's Imperial Army: Its Rise and Fall, 1853–1945* (Lawrence: University Press of Kansas, 2009), 163–66.

3. Tomita Takeshi, *Senkanki no Nisso kankei: 1917–1937* (Tokyo: Iwanami Shoten, 2010), 268–69.

4. Ugaki Kazushige, *Ugaki nikki* (Tokyo: Asahi Shinbunsha, 1956), 48–49; Sakai Tetsuya, *Taishō demokurashī taisei no hōkai: Naisei to gaikō* (Tokyo: Tokyō Daigaku Shuppankai, 1992), 174.

5. In contrast, central army headquarters in Tokyo did not plan any military action north of the South Manchurian Railway, since intrusion into a region considered to be within the Russian sphere of influence might provoke a Soviet military response. See Mark R. Peattie, *Ishiwara Kanji and Japan's Confrontation with the West* (Princeton, NJ: Princeton University Press, 1975), 97–100.

6. George A. Lensen, *The Damned Inheritance: The Soviet Union and the Manchurian Crises, 1924–1935* (Tallahassee, FL: Diplomatic Press, 1974), 480–83.

7. Chong-Sik Lee, *Revolutionary Struggle in Manchuria: Chinese Communism and Soviet Interest 1922–1945* (Berkeley: University of California Press, 1983), 96.

8. Ian Nish, *Japanese Foreign Policy in the Interwar Period* (Westport, CT: Praeger, 2002), 109.

9. Vassili Molodiakov, "The Tripartite Pact and the Soviet Union," *Proceedings of the International Forum on War History* (National Institute of Defense Studies, 2010), 146. http://www.nids.mod.go.jp/english/event/forum/e2010.html.

10. Jonathan Haslam, *The Soviet Union and the Threat from the East, 1933–1941: Moscow, Tokyo and the Prelude to the Pacific War* (Basingstoke: Macmillan, 1992).

11. Yukiko Koshiro, *Imperial Eclipse: Japan's Strategic Thinking about Continental Asia before August 1945* (Ithaca, NY: Cornell University Press, 2013), 17.

12. Hattori, *Higashi Ajia kokusai kankyō no hendō to Nihon gaikō, 1918–1931*, 230.

13. Lu, *Agony of Choice*, 199–205.

14. Koshiro, *Imperial Eclipse*, 39–40.

15. On the disintegration of Meiji ideological orthodoxy, see Tetsuo Najita, *Japan: The Intellectual Foundations of Modern Japanese Politics* (Chicago: University of Chicago Press, 1974), 102–48.

Bibliography

Adibekov, Grant M., and Haruki Wada, eds. *VKP(b), Komintern i Iaponiia, 1917–1941*. Moscow: Rosspen, 2001.

Akiyama Kiyoshi. *Nihon no hangyaku shisō*. Tokyo: Gendai Shichōsha, 1968.

Anderer, Paul. "Kobayashi and Dostoevsky." In *A Hidden Fire: Russian and Japanese Cultural Encounters, 1868–1926*, edited by Thomas J. Rimer, 38–48. Stanford, CA: Stanford University Press, 1995.

Anno, Tadashi. *National Identity and Great-Power Status in Russia and Japan: Non-Western Challengers to the Liberal International Order*. New York: Routledge, 2018.

Aoki Seiichi. "Shakai seikatsu no kekkan ni yotte." In *Roshia hihyō* (1919). Reprinted in *Taishō daizasshi*, 134–35. Tokyo: Ryūdō Shuppan, 1978.

Aoyama, Tomoko. "Japanese Literary Responses to the Russo-Japanese War." In *Russo-Japanese War in Cultural Perspective, 1904–05*, edited by David Wells and Sandra Wilson, 60–85. London: Palgrave Macmillan, 1999.

Arahata Kanson. *Arahata Kanson jiden*. Tokyo: Iwanami Shoten, 1975.

——. "Shindikarizumu no hatan." *Nihon rōdō shinbun*. February 10, 1921.

Arima Manabu. *"Kokusaika" no naka no teikoku Nihon: 1905–1924*. Tokyo: Chūō Kōronsha, 1999.

——. "Takabatake Motoyuki to kokka shakaishugi ha no dōkō." *Shigaku zasshi* 83, no. 10 (1974): 1–28.

Asada Masafumi. *Shiberia shuppei: Kindai Nihon no wasurerareta shichinen sensō*. Tokyo: Chūō Kōron Shinsha, 2016.

——. *Nichiro kindaishi: sensō to heiwa no hyakunen*. Tokyo: Kōdansha, 2018.

Asukai Masamichi. *Kindai bunka to shakaishugi*. Tokyo: Shōbunsha, 1970.

——. "Roshia daiichiji kakumei to Kōtoku Shūsui." *Shisō* 520 (1967): 1–21.

——. "Roshia kakumei to Nikō jiken." In *Taishōki no kyūshinteki jiyūshugi: Tōyō keizai shinpō wo chūshin toshite*, edited by Inoue Kiyoshi and Watanabe Tōru, 265–306. Tokyo: Tōyō Keizai Shinpō, 1972.

——. "Roshia kakumei to Ōsugi Sakae." *Gendai Riron* 4, no. 10 (1967): 34–42.

Bamba Nobuya. *Pacifism in Japan: The Christian and Socialist Tradition*. Kyoto: Minerva Press, 1980.

Bartlett, Rosamund. "Japonisme and Japanophobia: The Russo-Japanese War in Russian Cultural Consciousness." *Russian Review* 67, no. 1 (2008): 8–33.

Baryshev, Eduard. *Nichiro dōmei no jidai, 1914–1917: "Reigaitekina yūkō" no shinsō*. Fukuoka: Hanashoin, 2007.

Beard, M. Charles. *Cross Currents in Europe Today*. Boston: Marshall Jones, 1922.

Beasley, William G. *Japanese Imperialism, 1894–1945*. Oxford: Oxford University Press, 1991.

Beckmann, George M., and Genji Okubo. *The Japanese Communist Party, 1922–1945*. Stanford, CA: Stanford University Press, 1969.

Berton, Peter. *Russo-Japanese Relations, 1905–1917: From Enemies to Allies*. London: Routledge, 2012.

Berton, Peter, and Paul F. Langer. "Nobori Shomu: A Pioneer in Russo-Japanese Cultural Relations." In *The Russian Impact on Japan: Literature and Social Thought. Two Essays*, ed. Nobori Shomu et al., 13–20. Los Angeles: University of Southern California Press, 1981.

Berton, Peter, Paul F. Langer, and Rodger Swearingen. *Japanese Training and Research in the Russian Field*. Los Angeles, CA: University of Southern California Press, 1956.

Bisher, Jamie. *White Terror: Cossack Warlords of the Trans-Siberian*. London: Routledge, 2005.

Brandt, Conrad. *Stalin's Failure in China, 1924–1927*. Cambridge, MA: Harvard University Press, 1958.

Carr, E. H. *A History of Soviet Russia: The Bolshevik Revolution 1917–1923*. Harmondsworth, UK: Penguin Books, 1966.

Coox, Alvin D. *Nomonhan: Japan against Russia, 1939*. Stanford, CA: Stanford University Press, 1985.

Crump, John. "Anarchist Communism and Leadership: The Case of Iwasa Sakutarō." In *Leaders and Leadership in Japan*, edited by Ian Neary, 155–74. London: Routledge, 1996.

——. *Hatta Shūzō and Pure Anarchism in Interwar Japan*. New York: Palgrave Macmillan, 1993.

——. *The Origins of Socialist Thought in Japan*. London: St. Martin's Press, 1983.

Daba Hiroshi. "Gotō, Ioffe kōshō zengo no Gen'yōsha, Kokuryūkai." *Takushoku daigaku hyakunen shi kenkyū*, no. 6 (2001): 30–45.

Dirlik, Arif. *Anarchism in the Chinese Revolution*. Berkeley: University of California Press, 1991.

Drea, Edward J. *Japan's Imperial Army: Its Rise and Fall, 1853–1945*. Lawrence: University Press of Kansas, 2009.

Dunscomb, Paul. *Japan's Siberian Intervention, 1918–1922: "A Great Disobedience against the People."* Lanham, MD: Lexington Books, 2011.

Duus, Peter. *The Abacus and the Sword: The Japanese Penetration of Korea, 1895–1910*. Berkeley: University of California Press, 1995.

——. "Liberal Intellectuals and Social Conflict in Taishō Japan." In *Conflict in Modern Japanese History*, edited by Tetsuo Najita and Victor J. Koschmann, 412–40. Princeton, NJ: Princeton University Press, 1982.

——. "Ōyama Ikuo and the Search for Democracy." In *The Dilemmas of Growth in Prewar Japan*, edited by James W. Morley, 423–58. Princeton, NJ: Princeton University Press, 1971.

——. "Whig History, Japanese Style: The Min'yūsha Historians and the Meiji Restoration." *Journal of Asian Studies* 33, no. 3 (1974): 415–36.

Duus, Peter, and Irwin Scheiner. "Socialism, Liberalism, and Marxism, 1901–1931." In *The Cambridge History of Japan*, edited by Peter Duus, 6:654–710. Cambridge: Cambridge University Press, 1989.

Elleman, Bruce A. "The Soviet Union's Secret Diplomacy concerning the Chinese Eastern Railway, 1924–1925." *Journal of Asian Studies* 53, no. 2 (1994): 459–86.

Enomoto Takeaki. *Shiberia nikki*, 3 vols. Tokyo: Kaigun yūshūkai, 1935.

Esselstrom, Erik. *Crossing Empire's Edge: Foreign Ministry Police and Japanese Expansionism in Northeast Asia*. Honolulu: University of Hawaii Press, 2009.

——. "Rethinking the Colonial Conquest of Manchuria: The Japanese Consular Police in Jiandao, 1909–1937." *Modern Asian Studies* 39, no. 1 (2005): 39–75.

Eudin, Xenia J., and Robert C. North, eds. *Soviet Russia and the East, 1920–1927: A Documentary Survey*. Stanford, CA: Stanford University Press, 1957.

Ferguson, Joseph. *Japanese-Russian Relations, 1907–2007*. London: Routledge, 2008.

Fitzpatrick, Sheila. *The Russian Revolution*. Oxford: Oxford University Press, 2008.

Fletcher, William M. *Search for a New Order: Intellectuals and Fascism in Prewar Japan*. Chapel Hill: University of North Carolina Press, 1982.

Fujii Tadashi. *Nihon shakaishugi dōmei no rekishiteki igi*. Tokyo: Ōtsuki Shoten, 1978.

Fujiwara Akira. "Nihon guntai ni okeru kakumei to hankakumei." *Hitotsubashi University, Departmental Bulletin*, no. 10 (March 1969): 85–123.

Fuke Takahiro. *Mitsukawa Kametarō: Kōgai no kokorozashi nao sonsu*. Tokyo: Mineruva Shobō, 2016.

——. *Nihon Fashizumu ronsō: Taisen zen'ya no shisōkatachi*. Tokyo: Kawade Shobō, 2012.

——. "Sen kyūhyaku nijū nen shoki Nihon ni okeru Itaria fashizumu kan no kōsatsu." *Bunmei kōzō ron*, no. 3 (2007): 1–33.

——. "Sen kyūhyaku sanjū nendai shoki Nihon ni okeru kokka shakaishugi undō: Sono nachi tōron to 'fashizumu' ron ni shōten wo atete." *Shigaku zasshi*, no. 118 (April 2009): 1485–508.

——. "Sen kyūhyaku nijū nendai kōki ni okeru Takabatake Motoyuki no Itaria fashizumu ron ni tsuite." *Kirisutokyō shakai mondai kenkyū*, no. 56 (2008): 41–76.

——. *Senkanki Nihon no shakai shisō: "Chō kokka" he no furontia*. Kyoto: Jinbun Shoin, 2010.

Fukuda Tokuzō. "Nihon ni shakaishugi okoru naki ya." *Kyokutō jihō*, October 14, 1917.

——. *Reimeiroku*. Tokyo: Daitōkaku, 1920.

——. "Rōnō Roshia wo ika ni miru ka oyobi sono taisaku ika." *Chūō Kōron* (June 1919).

——. "Tadashiki rikai wo yōsu." In *Taishō daizasshi*, 132–33. Tokyo: Ryūdō Shuppan, 1978.

Fumoto Shinichi. "Russia's Expansion to the Far East and Its Impact on Early Meiji Japan's Korea Policy." In *Russia and Its Northeast Asian Neighbors: China, Japan, and Korea, 1858–1945*, edited by Kimitaka Matsuzato, 1–14. Lanham, MD: Lexington Books, 2018.

Gaimushō [Japanese Foreign Office]. *Nihon gaikō bunsho*. Vol. 1. Tokyo: Nihon Kokusai Kyōkai, 1953–64.

Gaimushō Hyakunenshi Hensan Iinkai, ed. *Gaimushō no hyakunen*. Vol. 1. Tokyo: Hara Shobō, 1969.

Gao, Bai. *Economic Ideology and Japanese Industrial Policy: Developmentalism from 1931 to 1965*. Cambridge: Cambridge University Press, 1997.

Garon, Sheldon. *The State and Labor in Modern Japan*. Berkeley: University of California Press, 1987.

Geifman, Anna. *Thou Shalt Kill: Revolutionary Terrorism in Russia, 1894–1917*. Princeton, NJ: Princeton University Press, 1996.

Gluck, Carol. *Japan's Modern Myths: Ideology in the Late Meiji Period*. Princeton, NJ: Princeton University Press, 1985.

Golovnin, Vasily. *Memoirs of a Captivity in Japan, 1811–1813*. Oxford: Oxford University Press, 1973.

Goodman, David G., and Miyazawa Masanori. *Jews in the Japanese Mind: The History and Uses of a Cultural Stereotype*. Lanham, MD: Lexington Books, 2000.

Gordon, Andrew. *Labor and Imperial Democracy in Prewar Japan*. Berkeley: University of California Press, 1991.

Gregor, James. *Marxism, Fascism, and Totalitarianism: Chapters in the Intellectual History of Radicalism*. Stanford, CA: Stanford University Press, 2009.

Gupta, Suman. *Marxism, History, and Intellectuals: Toward a Reconceptualized Transformative Socialism*. Madison, NJ: Fairleigh Dickinson University Press, 2000.

Hagiwara Shintarō. *Takao Heibē: Eikyū kakumei he no kishi.* Tokyo: Riberutēru no Kai, 1972.

Hama, Yukiko. "Russia from a Pan-Asianist View: Saburo Shimano and His Activities." *Ab Imperio,* no. 3 (2010): 227–43.

Han, Jung-Sun N. "Envisioning a Liberal Empire in East Asia: Yoshino Sakuzō in Taisho Japan." *Journal of Japanese Studies* 33, no. 2 (2007): 357–82.

Hara Takashi. *Hara Takashi nikki.* Edited by Hara Kei'ichirō. Tokyo: Kengensha, 1951.

Hara Teruyuki. "Japan Moves North: The Japanese Occupation of Northern Sakhalin (1920s)." In *Rediscovering Russia in Asia: Siberia and the Russian Far East,* edited by Stephen Kotkin and David Wolff, 55–67. Armonk, NY: M. E. Sharpe, 1995.

——. "The Korean Movement in the Russian Maritime Province, 1905–1922." In *Koreans in the Soviet Union,* edited by Dae-sook Suh, 1–23. Honolulu: University of Hawaii Press, 1987.

——. "Kyokutō Roshia ni okeru Chōsen dokuritsu undō to Nihon." *Sanzenri,* no. 17 (February 1979): 47–53.

——. "Nichiro sensōgo no Roshia kyokutō—chiiki seisaku to kokusai kankyō." *Roshia shi kenkyū,* no. 72 (2003): 6–22.

——. "Nikō jiken no shomondai." *Roshia shi kenkyū,* no. 23 (1975): 2–17.

——. *Shiberia shuppei: Kakumei to kanshō 1917–1922.* Tokyo: Chikuma Shobō, 1989.

Hashikawa Bunzō. "Kokka shakaishugi no hassō yōshiki: Kita Ikki, Takabatake Motoyuki wo chūshin ni." *Nihon seiji gakkai nenpō seijigaku* (December 1968): 104–38.

Hashiura Tokio. *Hashiura Tokio nikki.* Tokyo: Ganshisha, 1983.

Haslam, Jonathan. *The Soviet Union and the Threat from the East, 1933–1941: Moscow, Tokyo, and the Prelude to the Pacific War.* Basingstoke, UK: Macmillan, 1992.

Hata, Ikuhiko, and Alvin D. Coox. "Continental Expansion, 1905–1941." In *The Cambridge History of Japan,* edited by Peter Duus, 6:271–314. Cambridge: Cambridge University Press, 1989.

Hattori Ryūji. *Higashi Ajia kokusai kankyō no hendō to Nihon gaikō, 1918–1931.* Tokyo: Yūhikaku, 2001.

Havens, Thomas R. H. "Japan's Enigmatic Election of 1928." *Modern Asian Studies* 11, no. 4 (1977): 543–55.

Hobsbawm, E. J. *The Age of Extremes: A History of the World, 1914–1991.* New York: Vintage, 1996.

Hofmann, Reto. *The Fascist Effect: Japan and Italy, 1915–1952.* Ithaca, NY: Cornell University Press, 2015.

Hori Shigeru. "'Kokka shakaishugisha: Takabatake Motoyuki to 'Kakushin Kanryō.'" *Seiji keizai shigaku,* no. 566 (2014): 1–23.

Hosoya Chihiro. "Japan's Foreign Policy toward Russia." In *Japan's Foreign Policy, 1868–1941: A Research Guide,* edited by James W. Morley and James B. Crowley, 340–406. New York: Columbia University Press, 1974.

——. "Nihon to Koruchāku seiken shōnin mondai." *Hitotsubashi daigaku hōgaku kenkyū,* no. 3 (1961): 13–135.

——. *Shiberia shuppei no shiteki kenkyū.* Tokyo: Iwanami Shoten, 2005.

Hoston, Germaine. "Marxism and National Socialism in Taishō Japan: The Thought of Takabatake Motoyuki." *Journal of Asian Studies* 44, no. 1 (1984): 43–64.

——. *Marxism and the Crisis of Development in Prewar Japan.* Princeton, NJ: Princeton University Press, 1986.

——. *The State, Identity, and the National Question in China and Japan.* Princeton, NJ: Princeton University Press, 1994.

——. "Tenkō: Marxism and the National Question in Prewar Japan." *Polity* 16, no. 1 (1983): 96–118.

Humphreys, Leonard A. *The Way of the Heavenly Sword: The Japanese Army in the 1920s*. Stanford, CA: Stanford University Press, 1995.

Hwang, Dongyoun. *Anarchism in Korea: Independence, Transnationalism, and the Question of National Development, 1919–1984*. New York: State University of New York Press, 2016.

——. "Beyond Independence: The Korean Anarchist Press in China and Japan in the 1920s and 1930s." *Asian Studies Review* 31, no. 1 (2007): 3–23.

Hyndman, Henry. *The Evolution of Revolution*. London: Hyndman Literary Trust, 1920.

Inoue, Takutoshi, and Yagi, Kiichirō. "Two Inquiries on the Divide: Tokuzo Fukuda and Hajime Kawakami." In *Economic Thought and Modernization in Japan*, edited by Sugihara Shiro and Tanaka Toshihiro, 60–77. Cheltenham, UK: Edward Elgar, 1998.

Inumaru Gi'ichi. *Daiichiji kyōsantō shi no kenkyū: Zōho Nihon kyōsantō no sōritsu*. Tokyo: Aoki Shoten, 1993.

Iriye, Akira. *After Imperialism*. Cambridge, MA: Harvard University Press, 1965.

Ishikawa, Yoshihiro. "Chinese Marxism in the Early 20th Century and Japan." *Sino-Japanese Studies*, no. 14 (April 2002): 24–34.

——. *The Formation of the Chinese Communist Party*. New York: Columbia University Press, 2013.

Itō Akira. *Tennōsei to shakaishugi*. Tokyo: Keisō Shobō, 1988.

Itō Masanori. "Shiberia shuppei go no tōshin tetsudō mondai (1924–1928): Nisso kankei no ichi sokumen." *Sophia Historical Studies* 36 (1991): 29–50.

Itō Narihiko. "Nihon shakaishugi undō to Rōsa Rukusenburugu." *Shisō* (October 1971): 39–55.

Itō Noe. "Museifu no jijitsu." In *Itō Noe zenshū*. Vol. 2. Tokyo: Gakugei Shorin, 2000.

Itō Takashi. *Shōwa shoki seiji shi kenkyū*. Tokyo: Tokyo Daigaku Shuppankai, 1969.

Ito Yushi. *Yamaji Aizan and His Time: Nationalism and Debating Japanese History*. Leiden: Brill, 2007.

Iwamura Toshio. *Kominterun to Nihon kyōsantō no seiritsu*. Tokyo: San'ichi Shobō, 1977.

Izao Tomio. "Shiberia shuppei kōzō no henyō: Terauchi naikaku oyobi gaikō chōsakai wo chūshin ni shite." *Hōsei kenkyū* 66, no. 4 (2000): 153–84.

——. "Shiberia shuppei ron no kōzō to haikei." *Kyūdai hōgaku*, no. 78 (1999): 325–61.

——. *Shoki Shiberia shuppei no kenkyū: "Atarashiki kyūseigun" kōsō no tōjō to tenkai*. Fukuoka: Kyūshū Daigaku Shuppankai, 2003.

Jansen, Marius. *The Japanese and Sun Yat-Sen*. Cambridge, MA: Harvard University Press, 1954.

Japan Weekly Chronicle. October 27, 1927; March 8, 1928.

Kan, Dokusan. "Nihon teikokushugi no chōsen shihai to Roshia kakumei." *Rekishigaku kenkyū*, no. 329 (1969): 37–76.

Karl, Rebecca. "Creating Asia: China in the World at the Beginning of the Twentieth Century." *American Historical Review* 103, no. 4 (1998): 1096–118.

Kasza, Gregory J. "Fascism from Below? A Comparative Perspective on the Japanese Right, 1931–1936." *Journal of Contemporary History* 19, no. 4 (1984): 607–29.

——. *The State and the Mass Media in Japan, 1918–1945*. Berkeley: University of California Press, 1993.

Katō Tetsurō. "1922-nen 9-gatsu no Nihon kyōsantō kōryō." *Ōhara shakai mondai kenkyū zasshi*, no. 481 (1998): 43–60 (pt. 1); no. 482 (1998): 38–57 (pt. 2).

——. *Mosukuwa de shukuseisareta Nihonjin: 30-nendai Kyōsantō to Kunisaki Teidō,*
Yamamoto Kenzō no higeki. Tokyo: Aoki Shoten, 1994.

Kayahara Kazan. "Konton yori konton he." In *Roshia hihyō* (1919). Reprinted in *Taishō*
daizasshi, 137–38. Tokyo: Ryūdō Shuppan, 1978.

Kemuyama Sentarō. "Raido wo itashimeyo." In *Roshia hihyō* (1919). Reprinted in
Taishō daizasshi, 135. Tokyo: Ryūdō Shuppan, 1978.

Kennan, George. *Soviet-American Relations, 1917–1920.* Princeton, NJ: Princeton University Press, 1956.

Khuri-Makdisi, Ilham. *The Eastern Mediterranean and the Making of Global Radicalism, 1860–1914.* Berkeley: University of California Press, 2010.

Kikuchi Masanori. *Roshia kakumei to Nihonjin.* Tokyo: Chikuma Shobō, 1973.

Kim, Key-hiuk. *The Last Phase of the East Asian World Order: Korea, Japan, and the*
Chinese Empire, 1860–1882. Berkeley: University of California Press, 1980.

Kindai Nihon Shiryō Kenkyūkai, ed. *Tokubetsu yōshisatsujin jōsei ippan.* Zoku (Vol.) 2.
Tokyo: Meiji Bunken Shiryō Kankōkai, 1957.

Kitaoka Shin'ichi. *Gotō Shinpei: Gaikō to bijon.* Tokyo: Chūō Kōronsha, 1988.

Kobayashi Hideo and Rūji Sasaki. "Fuyu no jidai kara no dakkyo: Jūgatsu kakumei to
Nihon." *Rekishigaku kenkyū,* no. 515 (April 1983): 35–38.

Kobayashi Yukio. *Nisso seiji gaikōshi: Roshia kakumei to Chian ijihō.* Tokyo: Yūhikaku,
1985.

Kolakowski, Leszek. *Main Currents of Marxism: Its Origins, Growth, and Dissolution.*
Oxford: Oxford University Press, 1978.

Kondō Eizō. *Komuminterun no misshi.* Tokyo: Bunka Hyōronsha, 1949.

Kondō Kenji. *Ichi museifu shugisha no kaisō.* Tokyo: Heibonsha, 1965.

Konishi, Sho. *Anarchist Modernity Cooperatism and Japanese-Russian Intellectual Relations in Modern Japan.* Cambridge, MA: Harvard University Asia Center, 2013.

Koshiro, Yukiko. *Imperial Eclipse: Japan's Strategic Thinking about Continental Asia*
before August 1945. Ithaca, NY: Cornell University Press, 2013.

Kublin, Hyman. *Asian Revolutionary: The Life of Sen Katayama.* Princeton, NJ: Princeton
University Press, 1964.

——. "Japanese Socialists and the Russo-Japanese War." *Journal of Modern History* 22
(December 1950): 322–39.

——. "The Origins of the Japanese Socialist Tradition." *Journal of Politics* 14, no. 2
(1952): 257–80.

Kume Shigeru. *Kieta shinbun kisha.* Tokyo: Yuki Shobō, 1968.

Kuo, Heng-yu, and M. L. Titarenko, eds. *VKP(b), Komintern i Kitai.* Moscow: Buklet,
1994.

Kurokawa Iori. *Teikoku ni kōsuru shakai undō: Daiichiji Nihon Kyosantō no shisō to*
undō. Tokyo: Yūshisha, 2014.

Kurono Taeru. *Teikoku kokubō hōshin no kenkyū: Riku-Kaigun kokubō shisō no tenkai*
to tokuchō. Tokyo: Sōwasha, 2000.

Kurosawa Fumitaka. "Edo, Meiji ki no Nichiro kankei: Roshia imēji wo chūshin ni."
Nihon rekishi 802, no. 3 (2015): 53–72.

——. "Meiji sue, Taishō shoki no Nichiro kankei: Teki ka mikata ka, hatamata tomo
ka?" *Journal of the Diplomatic Archives* 30, no. 3 (2017): 57–74.

Large, Stephen S. *Organized Workers and Socialist Politics in Interwar Japan.* Cambridge: Cambridge University Press, 1981.

Lee, Chong-Sik. *Revolutionary Struggle in Manchuria: Chinese Communism and Soviet*
Interest 1922–1945. Berkeley: University of California Press, 1983.

Lenin, Vladimir I. "Backward Europe and Advanced Asia." *Pravda,* May 18, 1913.
Marxist Internet Archive. http://www.marxists.org.

——. *Essential Works of Lenin*. New York: Dover Publications, 2012.

Lensen, George. *The Damned Inheritance: The Soviet Union and the Manchurian Crises, 1924–1935*. Tallahassee, FL: Diplomatic Press, 1974.

——. "Early Russo-Japanese Relations." *Far Eastern Quarterly* 10, no. 1 (1950): 2–37.

——. "Japan and Tsarist Russia—the Changing Relationships, 1875–1917." *Jahrbücher für Geschichte Osteuropas* 10, no. 3 (1962): 337–48.

——. *Japanese Recognition of the USSR: Soviet-Japanese Relations, 1921–1930*. Tokyo: Sophia University, 1970.

——. *The Russian Push toward Japan: Russo-Japanese Relations, 1697–1875*. Princeton, NJ: Princeton University Press, 1959.

Linkhoeva, Tatiana. "New Revolutionary Agenda: The Interwar Japanese Left on the 'Chinese Revolution.'" *Cross-Currents* 6, no. 2 (2017): 83–104.

Lu, David J. *Agony of Choice: Matsuoka Yōsuke and the Rise and Fall of the Japanese Empire, 1880–1946*. Lanham, MD: Lexington Books, 2002.

Mackie, Vera. "Motherhood and Pacifism in Japan, 1900–1937." *Hecate* 14, no. 2 (1988): 28–49.

Malozemoff, Andrew. *Russian Far Eastern Policy 1881–1904 with Special Emphasis on the Causes of the Russo-Japanese War*. New York: Octagon Books, 1977.

Marshall, Byron. *Capitalism and Nationalism in Prewar Japan: Ideology of the Business Elite, 1868–1941*. Stanford, CA: Stanford University Press, 1967.

Matsumoto Ken'ichi. *Ōkawa Shūmei*. Tokyo: Iwanami Shoten, 2004.

Matsuo Takayoshi. "Daiichiji taisengo no fusen undō." In *Taishōki no seiji to shakai*, edited by Inoue Kiyoshi, 159–204. Tokyo: Iwanami Shoten, 1969.

——. "Sōritsuki Nihon kyōsantō no tame no oboegaki." In *Kyoto daigaku bungakubu kenkyū kiyō*, no. 19 (March 1979): 67–168.

——. "Wasurerareta kakumeika Takao Heibē." *Shisō*, no. 577 (July 1972): 88–113.

Matsuura Masataka. *"Dai Tōa Sensō" wa naze okita no ka: Han Ajia shugi no seiji keizaishi*. Nagoya: Nagoya Daigaku Shuppankai, 2010.

Matsuzawa, Hiroaki. *Nihon shakaishugi no shisō*. Tokyo: Chikuma Shobō, 1973.

McDermott, Kevin. "The History of the Comintern in the Light of New Documents." In *International Communism and the Communist International, 1919–43*, edited by Tim Rees and Andrew Thorpe, 31–40. Manchester, UK: Manchester University Press, 1998.

McDermott, Kevin, and Jeremy Agnew. *The Comintern: A History of International Communism from Lenin to Stalin*. Basingstoke, UK: Macmillan, 1996.

Mcquade, Joseph. "The *New Asia* of Rash Behari Bose: India, Japan, and the Limits of the International, 1912–1945." *Journal of World History* 27, no. 4 (2016): 641–67.

Mikhailova, Yulia. "Soviet-Japanese Studies on the Problem of the Meiji Ishin and the Development of Capitalism in Japan." In *War, Revolution, and Japan*, edited by Ian Neary, 33–38. London: Routledge, 1993.

Miki Kiyoshi. "Shesutofuteki fuan ni tsuite." *Kaizō* (September 1934): 392–405.

Miller, Owen. "The Idea of Stagnation in Korean Historiography from Fukuda Tokuzō to the New Right." *Korean Histories* 2, no. 1 (2010): 3–12.

Mimura, Janis. *Planning for Empire: Reform Bureaucrats and the Japanese Wartime State*. Ithaca, NY: Cornell University Press, 2011.

Mitani Taichirō. *Nihon seitō seiji no keisei: Hara Kei seiji shidō no tenkai*. Tokyo: Tōkyō Daigaku Shuppankai, 1995.

Mitchell, Richard H. *Janus-Faced Justice: Political Criminals in Imperial Japan*. Honolulu: University of Hawaii Press, 1992.

——. "Japan's Peace Preservation Law of 1925: Its Origins and Significance." *Monumenta Nipponica* 28, no. 3 (1973): 317–45.

Mitsukawa Kametarō. *Mitsukawa Kametarō: Chiiki, chikyū jijō no keimōsha.* Edited by Christopher W. Szpilman. Tokyo: Takushoku Daigaku Shuppankyoku, 2001.

———. *Mitsukawa Kametarō shokanshū: Kita Ikki, Ōkawa Shūmei, Nishida Mitsugi ra no shokan.* Edited by Yūichi Hasegawa, Christopher W. Szpilman, and Imazu Toshiaki. Tokyo: Ronsōsha, 2012.

———. *Sangoku kanshō igo.* Edited by Yūichi Hasegawa. Tokyo: Ronsōsha, 2004.

———. *Sekai gensei to Dai Nihon.* Tokyo: Kōchisha Shuppanbu, 1926.

———. "Shingunkoku Roshia no shutsugen to Nihon." *Chūgai*, no. 1 (June 1921).

———. "Taihō kensetsu no risō." In *Shakai kyōiku kenkyūjo rīfuretto.* Tokyo: Shakai Kyōiku Kenkyūjo, 1925.

Mochizuki, Tetsuo. "Japanese Perceptions of Russian Literature in the Meiji and Taisho Eras." In *A Hidden Fire: Russian and Japanese Cultural Encounters, 1868–1926*, edited by J. Thomas Rimer, 17–21. Stanford, CA: Stanford University Press, 1995.

Molodiakov, Vassili [Vasilii]. *Goto Simpei i russko-iaponskie otnosheniia.* Moscow: AIRO, 2006.

———, ed. *Katsura Taro, Goto Simpei i Rossiia: Sbornik dokumentov 1907–1929.* Moscow: AIRO, 2005.

———. *Rossiia i Iaponiia:V poiskakh soglasiia, 1905–1945.* Moscow: AIRO, 2012.

———. *Rossiia i Iaponiia: Zolotoi vek (1905–1916).* Moscow: Prosveshchenie, 2008.

———. "The Tripartite Pact and the Soviet Union." *Proceedings of the International Forum on War History (National Institute of Defense Studies)* (2010): 145–52.

Morley, James. *The Japanese Thrust into Siberia, 1918.* New York: Columbia University Press, 1957.

Morris-Suzuki, Tessa. "Lines in the Snow: Imagining the Russo-Japanese Frontier." *Pacific Affairs* 72, no. 1 (1999): 57–77.

Morris, Ivan. *Nationalism and the Right Wing in Japan: A Study of Post-War Trends.* Westport, CT: Greenwood Press, 1974.

Murata Yōichi. ed. *Shiryōshū Kominterun to Nihon.* Tokyo: Ōtsuki Shoten, 1986.

———, ed. *Shiryōshū shoki Nihon kyōsantō to Kominterun.* Tokyo: Ōtsuki Shoten, 1993.

Murobuse Kōshin. "Kageki shisō to Nihon." *Roshia hihyō* (1919). Reprinted in *Taishō daizasshi*, 138–39. Tokyo: Ryūdō Shuppan, 1978.

———. "Kokka shakaishugi no hihyō." *Hihyō* (July 1919).

Najita, Tetsuo. *Japan: The Intellectual Foundations of Modern Japanese Politics.* Chicago: University of Chicago Press, 1974.

Nakamura Yoshihisa and Tobe Ryoichi. "The Imperial Japanese Army and Politics." *Armed Forces and Society* 14, no. 4 (1988): 511–25.

Nakano Seigō. "Nichiro shinkō no shinkachi." *Warekan* (March 1925).

Narangoa, Li. "Japanese Geopolitics and the Mongol Lands, 1915–1945." *European Journal of East Asian Studies* 3, no. 1 (2004): 45–67.

Nicolaevsky, Boris. "Russia, Japan, and the Pan-Asiatic Movement to 1925." *Far Eastern Quarterly*, no. 3 (1949): 259–95.

Nish, Ian. *Japanese Foreign Policy in the Interwar Period.* Westport, CT: Praeger, 2002.

———. *The Origins of the Russo-Japanese War.* London: Routledge, 1985.

Nobori Shomu and Akamatsu Katsumaro. *The Russian Impact on Japan: Literature and Social Thought. Two Essays.* Los Angeles: University of Southern California Press, 1981.

Nolte, Sharon H. *Liberalism in Modern Japan: Ishibashi Tanzan and His Teachers, 1905–1960.* Berkeley: University of California Press, 1986.

Nomura Kōichi. "Tairiku mondai no imēji to jittai." In *Kindai Nihon seiji shisōshi*, Vol. 4, edited by Matsumoto Sannosuke and Hashikawa Bunzō, 52–108. Tokyo: Yūhikaku, 1970.

Notehelfer, F. G. *Kōtoku Shūsui: Portrait of a Japanese Radical*. Cambridge: Cambridge University Press, 1971.

Ōba Kakō. "Kagekihashugi to Minshūshugi." In *Roshia hihyō* (1919). Reprinted in *Taishō daizasshi*, 136–37. Tokyo: Ryūdō Shuppan, 1978.

Ogino Fujio. *Shoki shakaishugi shisōron*. Tokyo: Fuji Shuppan, 1993.

Oguma, Eiji. *A Genealogy of Japanese Self-Images*. Melbourne, VIC: Trans Pacific, 2002.

Oguri Katsuya. "Chian ijihō hantai ron no shosō." *Hōgaku kenkyū* 68, no. 1 (1995): 509–37.

Oikawa Eijiro. "The Relation between National Socialism and Social Democracy in the Formation of the International Policy of the Shakai Taishuto." In *Nationalism and Internationalism in Imperial Japan: Autonomy, Asian Brotherhood, or World Citizenship?*, edited by Dick Stegewerns, 197–228. London: RoutledgeCurzon, 2003.

Oka, Yoshitake. *Konoe Fumimaro: A Political Biography*. Tokyo: University of Tokyo Press, 1983.

Okamoto Hiroshi. "Taishō shakaishugi no kokusai ninshiki to gaikō hihan. Yamakawa Hitoshi no baai." In *Nihon gaikō no kokusai ninshiki: Sono shiteki tenkai*, no. 51 (1974): 87–108.

Okamoto, Shumpei. *The Japanese Oligarchy and the Russo-Japanese War*. New York: Columbia University Press, 1970.

Ōkawa Shūmei. "5/15 Jiken jinmon chōsho." In *Ōkawa Shūmei zenshū*. Vol. 5. Tokyo: Kankōkai, 1962.

——. "Atarashiki sekai sen." *Kaihō* (May 1920).

——. *Fukkō Ajia no shomondai*. Tokyo: Meiji Shobō, 1939.

——. "Sovieto renpō no taigai seisaku." In *Ōkawa Shūmei zenshū*. Vol. 4. Tokyo: Kankōkai, 1962.

Okudaira Yasuhiro, ed. *Gendaishi shiryō*. Vol. 45: *Chian ijihō*. Tokyo: Misuzu Shobō, 1973.

Ono, Keishi. "The Siberian Intervention and Japanese Society." In *Japan and the Great War*, edited by Oliviero Frattolillo and Antony Best, 93–115. London: Palgrave Macmillan, 2015.

Ōsugi Sakae. *Ana-Boru ronsō*. Tokyo: Dōjidaisha, 2005.

——. "Chishiki kaikyū ni atau." *Rōdō undō*. January 1920.

——. *Nihon dasshutsuki*. Tokyo: Iwanami Shoten, 1971.

——. "Nihon no unmei." In *Ōsugi Sakae shū: Kindai Nihon shisō taikei* 20:256–57. Tokyo: Chikuma Shobō, 1974.

——. *Ōsugi Sakae zenshū. Roshia kakumei ron*. Vol. 7. Tokyo: Gendai Shichōsha, 1963.

——. "Rōdō undō no seishin." *Rōdō Undō*, no. October (1919).

——. "Tettei shakai seisaku." *Rōdō undo* (November 1919).

Ōyama Ikuo. "Rokoku kagekiha no jisseiryoku ni taisuru kashōshi to kono seiji shisō no kachi ni taisuru kadaishi." *Chūō kōron* (May 1918).

——. "Sekai no minshūkateki keikō to Rokoku kakumei." *Chūō kōron* (April 1917).

Pak, Boris. *Koreitsy v Rossiiskoi imperii*. Moscow: Moskovskii gosudarstvennyi universitet, 1993.

——. *Koreitsy v Sovetskoi Rossii: 1917–konets 30-kh godov*. Irkutsk: Irkutskii gosudarstvennyi pedagogicheskii institut, 1995.

Peattie, Mark R. *Ishiwara Kanji and Japan's Confrontation with the West*. Princeton, NJ: Princeton University Press, 1975.

Podalko, Petr. *Iaponiia v sud'bakh rossiian: Ocherki istorii tsarskoi diplomatii i rossiiskoi diaspory v Iaponii*. Moscow: Institut vostokovedeniia Rossiiskoi akademii nauk, 2004.

Popov, Nikita A. *Oni s nami srazalis' za vlast' sovetov: Kitaiskie dobrovol'tsy na frontakh grazhdanskoi voiny v Rossii (1918–1922).* Leningrad: Lenizdat, 1959.

Riddell, John. *To See the Dawn: Baku, 1920—First Congress of the Peoples of the East.* New York: Pathfinder, 1993.

Saaler, Sven. "Fukushima Yasumasa's Travels in Central Asia and Siberia: Silk Road Romanticism, Military Reconnaissance, or Modern Exploration." In *Japan on the Silk Road: Encounters and Perspectives of Politics and Culture in Eurasia,* edited by Selçuk Esenbel, 69–86. Leiden: Brill, 2018.

——. "Pan-Asianism in Modern Japanese History: Overcoming the Nation, Creating a Region, Forging an Empire." In *Pan-Asianism in Modern Japanese History: Colonialism, Regionalism, and Borders,* edited by Victor Koschmann and Sven Saaler, 1–18. London: Routledge, 2007.

Sablin, Ivan, and Kuchinsky, Alexander. "Making the Korean Nation in the Russian Far East, 1863–1926." *Nationalities Papers* 45, no. 5 (2017): 798–814.

Saich, Tony. *The Origins of the First United Front in China: The Role of Sneevliet.* Leiden: Brill, 1991.

Sakai Tetsuya. "The Soviet Factor in Japanese Foreign Policy, 1923–1937." *Acta Slavica Iaponica* 6 (1988): 27–40.

——. *Taishō demokurashī taisei no hōkai: Naisei to gaikō.* Tokyo: Tokyō Daigaku Shuppankai, 1992.

Sakai Toshihiko, "Shiberia teppei no yōkyū." *Shinshakai hyōron* (June 1920).

——. "L. F. kai no kūki." *Shinshakai hyōron* (July–August 1920).

Sakamoto Masako. *Zaibatsu to teikokushugi: Mitsui Bussan to Chūgoku.* Kyoto: Mineruva Shobō, 2003.

Satō Masaru. *Takabatake Motoyuki no bōrei: Aru kokka shakaishugisha no kikenna shisō.* Tokyo: Shinchōsha, 2018.

Saveliev, Igor. "Militant Diaspora: Korean Immigrants and Guerrillas in Early Twentieth Century Russia." *Forum of International Development Studies* 26 (2004): 147–62.

Saveliev, Igor, and Yuri Pestushko. "Dangerous Rapprochement : Russia and Japan in the First World War, 1914–1916." *Acta Slavica Iaponica* 18 (2001): 19–41.

Saville, John. *The Politics of Continuity: British Foreign Policy and the Labour Government, 1945–46.* London: Verso Books, 1993.

Scalapino, Robert A. *The Japanese Communist Movement, 1920–1966.* Berkeley: University of California Press, 1967.

Schimmelpenninck van der Oye, David. *Toward the Rising Sun: Russian Ideologies of Empire and the Path to War with Japan.* DeKalb: Northern Illinois University Press, 2001.

Schlesinger, Jonathan. *A World Trimmed with Fur: Wild Things, Pristine Places, and the Natural Fringes of Qing Rule.* Stanford, CA: Stanford University Press, 2017.

Seki Shizuo. *"Taishō" saikō: kibō to fuan no jidai.* Kyoto: Mineruva Shobō, 2007.

Shea, George T. *Leftwing Literature in Japan: A Brief History of the Proletarian Literary Movement.* Tokyo: Hosei University Press, 1964.

Shibata Yoshimasa. "Shiberia shuppeiki tairo bōeki gyōsha shiensaku to Nichiro jitsugyō kabushiki gaisha no katsudō." *Tōyō kenkyū* 195, no. 1 (2015): 1–45.

Shulatov, Yaroslav. "Chōsen mondai wo meguru Nichiro kankei (1905–1907)." *Surabu kenkyū,* no. 54 (2007): 183–205.

Siniawer, Eiko M. "Liberalism Undone: Discourses on Political Violence in Interwar Japan." *Modern Asian Studies* 45, no. 4 (2011): 973–1002.

——. *Ruffians, Yakuza, Nationalists: The Violent Politics of Modern Japan, 1860–1960.* Ithaca, NY: Cornell University Press, 2008.

Skya, Walter. *Japan's Holy War: The Ideology of Radical Shinto Ultranationalism.* Durham, NC: Duke University Press, 2009.

Smith, Henry D. *Japan's First Student Radicals.* Cambridge, MA: Harvard University Press, 1973.

Stanley, Thomas. *Ōsugi Sakae, Anarchist in Taishō Japan: The Creativity of the Ego.* Cambridge, MA: Council on East Asian Studies, Harvard University, 1982.

Stephan, John J. *The Russian Far East: A History.* Stanford, CA: Stanford University Press, 1994.

Sternhell, Zeev. "The 'Anti-Materialist' Revision of Marxism as an Aspect of the Rise of Fascist Ideology." *Journal of Contemporary History* 22, no. 3 (1987): 379–400.

Storry, Richard. *The Double Patriots: A Study of Japanese Nationalism.* Boston: Houghton Mifflin, 1957.

Suda Teiichi. "Shihaisō ni okeru seiji rinri no keisha: Nisso kōshō shi wo chūshin toshite." *Shisō,* no. 391 (1957): 75–87.

Suny, Ronald G. *The Soviet Experiment: Russia, the USSR, and the Successor States.* Oxford: Oxford University Press, 1998.

Swearingen, Rodger, and Paul Langer. *Red Flag in Japan: International Communism in Action, 1919–1951.* New York: Greenwood Press, 1968.

Szpilman, Christopher. "Between Pan-Asianism and Nationalism: Mitsukawa Kametarō and His Campaign to Reform Japan and Liberate Asia." In *Pan-Asianism in Modern Japanese History: Colonialism, Regionalism and Borders,* edited by Victor Koschmann and Sven Saaler, 87–100. London: Routledge, 2007.

——. "The Dream of One Asia: Ōkawa Shūmei and Japanese Pan-Asianism." In *The Japanese Empire in East Asia and Its Postwar Legacy,* edited by Harald Fuess, 49–63. Munich: Iudicium Verlag, 1998.

——. "Kaidai." In *Mitsukawa Kametarō: Chiiki, chikyū jijō no keimōsha,* edited by Christopher Szpilman. Vol. 1, 441–75. Tokyo: Takushoku Daigaku Shuppankyoku, 2001.

——. "Kanokogi Kazunobu: Pioneer of Platonic Fascism and Imperial Pan-Asianism." *Monumenta Nipponica* 2, no. 2 (2013): 233–80.

——. "Kita Ikki and the Politics of Coercion." *Modern Asian Studies* 36, no. 2 (2002): 467–90.

——. "Mitsukawa Kametarō: A Brief Biographical Sketch." In *Mitsukawa Kametarō: Chiiki, chikyū jijō no keimōsha,* edited by Christopher Szpilman. 512–20. Tokyo: Takushoku Daigaku Shuppankyoku, 2001.

——. "The Politics of Cultural Conservatism: The National Foundation Society in the Struggle Against Foreign Ideas in Prewar Japan, 1918–1936." PhD diss. New Haven: Yale University, 1993.

Takabatake Motoyuki. *Hihan marukusushugi.* Tokyo: Nihon Hyōronsha, 1929.

——. *Jiko wo kataru.* Tokyo: Jinbunkai shuppanbu, 1928.

——. "Kageki undō torishimari hōan: Seitō katsu yūkō." *Kaihō* (April 1922).

——. "Kagekiha no tachiba wo ronzu." *Kokka shakaishugi,* no. 4 (August 1919).

——. "Kakumei kachū no rodoku." *Shinshakai* (May 1917).

——. "Kokka shakaishugi de yuku." *Kaizō* (March 1923).

——. "Kokka shakaishugi no irowake." *Kokka shakaishugi* (April 1, 1919).

——. "Marukusu mujun to Kawakami Hajime no mujun." *Kaihō* (November 1921).

——. "Mussorini wa hi kōshitsu chūshin shugisha." *Yomiuri shinbun* (December 1927).

——. "Nichibei mondai hihan," *Shūkan Nihon* 6 (April 1924).

——. *Nihon shakaishugi taigi.* Tokyo: Nihon Shakaishugi Kenkyūjo, 1932.

——. "Rōdōsha ni kokka arashimeyo." *Kokka shakaishugi* (April 1919).

——. "Rōnō teikokushugi no kyokutō shinshutsu." *Kaizō* (April 1927).

——. "Rōsōkai to Reimeikai." *Shinshakai* (February 1919).

——. "Shakaishugi kenkyū mondai." *Kokka shakaishugi* (June 1919).

——. "Shōhisha hon'i no taishū undō." In *Genmetsusha no shakaikan*. Tokyo: Daitōkaku, 1923.

——. "Tachiba no tachiba kara no seiji undō to keizai undō." *Shinshakai* (May 1918).

——. "Teikokushugi no shinkyū." *Shunjū* (December 1927).

Takeuchi Yoshimi. *Nihon to Ajia*. Tokyo: Chikuma Shobō, 1993.

Tanaka Masato. *Takabatake Motoyuki: Nihon no kokka shakaishugi*. Tokyo: Gendai Hyōronsha, 1978.

Tanaka Sōgorō. *Kita Ikki: Nihonteki fashisuto no shōchō*. Tokyo: Miraisha, 1959.

Tang, Peter. *Russian and Soviet Policy in Manchuria and Outer Mongolia, 1911–1931*. Durham, NC: Duke University Press, 1959.

Tanin, O., and E. Yohan. *Militarism and Fascism in Japan*. New York: International Publishers, 1934.

Teramoto Yasutoshi. *Nichiro sensō igo no Nihon gaikō: Pawā poritikusu no naka no Man-Kan mondai*. Tokyo: Shinzansha, 1999.

Tierney, Robert T. *Monster of the Twentieth Century: Kōtoku Shūsui and Japan's First Anti-Imperialist Movement*. Berkeley: University of California Press, 2015.

Tikhonov, Vladimir. "A Russian Radical and East Asia in the Early Twentieth Century: Sudzilovsky, China, and Japan." *Cross-Currents: East Asian History and Culture Review*, no. 18 (2016): 51–76.

Tipton, Elise. *The Japanese Police State: The Tokkō in Interwar Japan*. Honolulu: University of Hawaii Press, 1990.

Togawa, Tsuguo. "The Japanese View of Russia before and after the Meiji Restoration." In *A Hidden Fire: Russian and Japanese Cultural Encounters, 1868–1926*, edited by Thomas J. Rimer, 214–27. Stanford, CA: Stanford University Press, 1995.

Tomita Takeshi. "Roshia Kakumei to Nihonjin." *Shisō* 1119 (July 2017): 97–115.

——. *Senkanki no Nisso kankei: 1917–1937*. Tokyo: Iwanami Shoten, 2010.

Tomita Takeshi and Wada Haruki, eds. *Shiryōshū Kominterun to Nihon kyōsantō*. Tokyo: Iwanami shoten, 2014.

Tsurumi, Patricia E. "Feminism and Anarchism in Japan: Takamure Itsue, 1894–1964." *Bulletin of Concerned Asian Scholars* 17, no. 2 (1985): 2–19.

Tsurumi Yūsuke. *Gotō Shinpei*. Tokyo: Fujiwara Shoten, 2004–6.

Tsuzuki, Chushichi. "Kotoku, Osugi, and Japanese Anarchism." *Hitotsubashi Journal of Social Studies* 3, no. 1 (1966): 30–42.

Uchida Kōsai. *Uchida Kōsai kankei shiryō shūsei*. Edited by Michihiko Kobayashi. Tokyo: Kashiwa Shobō, 2012.

Uehara Yūsaku. *Uehara Yūsaku nikki*. Tokyo: Shōyū Kurabu, 2011.

Uesugi Shinkichi. "Kokutai no seika wo hatsuyō." *Kaizō* (March 1923).

Ugaki Kazushige. *Ugaki nikki*. Tokyo: Asahi Shinbunsha, 1956.

Ul'ianovskii, Rostislav. *Komintern i Vostok: Bor'ba za leninskuiu strategiiu i taktiku v natsional'no-osvoboditel'nom dvizhenii*. Moscow: Nauka, 1969.

Umeda Toshihide. *Shakai undō to shuppan bunka: Kindai Nihon ni okeru chiteki kyōdōtai no keisei*. Tokyo: Ochanomizu Shobō, 1998.

Umemori, Naoyuki. "The Historical Context of the High Treason Incident: Governmentality and Colonialism." In *Japan and the High Treason Incident*, edited by Masako Gavin and Ben Middleton, 52–63. London: Routledge, 2013.

Varneck, Elena, and Fisher, Harold, eds. *Testimony of Kolchak and Other Siberian Materials*. Stanford, CA: Stanford University Press, 1935.

Vatlin, Aleksandr Iu. *Komintern: Idei, resheniia, sud'by*. Moscow: Rosspen, 2009.

Voitinsky, Grigory. "Bourgeoisie and the Remnants of Feudalism in Japan." *Novyi Vostok*, no. 4 (1925), 122–28.

——. "The Class War in Japan." *Communist Review* 3, no. 8 (1922). Marxist Internet Archive. http://www.marxists.org.

Wada Haruki. "Japanese-Russian Relations and the United States, 1855–1930." In *A Hidden Fire: Russian and Japanese Cultural Encounters, 1868–1926*, edited by Thomas J. Rimer, 201–13. Stanford, CA: Stanford University Press, 1995.

——. "Koreans in the Soviet Far East, 1917–1937." In *Koreans in the Soviet Union*, edited by Dae-Sook Suh, 23–59. Honolulu: University of Hawaii Press, 1987.

——. *Nikorai Rasseru*. Tokyo: Chūō Kōronsha, 1973.

Wakabayashi, Bob Tadashi. *Anti-Foreignism and Western Learning in Early-Modern Japan: The New Theses of 1825*. Cambridge, MA: Council on East Asian Studies, Harvard University, 1986.

Wakeman, Frederic E. *Policing Shanghai, 1927–1937*. Berkeley: University of California Press, 1995.

Ward, Max. "The Problem of "Thought": Crisis, National Essence and the Interwar Japanese State." PhD diss. New York: New York University, 2011.

Waswo, Ann. "The Transformation of Rural Society, 1900–1950." In *The Cambridge History of Japan*, edited by Peter Duus, 6:539–605. Cambridge: Cambridge University Press, 1989.

Watanabe Haruo, *Katayama Sen to tomo ni*. Tokyo: Wakōsha, 1955.

Watanabe Tōru. "Roshia kakumei to Nihon rōdō undō." *Gendai no riron* 4, no. 10 (1967): 21–33.

Whiting, Allen S. *Soviet Policies in China, 1917–1924*. New York: Columbia University Press, 1954.

Wilbur, Clarence M., and Julie Lien-ying How. *Missionaries of Revolution: Soviet Advisers and Nationalist China, 1920–1927*. Cambridge, MA: Harvard University Press, 1989.

Wilson, George M. *Radical Nationalist in Japan: Kita Ikki, 1883–1937*. Cambridge, MA: Harvard University Press, 1969.

Wilson, Sandra. "The Comintern and the Japanese Communist Party." In *International Communism and the Communist International, 1919–43*, 285–307. Manchester, UK: Manchester University Press, 1998.

——. "The Russo-Japanese War and Japan: Politics, Nationalism, and Historical Memory." In *The Russo-Japanese War in Cultural Perspective, 1904–05*, edited by David Wells and Sandra Wilson, 160–93. London: Palgrave Macmillan, 1999.

Wolff, David. "Open Jaw: A Harbin-Centered View of the Siberian-Manchurian Intervention 1917–1922." *Russian History* 36, no. 3 (2009): 339–59.

Wray, William D. "Asō Hisashi and the Search for Renovation in the 1930s." *Papers on Japan*, no. 5 (1970): 55–99.

Xu, Guoqi. *China and the Great War: China's Pursuit of a New National Identity and Internationalization*. New York: Cambridge University Press, 2004.

Yamabe Kentarō, ed. *Gendaishi shiryō*, vol. 19–20. Tokyo: Misuzu Shobō, 1967–68.

Yamabe Kentarō, and Takemura Eisuke. "Jūgatsu kakumei ga Nihon ni ataeta eikyō." *Zen'ei*, no. 135 (December 1957): 124–48.

Yamaizumi Susumu. "Ōsugi Sakae, Kominterunu ni sōgūsu." *Shoki shakaishugi kenkyū*, no. 15 (2002): 86–121.

Yamakawa Hitoshi. "Bōfū no mae." *Shinshakai* (December 1917).

——. "Jihyō." *Shinshakai* (April 1917).

——. *Shakaishugi no tachiba kara: Demokurashii no hanmon*. Tokyo: Mita Shobō, 1919.

——. "Waga kuni ni okeru Marukushizumu no hattatsu." *Kaizō* (March 1933).

——. *Yamakawa Hitoshi jiden*. Edited by Yamakawa Kikue and Yamakawa Shinsaku. Tokyo: Iwanami Shoten, 1961.

——. *Yamakawa Hitoshi zenshū*. Edited by Yamakawa Kikue and Yamakawa Shinsaku. Tokyo: Keisō Shobō, 1966.

Yamamuro Shin'ichi. *Nichiro sensō no seiki: Rensa shiten kara miru Nihon to sekai*. Tokyo: Iwanami Shoten, 2005.

Yamanouchi Akito. "Borisheviki bunken to shoki shakaishugi, Sakai, Takabatake, Yamakawa." *Shoki shakaishugi kenkyū*, no. 10 (1997): 101–15.

——. *The Early Comintern and Japanese Socialists Residing Abroad: A Transnational Network*. Kyoto: Mineruva Shobō, 2007.

——. "The Early Comintern in Amsterdam, New York, and Mexico City." *Shien*, no. 147 (2010): 99–139.

——. "Katayama Sen: Zaibei nihonjin shakaishugidan to shoki Kominterun." *Ōhara Shakai mondai kenkyūjo zasshi*, no. 544 (2004): 36–68.

——. *Shoki Kominterun to Zaigai Nihonjin Shakai Shugisha: Ekkyōsuru Nettowāku*. Kyoto: Mineruva Shobō, 2009.

Yasukuni Ishiko. "Naze fashizumu ni yabureta ka, Yamakawa Hitoshi wo yomu." *Kagakuteki shakaishugi*, no. 173 (2012): 88–93.

Yonetani Masafumi. "Senjiki Nihon no shakai shisō: Gendaika to senji henkaku." *Shisō*, no. 882 (1997): 69–120.

Yoshimi Yoshiaki. "Senzen ni okeru Nihon fashizumu kan no hensen." *Rekishigaku kenkyū*, no. 451 (December 1977): 20–32.

Yoshimura Akira. *Nikorai sōnan*. Tokyo: Iwanami Shoten, 1993.

Yoshimura Michio. *Nihon to Roshia: Nichiro sengo kara roshia kakumei made*. Tokyo: Hara Shobō, 1968.

Yoshino Sakuzō. "Kageki shisō taisaku." *Chūō Kōronsha* (May 1919)

——. "Minponshugi, shakaishugi, kagekishugi." *Chūō kōron* (June 1919).

——. "Rokoku kakumei no sensō ni oyobosu eikyō." *Chūō kōron* (May 1917).

——. "Roshia no kakumei." *Chūō kōron* (April 1917).

——. "Seinen shōkō no mitaru Shiberia shuppei gun no jitsujō." *Chūō kōron* (May 1922).

——. "Tandoku kōwa ni yotte Rokoku wa nanimono wo toran tosuru." *Chūō Kōron* (January 1918).

Young, John W. "The Hara Cabinet and Chang Tso-Lin, 1920–21." *Monumenta Nipponica* 27, no. 2 (1972): 125–42.

Index

Abe Isoo, 34
Advisory Council on Foreign Relations, 49–52, 58
Akamatsu Katsumaro, 172, 206
Akao Bin, 116, 205
Alexander II, 32–33, 143, 154
Amakasu Masahiko, 116, 153
Amsterdam International Anarchist Congress, 130
Amur River Society. *See* nationalist organizations
ana-boru debate (*ana-boru ronsō*), 140, 142–43, 150–51
anarchism and anarcho-syndicalism: assassinations planned, 150, 155, 189; Chinese and Koreans in Japan, 137; demise of, 154; impact of Russian Revolution, 135–36; international influence, 137–39, 152; labor unions and, 136; "pure" anarchism, 150, 156–57; response to Kōtoku's execution, 131; split with Bolsheviks, 140, 142–43, 148, 151, 157; terrorism, 128, 130; working-class and veteran socialist split, 145–46. *See also* Morito Incident (1921); Taishō anarchism
anarchist organizations: Hokufūkai (North Wind Society), 136, 145; Kokuren (Black Youth League), 155, 157; Shakaishugi Dōmei (Socialist League), 136–37; Zenkoku Jiren (All-Japan Libertarian Federation of Labor Unions), 144, 155, 157; Zenkoku Rōdō Kumiai Jiyū Rengōkai, 144
Anderer, Paul, 31
Anglo-Japanese alliance, 29, 172
anticapitalism, 129, 186, 192, 195, 197, 206–7
Anti-Comintern Pact of 1936, 80, 216
anticommunism, 8, 100–102, 211. *See also* Peace Preservation Laws
Anti-Immigration Act of 1924 (United States), 3, 197–98
Anti-Radical Bill (1922), 118, 198
Antonov, Vasily, 67–68, 76
Aoki Seiichi, 108–9
April Theses of 1917 (Lenin), 133
Arahata Kanson: Beijing meeting with Ioffe, 148; Fourth Comintern Congress, 163;

improper use of funds, 151; against legal proletarian party, 165, 171; police crackdown effect, 175; prison after Red Flag Incident, 130; split with Comintern, 181; worked at Baibunsha, 132
Araki Sadao, 7, 55, 79, 214
Arishima Takeo, 31
Asō Hisashi, 206–7
Asukai Masamichi, 139, 158

Bakunin, Mikhail, 35, 152–53
Bak Yeol, 137, 155
Beard, Charles A., 83–84
Beijing Convention of 1860, 17
Benyovsky, Maurice, 15–16
Berkman, Alexander, 135, 140
"Bethink Yourself!" (Tolstoy), 34
Bill for the Control of Extreme Social Movements, 113–14
Bolshevik leadership, 1, 5–6, 44, 56, 76, 166–67, 190
Bolsheviks: Asian policy, 166–67; attacks by Cossacks and tsarist army officers, 46–47; and CER, 46, 61; dictatorship of the proletariat, 45, 135; diplomacy with, 79–80; dual goals of, 62; imperialism, war on, 1–2; Japanese debts cancelled, 49, 78; Japanese government split on relations, 47; Japanese view of, 52; and Koreans, 62–63; and Provisional Government, 41, 133; statism and nationalism, 95, 108; thought to be aligned with Germany, 41; view of Japan, 2; world revolution, 1, 110–11. *See also* Comintern; communist ideology; October Revolution (1917)
"Bolsheviks and World Peace" (Trotsky), 71
Bolshevism. *See* communist ideology
Borodin, Mikhail, 87
British Labour Party: Hands off Russia Committee, 172; model for Asian communism, 178
buffer state, 54, 59–60, 96
Bukharin, Nikolai, 95, 97, 133, 148, 160, 181, 208
Bukharin Theses of 1922, 163–64, 168–71, 180

Studies of the Weatherhead East Asian Institute
Columbia University

Selected Titles

(Complete list at: http://weai.columbia.edu/publications/studies-weai/)

Residual Futures: The Urban Ecologies of Literary and Visual Media of 1960s and 1970s Japan, by Franz Prichard. Columbia University Press, 2019.

Down and Out in Saigon: Stories of the Poor in a Colonial City, by Haydon Cherry. Yale University Press, 2019.

The Power of Print in Modern China: Intellectuals and Industrial Publishing from the End of Empire to Maoist State Socialism, by Robert Culp. Columbia University Press, 2019.

Beyond the Asylum: Mental Illness in French Colonial Vietnam, by Claire E. Edington. Cornell University Press, 2019.

Borderland Memories: Searching for Historical Identity in Post-Mao China, by Martin Thomas Fromm. Cambridge University Press, 2019.

Sovereignty Experiments: Korean Migrants and the Building of Borders in Northeast Asia, 1860–1949, by Alyssa M. Park. Cornell University Press, 2019.

The Greater East Asia Co-Prosperity Sphere: When Total Empire Met Total War, by Jeremy A. Yellen. Cornell University Press, 2019.

Thought Crime: Ideology and State Power in Interwar Japan, by Max Ward. Duke University Press, 2019.

Statebuilding by Imposition: Resistance and Control in Colonial Taiwan and the Philippines, by Reo Matsuzaki. Cornell University Press, 2019.

Nation-Empire: Ideology and Rural Youth Mobilization in Japan and Its Colonies, by Sayaka Chatani. Cornell University Press, 2019.

Fixing Landscape: A Techno-Poetic History of China's Three Gorges, by Corey Byrnes. Columbia University Press, 2019.

The Invention of Madness: State, Society, and the Insane in Modern China, by Emily Baum. University of Chicago Press, 2018.

Japan's Imperial Underworlds: Intimate Encounters at the Borders of Empire, by David Ambaras. Cambridge University Press, 2018.

Heroes and Toilers: Work as Life in Postwar North Korea, 1953–1961, by Cheehyung Harrison Kim. Columbia University Press, 2018.

Electrified Voices: How the Telephone, Phonograph, and Radio Shaped Modern Japan, 1868–1945, by Kerim Yasar. Columbia University Press, 2018.

Making Two Vietnams: War and Youth Identities, 1965–1975, by Olga Dror. Cambridge University Press, 2018.

A Misunderstood Friendship: Mao Zedong, Kim Il-sung, and Sino–North Korean Relations, 1949–1976, by Zhihua Shen and Yafeng Xia. Columbia University Press, 2018.

Playing by the Informal Rules: Why the Chinese Regime Remains Stable despite Rising Protests, by Yao Li. Cambridge University Press, 2018.

Raising China's Revolutionaries: Modernizing Childhood for Cosmopolitan Nationalists and Liberated Comrades, by Margaret Mih Tillman. Columbia University Press, 2018.

Buddhas and Ancestors: Religion and Wealth in Fourteenth-Century Korea, by Juhn Y. Ahn. University of Washington Press, 2018.

Idly Scribbling Rhymers: Poetry, Print, and Community in Nineteenth Century Japan, by Robert Tuck. Columbia University Press, 2018.

China's War on Smuggling: Law, Economic Life, and the Making of the Modern State, 1842–1965, by Philip Thai. Columbia University Press, 2018.

Forging the Golden Urn: The Qing Empire and the Politics of Reincarnation in Tibet, by Max Oidtmann. Columbia University Press, 2018.

The Battle for Fortune: State-Led Development, Personhood, and Power among Tibetans in China, by Charlene Makley. Cornell University Press, 2018.

Aesthetic Life: Beauty and Art in Modern Japan, by Miya Elise Mizuta Lippit. Harvard University Asia Center, 2018.

Where the Party Rules: The Rank and File of China's Communist State, by Daniel Koss. Cambridge University Press, 2018.

Resurrecting Nagasaki: Reconstruction and the Formation of Atomic Narratives, by Chad R. Diehl. Cornell University Press, 2018.

China's Philological Turn: Scholars, Textualism, and the Dao in the Eighteenth Century, by Ori Sela. Columbia University Press, 2018.

Making Time: Astronomical Time Measurement in Tokugawa Japan, by Yulia Frumer. University of Chicago Press, 2018.

Mobilizing without the Masses: Control and Contention in China, by Diana Fu. Cambridge University Press, 2018.

Post-Fascist Japan: Political Culture in Kamakura after the Second World War, by Laura Hein. Bloomsbury, 2018.

China's Conservative Revolution: The Quest for a New Order, 1927–1949, by Brian Tsui. Cambridge University Press, 2018.

Promiscuous Media: Film and Visual Culture in Imperial Japan, 1926–1945, by Hikari Hori. Cornell University Press, 2018.

The End of Japanese Cinema: Industrial Genres, National Times, and Media Ecologies, by Alexander Zahlten. Duke University Press, 2017.

The Chinese Typewriter: A History, by Thomas S. Mullaney. The MIT Press, 2017.

Forgotten Disease: Illnesses Transformed in Chinese Medicine, by Hilary A. Smith. Stanford University Press, 2017.

Borrowing Together: Microfinance and Cultivating Social Ties, by Becky Yang Hsu. Cambridge University Press, 2017.

Food of Sinful Demons: Meat, Vegetarianism, and the Limits of Buddhism in Tibet, by Geoffrey Barstow. Columbia University Press, 2017.

Youth for Nation: Culture and Protest in Cold War South Korea, by Charles R. Kim. University of Hawaii Press, 2017.

Socialist Cosmopolitanism: The Chinese Literary Universe, 1945–1965, by Nicolai Volland. Columbia University Press, 2017.

The Social Life of Inkstones: Artisans and Scholars in Early Qing China, by Dorothy Ko. University of Washington Press, 2017.

Darwin, Dharma, and the Divine: Evolutionary Theory and Religion in Modern Japan, by G. Clinton Godart. University of Hawaii Press, 2017.

Dictators and Their Secret Police: Coercive Institutions and State Violence, by Sheena Chestnut Greitens. Cambridge University Press, 2016.

The Cultural Revolution on Trial: Mao and the Gang of Four, by Alexander C. Cook. Cambridge University Press, 2016.

Inheritance of Loss: China, Japan, and the Political Economy of Redemption after Empire, by Yukiko Koga. University of Chicago Press, 2016.

Homecomings: The Belated Return of Japan's Lost Soldiers, by Yoshikuni Igarashi. Columbia University Press, 2016.

Samurai to Soldier: Remaking Military Service in Nineteenth-Century Japan, by D. Colin Jaundrill. Cornell University Press, 2016.

CPSIA information can be obtained
at www.ICGtesting.com
Printed in the USA
BVHW082128310120
571144BV00001B/28